The Damp Garden

THE DAMP GARDEN

Beth Chatto

Drawings by Margaret Davies

J. M. Dent & Sons Ltd
London Melbourne

First published 1982
First published in paperback 1986
© Beth Chatto 1982

Photoset in VIP Times New Roman
by D. P. Media Limited, Hitchin, Hertfordshire
Printed and bound in Great Britain
by Mackays of Chatham Ltd
for J. M Dent & Sons Ltd
Aldine House, 33 Welbeck Street, London W1M 8LX

British Library Cataloguing in Publication Data

Chatto, Beth
    The damp garden
    1. Gardening – Great Britain
    2. Wetland flora
    I. Title
    635.9′55   SB454

    ISBN 0-460-02457-4

Contents

List of Colour Plates

List of Line Drawings

Acknowledgments

I am grateful to many people who have helped and encouraged me to write this book, both directly and indirectly. Most of all, to my husband. Throughout our life together I have absorbed, like a sponge, talk of plants and their habitats. From Andrew's patient, lifelong study I have learnt much that I know about plants and their needs. It is a never-ending study for us both, from books, and from practical experience in our own particular environment.

I am glad to have this opportunity to give credit to my staff, whose enthusiastic and conscientious teamwork brings my plans and ideas to life. In winter as well as summer time their wholehearted involvement and hard work have made my gardens grow. Fine plans would be of little use without such support.

I would like too to say thank you sincerely to our visitors and postal friends from far away. Without them the gardens would not have developed, or could continue. Their appreciation of our efforts gives us fresh energy and inspiration to do better.

I am much indebted to Graham S. Thomas for his sound and constructive criticism of my manuscript. With much patience, and far greater experience he has spared me from many pitfalls which strew the path of would-be horticultural writers. But I begin to think that a gardening book, like gardens, does not exist that has no flaws!

My two books, *The Dry Garden* and now *The Damp Garden* gain something very special with the exquisitely sensitive drawings of Margaret Davies. She involves herself so completely with my ideas and feelings about plants and design that sometimes I feel we are two parts of one whole.

The lovely photographs come from the discerning eyes and steady hands of Michael Warren.

Introduction

In my first book, *The Dry Garden*, I described how we made a garden on poor sand and gravel soil in an area of the country where the average rainfall is around 20–22 in./250–300 mm a year. I also have some very damp land on the same site, and would like to tell the story of its development as a garden, so that I may describe not only the many beautiful plants which previously I had no chance of possessing, but also the trials and errors which occurred as I laboriously learnt something of the art of managing a boggy meadow.

I live in a highly developed part of the country and sometimes feel sad that many young people growing up today will not have the evocative memories that those of us have who were children before the Second World War – of playing and wandering in copsey places, dusty lanes or wet-legged meadows, where each season we looked out for the flowering plants that we took for granted would always be there, part of our world, part of the fabric of our lives. When I was a child a hedge, together with the ditch that had provided the soil bank on which the hedge had been planted generations before, provided the shelter and spring-moist atmosphere needed by sweet violets and pale clumps of primroses. On the dusty roadside verges we found tall purple knapweed, scabious, yellow toadflax and great stands of cow parsnip, their star-topped seed heads always used to make 'fairy wands' in autumn. In spring the shining golden King Cups edged the little brook meandering through the low-lying damp meadows, dotted about with lilac Lady's Smock and contented cropping cows. As the summer days lengthened we would look out for the tiny baby frogs which, disturbed by our plunging through the long grass, would leap ahead of us like grasshoppers, tiny clammy-wet creatures, appealing because they were so vulnerable. As we chased them we stumbled across a colony of slender spotted orchids, a rare sight even in those days, golden days of childhood.

But as I grew up the Big Machines moved in. The utilization of the land was under constant revision. Greater efficiency in farming decimated the hedges and drained and ploughed the water-meadows; networks of new roads had to be made, conurbations of new homes built – all of this has created very different associations.

Many people will be growing up, making homes and starting gardens who have not had these carefree nature lessons when we unconsciously absorbed something of the needs of plants. I had never heard the word ecology in those days, nor did I connect wild plants with gardening as I understood it then. But before long I was involved in making an ecological survey of our local salt marshes as part of my college studies. With the highly informed help of Andrew, my future husband, I started an interest which has lasted all my life, and directly influenced my gardening. By studying the marshes in detail I learnt how marvellously plants adapt themselves to their environment, and also how that environment can change in a matter of a few yards, and that each differing section has a slightly modified plant community.

Plants edging sea water have one particular problem and that is salt, both in the air and the soil. So, curious as it may sound, they have to adapt themselves to take in and preserve fresh water. Where the salt content is very high, such as round the little pools that are left by the tide, where the sun evaporates the water causing a build-up of salts, very few plants can cope. But one has and that is *Salicornia europaea*, the Marsh Samphire. Colonies of these little succulent jointed stems, glass-green, sometimes red when starved, edge these salty pans. We used to munch a few, then pick out the brightest green to take home and eat, cooked, with melted butter. At one time they could be found, sometimes bunched as Poor Man's Asparagus, in London markets.

As we moved across the marsh from the areas of high salt concentration to the fresh water plants inland we could see a pattern emerging in the bands of colour and textures, as the changing conditions caused changes in the plant communities.

Salt marshes may seem a long way from cultivated gardening, but I learnt important lessons there. Plants have adapted themselves to almost every kind of condition, no matter how unpromising. They will tolerate a great deal. But they are also sensitive and will not establish themselves in a situation that differs markedly from their natural environment. As conditions change in my own garden from dry gravel to silt, from damp to bog, so I must consider what I will plant that will tolerate the change.

I would like in this book to discuss most of the plants that I grow which are omitted from *The Dry Garden*. While many, or most of them, do not need, and would not thrive in, really wet conditions, neither will any of them tolerate drought during the growing period. They require soil that does not dry out and, in some cases, a sheltered environment, providing some shade from direct hot sunlight and shelter from wind, which can cause immediate wilting of large soft foliage, even though there be ample moisture underfoot.

While I shall certainly discuss the making of my ponds, and the plants I have put in and around them, I do not propose to describe how pools in general, either natural or artificial, may be constructed. Nor shall I describe more than a fraction of the plants that actually grow in water. I have too little experience of either, and shall stick in the main to the things I have learnt through trial and error.

The most comprehensive book that I have on this specialized subject which I am evading is *Water Gardening*, by Frances Perry. There are practical ideas in it for everyone, from the most modest garden to the most expansive. The sensitive use of water and plants combined is evident everywhere. To look as natural as possible, to fit into the surroundings like the final piece in a jigsaw puzzle, that is, for me, the art of bringing water into the garden. It does not have to be a lake. A picture in Mrs Perry's book which especially delights me is of two wooden tubs containing small water-lilies, surrounded by rushy leaves, all most harmonious, a focal point for the background. Underneath is a little verse:

> A garden should be rather small
> Or you will have no fun at all.
>   Reginald Arkell

Seeing the picture of these tubs reminds me of another picture which we have of the great Amos Perry as a boy (1897), tightly buttoned up in overcoat and topped with a hat, standing beside his row of little water butts containing lilies. This world-famous nursery began at Weeley, the next village down the road from us. Alas! before my time.

The first, and ever memorable, visit I made to Chelsea was soon after the Second World War. Then, and on other occasions, I always made my way to Perry's Water Garden stand, to be carried away by the magical effect of plants that were far beyond me, entranced by the naturalness of the designs, an oasis of green surrounded by masses of hot colours.

I have been dipping into Mrs Perry's book and several of the firm's old catalogues – in a photograph showing the proud owners of a 'Rock and Water Garden' the style of dress suggests the thirties, *and* the prices too, sixpence and ninepence for most plants, while something special like *Orchis foliosa* was five shillings. (Wages on the farm in those days were thirty shillings a week.) I remember in the forties we bought a small round tuber of *Arisaema candidissimum*, about the size of the top of my finger – we felt very dissipated, but we treasured it, and called it the 'Five Shilling Plant' for years. But how can such a plant ever be anything but a luxury? I know no one who has a large stock of this lovely plant. Someone must spend patient years to build it up and then find enough people aware of it to seek it out.

Losing myself in these treasured old catalogues and Mrs Perry's book, I recognize many plants that have become familiar to me since I started my Damp Garden, but I am impressed also by the vast number that I have still neither heard of nor seen. In those far-off days the wealth of plants offered in such a specialized field makes my head spin – think of the propagation and maintenance alone.

For those who may be overwhelmed by such a choice I would recommend the Wisley Handbook No. 29, *Water Gardens* by Ken Aslet. This is a delightful little book, giving you the names and habits of the best-known and best-loved water plants. As well as providing very good instructions, with illustrations, for the construction of pools that most of us could envisage in our gardens, there is also plenty of sane advice. I like the list of equipment that comes in handy, like floating plastic bowls and waders. We have spent many warm summer afternoons wading to pull out barrow-loads of water plants that have flourished too well. Even desirables like water-lilies, or *Pontederia cordata*, the Blue Pickerel Weed, can, almost without your noticing it, make ever-widening clumps or rafts of foliage until you suddenly realize that the proportion of plant to water is the wrong way round.

So often it is after the event that we read these wise and experienced people's books, full of sound advice that would have prevented us from spending hours, not to say weeks, on wasted effort.

It is especially important in an ideal growing medium like tepid water *not* to plant things which will rapidly multiply so that the water vanishes. A frightening little surface smotherer is *Azolla caroliniana*, Fairy Moss, looking like pink duckweed. It is the prettiest thing for an indoor pool or aquarium, or perhaps a tiny outdoor pool where you can control it. But let one minute piece dangle its little roots below the surface of a large stretch of water and you will find it covering the entire surface in one season. Not only is this unattractive, it is dangerous. I have seen large stretches of the wide land-draining ditches in Holland covered with it, where perhaps a tiny piece has been flung away, attached possibly to some discarded plant. It is always wise to examine carefully water plants bought in from a nursery, where they may keep this charming menace for its proper use – in small, controlled tanks. Fortunately it comes from warmer climates than ours, so a really hard winter may dispose of it. But I would not trust that some small piece does not survive, lurking in the frost-free muddy bottom of the pond, to float to the surface in spring.

Another charming invader that I came to rue the day I chose to plant it was *Villarsia* or, more correctly, *Limnanthemum peltatum*. A British native, the leaves make one think it is a miniature form of water-lily. Small, round and slightly mottled brown, they float up and lie flat on the surface, while the bright yellow flowers are pushed up 2 or 3 in./50 or 80 mm above the level of the water, shaped rather like convolvulus. Very pretty. But they have roots like bootlaces which interlace in the mud, in shallow water, and before you know where you are the water is covered. A scattering of leaves on water is delightful, a carpet is a bore. I thought I had finally eradicated it from my shallow ponds (or rather Harry had, who did all the wading and pulling among slimy mud). But we have not managed this. It is still an annual job to dig and haul as much out as we can see in the disturbed muddy water. But I have now planted it in a pond that quickly drops to 9 ft/3 m deep, and so far it is restricted to the shallow edge. One has to find out the most favourable depths in which to plant all water plants. Some will only stand a few inches, others several feet.

I have strayed away from my point which is to explain what I am hoping to do and why. I think, too, I am trying to convince myself that there might be room for yet another book about moisture-loving plants. I could be very discouraged by having beside me Alan Bloom's excellent book *Moisture Gardening*. His garden was established, and his name as a great plantsman was known in Europe and the United States before I had begun to be a gardener. Now, to my delight, we sometimes exchange visits – and plants – and enjoy wandering round each other's gardens. I often say that one lifetime is not nearly enough to learn about plants. With people like Mr Bloom I feel that I have been given extra time, so generously does he share his great stores of knowledge and experience.

Gardens are like paintings, individual to their creator, so our two gardens are in no way alike, although we grow many of the same plants. I have learnt much from the garden at Bressingham and shall continue to do so, I hope. But gardens, unlike paintings, are never completed. There must be change, both in planting and design. New plants are introduced, sometimes old ones are banished. The permutations of groupings are endless.

Again, because of the different nature of our sites, together with the fact that he was already a master and I was a novice, we tackled the job of making damp gardens quite differently. I am not sure that if I had read his book twenty years ago (fortunately it wasn't written then) I should have dared to begin. But, assuredly, if I had I would have saved myself several false starts. His book is invaluable to people considering how to prepare their site for moisture gardening. He describes forthrightly the kind of conditions that are *not* suitable, reminding me of occasional visitors who come to me for advice on what they should plant in a water garden, adding as an afterthought that the level of water drops 3 ft/1 m in summer! Sometimes it is a farm pond, sometimes a moat, sometimes a river in full spate whirling past the bottom of the garden. Another time it may be a low-lying piece of puddled clay that is wet and soggy all winter, but bone dry and fractured in summer.

None of this, of course, will do—at least, not as it stands. Soil for damp-loving plants must not be allowed to dry out during the growing season, when the plants will be seeking moisture. At the same time, for the vast majority, neither must it be waterlogged. This formula of moisture-holding properties allied to good drainage sounds impossible, but Mr Bloom explains it very clearly in *Moisture Gardening*. I have described how we have dealt with badly drained soils in Chapter 7.

I have never lived in an area where the average rainfall is over 20 in./250 mm, so what the summer growing conditions are like where you have 40 in./500 mm plus, I cannot imagine. But books like A. T. Johnson's *A Woodland Garden*, which was based on his garden somewhere in wet Wales, lead me to think that many of the plants grown both at Bressingham and in my own garden can be grown naturally in some favoured parts of the country without necessarily contemplating irrigation.

In East Anglia we are so plagued by regular periods of drought, aggravated by the desiccating winds which inevitably follow a welcome summer shower, that I may appear to be making an undue fuss about site conditions, but I think not. So I read with great interest and admiration Mr Bloom's methods of underground irrigation, of creating a system of water-carrying pipes, in some cases laid on polythene, but always ensuring that water-logging could not occur. The advantages and hazards of overhead irrigation are also considered.

If Damp Gardening sounds like hard work I can assure you that, unless nature provides for you, initially, it is. Both the careful preparation of the site and the subsequent management of the soil (ideally suited for the germination of weeds) require considerable effort, followed by skilful planting. But when it is successful I think it is possibly one of the most beautiful forms of gardening.

Perhaps the best place to seek knowledge is to go and see the plants growing in their native environment. I have done no serious plant collecting, but holiday trips abroad have been an inspiration for plantings made many years later. My first trip to the Swiss Alps resulted in unforgettable memories of some of the plants which we were struggling to grow, flourishing in their native home. *Sedum*, *Sempervivum*, *Dianthus* and *Euphorbia*, *Potentilla* and thymes were no problem at home, and on the hot rocky slopes we saw them in profusion with achilleas, *Biscutella*, and linarias which we knew we could grow. But the rich, low-lying valley meadows were a different matter. Fed by melting snow from the glaciers at the head of the valley were many desirable flowers and grasses just about to be cut for hay. Snowy masses of *Chrysanthemum alpinum*, indigo-blue *Phyteuma*, large pink pokers of *Polygonum bistorta* with occasional clumps of the pale yellow Globeflower, *Trollius europaeus*, in the really boggy places—none would be happy in Essex drought. Much higher, where the short turf is still watered from below though the sun may be hot in a clear blue sky, we found *Geum montanum*, several species of orchid and, of course, many kinds of gentians, including the stately *Gentiana lutea* whose roots are used to flavour a famous mountain liqueur. Here I saw for the first time the orange daisy-flowered *Arnica montana*. With memory prompting me I bent my head and put my nose into the sun-warmed petals, and in a moment the curious long-remembered smell carried me back to my childhood and a small dark green bottle with faded label, 'Tincture of Arnica', kept inside the case of the mantelpiece clock, to soothe bumps and bruises. Before leaving that mountain village I had to buy a bottle to take home to treat my own small daughters' bruises.

Beside tumbling brooks we saw *Aruncus dioicus* and *Thalictrum aquilegifolium* arching their feathery flower heads over the water. Although they do not need boggy soil in English gardens neither will they flourish in parched conditions. *Primula farinosa* was always to be found in the really wet soil at the edge of little runnels of water.

There were far, far more. But in those early days, although I saw them with my eyes, I did not have the knowledge to comprehend them.

1 *Starting from Scratch*

First I must show you the site as it was. Twenty-one years ago we stumbled through it one late November afternoon, making the final decision that this isolated and derelict piece of land was going to become our home. Several fine oaks threw rugged silhouettes against the skyline, supported by a couple of towering dark hollies alive with quarrelsome sparrows fighting over accommodation. Mountainous piles of blackberries ran into wickedly prickly thickets of sloes, with nettles and marsh thistles filling the remaining spaces.

The hollow was long and narrow, with a spring-fed ditch running from north to south down the centre. The Water Board sent a couple of men along it once in a while to clear it because the free flow of water was vital to the drainage of the fields which surrounded us. Gradually the ditch had deepened and low banks of mixed clay and gravel had built up alongside to be colonized by Rosebay Willowherb, nettles and coarse grasses until the next spring-clean. A stately alder rose out of a muddle of stunted oaks while a group of Arthur Rackham-like willows visually closed the northern end.

Most of Essex is dead flat; in any case, few builders would consider putting a house into a swamp. But here, for us—if we could persuade a builder to build us a house—was the possibility of making a garden on different levels, with running water and, perhaps one day, a pond.

For those who have real valleys I hasten to repeat that ours is a very shallow depression. This whole area was probably formed about 10,000 years ago by a melting ice sheet that lay to the north-west of Colchester. During the last Ice Age it had ground its way over northern England to deposit, as it melted, a layer of clay many feet thick, incorporating nodules and grains of chalk from the hills it had passed over. This layer is what we call chalky boulder clay. It did not come to the east of Colchester but the melting ice water did, gushing over the east coastal strip and laying down banks of gravel where the current was strongest, sand and silt where it was shallow. All these gradations of soil lay on twelve acres of land, part of which we proposed to use. Subsequently our small stream cut itself a shallow course through the gravels and silt to the ancient London clay which lies beneath us.

The wasteland was overgrown by different groupings of plants, because of the different soil types, reminding me of the salt marshes which varied from salt to fresh water. We had willows and marsh thistles in the wet hollow, tall stands of bracken on the drier sandy slopes, wild roses, sorrel and bare stones on the uppermost gravels. Overall the soil was acid. An analysis showed it to be as low as 0.4 in places.

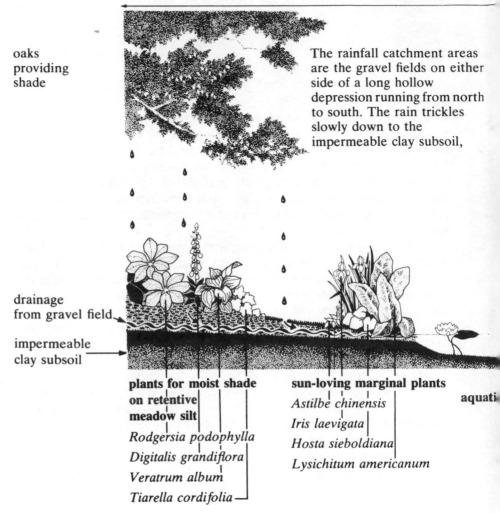

oaks
providing
shade

The rainfall catchment areas
are the gravel fields on either
side of a long hollow
depression running from north
to south. The rain trickles
slowly down to the
impermeable clay subsoil,

drainage
from gravel field

impermeable
clay subsoil

**plants for moist shade
on retentive
meadow silt**

Rodgersia podophylla
Digitalis grandiflora
Veratrum album
Tiarella cordifolia

sun-loving marginal plants

Astilbe chinensis
Iris laevigata
Hosta sieboldiana
Lysichitum americanum

aquati

A. A section across the garden showing soil conditions which have
produced the damp garden and the dry garden

On either side of the ditch, unseen beneath the tangles of undergrowth,
were springs which enter our land from east and west. The cultivated
farmland which lies on either side of us is several feet higher, possibly
20 ft/6 m higher, than the lowest level of the garden and is, predominantly, a
gravel soil overlying the clay base. The rainfall, especially the winter rain,
trickles very slowly down through this open-textured soil to the clay
beneath, which it cannot easily penetrate. So water runs along the surface of

The Dry Garden

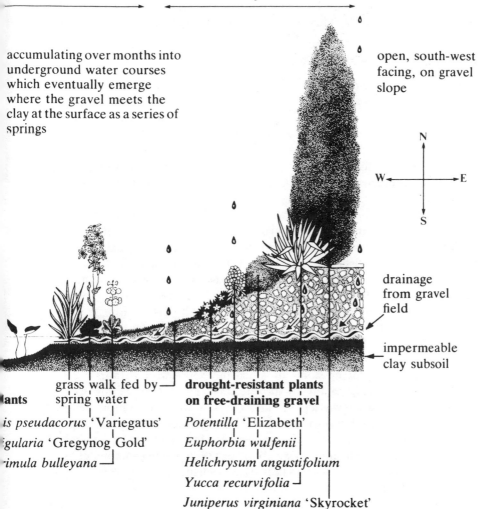

accumulating over months into underground water courses which eventually emerge where the gravel meets the clay at the surface as a series of springs

open, south-west facing, on gravel slope

N
W——|——E
S

drainage from gravel field

impermeable clay subsoil

grass walk fed by spring water

drought-resistant plants on free-draining gravel

lants

is pseudacorus 'Variegatus'
gularia 'Gregynog Gold'
imula bulleyana

Potentilla 'Elizabeth'
Euphorbia wulfenii
Helichrysum angustifolium
Yucca recurvifolia
Juniperus virginiana 'Skyrocket'

the clay, joining up into underground tributaries which eventually find their way on to our land, emerging finally at the ditch level as a row of springs. The ditch was thus continuously fed by water that had fallen months previously. With our few inches of summer rainfall either blown away by devilish winds, or dried up the next day by the sun, the thought of all this underground water was intoxicating.

Twenty-one years ago we could see very little of it, but as we squelched our way up through the hollow that long-ago November evening, the white mist curling among the russet stands of head-high bracken and mouldering the last of the blackberries, I felt that this place was right for us. I had no idea of the way the garden would evolve, but I could hardly wait to make a start.

Clearing the Site

The first thing to decide was where our house should stand. Among our friends was a young architect who, on being taken to the site, immediately saw the possibilities. The result was a plan for a simple, low-lying, split-level house to be built into the warm west-facing bank, at that time overlooking the ditch. Months of planning and preparations went by. At the same time I was busy in my Colchester garden, boxing up seedlings and cuttings, trying to preserve as much as I could of the first seventeen years of our gardening life together.

Eventually the day came when we followed the bulldozer down the quarter mile headland (unmade farm roadway) which led from the main road through the farm to our wilderness. The last hundred yards or so ran along an old boundary hedge. We stopped at an ancient pollarded oak with a magnificent umbrella head. Between this bastion and an equally ancient holly, yards on at the top of a slope, was the place where our house would stand. Old rabbit netting and barbed wire—which years before had kept grazing cows in the damp hollow from invading our land—had to be cut. We cut, and tugged, and tore ourselves, but by the end of the day a roadway had been levelled out of the headland, and three shallow platforms had been made on the south-facing slope on which the house would stand.

Next day, Percy, on the bulldozer, started to clear the site for the garden. In some ways it was a pity. I know that my husband, a more devoted naturalist than I am, thinks so. And a speck deep inside me can see his point of view. For so many years this piece of land had been a haven for all kinds of creatures. One early morning a vixen had been seen playing with her cubs. A badger had a set up on the warm sandy bank, well hidden by bramble tangles and bracken beds. Grass snakes sunned themselves on the remains of straw bales. But not all was idyllic. Lazing one day on the edge of the ditch, fascinated by caddis worms, teasing them perhaps by giving them bits of stick to embellish their pebbly coats, my reverie was shattered by the screams of a rabbit being chased relentlessly through the brushwood by a stoat. Now Humans were invading, for better or worse!

It always alarms me how quickly large machines change the landscape. Within a few hours the impenetrable tangle of blackthorn was crushed into a vast heap to be burnt. We had marked the straight limbed oaks we wished to keep, and the hollies, of course, were not touched. The alder stood alone now on the edge of the ditch. Opposite it, some distance away, was the vast oak complemented by the equally massive holly. Between these trees and the site where the house would stand there was nothing, not a blade of grass. The ditch, several feet deep, lay parallel to the house site but separated from it by a level stretch of moist silt.

At the very end of this long tongue-shaped piece of land we had a small reservoir, made several years previously to irrigate the farm. It had been constructed by scooping out the 'valley' bottom, and piling the clay across the end, so collecting the spring water that ran down through our land. A large outflow pipe took the excess water further downstream through an alder wood. Some repair work was being done to this at the same time as we were bulldozing. The owner of the drag-line at work there walked over to see what was going on. Immediately he saw it from *his* viewpoint. 'I know what you want, Mrs Chatto!' he said. 'A nice Lily Pond.' 'Yes,' I said, uncertainly. 'That would be nice.' Looking at the large empty area we had created—the straight line of the ditch, the unfamiliar scale of the few huge trees we had left—I could not be helpful. However, he was not a man to let the grass grow under his feet. In no time his vast machine was trundling over my 'garden' as easily as a wheelbarrow. He dipped the large scoop into the ditch a number of times, brought out several tons of bright yellow clay and laid it around the edge of a large muddy hole. It seemed a huge hole at the time, and the pile of clay looked totally unmanageable. Percy's fire of brushwood was sending up sparks like fireflies into the dusk. Both machines moved off home.

I was pleased with the cleared ground. The soil, soft black silt, full of humus from decades of falling leaves, looked good. We knew what we would do next with that. But 'Mrs Chatto's Lily Pond' was not right. I could not tell myself why, but I knew it was wrong.

Soil Preparation

The next tool we used was our own tractor, with the subsoiler attached. Land that has lain for a long time can become very compacted, roots cannot easily penetrate, there may be bad drainage and certainly lack of air. When breaking up a new piece of ground we always use the subsoiler, a great curved piece of strong steel, facing forward, which, drawn behind the tractor, sinks in about 2 ft/600 mm deep, bursting up the compacted soil. I love to walk behind the tractor and watch the soil lift and crack on either side of the deep spike. The soil has to be right. If it were very wet the tool would just slide through like butter—which might be useful to start off some drainage—but when it is the right degree of dampness the land fractures, which is better.

In many gardening books double digging is recommended to open up the soil. It is not always easy nowadays to find someone, able and willing, to do this heavy work. But I do think in entirely new gardens, where the soil may have been compacted by very heavy machinery, perhaps to level the site before building, some deep digging should be done initially—if not overall, then for individual trees and shrubs. Simply by doing that I have, on occasion, in gardens where I have been asked to help, had an unwelcome shock finding all kinds of unexpected features beneath soil level (like large pieces of buried hardboard, or the swillings out of the concrete mixer which had set like a laid path, a foot beneath the surface). Once the hard pan, whatever it may consist of, has been broken I would prefer to maintain the texture of the soil by adding as much humus as possible to the top layer, and allowing the worms and soil bacteria to build up the soil structure.

With our subsoiling done this is how things stood. Three shallow platforms represented the house. All the land on the house side of the ditch had been cleared (apart from the marked trees). From its west side the house overlooked the ditch, beyond which were still the dark masses of blackthorn, and overtopping them was the ancient farm boundary hedge containing oaks, a crab apple, holly and hazelnut. Crowning them all was the finest oak in the district. I felt puny beneath it.

The next thing was to decide where the paths should go. At that time I felt rather nonplussed by the size of the area cleared and its absence of features. I had never before started a garden from scratch. It was a bit like facing these large empty sheets of foolscap and wondering where to go next. So I was thankful to follow Andrew's ideas, which were based very much on ecological groupings rather than park-like landscaping.

We had in mind to create several different gardens, influenced by our memories of plants in the wild and subsequent reading of plant associations. So, the area between the alder and the large oak was to become a Shade Garden. The Lower Ditch area which ran alongside would become a Water Garden. The open silty soil on the south side of the house would, for the time being, act as a nursery bed until we had sorted ourselves out. The fairly level areas of starved gravel which approached the house and lay all round it on its upper levels could only become our Mediterranean Garden, the making of which I have described in *The Dry Garden*. 'The Lily Pond', although lying across that part of the ditch which flowed past the west window of the house, I managed to ignore. Quite soon, as a gesture, I planted a large Pampas Grass on the edge of it, but I could not imagine what else to do and anyway there were more important things to be done—like the paths.

By now I have learnt one or two useful tips about paths. When starting from scratch paths need to have a definite objective, and to return if possible by a different route. By their very nature they make openings among the screen of trees and shrubs to be planted, so make sure the path will lead your eye as well as yourself to a pleasant vista. Again it is wise to follow the contours of the land and let your path take the gentler slopes, remembering that before long you will be pushing a heavy barrow up or down the slope. Andrew had these things in his mind as we shuffled our paths in the soft soil. We left a much wider curving strip throughout the whole length of the garden alongside the ditch. Later we sowed it all down by hand with a fine grass seed mixture. Much later the narrow grass paths and the beds they contained were simplified as the garden developed, and I began to get a feeling of the scale of the garden to come. But initially it was right that we designed to a scale we could manage ourselves.

Although the land had been broken up by the subsoiler it still had to be levelled and dug. It was full of roots, especially blackthorn and bracken. We

had several men working on our fruit farm (of which this patch of land was
the wasteland, too wet, or too dry, to plant commercially). But there was
rarely time in the year when they could easily be spared. So we did our own
digging. There was plenty of time. The house took nearly a year to build. I
thought at the time that the garden would take the rest of my life. (Now I
know that one lifetime is not half enough.) After seventeen years of chalky
boulder clay in my Colchester garden, only seven miles away, I found it very
enjoyable to dig in this soft, almost stoneless soil, full of the leaf-mould of
ages. I took pleasure in following down as deep as I could the black rope-like
roots of bracken which in places interwove the soil like a fishing net. Since
then I have learnt that it can be killed by spraying with a weedkiller like
'Asulox', but that is not a quick process either; it takes months to be
effective. However, it is the thing to do if you happen to be a hill farmer and
are trying to clear extra grazing land.

    In small areas, where digging is possible, it is I think the best way, for
breaking as much of the root as you can causes the milky-white sap inside to
bleed and so helps the destruction of whatever you leave behind. For years
afterwards odd pieces of bracken appeared in my garden; some still do. I try
to remember to weed them out when the frond is mature, pulling the stem
away from the deep root, so wounding it again. Gradually it dies out. For
those who may wonder why I am so intent on the destruction of something
which looks so attractive, especially in spring uncurling among bluebells, I
will say more explicitly that left to itself it forms dense tangles, more than
head high, much too rampant for a garden. Proper ferns are a different
matter, and will come later.

    As the digging progressed we ferried over our boxes of plants, small
shrubs and young trees, and planted them in rows, in a nursery area, till we
had time to sort them out. Almost the first night the local rabbits found the
new menu to their taste, so we hastily erected some old netting as an
enclosure. But before we could contemplate any permanent planting we
had to face up to the trouble and expense of putting a proper rabbit-
proof fence around the perimeter of the area we thought then was to be our
new garden.

The First Shade Bed

Thus far you may have felt excluded by so much attention to preparations,
especially with earthmoving machinery—although I can assure you that the
cost, in relation to the type of work done and the time saved, was not
exorbitant. But now I propose to tell you something of the making of our
first Shade Bed, which in itself could be a complete small garden for
someone who has a shady site and soil that does not dry out excessively. Of
course sometimes, by the very nature of being shady, gardens are often dry
as well. This is especially the case where there is too much root competition
from trees and shrubs, and too low rainfall in the growing season. Where
every inch is precious I have been told of an idea to keep questing roots out

of a bed particularly desired for choice plants. It is to dig down a deep slit trench, as close to the trees or shrubs as you dare, and insert a sheet of corrugated asbestos, or even high-gauge black polythene.

The soil of my first Shade Bed was deep and black, with a damp area along the lower side where a spring ran just below grass level. At one point, when digging an extra-deep hole for a shrub, we hit the old land drain which had been laid long, long ago to carry this spring off the land above. Not pipes as we use today but tile drains, that is, a pipe made in two halves, one lying on the other, like a lid. We also came across the curious greyish-white substance called 'gley', caused by the humus acids from the top layer of soil bleaching the silty soil beneath. We wondered immediately if anything would grow on such barren-looking soil, but elsewhere it had been thrown on the surface by the bulldozing, and within weeks the finest crop of Fat Hen, a common farm weed, was thriving in it.

The first tree we planted to create shade was *Paulownia imperialis*, native to the warm temperate parts of China. It is mostly seen now planted, as the Chinese have destroyed most of their natural forests to make way for crops. It is a member of the foxglove family and its flowers, carried on long upcurved shoots, look like large, frill-lipped, pale blue foxgloves. In early June they open from soft chamois velvet buds, with no leaves unfurled to detract from their exotic beauty. Visitors seeing the first flowers dropped on the green grass wonder where they have come from, looking in vain from left to right, not thinking to look at the great tree above their heads. Some years the branches sweep down to eye level and then we are all bewitched. Our tree loved the rich, deep soil and shot up like a rocket, all of 6 ft/2 m a year. But it has paid the price for such exuberance, for twice now several large, brittle limbs have been torn off by autumn gales. Rough pruning! The large, soft, heart-shaped leaves, which do not expand fully till mid June, make pretty dappled shade for the large bed beneath.

Beyond it we planted *Davidia involucrata*, which has never done well. I know they can take as long as thirty years to dangle those large white flower bracts, but this one does not make good growth. I wonder what is troubling it. Is the soil too acid? More trees planted for shade were *Liriodendron tulipifera*, *Catalpa bignonioides*, *Liquidambar styraciflua*, a pink-flowered *Robinia* (torn to pieces by wind), *Picea omorika* and *Ginkgo biloba*. What a list, far too many for the space available, and there were shrubs as well. The blue-berried *Symplocos paniculata* was ruined by the sticky spit from aphids in the oak above. A *Neillia* made a thicket of stems (useful for pheasant cover, in suitable places), pretty in leaf and flower, but menacing here.

Something which I do greatly regret was *Rhus trichocarpa* which had to go when this area had to be replanned. We tried to move it with great care, but without success. I must find room for one again soon. It had the most brilliant of all orange-scarlet leaves in autumn.

I have found that though, in places, I have underground moisture, I do have to restrict the number of trees and shrubs that suck it up greedily in dry summers, leaving my plants between famished.

At the beginning some shade was already provided by the high canopy of alder and oak, so I planted great clumps of hostas backed by tall stands of Solomon's Seal, *Polygonatum × hybridum*, and the common fern, the Male Fern, *Dryopteris filix-mas*. Among them, for ground-cover, I planted *Tiarella cordifolia* and *Geranium endressii*, both of which spread quickly, making a carpet of pretty foliage as well as providing a foam of white or pink flowers in spring. Lily-of-the-Valley seemed the right thing to plant, bluebells were already there (why not keep them?) and the Welsh Poppy, *Meconopsis cambrica*, in orange and lemon, added to a spring picture of simple charm. *But* the bluebells and Lily-of-the-Valley spread far too well, pushing their way through clumps of *Tellima* and jostling poor Bowles' Golden Grass, *Milium effusum* 'Aureum', almost out of existence. The poppies too were into everything. After a few years my ruthless character could stand it no longer and all those invasive creatures had to come out and be banished to places where I felt they could do less damage.

The upper side of this bed was drier, partly because of tree roots, so I planted it with things that enjoyed the spring and early summer moisture. Pretty little *Corydalis solida* is very welcome there early in the spring, while erythroniums have increased well. *Erythronium dens-canis*, and *E.* 'White Beauty' do especially well. They come up through carpets of the little purple-leafed *Viola labradorica* which I find invaluable for awkward conditions. Dwarf vincas and *Cotula squalida* are the only things that have made a satisfactory carpet over the roots of *Acer davidii*. This is a most beautiful small tree, especially in winter when its green and white striped bark is tinted red and all the young twigs are coral against a blue sky. I think it should be in grass. It makes such a loofah-like mat of roots.

On the lower damper side of this bed are hybrids of *Primula vulgaris*; *P.* 'Garryarde Guinevere' and *P.* 'Lady Greer' look well mixed up in backgrounds of pink- and purple-leafed ajugas. Very striking too are a few clumps of Cowichan polyanthus. I love best the darkest garnet colours, velvet soft, with the merest glint of a golden eye. Various forms of *Anemone nemorosa*, including the fragile-looking lilac-blue bowls of *A.n.* 'Robinsoniana' run now with *Tiarella*, while *Potentilla rupestris* looks right with sprays of pure white flowers on rosy-pink stems. *Heucherella* 'Bridget Bloom' has settled happily and flowers over a long season in this bed, but the ordinary heucheras would not put roots down into the sour black silt.

In a drier section, where a big oak root may be coming near the surface, epimediums have made most satisfying thickets of growth. Especially easy is *E. × versicolor* 'Sulphureum' and nothing is more beautiful in the spring when, if you have remembered to cut off the old leaves in February, it will be covered with nodding sprays of tiny primrose-yellow flowers; heart-shaped leaves most tenderly suffused with tan over pale green will quickly follow. As the leaf strengthens the colour drains away, to become russet again with autumn frosts, remaining so all winter. I have other delicate epimediums to tell you of in more favoured spots elsewhere, but I value none more than this.

Thalictrum aquilegifolium was an easy settler, holding its large mauve-pink or white powder puffs high above most things. Its green seed heads also add something to the scene among stands of *Lilium tigrinum* and dark blue *Aconitum*. *Thalictrum* seedlings appear where I would not think of putting them, and grow to an astonishing height, peering through the lacy foliage of the golden cut-leafed elder, *Sambucus racemosa* 'Plumosa Aurea'.

Camassia leichtlinii has also seeded generously in among hostas with tall graceful stems of pale cream-coloured stars. Not quite so delicate, but much admired, is the rare double form *C.l.* 'Semiplena'. This need a deep, rich soil to make the large bulbs which send up stout stems, over 5 ft/1.5 m tall, heavily set with double cream rosettes. Snowdrops—among which appeared a particularly fine looking one, tall stemmed with globular flowers and grey leaves, given various names by enthusiasts so I am still no wiser—I planted and divide every few years to build up stock. Ivory-white *Narcissus* 'Thalia', and *N.* 'Tresamble' please me more than too much bright yellow, looking especially lovely among the forget-me-not blue of *Brunnera macrophylla*, whose large leaves handsomely cover the gaps when both flowers have long gone.

For autumn glory colchicums, including the peerless *Colchicum speciosum* 'Album', slowly multiplied.

The Ditch

Alongside this Shade Bed, separated by a wide curving grass walk, ran the ditch, about 1 yd/1 m wide with fairly shallow sloping banks. We had no experience of growing water-side plants, and we made the usual mistakes. Probably the worst was being in too much of a hurry and not making proper preparations. But to begin with it did not show up too badly.

The worst weeds along the bank-side were rushes, grasses of course, and nettles. Although we had dug the roots out initially the soil was full of weed seed, and in those early days we had no ideas about mulching—at least we had seen hop waste used at Kew Gardens, but considerable effort among local breweries produced not even a whiff. It seemed it all went to fertilizer firms, in which case we could not afford it, not in the amounts we would be needing. We could only cope with the weed problem on this especially difficult type of soil, where native weeds germinate freely and rapaciously smother newcomers, by planting large and vigorous co-operators who would do some of the work for us.

We planted quick-growing shrubs like *Cornus alba* 'Westonbirt' whose china-blue berries set among crimson autumn leaves are followed by brilliant red stems all winter. The lovely green and gold variegated *Cornus alba* 'Spaethii' made a great shrub more than 8 ft/2.5 m high, and far more across. Several bushes of *Viburnum opulus* 'Xanthocarpum' looked charming in early summer covered with lacy 'maid's caps', while in autumn we seemed to have weeks of pleasure from the large clusters of marble-sized berries, butter-yellow, gradually turning transparent amber. The crimson-fruited

Viburnum opulus was there as well. So too was *Viburnum betulifolium* which made an enormous screen, but was most reluctant to berry. Why, I wonder? Thinking the first plant needed company, perhaps from a different clone, we bought two more, which shot up with equal vigour, but only an occasional bough was hung with the characteristic tiny glittering berries (see page 109).

We planted *Aralia elata*, the Japanese Angelica Tree, which makes in one season tall, linen-proplike prickly stems topped with handsome pinnate leaves, the second year producing a froth of white blossom followed by wide heads of tiny purple-black berries on crimson stems. But this too had to go further afield. Its suckering habit was insufferable among border *Phlox*, Black-eyed Susan, *Rudbeckia newmanii*, and other robust perennials.

Polygonum campanulatum was a great success. A rapid colonizer with surface roots so not a menace, it makes ideal ground-cover in damp soil where something large is needed. In spring it appears as a close cover, but during the summer the crowded stems elongate to about 3 ft/1 m. All late summer and autumn they are topped with loose heads of tiny rose-pink flowers.

Polygonum sachalinense we planted also, and magnificent it looked in its wild setting. Great jointed bamboo-like stems, 10–12 ft/3–4 m high, carry large oval green leaves while strings of typical white flowers emerge from every leaf axil. But it is a formidable underground worker so beware of putting it anywhere you would regret.

Polygonum cuspidatum, and *P.c.* 'Compactum', originally introduced as *P.* 'Reynoutria' were both there, invincible among native weeds but practically ineradicable themselves—a pity, because they are both very handsome. They had to be removed, but fortunately I could find for them a distant wilderness where I hope I shall not live to regret my decision. Tall grasses like *Miscanthus sacchariflorus*, *M. sinensis* 'Gracillimus' and *M.s.* 'Zebrinus' made splendid contrast in form to these gigantic herbs.

Having read that *Rheum palmatum* looked splendid among water-side plantings I tried to establish some pieces, but they looked more and more miserable. When I dug them up I found their great crowns were rotting. The soil was too wet for them. However, in later years I have planted more, not far from the water, but on raised ground so there is no danger of water-logging. They do look almost tropical in luxuriance, and are needful near the lush water-side plants, especially if *Gunnera* is not easily obtainable.

We had prepared a rich, deep bed for *Gunnera scabra* which was making good headway until we had a particularly cold winter. Our plant was being so slow to produce those rusty-backed funnels of new leaves that we went to investigate and found that a family of water rats had lived all winter in its huge starchy heart and eaten it out, leaving, like a cheese, the outer rind. Offshoots did survive, but it was a wasted year or so. I have also had *Phormium tenax* chewed off at their heavy bases by these little creatures. When we first began the garden they were so unused to humans they were quite fearless. Not at all repulsive, like the scabby land rats against whom we wage incessant war, they are neat little creatures, with sleek brown coats and shining beady eyes. Endearing, in fact, as Ratty himself. But their eating habits are as deadly to water gardeners as are rabbits elsewhere. We had to deal with the problem in due course.

Naturally I tried to grow candelabra primulas, and blue *Meconopsis* (of all things in windy Essex!), but the situation was not sufficiently under control. Anything small was eventually lost, either because I could not give it enough attention, or because the coarseness of the soil did not favour it.

I should not like to forget to mention a plant that I associate very much with the early days of the Damp Garden. We had planted the Himalayan *Impatiens roylei*. When well grown this imposing annual makes transparent stems, as thick as your wrist at the base, standing easily 6–8 ft/2–3 m tall. In late autumn its curious sweet scent floats on the moist air of still evenings. I stand and look into its extraordinary shaped flowers, made in two parts which open like a medieval knight's hinged helmet. Andrew takes a ripe pointed seed pod and puts it in my hand, telling me to hold it close—knowing that in a few seconds I will jump in alarm as it bursts like a broken spring to toss its seeds for yards. That is the trouble. We had, at times, forests of seedlings. In our primitive beginnings it did not matter. It looked in keeping. But as I wished to grow more and more unusual plants I knew it would have to be checked.

Now we tend to weed out every seedling we find so that sometimes I am concerned that there seems not to be a single plant left. But I need not worry. Tucked into the wilder places, perhaps around the great clumps of bamboo, enough seedlings escape to flower and toss their seeds where no harm can be done.

2 *The First Seven Years*

By midsummer 1960 the house was finished, and as much of our seventeen years of collecting as we could decently manage was heeled in, lined out, or comfortably planted somewhere. Initially I think it was a rather traumatic experience for our two young daughters to have a new house surrounded by so much empty space. They had grown up in a sheltered, rather formal garden, with a brick-pillared pergola of roses, tidy lawns, a summerhouse to play in. *I* was sustained by the endless possibilities of this new project but I was jolted abruptly into someone else's point of view one day by the youthful realist who commented that Mother's garden was a muddy field full of sticks.

Paving and Planting round the House

To try to create a more civilized atmosphere we turned from planning and planting to contemplating the ruts, humps and hollows that lay around the house. We had not had anything done by the builder. For one thing we had to decide what we wanted, and for another we had to have what we could afford. The land was sloping, and likely to be damp, especially on the lower levels, so paving was the obvious choice. Grass around the house would have been impossible to manage.

The lower side of our split-level house consists of our living quarters. Glass doors led out onto a platform made by the bulldozer across the slope which fell away on the west side to a wide level stretch of grass. At the far end of the platform another slope led up and around the bedroom wing which looked onto the Dry Garden-to-be.

We hired a cement mixer, staked out levels so that rain water would run away from the house and, armed with boards of various lengths, we created a pattern of squares of various sizes, arranged randomly, laid in situ. We made the amateur's mistake of not using sufficient reinforcement at the base beneath our concrete, so that over the years there has been some movement of the blocks, but on the whole it looks good and has worn well.

Leading both up and down from this terrace we made flights of steps to fit the levels, making sure that they measured the right number of paces required. It is very disconcerting to find yourself with foot in mid-air and nowhere to put it. We carried on, in similar fashion, all round the house, leaving room beneath the walls for planting. We could now step out without risk of breaking our backs. There was also a sizeable area of outdoor living space in which to eat, read or sunbathe—for those who had time, and weather!

Already planted on this south-facing terrace was *Magnolia* ×
soulangiana. Only a year or so previously we had heard Mr Graham Thomas
talking about gardening at our local grammar school. He told us that
magnolias should be moved in spring. Of course they might be in flower, but
that was not important, it was the roots that mattered. Move them in winter
and they could rot in the cold soil, move them when the soil was warm, the
sap moving, and they would get away. What good advice! We had a young
tree, established about three years in our old garden. I could not bear to
leave it. So, with its seven blooms, we carefully dug it up and replanted it on
our terrace-to-be, watched in disbelief by tilers and carpenters who came
down off their ladders to view the operation. The tree has never looked
back. Now it almost dwarfs the terrace. In spring the bedroom windows look
into its great branches of blossoms, and wrens make nests in *Hedera helix*
'Discolor' (so charmingly stippled with white we call it *Hedera* 'White Lace')
which I planted at its base; it now fans a circle of tendrils across the shaded
paving.

With so much empty space there had to be more trees to create a
framework for the house, to shelter the plants I hoped I could grow. I
sometimes say it is not difficult to cover the bare earth when making a new
garden; much more patience is needed to paint the sky. Time dragged as I
waited for the trees to reach the roof level of our low-pitched mushroom-
like house.

Another interesting problem was to change the unfamiliar scale created
by a three-hundred-year-old oak dominant under a wide Essex sky, set in
undefined space. I felt this most keenly one day when I carried a handful of
snowdrops in green leaf and planted them beneath the oak. I stood back to
admire the effect and felt chilled by the loneliness of that little bunch. There
needed to be many frames within frames to ease the transition in time and
space. An oak wood, with trees of mixed years, with ivy curled round their
trunks and carpeting the ground below, becomes with time the setting for a
ballet of snowdrops, bunched and drifting to catch your breath.

The *Magnolia* was planted. Adding to it, to make a screen for the
terrace from the grass walk below, we planted *Pseudolarix amabilis*, the
Golden Larch. Larches tend to get their heads blown out by our savage east
winds. We hoped the house and the lie of the land would shelter this rarely
planted tree so that we should have the pleasure of its warm yellow needles
in autumn. Great contrast in colour and form was in mind as we planted one
of my cuttings of *Chamaecyparis lawsoniana* 'Ellwoodii'. Supposedly slow
growing it is now, after nineteen years, a monumental column, standing
halfway down a shallow flight of steps, at least 20 ft/6 m high, 6 ft/2 m
across. It has a noble architectural quality, complementing the lines of the
house. For several small birds it provides a high-rise dwelling, with nests at
all levels, busily attended by anxious parents who chatter desperately against
the cat who can wait, patiently, on the sun-warm terrace.

Beyond the steps we planted a Chinese Crab Apple, *Malus hupehensis*,
grown from a tiny cherry-like apple. It has made a fine tree whose domed

head of twiggy branches is loaded with cup-shaped white blossoms in late May. Blackbirds and thrushes feast on the fruit in autumn. A fastigiate yew, *Taxus baccata* 'Fastigiata', and *Picea omorika*, that beautiful Balkan Spruce so good for areas that need grace without demanding too much space, add comforting columns of green in winter.

We made several false starts with the rest of the planting. There were yellow kniphofias with gigantic blue campanulas, and other muddles of herbaceous plants. Orange lilies came and went. We were overwhelmed by our inability to keep so much new planting clean. I felt that we must have plants as a surround to the terrace which remained effective with the minimum of time spent, to provide a peaceful view from the house. So I thought of heathers. 'What a waste of good soil,' you may be saying. Perhaps. But let me add quickly that heathers die very easily of drought here on excessively drained soil, with minimal summer rainfall whisked away by inevitable wind. Around my *Malus* then, which lifts its light shade well above them, I planted tree heathers. *Erica arborea*, with *E. lusitanica* which is not unlike it but always seems to be finer in spring when its great boughs of greenery, soft and light green, are crowded with tubular white flowers out of pink-tinted buds.

I liked *Erica terminalis*, the Corsican Heath, with its very upright growth, with long straight tips bearing rose-coloured flowers in late summer which, fading to a warm brown, were good to pick in winter. But my bush became elbowed out of the way by *Erica arborea* before I was aware of the damage done. It is difficult when planting to imagine that tiny potfuls may well need spacing at 10 ft/3 m intervals—and still these great heathers will collide.

Erica mediterranea makes a smaller, denser bush, a darker, pewter-green, separating the giants in the background from the low mounds in the foreground. Here various forms of *E. carnea*, *E. ciliaris*, *E. cinerea*, and *E.* × *darleyensis* provide colour for much of the year. They do need clipping over occasionally, after they have flowered. I confess I have neglected to do this the last year or so. My attention has been given to making new plantings elsewhere, but although they have demanded so little attention over fifteen years, the recent dwindling attention is noticeable. They lack that cared-for look which is desirable, as opposed to the short-back-and-sides look which can be the result of too much scissoring, too frequently.

Pernettyas go well with heathers. They help with smothering weeds, while their marble-sized berries in shades of lilac-pink, ruby-red and white are a joy to pick in late autumn, perhaps to put with the Kaffir lilies, *Schizostylis coccinea*, which are also in flower at the base of the bed where the springs are coming near to the surface.

A selected seedling of *Euphorbia characias wulfenii* makes interesting contrast to the fine-leafed heathers and dense sprawling mound of *Juniperus communis* 'Hornibrookii' (there are eleven pages of junipers in Hillier's *Manual*!) which creeps over a little rounded platform between two flights of steps. The *Euphorbia*, looking as though it has dropped from the

Mediterranean Garden above, links the two, and for months lights up an area of muted greens with large spiralling heads of luminous yellow-green.

Erica australis I would not be allowed to forget if I were writing this in spring. It is the finest of tree heathers, so large are its flowers, so heavily clustered that the leaves are hidden, the boughs bent beneath them—but, coming from Spain and Portugal, it is not very hardy. Tucked down on my west-facing bank it has survived yet. *Cistus*, which I thought would look so well here, did both look and grow *too* well. The first hard winter killed their sappy growth stone-dead, while stringy shrubs, half-starved elsewhere, had their foliage seared but survived.

Hebes, I thought, would make another change in colour and texture of foliage. Among the 'whipcords' *Hebe ochracea*, which for years we called *H. armstrongii* (in company with most other folk), makes somewhat open bushes of very upright branches. It has done away with leaves and instead makes do with masses of cord-like stems atop the woody branches, of a peculiarly arresting shade of dull gold. It is beautiful, especially in winter among heathers.

Hebe recurva I prefer to *H. pagei*, although I do use the latter as ground-cover. But *H. recurva* makes a neat, round bush set with slightly larger, more pointed blue-grey leaves. When in flower, with heads of nutmeg-brown buds opening to little white flowers, it is a delight. Behind these a background is made with *Hebe* 'Amy'. I am not certain that is the correct name, but it is not uncommon, being much valued for its beautiful young growth, which is shining burgundy. Although rather tender, like most large-leafed hebes, it has survived here for more than ten years, in company with a great *Rosa rubrifolia*, glorious in new leaf, all pewter and rose, clustered with hips which turn from leaden-purple to crimson as the nights draw in. As I stand below on the grass several arching clumps of *Libertia formosa* mask the long legs of the rose, and throw up stiff straight stems of little white flowers which repeat an upward movement through the rose to the *Magnolia* stretched high above them.

Another group I enjoy is to my right as I stand indoors looking out of my west window, separated from me by a narrow path. Originally I planted a fine quince, called 'Vranja' (I think it was from Hungary), imagining the golden globular fruit I would pick to make quince jelly and scented bowls of apple mousse. I did keep the tree long enough to do a little of that. But I was disappointed with its ungainly shape, in which it persisted however I tried to prune it. In an old garden I remember seeing a 'common' quince having made a most attractive gnarled yet compact head. I could see no sign of that in my tree, however long I waited. What was more the fruits, all too quickly and often before I picked them, became damaged by large patches of brown rot which again ruined my vision of perfection as well as limiting the store-cupboard. The flowers, incidentally, were very pretty, unexpectedly large pink and white cups, but not pretty enough to stay the day of execution. Up it came, and in its place I planted *Prunus subhirtella* 'Autumnalis Rosea'. This year I shall see for the first time branches of delicate pink blossom stretching across the window. Quite apart from having waited long enough for the branches to reach my view, this is also the first year that I have kept the bullfinches from eating all but about ten buds. Each winter our last thought before packing up the garden for Christmas has been to spray with bird repellent those things we would choose to keep. Last year, early in January, an inspection found that bitter or not, most buds of my *Prunus*, and all the forsythias, were hollow shells. This year I strung them with glitter-bangs and milk bottle tops threaded on string. Most unsightly, but the buds are still there. I would like to think that I was successful—but I have not noticed bullfinch damage anywhere this year yet, not even the fat pear buds which are great favourites.

Beneath my 'Spring Cherry' are now established clumps of the Christmas Rose, *Helleborus niger*. Although it is supposed to favour a limy soil it has done well here in soil which is drained (at the top of the shallow bank) yet retains moisture well enough. Not knowing what else to do with it I planted *Sisyrinchium striatum* 'Variegatum' beneath the tree (it scarcely casts shade), and together with *Veronica teucrium* 'Crater Lake Blue' these two have made the prettiest picture—especially as when it comes up to flower the *Sisyrinchium* is more cream than green, a striking vertical in a brilliant blue sea.

To rest my mind from writing I turned to that great gardening poet, V. Sackville-West, who made gardens with words as no one can, and gave sound advice in good plain English too. I think I may have found the answer to my quince trouble. She writes that the quince is subject to fungus attacks, including one which attacks leaves and fruits, whose alternative host is the Savin Juniper. I do not know whether my tree had this disease but a wide-spreading Savin Juniper, *Juniperus sabina*, flares across the grass only a few yards from where my quince tree grew. A page or two away I learn that *Prunus subhirtella* can be grown from young summer shoots. I must try that—it almost feels as though she had looked over my shoulder to give me a hand with my gardening.

Beginning the Water Gardens

With the rest of the garden under way I looked again at the Lily Pond and thought I knew what was wrong with it. It was the wrong shape—too small for its setting, too round. It was a heady spring day, long white clouds in a blue sky. Suddenly I saw that, instead of a small round pond, I needed a long stretch of open water to repeat the shape of my white-boarded house, to reflect the clouds and the majestic oak which stood almost opposite the house. I broke the good news to Andrew who, while not exactly discouraging, thought it was out of the question. The expense would forbid it.

Then one of those curious coincidences happened which make you feel as though life is already mapped out for you, and you are merely following the white line. Within a few days, who should I meet in the village but my friend with the drag-line. He began it. How was the Lily Pond? What could I say? I said, 'Why don't you come and have a look at it?' The end of an entertaining and reassuring morning, during which Mr C. walked up and down our hollow (hanging on to a vibrant hazel twig), was that he could easily do what I wanted for £20! Twenty pounds then was worth a great deal more than it is today, but that morning to me it seemed very reasonable to drown a lot of weedy rubbish, to get rid of the dry steep sides of the ditch, to have shallow boggy edges. I could already see primulas—in sheets!

Once again the drag-line, that huge and seemingly cumbersome machine, edged its way delicately down the garden entrance slope, followed by a bulldozer, for we had decided to go further and open up the opposite side beyond the pond as far as the ancient boundary hedge. There was already a crossing over the ditch made above a small brick culvert. It was decided to open up this little dam and raise the level of the water by ramming wet clay into the culvert, lay new pipes at a higher level and replace the topsoil. This would cause the running water to flood the land behind. It was also decided, because of the gentle slope of the land, that instead of making one long sheet of water we would divide it by two dams placed across the middle, so forming a second and third pond at slightly higher levels. This meant moving the minimum of soil. The effect when done was, and still is, just as I wished. But it might have been better if several feet of clay had been removed from the bottom of the ponds, as they are rather shallow, and I fear for them silting up. However, to cart away the abominable clay would have entailed expense we could not afford—and where to?

I am always in a state of dither when the drag-line is at work. So much happens so fast. Can I visualize how it will look when the piles of oozing scooped-up clay, heaped to make dams across the middle of three seemingly vast scraped holes, have settled and the water has found its new level? It must not come too high and flood the grass walk below the house. At the same time will it be high enough to cover a particularly awkward wet patch?

While the topography of the garden was being remade the bulldozer was making short work of the wilderness beyond. Great thickets of black-thorn to which we had become accustomed, even admired for a brief space when 'frosted' with blossom in April's blackthorn winter—all were being swept away, and a new wide expanse of brown meadow silt was being exposed. For the first time we could see all of the boundary trees—six oaks, a couple of immense hawthorns, a fine crab apple and several decrepit hazel-nut bushes.

It was no use being impatient at this stage. The land had to settle. During the summer we let the meadow silt run down to its native grasses, and while there were undesirables like great prickly rosettes of marsh thistle, and soft grass, *Holcus mollis*, which makes enormous floppy tussocks, so big that one will fill a barrow—we managed to control it well enough for the time being with our old farm Hayter pulled behind the tractor.

My first bog borders lay between the mown grass and the edge of the water where we could see them from the house. We dug and carted away in barrows as much of the clay as we had the strength and willpower to do. It was not a great deal. Then we carted as much decent topsoil and rotted compost as we could find and piled that on top to hide the beastly yellow stuff.

Next we thought about suitable trees. We planted three Swamp Cypresses, *Taxodium distichum*, tiny things, knee high, and a *Metasequoia glyptostroboides*, or Dawn Redwood as many people, understandably, would prefer to call it. Both of these are leaf-losing conifers; both take, like ducks, to water. The Swamp Cypress, from the Everglades of Florida, has smaller frond-like leaves, soft and mossy-green. Before they drop in autumn they slowly turn a rich foxy-brown. Knowing they would take many years before they made their mark in the landscape we planted quick growing willows to give some height. The great oak still remained aloof in the background, so to bring it into the garden I planted a Weeping Willow, *Salix* 'Chrysocoma' between it and the water. By the water's edge I planted *Gunnera scabra*. Today the willow makes a tumbling mass half the height of the oak. It unites visually with the oak from across the water, and together with the vast parasols of the *Gunnera* leaves they create a harmonious group in scale with their surroundings.

When the dams were sufficiently settled they were prepared for grass. This was Harry's job. Harry has, over the years, made it possible for me to follow behind his careful preparations and plant my garden. Halfway across one of the dams, which lies opposite my bedroom window, we planted a *Salix matsudana* 'Tortuosa', better known as the Twisted Willow. On the whole I do not like 'tortured' plants. I think the contorted hazelnut is shockingly hideous in summer, its poor leaves so twisted and malformed that one immediately thinks it must be riddled with aphids. In winter, of course, it is a different matter; there is something attractive about those corkscrew curling twigs and branches. But where to plant it, so that you will not come across it in summer?

The Twisted Willow is not nearly so deformed, but I think *it* is best in winter, when every gracefully curling branch and twig sparkles as the sun is reflected from its polished surfaces. The young leaves, slightly twisted, look particularly pleasing if you cut a few boughs in early January, bring them into the house, and let a jugful become an indoor mini tree, decked in the tenderest green leaves long before the buds have burst outside.

Near the first little dam we planted *Prunus* 'Tai Haku', the Great White Cherry, well above the water on a little bank. Among earlier tree plantings we had had a *Liquidambar styraciflua*, the Sweet Gum, but in autumn it never managed more than the dirtiest of nettle-green colouring where I had expected a warm conflagration of crimson and scarlet. From somewhere I had obtained seed, and now with several little saplings to choose from I picked out the one which looked most promising and planted it in a group with the white-flowered cherry and another *Metasequoia*. They have all grown into a most companionable group: the *Metasequoia* rapidly made a tall slender accent, as lovely in winter with its cinnamon-brown bark as it is in summer clothed in larch-green. The leaves of the *Liquidambar* glow like garnets in the short days of autumn, a total contrast to the ice-white clusters of cherry blossom in spring. They grow to the constant sound of water as it falls from the hidden pipe laid beneath the little grassed dam, and drops several feet into the widened ditch, over which they cast a cool shade. For long enough the steep sides of the bank and the sight of the pipe emerging from it bothered me. But I planted *Hedera helix* 'Cristata' thickly and soon both bank and pipe were disguised by a green shawl of crinkled leaves, which solved my weeding problem in that awkward area.

We came at last to the exciting moment of putting herbaceous plants into the damp soil. Water does not travel far sideways in heavy soil, so it remains really wet a comparatively short distance from the water's edge. Here we planted various forms of marsh marigold, *Caltha palustris* and *C.p.* 'Flore Pleno', the double-flowered form which makes such a long-lasting display but does not, to my mind, have quite the charm of our common King Cup with its brownish stems forming a graceful mound, each single cup filled with a boss of rich gold stamens. With heaps of wet ground to cover perhaps my favourite is *Caltha polysepala*. Planted on the edge of a low wet place it will root itself into the soil, or fling out yard-long stems which root into the water, eventually making great rafts many feet across if you will let it. The large round leaves stand up well above the water, no less handsome than the leaves of water-lilies, perfect to unite large areas of land and water.

The Water Forget-me-not, *Myosotis palustris*, quickly settled in, seeded and made drifts of blue among the spring golds. Water iris, especially *Iris laevigata*, *I. versicolor* and the handsome *I.v. kermesina*, also multiplied.

We had decided that large herbs would, on the whole, stand a better chance of survival than anything more refined. The largest we were aware of then was *Eupatorium purpureum*, whose dark plum-coloured stems easily soar over 8 ft/2.5 m, topped with wide flat heads of fuzzy cinnamon-pink flowers.

Members of the meadowsweet family were another obvious choice, especially *Filipendula rubra* 'Venusta' which sent its strong roots down into the clay, spreading around its tall stems set with dark vine-like leaves. As time has passed one of the prettiest sights now, in summer, is that of the fluffy pink heads, like candyfloss, poised high against the fresh green columns of the Swamp Cypresses. Not so tall, and keeping itself in a well-controlled clump, is the pale pink form of *Filipendula purpurea* (*Spiraea palmata*). Close again to the water I planted my two favourites of the European mountain meadows, *Trollius europaeus* with *Polygonum bistorta* 'Superbum', the soft yellow globes and thick pink pokers reflected in the dark water. The *Polygonum*, with its mounds of great dock-like leaves (always causing the same kind of tediously obvious comment—as does *Gunnera*) is invaluable ground-cover in wet clay soil.

Along the mown grass edge, furthest away from the water, I planted hostas. Especially handsome was *H. sieboldiana elegans*—its quilted bluish leaves make an incomparable focal point—while the exquisite grass, *Molinia coerulea* 'Variegata', almost steals that honour, especially in the autumn when it becomes almost totally white.

It is not easy to find plants which remain evergreen by the water-side. Most disappear completely, so that the contrast between summer lushness and the desolate drabness of winter can be painful. I value both the Pampas Grass, *Cortaderia selloana*, and *Phormium tenax* for their big bold outlines, in winter especially when they help to take the eye off the empty wastes.

I try to leave the tall stately clumps of *Miscanthus* for as long as I can in the winter. In autumn they withdraw their colour, becoming columns of palest straw. *Miscanthus sinensis* 'Gracillimus' survives the wintry gales with scarcely a curling wisp out of place, elegant to the end, but the 10 ft/3 m (and more) stems of *Miscanthus sacchariflorus* fluttering with tattered ribbons have usually to be cut down before they have made a fine mess.

All of these plants, in their season, add something to the varied pattern of leaves and flowers at the water's edge. But there are two plants which for me are high points in the design. From spring to autumn they dominate.

The first is *Lysichitum americanum*, the Bog Arum. In early April, when the cold wet soil is bare but for twigs and dead leaves, cobra-like heads emerge, tipped and shaded with green. As this fades away the huge spathes reflect rich yellow in the clear water. Inside are sheltered slim spadices which slowly form green club-like heads of seed, caviare for my friends the water voles. There is more to come. At this time only the very tips of the leaves are showing at the base of the thickly clustered flower stems, but surging up from 3 ft/1 m or more below the sodden clay they come, pushing aside the spent spathes, and making a leaf cluster, shining green, as spectacular as any flower for months to come. Thinking how to describe these impressive leaves, I am reminded of one, in a group of young students, who irreverently rocked with mirth at the enormous 'spinach' which had suddenly caught his eye and imagination. Recovering my balance I appreciated that he had noticed the plant, and am grateful now for the simile because they are not unlike a well-grown Spinach Beet, though four times as big, and stronger and smoother in texture.

The second and most dramatic plant by the water-side is *Gunnera*, whose enormous leaves, 4–6 ft/1.2–2 m across, can stand more than head high, offering shelter from a sudden shower of rain. Not everyone admires it. Its sheer size, rasping texture and outlandish fruiting body undoubtedly contributed to the emotion of a lady who observed, matter of factly, that it really was quite hideous. Although I could not agree with her I was amused by this unexpected opinion in place of the usual comment of 'Oh, look at this gigantic rhubarb', which of course it is not.

Our plants came originally from a garden in the last sad stage of decay. The shallow moat had vanished completely beneath a meadow of rush and water grasses, the flowering plants were long gone. Once or twice a year the banks were scythed. Tidied up with the rest (maybe in full leaf, but no matter), were the remnants of *Gunnera scabra*, their huge parasols reduced to pygmy proportions. I could not believe they were the real thing. But time, and care (with annual dressings of old muck) healed, and they recovered their majestic grandeur. Without them, and the towering feathery pennants of Pampas Grass, *Cortaderia selloana* 'Sunningdale Silver', the scale of the garden could overwhelm smaller plants. (I may have said it before but in a smaller setting I would probably use an ornamental rhubarb in place of *Gunnera*.)

Our first plants were of *Gunnera scabra* (*G. chilensis*). It grows wild in Chile, with *Cortaderia selloana*, backed by a forest of the Antarctic Beech, *Nothofagus*, while feathered stems of climbing bamboo disappear above them. This spectacular scene is illustrated in *Die Vegetation der Erde*, by Dr Karl Reiche, who stands four-square beside his photographic paraphernalia, dwarfed by these giants among plants. This wonderful picture stretches the mind, and is the answer to a sensitive gardener who, when advised by me to plant Pampas Grass as a feature near her water garden, ventured hesitantly that it might look suburban. In the wrong setting it might look out of place, but suburban never!

In the wild *Gunnera scabra* stays near the shelter of the forest, but the Pampas Grass can also be found alongside water courses, all over the wide pampas, or prairies, where there is little but grass and sky for miles and miles. *Gunnera manicata*, which grows even larger and taller than *G. scabra*, comes from southern Brazil, which is considerably warmer. It is necessary to cover both forms well, to shelter the coconut-sized resting buds which have no outer protection, only the first leaf wrapped round like a parcel. When the plants are young additional comfort like straw or bracken will be needed, but we saw down the stout prickly stems of our established plants and turn them upside down over the spreading crowns like a great bonfire. By early April the upturned funnels of folded leaves are pushing through the battered remains. We remove them. But sometimes late May frosts have killed the new leaves; they stand crisply mummified while I wait anxiously to see what will happen next. Within a few weeks new leaves have emerged from hidden reserves and the show is on, a little later.

My second, narrower bed beside the water I filled at last with primulas. *Primula japonica*, *P. pulverulenta*, *P. florindae* and *P. bulleyana*, mixed up with *Iris kaempferi*, the little double *Cardamine* and a few astilbes. It was colourful—too colourful for my liking, too many star-performers grouped together. However, we pressed on, and before long we had made borders round two of the ponds, so tempting was it not to waste any damp ground.

Beguiled by a picture in Frances Perry's book, *Water Gardening*, that has haunted me for years, showing a great curve of lake-side with at least a thousand blooms of Arum Lily (*Zantedeschia aethiopica*) I planted two or three clumps. We made shallow baskets of old wire netting, filled them with upturned turves, well-rotted muck and topsoil, set the roots among it and lowered the lot into the water, hoping the water rats would not get them. They have established and increased, but I shall never see the luxuriance of that mysterious garden in the picture—could it be a warmer district than here?

B. *Menyanthes trifoliata* (foreground), *Zantedeschia aethiopica* (centre) and *Iris laevigata* (background)

Dealing with Water Voles

By now we had learnt a little about gardening in boggy land. The most frightening thing was the way the weeds grew. No thought of hoeing—everything had to be pulled, dug or slurped out of the squelchy ground or it immediately took root again. Along the water's edge knitting needle clumps of Common Rush, pretty as could be when young, became a major issue, back-breaking to lift with the slime running down the front of your anorak and into your wellington boots. Not only that, but the edge of the bed on which you have piled your precious topsoil crumbles down into the water as you prise out some particularly tenacious weed. Something had to be done.

There was another problem. It was the water rats, or more correctly, water voles, who were becoming too troublesome to be tolerated. Imagine, on one of our two soft, still summer evenings, that you are dreaming round the garden counting your blessings (and failures). Or, you are tearing yourself away from a bit of blissfully uninterrupted planting to go indoors to make supper. Suddenly either mood is shattered by the loud crunching of teeth on something not easily spared. It may be the fine stand of bamboo by the little wooden bridge now at the far end of the garden. It is almost bound to be water iris. Remains of enormous clumps of *Iris pseudacorus* have been seen to float on the surface like shredded wheat. In spring I have found heavy tillers of *Phormium tenax* that could be lifted out of the soil, baseless. I could go on, monotonously for you, maddening for me.

Riddling their way through the pond-side borders the water voles undermined the banks with their exits and entrances, below water level. The edges fell in, plants fell out. Even the lawns became undermined by these busy little bodies. What to do? Neither of us was born with guns in our hands, so although we possessed a four-ten we were not very efficient with it. The water voles plopped out of our plants as soon as they heard us coming and we did not have the cat's patience to wait. What is more, there were plenty of families both up- and downstream to come and take their places.

Then Andrew had a bright idea. We remembered the edging around the lakes at Kew Gardens, preventing the banks from disintegrating. They have driven in strong poles, of elm perhaps, vertically, and packed close together so that the finished effect, a few inches above water level, is a necklace of round wooden blocks (about 5 or 6 in./150 mm across as I remember), set all round the water's edge. This is called piling, and must be extremely laborious and expensive. We could not see our way to piling with wood (elm disease was then unknown to us). But we could make a substitute. We could lay our hands on old angle irons (new ones are costly), and we could buy, not too expensively, hollow concrete blocks. We would sink the blocks around the edge of the pond and stabilize them with an angle iron driven through both ends of the blocks into the hard soil beneath.

Once more Harry took over this heavy job. The flow of water had to be stopped by blocking the entrance culvert with clay, and our handy little pump chugged away for a day or so lowering the water level so that he could

C. A small group of water-side plants

see what he was doing. In most places two blocks deep were sufficient, making an 18 in./460 mm wall, with irons about 4 ft/1.2 m long driven through them. Sometimes three or four blocks were required where the hard bottom was deeper, and I saw irons 6 ft/2 m long disappear through the blocks to rest just at the top level of concrete. When finished the top of the blocks was about 2 in./50 mm above the water line, and I think Harry was as delighted with it as we were, having taken great care to make the curves natural and pleasing.

It may *sound* horrible. I must confess that throughout the operation I had felt Gertrude Jekyll's sensitive eye looking down on me in reproach. But, said I to myself, I must try to be practical as well as aesthetic. A garden is by its very nature chaos controlled (more or less), but we do not want that control too apparent.

As I had hoped, the hard edging soon weathered, plants flopped over it, *Iris* and *Pontederia* grew happily against it. I hardly think that, in most places, you would notice it. We decided to edge the dams as well; the final effect of neat mown grass walks crossing the broad stretches of water is very satisfying. They are pleasant places to sit, surrounded by lush plants, and to feed the ducks and watch a red-finned rudd surge beneath an astonished drake to tip him off course as both of them aim for the same crumb of bread.

On early summer mornings I often see a heron from my window, immobile in shallow water or marching stiffly up and down the dam, alert for the slightest sign of movement in the house. Sometimes I see him lunge like a spear, then throw up his head and struggle mightily to ease a big fish down his long neck. There are plenty of the native fish for him and to spare; he helps keep a natural balance. Sometimes the shallows look like marmalade with thousands of tiny suspended fish warming themselves in the sun. I like to think the kingfisher has a taste of those. One memorable day I walked back to my digging to find him, unbelievably, sitting on the handle of my spade.

After making the low support walls gardening around the ponds became much less hazardous. The sound of chewing ceased, and I could crouch on the narrow edge of the blocks to weed my beds in comfort.

3 *Expansion*

Start of the Shade and Meadow Beds

Looking from the house, across the ponds, the view disturbed me. It needed a more comfortable background. There was, of course, the great oak which dominates the garden wherever you stand. It stood at the end of the boundary row of miscellaneous oaks and oddments. Too many oddments. Elders, naturally, were seeded everywhere, with blackthorn suckers and Goat-willow between the glaring gaps. Beyond the gaps we have glimpses of the neighbouring farm, under plough, or golden with corn, while a distant mixed hedge of mature trees and brushwood adds considerably to the view. But I dread this being axed during some particularly cold spell when nothing more useful can be done. I felt we needed to plant more trees and shrubs, in groups, in the grass, and far enough away from the boundary not to be affected by overhead shade.

One warm day, walking over the rough grass discussing the proposed tree planting, someone dropped a hot match—in a flash the grass crackled and fire ran quickly ahead of us, in spite of damp soil underneath. Beating with branches and stamping our feet we had a hot and anxious time before it was controlled.

I shall not list the names of all the trees and shrubs we planted to make a windshield and background screen for our ponds. Suffice to say that plant we did, and as usual more than enough so that changes had to be made as crowding became apparent. The trees and shrubs were planted in rough grass, that is cut two or three times a year. I used to enjoy sweeping up the long grass with a big wooden rake, imagining I was on holiday in Switzerland as I 'toiled' up and down my slight slopes. The hay I piled around the trees to act as a mulch, leaving a few inches of bare ground round the base of the trunks so that mice would not be tempted to sit under cover and chew round the bark in winter.

As the trees grew the little round beds they stood in were enlarged to prevent too much root competition from the grass. One or two trees stood still for several years after planting. Feeling there was not much to lose I slit the bark vertically from top to bottom with a sharp knife. I was pleased to see the split widen and the trees begin to make new growth. Such a drastic method can be worth knowing if trees become bark-bound; an old countryman had shown me how to do it years before.

Seven years went by. By now Andrew's health had deteriorated too badly for him to continue running the farm. It had to be sold. The thought of leaving the wasteland and the garden well started I found unbearable. It was agreed that I could start a little nursery to help pay someone to help me. I had learnt to propagate many things for the garden. There were always plants to spare. So I began, with one girl, a few frames made from railway sleepers, and Harry, who asked to stay with me when the farm was gone.

An old way of life was over. A different life began. The garden had to be maintained, but alongside it I had to learn to balance the books. Making and selling plants had to have priority. However, I made time still to plant, and one day I planted both the green- and red-leaved forms of *Rheum palmatum* in two groups in front of my young trees. The effect was inspiring. There were already bulbs in the grass, the colchicums especially looked effective, but they had not suggested to me, as these handsome big leaves did, that too much of this moist meadow soil was wasted under grass. I had big groups of *Hosta*, with perhaps *Astilbe* or *Ligularia* in mind, with room to spare for plants unknown. I dragged hosepipes in a wide arc around one of my tree groupings, and asked Harry to clear the turf.

When I wish to extend the garden, I equip myself with all the hosepipes I can find in order to take away from one bed, or add to another. In case I have not made myself clear I should explain that a hosepipe laid on the ground is the easiest way of suggesting a new curving outline. I also have by me a bundle of small canes to push into the grass on either side of the hose to hold it in position here and there. Then I take a half-moon edging blade, make a shallow cut on either side of the hose, remove it and pick out the narrow strip of turf with a border fork. There is the new outline lying on the ground until such time as the rest of the turf can be removed, and the soil properly prepared for planting. By aligning the new curves with those already laid down you make sure that they flow naturally and easily, not fussily, like contrived scallops.

Then I was ill. For four months I did not see the garden or the nursery. When I returned it was with a few new ideas, including the following:

1. I am not indispensable.
2. It is a waste of energy worrying about what cannot be done tomorrow.
3. Much better to reserve my energy for what I can do today.
4. Simplify wherever possible, without sacrificing interest.
5. Use all available aids.

This may sound childishly obvious to you, but I was glad to have been shaken into seeing it for myself.

Before long the grass was cleared around all my young shrubberies. The uncovered soil appeared damp. In one place it was wet where a spring from the farmland behind came near the surface. The west wind was also a problem from this quarter, so I fastened a fine mesh Netlon windbreak to the rabbit netting fence which we had put behind the boundary oaks. I do not care for the look of it, but more recent plantings on the bank of holly, laurel, yew and *Cotoneaster* are beginning to hide it, and have themselves done better because of this protection from wind which blows uninterrupted across open fields.

Slowly the trees and shrubs became effective, and the water gardens too started to look attractive, so we began to take more interest in the grass. There is always too little time to care for it when all available help is required for more important jobs, but the time comes when poorly kept grass spoils the effect. Our trouble was that the land remained wet far too long in the spring. Often it was late May, and still the small Hayter would become stuck in wet places—I remember sinking in those same wet boggy places long years before we ever thought of making a home there when we went blackberrying along the mountainous bushes laden with fruit:

> And never was queen
> With jewelry rich
> As those same hedges
> From twig to ditch.

All of that delicious poem would stream through my mind as we filled our baskets to make dark jelly. Were strands from those drowsy afternoons binding us to this soil then? We were not aware of it.

Drainage is not a simple matter in fine close-textured soil. It packs down tightly, almost as bad as clay. To begin with we made T-shaped trenches across the wettest patches to pick up the water and carry it down to the ponds. We put in short land drainage pipes and covered them with gravel before filling in with topsoil. Then a particularly wet February showed that this was not enough, so Harry dug a deep ditch where the original ditch must have been made generations before to catch the line of springs from the adjoining land. It is always a pleasure to see a craftsman dig a good ditch, the sides so straight and clean, sloping slightly so that they do not immediately cave in. I would like to say that we found some relic of times long past, a coin perhaps, dropped from the pocket of the first digger of my ditch. But we did not. Only a rather curiously shaped green glass ginger-beer bottle with its rattling marble, and the name of its maker, and town, Colchester, moulded in the glass.

The banks of spoil were removed, to be used elsewhere. We never have waste soil. It is a precious commodity, whatever it may be like, and will inevitably come in handy one day. Often our problem is finding enough of the kind we want. If it is heavy it will go eventually to some place needing body. If it is the poorest gravel it will be ideal for draining wet land, or making up pathways. If it is a solid wet clay it is the only thing for repairing dams. The new ditch was a success, carrying away the surplus surface water, but not drying my tree and shrub plantings too much, or the grass walks which improved in texture.

The cleared ground around the shrubs was deeply dug to aerate it. Once more I had a new home for plants. But before I describe them I would like to tell you something of their neighbours.

The spine of trees and shrubs in the centre of the large, somewhat elliptical-shaped bed, is dominated by *Malus tschonoskii*. I love the shape of this wild apple from Japan. It is so upright you might think it a poplar when not in leaf, while the autumn colour is the most brilliant we have, the richest scarlet. In all these years I have never noticed the flowers (what a confession!) but flower it must, though inconspicuously, because in November I search the ground beneath for little yellow and red apples. We split a few and sow the pips. I did have several other wild crabs in this area, thinking it would be pretty to have a little grove of them flowering in the grass. But the blossom of most ornamental trees is so fleeting that unless you have parkland to fill I think the room they take is not justified. So, the broad-headed ones were removed.

Although it does take up a lot of room I kept *Parrotia persica*. This has made a great, wide, hazel-like shrub, but it provides a fine background for other things, and its autumn colour, especially now it has a little shelter and the new growth does not get so whipped about, is really magnificent. I like the funny little flowers too. Absurd for such an elephantine shrub, they are just little tufts of raspberry-red stamens.

Cryptomeria japonica, the Japanese Cedar, likes moist soil so I planted it at the dampest end. It has made a graceful pyramidal shape to which my eye is gratefully led in winter. Other evergreens which have interesting form are two or three *Picea omorika* which I probably use too much, but they are so beautiful, take up little room, and associate so well with soft-leaved trees and shrubs. So anxious have I been to make a screen that I have also planted different forms of *Chamaecyparis lawsoniana*, including *C.l.* 'Pendula', and *C.l.* 'Stewartii', though I am not really certain if they look right. But I must give them time. Too artificial looking trees, if I can use that phrase, can look out of place, especially in a very rural setting.

The same remark could apply to variegated hollies, but I have planted a couple in the back. They are very slow growing. (I cannot understand how rabbits can have such a passion for holly. Although the garden is surrounded by rabbit netting, inevitably the occasional youngster squeezes through, or a gate is left open, so every holly has to be individually netted.)

Mahonia japonica is slowly making bulk beneath the tall *Malus*; I love the odd leaves enamelled red in winter. Another evergreen I have planted is *Osmanthus delavayi*. 'One of China's Gems' says Hillier's *Manual*, but not in *my* garden. It sits looking very thwarted, which is not the same thing at all as being slow growing. In April, when properly grown, its twiggy neat-leaved branches are wreathed with clusters of small, white, tubular flowers, most sweetly scented. Perhaps my soil is too sour for it.

I planted *Stephanandra incisa*, and *S. tanakae*, both because I have seen them in other gardens looking a dream in autumn, their prettily shaped leaves a mass of honey-gold. But not with me.

These failures give me the space to try something else but meanwhile precious years have gone, and I still have gaps. However, only by trying, sometimes again and again, can you find what suits your soil.

I should think more young trees of *Acer palmatum*, the Japanese Maple, especially *A.p.* 'Dissectum' are planted and lost every year than almost anything else. They are under-storey large shrubs or small trees, from forests in Japan. They need a sheltered environment, especially from cold east winds, with moist, not waterlogged soil. I was given seed from the famous Westonbirt maples. I picked out the three strongest seedlings and, rather to my surprise, they hung on through several severe droughts and now make substantial growth. The character of my bed will change considerably when all these trees and shrubs look more mature.

Finally, on the old hazelnut bushes in the far background, I have threaded *Rosa filipes* which fills the air with scent from a tangle high above our heads, and the golden-leafed hop, *Humulus lupulus* 'Aureus', mingles both with it, and also trails its beautifully shaped golden leaves across the bed beneath and between dark green clumps of *Helleborus orientalis*.

Since my new bed looked very big, and the trees were still not big enough, I chose large herbs for the centre, hoping to provide height, bulk and colour – although not too much at a time! I planted *Eupatorium purpureum* again because it is so good. Nearby I liked the creamy plumed heads of *Aruncus dioicus* although they do not flower together. *Rheum palmatum* 'Atrosanguineum' looked sumptuous in the spring. First the scaly stumps produce large polished cherry-red buds, almost the size of a cricket ball. The enormous leaves then emerge, pleated and puckered, tinted dull purplish-red all over as the newly born human can be, but as they expand the reddish tinge fades away from the upper surface, lining the underside with soft magenta, a sight to warm your heart on a cold April evening. Good, rich, vegetable-garden type soil is all these great plants need to do well.

Ligularias soon fill up a large empty space. One of my favourites is *Ligularia przewalskii*. Its tall tapering spires of clear yellow flowers look very good rising 5 ft/1.5 m above the neighbouring plants. When I was planting this bed I had not yet come across the fine form called 'The Rocket'. I find this family, some members of it anyway, rather clannish, so I sometimes look for other members of the same family to keep each other company. (Red and puce astilbes look quite dreadful nearby I think!) So I planted *Senecio clivorum* 'Desdemona' whose beetroot-tinted foliage curiously does not clash with either the slender yellow spikes or the wide heads of rich orange daisy flowers of 'Desdemona'.

Polygonum amplexicaule 'Atrosanguineum' needs plenty of room because by autumn it can be 4 or 5 ft/1.5 m tall, a softly bulky plant crowded with thin tapers of tiny red flowers while occasional leaves become brilliantly coloured, with crimson, yellow, bronze and green markings, vivid as any tropical plant. On thinking over that statement I am wondering if the colour occurs more frequently on poorer soil. This plant takes over in midsummer from *Euphorbia griffithii* 'Fireglow'. Most euphorbias succeed in hot, sunny, well-drained situations, but this one, although happy in sunshine, revels in deep, rich soil. The spreading roots send up branched stems 1 yd/1 m high, with handsome red-veined leaves, and every tip shoot developing in succession a flat cluster of soft tomato-red flowers. I think it is because these flowers are small, held lightly, with green light reflected among them, that from a distance the colour appears to be soft rust.

Euphorbia sikkimensis also likes cool, damp conditions. You cannot overlook its new young shoots which appear so early in spring with the first gentian-blue flowers of *Pulmonaria angustifolia* 'Munstead Variety'. The smooth white underground shoots of the *Euphorbia* thrust up pale stems immediately topped with glass-red shoots, flower-like against the bare earth. They spend the rest of the summer growing green and tall, retaining red veins and stems. Then, suddenly, in late summer, you are surprised to see wide flat heads of gentle yellow-green flowers pushing above something else.

I planted astilbes but they did not look right, so they went elsewhere. *Cimicifuga*, however, looked magnificent but I cannot say I have it growing in abundance. How I wish I had. There are several different kinds, all most desirable. I am trying to build up stock, but it takes a long time. Perhaps I have not yet learnt the art. I have learnt that they dislike hot sun on their leaves, no matter how moist it may be underneath.

Hostas I chose as a buffer between these groups and because their bold foliage is a relief, both in shape and colour. In full sunlight I think that *Hosta sieboldiana*, or *H.s. elegans* is the most successful. They need plenty of humus, occasional dressings of old muck, and then time: many years of undisturbed growth to produce really huge leaves. I have one vast group which takes over quite easily from *Rheum palmatum* 'Atrosanguineum' which, when it has sent up its 6 ft/2 m spire of tiny carmine-red flowers, takes a rest and retreats rather shabbily into the background. I planted a big group of *Hosta fortunei* 'Albo-marginata'. It has producd plenty of large leaves and increased in girth, but it is in no way remarkable, the leaves remaining green with only a narrow white margin. Plants taken from the same group and planted elsewhere, in fairly dense shade, are unrecognizably different being boldly variegated with some of the hidden leaves almost entirely white.

I managed to germinate *Veratrum nigrum*, and gave it a place of honour. I almost think it is a plant you need to inherit, it takes so long to become stupendous. My single plant, with its curving pleated leaves, could have been sufficient alone, but when it sent up a tall dark stem topped with a proud branching head of maroon star-shaped flowers, I thought I had a treasure. Since then I have seen an established clump, inherited from a plant-minded mother-in-law, which stood taller than I, and was an experience to walk round. Then, idling one day with Farrer's *The English Rock Garden*, I began to read his opinion of these statuesque mountain plants. As often before his introduction led me to expect the ultimate in beauty, but he ended with explosive contempt for these flowers of 'unmitigated dinginess'. Such an unexpected emotion, expressed so forcibly, found me helpless with laughter. The cult of flower arranging has been responsible for helping us to look and see plant forms with fresh eyes. Certainly green, both in leaf and flower, has probably never before been so fashionable. Imagine the rush there would be now, if we could suddenly supply hundreds of *Veratrum viride*. Whatever would Farrer think?!

Two tall plants that found themselves foot-room before more permanent neighbours had covered the gaps were foxgloves and an Ornamental

Tobacco. I particularly love white foxgloves (*Digitalis purpurea* 'Alba') and allow some seedlings to settle where they will, thinning out too crowded colonies or removing any that threaten to spoil something more lasting. I have learnt to weed out any that have purple leaf stalks as these plants will have purple flowers. Pretty though they are in the wild, I care less for them in the garden. I have two other colour forms of the native foxglove which add something special to early summer flowers. One is primrose-yellow, the other soft apricot-pink. I bought the seed originally from Messrs Sutton. Among the young *Hosta* leaves, with yellow *Paeonia mlokosewitschii*, or white *Paeonia emodi*, they look serene. But I have had them seeded together with *Thalictrum aquilegifolium*, all poking their heads through the arching branches of *Rubus* 'Tridel' in bridal splendour, and the effect was devastating.

Nicotiana sylvestris I have lost sight of for several years, but I think I prefer it for its effect (where there is room) to *Nicotiana alata* (*N. affinis*) which is, I admit, a very pretty thing for flower arranging, with its loose stems of blotting-paper green flowers. But in the emptier days of my big borders I loved to see *Nicotiana sylvestris* with its handsome columns of large matt green leaves topped with elegant heads of long tubular white flowers, gleaming faintly in the falling dusk, scenting the damp air.

By the end of the first season the progress of this bed was so encouraging I felt that more could be done with an extra yard or so of grass round the edge than waste time mowing it. So the bed was extended. It has become a habit of mine to create the garden this way. In doing so I have found that I need to keep a comfortable balance between the width of the grass walks and the beds. Going back to my first damp border: I was now looking for low or medium-sized plants that would taper the profile of my big bed into the broad grass walk which separates it from the water garden.

Perhaps the plant which stands out most exotically as a feature now is *Rheum alexandrae*, that is, when it flowers—it is, unfortunately, rather reluctant to do so. Perhaps it needs a softer climate than we have in East Anglia. This relative of our common rhubarb and docks grows wild on the Chinese-Tibetan border, in damp mountain grassland. I first saw it at the Inverewe gardens, Ross-shire, where it was staged, dramatically, as foreground to a water garden. It was meant to take your breath away, and did. The leaves, not at all like the other big ornamentals, remind me in shape of the ribbed plantain, but shining, brighter green with wide pale veins. Stiff above them stand 3 ft/1 m stems, pagoda-like, with large parchment bracts sheltering the clusters of little dock-like flowers hidden beneath them. It was unlike any other flowering plant I had seen. I have planted it, now, in two different places. Where it is drier it flowers reasonably but looks discontented. Where the soil is much wetter the plants have increased, but have rarely flowered! There must be some place where it will do both well.

More cream, or rather soft yellow, accents are made with perennial foxgloves. *Digitalis lutea* perhaps has rather too small flowers for some people, but I find its close-set, narrow tubular flowers rather interesting.

D. *Rheum alexandrae* (foreground) with *Hosta sieboldiana*

Sometimes a hybrid appears in the garden crossed with *Digitalis lutea* and *D. purpurea*, the purple-flowered native which has escaped my eye. The off-spring is a pretty thing with slightly larger creamy flowers flushed with pink. It lasts quite well as a perennial. When I think of it I split it up, and it seems to appreciate this, as it cannot set seed itself. *Digitalis ferruginea* is as unlike our flamboyant native as could be. It has narrow smooth leaves, and sends up a wand-like stem set halfway down its length with little round buds. They open short roundish trumpets of copper-yellow, netted with brown veins. *Digitalis grandiflora* (*D. ambigua*) and *D. ciliata* I think have interbred in my garden. Both produce good-sized yellow flowers, with *Digitalis ciliata* making taller stems. Neither is less desirable than the other. They and their offspring, if such they be, all last in flower for weeks in midsummer. The semi-shady patches would be dull without them, and it is a relief to know they will stay where you put them and return next year.

Around the sunny edges I planted quick-growing carpeters like the ajugas. *Ajuga reptans* 'Burgundy Glow' has clustered leaves in warm shades of pink and cream, and I like to set it off with the darkest glossiest form I call *Ajuga reptans* 'Atropurpurea'. These bump into *Viola cornuta* in shades of blue and white, and all go as near as they dare to the big clumps of *Hosta*. Further along I planted a generous patch of my favourite *Astilbe* 'Sprite'. From spring to winter it is a joy. First comes its neat ferny bronze foliage followed by wide delicate sprays of shell-pink flowers not more than 1 ft/300 mm high. These slowly become russet-brown seed heads which remain to warm the chill of winter. Another virtue of *Astilbe* 'Sprite' is that it provides a buffer, as the hostas do, to keep the stranglers apart. Nearby is *Pratia treadwellii*. Little prostrate stems run about over the damp soil starred with stemless white flowers. By autumn they have become currant-sized pink berries nestling on a moss-green bed, remaining some time after the tiny leaves have gone.

This bed still receives full sunlight for much of the day, but both the background of oaks, and some of the new trees and shrubs do now afford welcome shade where it is needed. Such places provide a setting for the kind of planting I love best. There is a corner, shaded overhead, with *Cryptomeria japonica* and *Weigela florida* 'Foliis Purpureis' with chocolate leaves and dark pink flowers providing the background. Several crowns of a lace-like fern, *Polystichum setiferum* 'Acutilobum', make a frame for the dangling yellow flowers of *Uvularia grandiflora*. *Anemone nemorosa* 'Allenii' opens its lilac-blue saucers filled with golden stamens when touched by the sun, but when the sky clouds over their wine-stained buds nod modestly above the dark leaves of *Viola labradorica*.

The variegated *Hosta undulata* lightens this quiet scene and tones with another group created by *Hydrangea paniculata*, which I find less formidable than *H.p.* 'Grandiflora'. If you have never seen *Hydrangea paniculata* then try to imagine a cream-coloured lace-cap *Hydrangea*. Take a handful of these round lacy mats, each diminishing in size, and place them one above the other until you have a cone-shaped inflorescence separated by short lengths of stem, each mat consisting of an outer ring of large sterile flowers, the inside filled with small fertile flowers. With *Hydrangea paniculata* 'Grandiflora' the arrangement is similar, but all the flowers are sterile. It makes larger, more showy heads, but sometimes I think it looks overdone. Much depends, of course, on the setting to decide which one you prefer.

The driest and shadiest side of this bed looks best in spring when *Erythronium* 'Pagoda' and *Erythronium* 'White Beauty' delight me with their beautiful olive-mottled leaves and crowds of little lily-like flowers in yellow and cream. The deep rose-pink of *Dicentra formosa* takes over in May, and a *Dicentra oregona* hybrid provokes admiration all season with its pewter-blue ferny foliage. As intriguing is *Eomecon chionantha*, the Dawn Poppy. Its large rounded leaves have a waxy texture, jade-green above, bluish beneath. Several white flowers nod from each single stem, pure in shape and colour. But they are not very free flowering and the travelling roots can be a nuisance, especially if they run through something I value like the *Dicentra*. I shall have to re-make this section and put the Dawn Poppy where its leaves will be an asset, and its occasional flowers a bonus.

Another traveller is the variegated strawberry, *Fragaria vesca* 'Variegata', but it never really becomes a pest because it is so easily pulled up. It continues to look very pretty when some of the more showy plants have had their day.

Coping with Weeds

By the time most of this was planted I was beginning to worry about the amount of weeding I had set myself and my helpers. Not that I dislike weeding. I would go so far as to say that gardening without weeding would lose much of its charm. I think there is no better way of getting to know plants than working among them. Ensuring that they are not being attacked or invaded, you find yourself at close quarters, able to study exactly the petal formation, feel the texture of a leaf. You smell strange perfumes, aromatic or pungent from bruised leaves, emerging bulbs or disturbed roots. Sometimes you step on plants, smash your heel into a tender shoot, which is sickening of course. But crouched low among tall herbs you have a child's view of the garden. Like Alice in Wonderland, you feel yourself in another world—seeing a new garden from unfamiliar view points. Down to earth, you can curb invasions before the weak have fallen to the strong. You move things around, break something up—jobs which rarely get done by saying 'I shall go out and divide those . . .'! You learn to know your plant seedlings as well as the native weeds and rejoice when something unexpected appears; curse yourself also for having allowed pepper-pot seeders like poppies or foxgloves to make unnecessary work by scattering armies of their offspring in the wrong place. You find gaps and sense the kind of planting needed there.

Weeding can be both a delight and a lesson. It can also be a great bore. Or worse, a nagging worry, either because you feel you cannot cope and the sense of frustration saps your energy or, if you are fortunate enough to have some help, whether it be paid or blackmailed, it is maddening still to find yourself going three steps forward and two back because the same boring jobs have to be done too often. Weeding can be tiresome, very tiresome, or impossible. I infinitely prefer a large patch of nettles to the same area of annual meadow grass. With a border fork a nettle comes up easily enough, its tough yellow roots pull clean, leaving the soil behind. If it be inextricably wound into the roots of a shrub I leave it alone and just touch all the growing tips I can reach with a suitable weedkiller (diluted), squeezed from an old detergent dispenser. Although I would probably have given the dispenser a rinse, well-diluted detergent does not harm as a rule. It is sometimes recommended to use as a wetter on very smooth leaves like grasses. There is a weedkiller, however, which reacts with detergent to form a fertilizer, so it is always important to read every scrap of small print on the can before you begin.

Back to weeding by hand. The annual meadow grass, chickweed, groundsel *and* the rest, which soon form a tight turf, have to be hoed or forked and removed, taking away barrowloads of good topsoil. You leave the bed—there are other things to be done—for a month or six weeks and return to find the same misery. Even valued ground-cover plants like *Vinca*, *Hedera*, *Tiarella* and *Ajuga* can, if the conditions are poor for them, be overrun by the native inhabitants.

Where there is complete chaos I find the situation has only one solution. No more fiddling about. Remove carefully everything you still wish to keep and heel it in in a reserve border, which can be quite small. Dig out everything else thoroughly—plants infested with weed roots, all deep-rooted and running weeds—and any that cannot be eradicated by digging, such as bindweed or sorrel, have to be treated later with selective weedkiller. Next dig in anything nutritious that you can lay your hands on—garden refuse composted, well-rotted muck, a sprinkling of bonemeal and well-wetted peat. Peat itself, we are told, has no nutritional value but it does help enormously to improve the soil texture and conserve moisture. Organic fertilizers, like dried blood and bonemeal, are concentrated and costly. Used sparingly they add vital elements to the plants' diet, but without humus as well to improve the soil texture it would be like taking vitamin pills and little else.

I was concerned about the time spent doing unnecessary and unpleasant weeding, concerned too about the amount of topsoil being peeled off my garden like pieces of old carpet. So I made the momentous decision that I must spend money to reduce weeding to a pleasurable level in order to save ourselves time to do something more advantageous. I decided that once my beds were planted I must cover them with a sterile mulch which would depress germinating seedlings and prevent the removal of good soil. In addition, it would gradually improve the structure of the soil and conserve moisture.

Initially I bought coarse shamrock peat which was delivered in large wrapped bales. We broke them open onto a big sheet of polythene laid on the grass. Then, the bed having been freshly weeded, we used our weeding buckets to spread the peat, about an inch or more thick, all over the bare soil and among the herbaceous plants. I use baled straw, spread thickly, among trees and shrubs, or very large plants which could not be smothered, and in the centres or backs of borders where it would not be unsightly.

By the time I was ready to start another large bed I had discovered crushed bark. When pine logs are stripped in the Forestry Commission forests the bark is put into a pulverizer, where it is crushed to a very pleasant peat-like texture. We buy it from forests, fifty miles away, hiring a man and a high-sided lorry who can make the journey twice in one long day. Half the cost of the load is the transport; two loads cover my needs for twelve months and at the time of writing the sum I pay for it is less than one week's wages bill. So I consider it an economy. It is unwise to use freshly pulverized bark, however. I like to buy one year, let it stand in great heaps to decompose a little, and then use it the next year.

Now, after several years of using forest bark, I really have an aversion to naked soil. The reddish-brown bark looks attractive, footmarks do not show, and on warm days the bark smells delicious, bringing back memories of holidays in the Alps. Another advantage is that heavy rainfall cannot cap the surface of the soil. It follows that the structure beneath remains open, so water can trickle gently through the mulch into the soil beneath. Not least, the soil remains damp far longer than soil which is exposed to drying winds and sun.

It is not usually necessary to add fresh mulch every year, as it breaks down slowly. At the end of even the first year of planting I find that the plants have done so well that they themselves will be covering more than half the surface. And that is what I aim to have, my plants themselves providing natural soil-cover for most of the year.

How often do we apply it? Once we have thoroughly mulched a bed it could, in theory, last two or three years because the bark disintegrates very slowly. By the end of the growing season at least half of the original bare soil will have been covered by the plants themselves, which grow so much better having had protection for their roots instead of constant interference from forking and hoeing. The important thing is not to disturb that total cover; any little nodule of soil left on the surface will, when moist, sprout some kind of weed. However, I always have second and third thoughts about my planting, so inevitably there will be breaks made in the mulch where I have been putting in new finds, as they have become available. A bucketful, or barrowload, of fresh bark soon covers the disturbed patches. Sometimes, we put two layers on a new bed, the first shallow while the plants are still small, then when they have grown a little higher we add more. I make a point of walking by young plants to see that they have not been buried. Both the wind and scrapping birds can toss the bark about which can smother small plants as well as weeds. At the beginning of the new growing season it is a good idea to follow the spring clean-up with just enough bark to cover any bare patches of soil. There is no need to add it where the layer has not been disturbed. Try to watch plants that are heavy seeders. Fresh seed scattered onto the mulch will happily germinate down into the warm, damp medium. A mulch will only stifle seedlings that are struggling up from beneath it.

It would be wrong to give the impression that the garden becomes totally weed-free after mulching. There are always a few persistent scramblers for the light which manage to emerge triumphant, like chickweed, but most seedling weeds and especially annual meadow grass, which I consider *the* pest, are defeated. We walk over the beds to remove the survivors, carefully so as not to disturb the mulch, adding more if any soil is left showing. We paint any deep-rooted perennial weeds with diluted systemic weedkiller. Finally, the depth of mulch must be generous. It is false economy to apply a thin dressing—robust weed seedlings will thrust their way through it.

Another point to remember is to apply your mulch when the ground is thoroughly wetted deep down. Sometimes, in autumn, I feel that we need a good snowfall to wet the soil, because once my fine silt has dried out it can receive all the winter rain and still, in some places, be dry. But snow melts slowly and seems to sink everywhere. When it does snow we are soon frustrated for little work can be done, but there are advantages we cannot see at the time. Some springs, on my very dry soil, I have been unable to mulch because the soil was still too dry. Once the bark is put down it takes a tremendous amount of rain to wet it and the soil beneath. Like peat it absorbs a lot of water before it can begin to soak down into the soil.

More Planting in Sun and Shade

I have been trying to decide how I shall describe more of my damp loving plants, fearing that it may be as boring for me to write as it will be for you to read if I do not introduce it from a different angle. The beds which contain these plants are, in effect, one long continuous curving border, broken in two places by grass walks which enable you to see both shady and sunny aspects without having to take in all of one side at a time. Perhaps I should explain what I am hoping to achieve as I steer the garden through its various phases of development. A garden is never finished, never just as you think it should be. Rarely comes that magical moment, captured when everything is there together, the matured planting, the light and your state of mind. The next year you may stand at the same spot, but it will not be the same—the picture, and your mood, will have changed.

Whether your garden is very small or covers acres, there are perhaps a few basic principles of design which apply to both. I think a garden needs to have a sense of wholeness, a harmonious feeling overall. But that does not mean that the same pattern should be repeated throughout, still less that the same plants will be dotted about indiscriminately regardless of conditions. The tiniest garden can provide different conditions—a hot sunny patch, a cool shaded corner—which will provide areas for different themes. In simplest terms, the hot spot may be filled with silver- and grey-leafed plants, a scented *Cistus* or stately *Verbascum*. The dark corner could be restful all the year round using ferns, hellebores and trailing ivies. To place the plants in these two groups together would not necessarily be wrong, but some would do less well than others and, to my mind, they would not look so well. Grey-leafed plants are protected from the drying effect of hot sunlight by the felty covering over their leaves. The second group of plants are adapted to cool, dim conditions. Reduced to very simple examples it becomes basically commonsense. The interest begins when you start to search for all the subtle variations on the theme you have in mind which will fit your situation.

Again, consider shapes. A haphazard collection of trees and shrubs could become a monotonous hedge-like obstruction. I prefer to plant in groups, with spaces between so that you may see another view through the gaps. This gives depth to your design. I try to keep to this principle in a small garden, a small bed, even a sink garden. I make a dominant group, which is the main centre of interest, while every plant, large or small, contributes something to the shape as well as the colour of the design.

How has all this worked out in the second half of my long broken border, which is separated from the ponds by wide grass walks? The side which faces the ponds lies in the sun for much of the day, but the back of the border is cool and shady, overhung by the old oaks and sheltered by the groups of trees and shrubs along its centre. The soil remains fairly damp on the sunny side in all but exceptionally dry summers. The shady side is drier, more affected by roots. It is an indication of the type of soil, and the effect of springs coming nearer the surface, that the low-lying wide grass walks have remained emerald green ever since they were seeded down, while grass elsewhere in the garden, on the upper level, on gravel soil, burns biscuit brown without a fortnightly shower in summer. And that we rarely have!

Now, to return, once again, to the second half of the Long Border.

By the time I was ready to take up the turf and use the good soil beneath for more unusual plants, most of our original planting of trees and shrubs had passed the spindly stage and some were already making interesting features. A few, regretfully, had to be removed as we had made our usual error of putting too many in too little space. It might have worked if we had stayed with trees and shrubs. The major trees would have eventually shaded out the others, but trees can be lopsided, grown close against one another for a very long time without much harm to either. But mine is the constant search for root space, for the kind of tree that will allow plants to grow beneath or around them, hopefully during my lifetime. So a beech, maple and horse chestnut had to go. One would need a park to accommodate the many fine trees one would like to grow. On the other hand, in the average garden, with only ornamentals like flowering cherry or laburnum, attractive though they are, there is no touch of stateliness in the design. A tree which does, in time, add grandeur to the garden is *Quercus coccinea*, the Scarlet Oak. This tree is like *Liquidambar*, I suspect, in that seedlings from it vary in the intensity of autumn colour. Ours is not spectacular, but it has already made a young tree of noble aspect throughout the year. For a week or so in spring I think it is as beautiful as any blossoming tree, when the tiny emerging leaves are like little pleated fans, silvery pale, held against a blue April sky.

As a companion to the oak we planted *Liriodendron tulipifera*, the Tulip Tree, with its curious shaped leaves looking as though all the tips had been carefully cut off with scissors. We have not yet seen it flower—it has to be sufficiently mature to do so—but although the flowers are very beautiful, they can easily be missed. One day I was lucky enough to be at Kew at the right time to see a splendid isolated specimen in full flower, hundreds of upturned pale green cups painted inside with orange. Even in my garden now the rich honey colour of autumn leaves carries your eye above everything else.

In the shelter of the oak, hoping to protect it a little from cold spring frosts, I have planted *Pieris* 'Forest Flame', a presumed hybrid between *P. formosa forrestii* 'Wakehurst' and *P. japonica*. So often, no sooner have the young shoots unfolded in late April or May than they are reduced to pulp by a murderous frost. But sometimes we are lucky, and can marvel as the young terminal leaves go through a long phase of change, from polished red through tender pinks and cream to green. It is not surprising that everyone who sees it wants to possess it.

Much easier, and making fine bulk, is a purple-leafed hazelnut, *Corylus maxima* 'Purpurea'. The young pleated leaves open rich chocolate-purple, this colouring draining slightly in high summer, but lightening and brightening to reddish tones in autumn. As contrast to this heavy purple colouring I planted *Rubus idaeus* 'Aureus' beneath it. Now I have a carpet of cool yellow around the massed stems as this golden-leafed raspberry has sent its runners through the fine soil, producing fresh yellow foliage all summer on short stems, none more than 18 in./460 mm long.

For blossom and perfume there is *Syringa sweginzowii*, a Chinese Lilac of great elegance and charm. Its small oval leaves are not overpowering for the long loose panicles of palest pink tubular flowers which are carried on every shoot.

Rubus 'Tridel' forms part of this group. It makes a stout frame from which cascade arching branches garlanded with large white blackberry-like flowers. But although it is spectacular at its best, the flowering season is short. I think it may move on one day to a place where its exuberant growth can be allowed more space, in grass perhaps, with masses of the late-flowering, sweet-scented *Narcissus poeticus* 'Recurvus' beneath it.

I left the space beneath and immediately around this group of trees and shrubs free, except for *Rubus tricolor*, hoping it would cover the soil which becomes dry on the surface, partly because of roots, partly because the leaf canopy does not allow much of the light summer rain to penetrate. Now this rampageous ground-coverer is coping very well, and will need to be curbed when it reaches the boundary of its allotted space. I like the way it sends out long prostrate runners, then quickly fills the space between with side shoots so that before long you have a carpet of shining, dark green leaves, grey backed, with soft red bristles set all round the young stems. I have also planted it at the top of a very steep clay bank, where I think little else would flourish, and already it is beginning to hang down a curtain of trailing stems to hide the raw clay. Like all brambles it roots down at the tip, useful when you need more plants. Although rampant it is not difficult to control, being lax and soft to handle. Where space is limited watch it each spring, and cut back then if necessary. I have been told that this bramble is not very hardy. That may well be so in very cold and exposed districts. Here in East Anglia there is little between us and the bitter north-east winds from Russia, but my plants are sheltered among shrubs, partially protected by the straw mulches which are put down until the ground-covering plants have carpeted the empty spaces. Some years the overwintering leaves of *Rubus tricolor* have been singed by cold, but the plants have never suffered.

With these strong-growing trees and shrubs as the background and apex of one end of my bed I began to plant tall strong-growing plants just in front of their shade perimeter. *Macleaya cordata* I found had not liked my poor starved gravel elsewhere, so I thought I would try it here, in the sun. Its graceful heads of coral buds and pale creamy flowers look well among the rustling stems of *Miscanthus sinensis* 'Silver Feather'. This superb grass, 5 ft/1.5 m high, makes an elegant fountain (not so overpowering as *M. sacchariflorus* might have been) and it flowers regularly, pale fawn and brown feather dusters, folded and furled when wet, silken and silvery when dried in the wind.

Several inulas complete this group of herbaceous giants. *Inula magnifica* must be one of them. All of them have enormously long, coarse, but handsome dock-shaped leaves. All send up stout towering stems over 8 ft/2.5 m high; they can only be contemplated where they will have ample room. Among mine I have three distinctly different types of flower, but no one has yet been able to help me identify them with certainty. One has a tapering head of closely set, hard, knobby buds which open smallish yellow daisies in a spire, eventually forming an interesting seed head for decorating a large space like the church. I have planted some of these by the water-side where they look very suitable, in scale and form. Provided they are not situated where they catch the wind they remain stiffly upright without staking. My two other giant inulas each have similar foliage and majestic height, but one is topped with wide branching heads of large yellow daisies with the narrowest, almost thread-like petals; the other has orange petals, with brown centres. Nearer the front of the border I have placed another, *Inula hookeri*, more suited to smaller gardens, although it is invasive. It makes good cover because of this, with spreading clumps which send up many stems, about 2½ ft/760 mm topped with unusual furry green buds which open to greenish-yellow daisies.

Yet another similar plant is *Buphthalmum speciosum* (*Telekia speciosa* or *B. cordifolium*). Not so tall as the other giants, it has similar heads of large yellow fine-rayed daisies over great mounds of huge heart-shaped leaves. To retain their look of distinction watch for damage by slugs or snails for it is the perfection of the great leaves that contributes to the scene. Some of these great daisies are invasive, and could be a menace in unsuitable places, but they are ideal in rough grass where they can add drama to a scene that might be monotonous, but which would also be impractical to garden in detail.

Another great plant which could be used for the same purpose is *Rheum palmatum*. When I was thinking of what to use to bring the eye forward from the tall herbs in the background I chose an especially fine form, which may be *Rheum palmatum tanguticum*. This wonderful plant, which has much richer coloured foliage than *R.p.* 'Atrosanguineum', starts the season in a void before the tall herbs have begun to make their mark. Very early in spring the *Rheum* buds are unfolding, continuing to do so for weeks to come, so that gradually there is a huge overlapping pile of curved and slashed leaves, purplish-red and ruched above, raspberry-pink beneath, slowly maturing to green above but retaining the strong carmine tint on the undersides. From among this pile, one or two great reddish buds emerge, each with a single enveloping scale from which unfolds a 6–8 ft/2–2.5 m flowering stem dangling with tiny sprays of *white* flowers (not pink, as has *R.p.* 'Atrosanguineum'). This is a plant I have waited long to possess. For weeks, for months, its leaves remain an important feature, framing the view as you look beyond, diametrically, across the sloping grass and clear water, to another planted on the far side of the pond. Placed among plants with smaller fussier leaves, these noble plants have a stabilizing and architectural effect.

Towards the edge now of this large group is a planting of *Geranium maculatum*, a choice member of a family in which it is hard to choose a favourite. The cool lilac flowers in early summer are followed by mounds of parasol-shaped leaves, frilly-edged. They sometimes have rich orange and red tones in autumn. To complement this group I planted *Dicentra spectabilis* nearby. To mark the *Dicentra*, which fades away by late summer, are clumps of *Pulmonaria saccharata* 'Alba'. I was given this plant by Miss Elizabeth Strangman. It is so much better than *P. officinalis* 'Alba', which is a wishy-washy plant by comparison. (Poor thing! Why haven't I found a grouping that would enhance it?) But *Pulmonaria saccharata* 'Alba' has large trusses of pure white flowers followed by great rosettes of undulating dark green leaves handsomely spotted with white, decorating their share of the scene until winter withers them away. By early March the clustered flower buds will unfold, long before the basal rosettes appear, to charm no less than do the snowdrops.

I hope it is not becoming monotonous, my obsession with leaves, but if a plant has beautiful leaves, it is, I think, the best reason for growing it. If it has good flowers as well that makes two good reasons. Although not exactly short yet of room to grow plants I still have to be selective. Those that go off quickly in both leaf and flower must be placed where their absence is not noticeable, so plants which continue to furnish, even if it be with quite plain good green foliage, are welcomed. After all, nothing but spotted and splashed leaves herded together would be quite upsetting.

Most people know *Aruncus dioicus*, which is not unlike a huge *Astilbe*. It makes such a handsome stand of light green foliage, never troubled by pests. Like apple blossom, I like best the early stage before the great creamy plumes have all exploded into foaming flowers, when the sprays are delicately lined with tiny round buds, only a few breaking. Not everyone has had the chance to meet *Aruncus dioicus* 'Kneiffii'. It makes a smaller plant, with leaves so finely shredded you would not be blamed for failing to recognize it. Above this fretted frame are the same ivory plumes, reduced in scale.

To add body to this dainty group without overshadowing it I have planted *Heuchera cylindrica* 'Greenfinch'. For most of the year I enjoy its tidy clumps of heart-shaped leaves, beautifully mottled green and silver. By midsummer they break the low line of edging plants with a forest of straight stems a yard high, topped with closely set spikes of green flowers.

While thinking of related shapes it also helps to group together plants whose flowers look well together. On the cooler side of this corner group, close to the grass edge, is a combination of plants slowly forming a picture. These are three fritillaries which seem to prefer heavier soil than their Mediterranean cousins which flourish elsewhere on my sun-baked gravels. *Fritillaria meleagris* can still be found growing wild in a few damp, low-lying meadows in England. None has more sinister charm than this, our own Snake's Head Fritillary. Like the Lenten hellebores it can be found in all shades. Those with white tapering bells, squared at the shoulders, are faintly shaded and chequered with green. Others are dark greyish-plum, with occasional in-betweens of palest pink, delicately veined and patterned in minute mosaics.

Standing taller is *Fritillaria verticillata*, that is, those bulbs which will flower. Some years I have quite a lot of flowering stems, sometimes only a few. Perhaps I should dig them up more frequently and replace only the largest. They produce very narrow strap-like leaves along the flowering stem which become tendrils, with curling tips at the top of the stem. This adaptation may be a means of ensuring that they can haul themselves up into the sunlight when growing in the wild in grassy meadows. The flowers are shallow open bells, almost whitish-green, chequered inside with brown. The large angular seed heads surrounded by dried curling wisps of leaves are equally attractive.

All fritillaries seem to have very individual characters. I have special feeling for *Fritillaria pallida*. Shorter than the other two, it is sturdier looking, with thick stems set with broad wax-grey leaves which taper up the stem, bending with the weight of several large citron-yellow angular bells, overlaid with green and faint tan veining. If you tip them up you will see the tan repeated inside, around the base of the stamens.

For these treasures *Epimedium macranthum* provides a background of newly made leaves, small and heart-shaped, echoing with softest tan. Soon there will be sprays of little mauve-pink flowers, on thread-like stems, and the leaves will mature green.

Anemone blanda 'White Splendour' lives up to its name, although sometimes I think it is called 'Bridesmaid'. The ground is starred with masses of quite large, many-petalled white flowers over mounds of cut-leafed foliage, tinted purple. Well behind all these delicate creatures the handsome red leaves of *Rheum palmatum* 'Atrosanguineum' just unfolding make a strong accent.

In the same setting *Astrantia major* 'Sunningdale Variegated' produces clumps of almost strawberry-shaped leaves brilliantly variegated with cream, yellow and green. Much later in the year, in late summer and autumn, these will have faded to green, and the scene will have changed as the plant sends up tall, branching stems which carry hundreds of green and white posies, stained pink in the centre, for weeks and weeks.

Meanwhile, in spring, carpets of dark purple-leafed *Viola labradorica* cool the group and separate it from the starfish-shaped clumps of *Pulmonaria longifolia*, whose variegation is somewhat muted as it carries its clustered heads of small gentian-blue flowers.

A curious form of *Helleborus purpurascens* (I think that is what it is) sits on the edge of the group, massed with short, stout flower stems each carrying several smallish cupped flowers of a dingy, dusky purple. The insides are lined with greyish-green and filled with fresh green anthers set around dark purple ovaries. The subtle tones of *Primula* 'Garryarde Guinevere' seem just right with this strange plant. Purplish-brown stems carry heads of many light lilac-pink flowers, with leaves neat and narrow, shaded and veined maroon.

Another spring group is based on *Valeriana phu* 'Aurea', whose brilliant gold cut leaves set off *Euphorbia sikkimensis* with leaves, stems and veins in strong vermilion-red running through leafy soil. Cream and yellow erythroniums, including *Erythronium* 'White Beauty' and *E.* 'Pagoda', reflex their petals, each fluttering stem rising out of a boat-shaped base made by the broad succulent leaves, faintly marbled brown. *Erythronium revolutum* has not yet established itself so abundantly. As yet it has only one flower to a stem, a rich rosy-red, paling slightly at the tips of the pointed petals. *Dicentra formosa* 'Alba' marks this ephemeral little treasure with drooping clusters of greenish-white heart-shaped flowers held over spreading clumps of pale ferny foliage. In the background among the shrubs are creamy-white *Narcissus* 'Tresamble' and *N.* 'Thalia' making an entrance among pale gold ribbons of *Milium effusum* 'Aureum', Bowles' Golden Grass.

We have been led around the border to the Long Walk, shaded by the boundary oaks. Spring is the loveliest time here while there is still enough sunlight for flowers. Later in the year hostas and ferns, with shade-loving plants like *Actaea*, provide quieter patterns.

Euphorbia robbiae usefully invades the drier soil over the roots of shrubs while its running shoots appear through tight carpets of *Vinca minor* 'Bowles' Variety', both in flower together, although the *Euphorbia* lasts much longer.

Dominating another picture is the golden cut-leafed elder *Sambucus racemosa* 'Plumosa Aurea', forming a tender background for *Smilacina racemosa* whose softly pleated leaves clasp green stems which end in a fluffy spike of cream, freshly scented flowers. It is supposed to set red berries, and sometimes shows every sign of doing so, but although I watch, full of expectation, they never materialize—I don't know why. Some years it happens that the *Sambucus* and *Smilacina* have just expanded to perfection when *Paeonia obovata alba* raises among them her perfect round globes of white petals protecting precious crimson ovaries inside. All too ephemeral, these few perfect moments, but remembered for ever.

Paeonia emodi, although single, and white, is quite different. It makes a slowly increasing clump, the leaves as they appear being more dissected, richly shaded in browns and tan. Maturing green they form a large loose mound over which nod open shallow saucers filled with golden stamens.

Moist Shade Under the Oaks

I think it might be a good idea to leave the Long Border and take a look behind it, at the Shady Walk. It is unlike any of the rest of the garden, a long, slightly curving grass walk, enclosed on both sides, shaded by oaks overhead. It is formed by the back of the tree and shrub planting (part of which I have just been describing) on the east side, with a wide, gently sloping bank on the west. Spaced along the bank, on the top side, are the six ancient oaks. They provide welcome shade in summer for plants and people.

I have already described how we dug a ditch at the bottom of the bank to take away the surplus water entering the garden from our neighbour's gravelly field beyond. About four years ago I decided to pipe the ditch. It had been interesting actually to see the spring water coming off the field, entering the ditch about a foot down from the top of the soil level, showing wet patches and then little soil falls, sometimes a trickle of water, all adding up to a satisfactory flow at the ditch end during the wettest months of the year, remaining moist all summer. But cleaning out a ditch and scything the weeds and rough grass around it seemed rather a waste of time when this damp soil might be put to better use. There was, of course, a great debate as to the wisdom of laying pipes which might become impenetrably blocked with tree roots. What to do then? What a performance to have to dig them out from under all my plants! I decided to take the risk, and so far the water still falls out of the end pipe. But there remains in my mind the picture of ancient land drains so tightly packed with roots that not a drop could penetrate, so each winter I watch my end pipe a little apprehensively.

I bought 6 in./150 mm diameter pipes, made from a kind of porous substance (looking like breeze block material) which slot into one another. After they were laid we put thin bundles of willow around them, as well as gravel to prevent the fine-textured soil from settling too tightly around them. When all had settled I contemplated what I might do with a length of 125 yd/120 m of shaded soil, 12 yd/10 m wide. The soil can become quite dry at the top of the slope towards the field, but usually remains damp enough along the lower edge, against the grass walk. Howling draughts would be a problem as the west wind tore through the spaces between the oaks, so I erected a windbreak of fine-meshed Netlon, laid over the strongly made rabbit-proof fence which immediately helped the hollies and laurels which were already planted. Of course, I thought of rhododendrons, even tried a few, but apart from a few *Rhododendron ponticum* which seem to survive anywhere, I should have known better. Our very low rainfall and, much worse, the drying winds make conditions for rhododendrons intolerable. They are, in the main, mountain shrubs and trees, adapted to living in the cool, damp atmosphere of the cloud belts. There *are* sheltered gardens in East Anglia, perhaps in a hollow, under mature woodland, where they can be, indeed are, established, but I have no experience of such gardening. I know it is much more difficult than in the West Country where the rainfall is higher, the winds less desiccating.

Although limited by the conditions, I wanted to add a little more interest to my background of evergreens. I planted *Mahonia* × *media* 'Charity' for its stately habit and distinctive long spiny leaflets, as much as for the long clusters of yellow scented flowers which open in autumn.

Cotoneaster 'Rothschildianus' has made a wide spreading bush and now causes comment with its trusses of creamy-yellow berries. *Viburnum tinus* is very accommodating. It makes a rounded comfortable-looking bush, easily controlled by pruning if need be, and modestly smothers itself with clusters of brownish-pink buds and lacy white flowers. Too easily overlooked, even dismissed by those who 'must' have colour, it is hard to fault when you have time to stand and really look at it. I have several forms. 'Eve Price' is more compact, and planted where there is plenty of light is very attractive when smothered with much deeper toned buds and pinkish flowers. *Viburnum tinus* 'Lucidum' has larger glossy green leaves with slightly bigger flowers than the common form. Another form, *V.t.* 'Gwenllian', produces the largest pearl-like blue-black berries when the late flowers are not damaged by harsh winters. Finally, I have a few small plants of the variegated form, but they make slow headway, often being damaged by hard frosts.

The most showy evergreen, and in spring the dominating plant along the whole border, is *Taxus baccata* 'Washingtonii'. I only guess that to be the name of my really magnificent Golden Yew. I was given a cutting about twenty years ago, from an old overgrown garden. It took almost two years to root, but is now a splendid shrub 10 × 10 ft/3 × 3 m. It is most striking in spring and early summer when all its new shoots are bright yellow.

I planted *Photinia* × *fraseri* 'Red Robin', which I hoped would provide a warm background with all its young tip shoots enamelled red. It may slowly make a good framework, but although it grows well its tender brilliant shoots are often damaged by late spring frosts.

At the rough end, against a background of dark holly, I planted *Rubus cockburnianus*. This 'ghost' bramble has spread into a large clump. I cut it down to ground level every spring when it quickly throws up strong arching stems which arrive at about 5 or 6 ft/2 m and then branch, letting the tips cascade to the ground. The leaves are pretty, being soft and finely cut. But in winter, when the leaves have gone, you find yourself with a gigantic 'bird cage', every purple stem coated with waxy-white bloom.

Rubus thibetanus is smaller and daintier with very pretty fern-like leaves of a whitish-grey colour. It does not create the same huge cage-like effect, but neither does it demand so much space. Dull neglected corners, where there is plenty of room, could easily be transformed by these ornamental brambles. The new canes are brighter and better formed if the old ones are cut down each spring. I like to add a few coloured-stemmed dogwoods, forms of *Cornus alba*, for contrast all the year round.

During the past two or three years I have been much occupied with this Long Shaded Bed. In the patches which retain moisture the longest, I have accumulated shade lovers which will not stand drought. I think some moisture from the spring-line below must rise in the soil by capillary action. Apart from the fact that suitable peat blocks are not easily available here, I did not think the site was suitable for peat gardening. However, we did work a little well-wetted peat into the soil before I started to plant. For more favoured parts of the country the plants I have chosen to put here may not all sound so very exotic, but I could scarcely grow them at all if I did not have this sheltered haven. It is still an experimental border, where I am getting to know plants which were unfamiliar to me.

Now there is scarcely a day in the year when I do not wander over the Long Walk bank. I can walk over it because I keep it well mulched, with straw around the trees and shrubs on the upper level where it joins the field of the neighbouring farm at the back—and with crushed bark among my treasured plants that benefit from damper soil as the bed falls towards the grass walk that edges it.

Before the New Year the bracts and first flower buds of *Helleborus foetidus* are glimmering palest green, but more surprising is a wild daffodil opening its first perfect little flower. It was brought home from Calabria, along the north coast of Spain, over thirty years ago by my old friend Sir Cedric Morris. When it had increased a little he generously gave me a bulb or two. Gradually over the years we have built up a small stock. Standing about 8–10 in./250 mm high they have the charm of being miniature without being too close to the ground. With an appropriate setting their free-flowering clumps look very effective. In another part of the garden they are spilling out of *Erica cinerea* 'Golden Drop' whose yellowish foliage becomes tinted with vivid reds and scarlet in winter, quite an astonishing combination. I almost always pick a few of these little daffodils for Christmas Day, and they continue to bloom until the middle of March. If we have very severe frost they collapse and lie like sticks stuck to the frozen soil. But when the thaw comes they stand erect again, quite unharmed. This delightful addition to the garden was given an Award of Merit by the Royal Horticultural Society and has been named after Sir Cedric, *Narcissus minor* 'Cedric Morris'.

Every spring I split up more of my snowdrop clumps to spread them along this boundary border. I am not yet a snowdrop fanatic, but I do enjoy finding really distinctive ones. There are several different double forms as well as some handsome tall-stemmed single ones, probably *Galanthus elwesii*. *Galanthus nivalis* 'Viridapicis' is slowly increasing, and so too is an extraordinary snowdrop which appeared, as from nowhere. Maybe it is a seedling, maybe it came with another plant. The size is exceptional. Each rounded petal is 1½ in./37 mm long, and although it is difficult to measure across the deep curve of each petal I make it to be 1 in./25 mm in width. The warmth of the room releases its sweet delicate perfume. I dug a potful of flowering bulbs in late March 1981 and sent them to the RHS fortnightly show. There they were seen by Richard Nutt who wrote to me that it was an 'impressive late-flowering form of *Galanthus byzantinus*'.

By February I am looking for the Lenten roses. I have planted my different colour forms of *Helleborus orientalis* in groups spaced along the length of my partly shaded border. I think they look better, the dusky purples together, then the soft pink and old-rose shades, and finally the spotted pink and white forms. I had also thought that the seedlings might be more likely to come true. I think they do on the whole. But the only sure way to repeat an especially fine form is to break it up in March, cut off all those magnificent flowers, and plant out small individual pieces. It takes a long time to grow a plant big enough to split, say into ten or more pieces— and I found it took a lot of courage to split my best and most handsome plants, because again it takes several years for each piece to become so fine again.

I have been privileged to obtain new blood for my hellebore collection from Eric Smith, who has devoted much care and patience to propagating good seedlings. Among his plants is a lovely white one, very aptly called 'Cygnus', with pointed petals shaped like a swan's head in bud, but opening into a large, wide open bell with a green centre.

The bright yellow leaves of *Valeriana phu* 'Aurea' make strong contrast near the brooding purple hellebores, and so too do my Jack-in-Green primroses. I originally grew my plants from seed, keeping only the shades of yellow, some so pale they are almost white. The savage magentas I find too difficult to place.

The old fashioned laced polyanthus primulas, reminding me of some forms of *Primula auricula*, flourish in a piece of really heavy soil helped out with a liberal spadeful of compost. They too vary from seed. I have selected two forms, one with a narrow gold edge, the other a fine silver edge. Both have a base colour of darkest mahogany-crimson, with a yellow-green eye. I find that the plants deteriorate badly if left alone. It seems to be vital to dig them up every second year, split them and replant them in fresh soil. Just after flowering is supposed to be the right time, but I try to do a few as soon as I can in early spring, cutting off the flower buds and then replanting them in fresh soil. The unrooted shoots I put into a pan on the propagating bench and within a week or two they are making little roots. I find that by the time the flowers are over it will have become too warm or too dry, and the large leaves have to be cut back severely to check transpiration. However, they can be divided then, provided the wounded plants are sheltered, preferably under cover, and not allowed to dry out.

I tend to say that the common celandines are a menace in my garden. Certainly on the ever-moist lower levels they are everywhere, opening their glistening yellow saucers the minute the sun warms them. But I really do not think they do any harm as they are mostly among big perennials which cover the soil later in the season, and once I have stopped worrying about them as weeds I have to admit that they are very pretty. I have three more which I actively encourage. One, with orange flowers, is unfortunately favoured by some predatory creature. I suspect the moorhens, and have to make a web of black cotton over the plants. Another has double yellow flowers with a greenish centre; and lastly I was given a plant by Mrs Joan Elliott, which has burnished bronze leaves. Mrs Elliott has a gift for stepping out of her car and within yards, and with the least effort, spotting something unusual. Needless to say (so far anyway) this intriguing plant has not spread itself around with any degree of generosity.

In early spring several sorts of *Corydalis* appear suddenly and as suddenly are gone. The first to arrive is *Corydalis bulbosa*. The long spurred flowers closely set in a short spire are soft magenta with pale silvery throats. Flowering at the same time is a form which I think may be *Corydalis bulbosa marshalliana*. It has a delicate colour scheme, greenish-yellow buds opening to ivory-white flowers, while the mahogany-brown bracts peeping out among the clustered flowers repeat the colour of the stem. *Corydalis solida*, producing clusters of blue-mauve flowers, comes a week or two later, good company for the well-known Dog's Tooth violets, the cyclamen-purple *Erythronium dens-canis*.

Narcissus pallidus is among the earliest of the daffodils thrusting skywards its pale lemon trumpets, while the crowded clumps of *Narcissus minor*, or they may be *N. minimus*, barely lift their buds above the soil before they are opening bright yellow flowers.

Every day during March, it seems, a new flower or shoot appears. In these early spring days we are keenly aware of the surging plant life which ferments just below the soil. The first folded tips of leaves breaking the surface, the soft veils of pale yellow appearing over the willows as their buds swell and break, the haunting perfume of *Daphne odora* drifting from the foot of the warm walls of the house across the garden towards the chill marble perfection of the snowdrops—these are among the most magical moments of the year, though the soil be still cold and wet, the grass sodden beneath my feet.

Coptis trifolia seems a fragile thing to be about so early. It makes a neat carpet of finely cut leaves topped with little rounded white flowers on thin stems. I have in mind to make a raised bed along a shady wall where I can linger over such plants.

Cardamine trifolia could also be placed on the wall bed, but while remaining dainty it is also well suited as an edging to my cool grass walk—it makes very tidy cushions of smooth trifoliate leaves which are often tinted purple by winter cold. By late March they are covered with heads of little white cruciform flowers. They are a miniature version of a splendid relative, *Pachyphragma macrophyllum*, which is sometimes wrongly called *Cardamine asarifolia*. This I have planted among the shrubs where, for a month at least, the frothy white flowers look like drifts of snow against the brown leaf litter. They are followed by large round leaves. In time, by seeding, I hope to have extensive carpets of these handsome plants beneath my shrubs.

All one kind of cover plant can be monotonous and deprive the garden of the interest that can be made by planting contrasting forms in reasonably large groups. I enjoy as contrast the dark green rosettes of *Euphorbia robbiae*, topped from spring to autumn with luminous heads of lime-green.

Several forms of *Symphytum* produce very pretty flowers, as well as thick mats and clumps of impenetrable foliage. *Symphytum grandiflorum* I find the least aggravating if I have been thoughtless about future plantings. They are all tempting to plant, because they are so useful in colonizing new ground. But the lovely blue-flowered *Symphytum caucasicum* must be kept to the outlying areas of the wild garden, where it is unlikely you will decide that this is just the place for something more precious, such as paeonies or hellebores. I think probably we can now exterminate most of our mistakes by some kind of weedkiller, but even that takes time, and we are not certain of all the risks.

Symphytum grandiflorum has croziers of little orange buds which open to creamy-yellow flowers. I have another plant which may be a form of *Symphytum grandiflorum*, but the flowers are much more showy, on taller stems held well above the leaves. They create a symphony of tender pink and blue. We used to call it 'the Red, White and Blue' Comfrey because all those colours can be seen in the unfurling buds. I have since discovered a form with entirely pink flowers and learnt that these two plants are called 'Hidcote Blue' and 'Hidcote Pink'.

Another comfrey, *S.* × *uplandicum* 'Variegatum', insists on sending up indifferent sprays of flowers as its first task of the year, no matter how often I cut them off, but then settles down to produce perhaps the most spectacular of variegated leaves for the rest of the growing season. Huge dock-shaped leaves mound themselves one above the other; each matt leaf is pale cream, shadowed and veined with soft grey-green. Such a plant needs a plain background. It could be provided by *Trachystemon orientale* which has similar shaped leaves of rich dark green. In early March this plant sends up naked pink stems which carry blue pointed flowers which are soon engulfed by the rapidly developing leaves. I value their solidarity which is easily contrasted again by big plantings of *Dryopteris filix-mas*, one of the easiest and most useful of ferns.

Rubus tricolor has already filled its allotted space under the old oaks. Provided the winter is not too severe it retains a beautiful carpet of polished dark green leaves. Each spring I have to remember to prune the long shoots back at least halfway to their source. Each tip will have already rooted, providing scores of new plants.

Over an old hawthorn stump I have planted *Clematis spooneri* 'Alba', mixed up with *Hedera colchica* 'Paddy's Pride'. The graceful tendrils and pure white flowers of the *Clematis* go well with the sharp acid tones of the large-leafed ivy. Below them is a planting of *Uvularia grandiflora*, a quiet little plant with drooping twisted bells of pale straw-yellow. The pale blue *Viola* 'Freckles' is clustered around it. The small pink and white pea-like flowers of *Lathyrus vernus variegatus* (which I have always called *Lathyrus albo-roseus*) join the group, and the pretty leaves and pinky-mauve flowers of *Epimedium macranthum* complete the spring picture. Violas thrive in cool soil, so the season is carried foward, after the white flowers of *Viola septentrionalis* have faded, by *Viola cornuta*, the little Horned Pansy of the Pyrenees. On tall slender stems its flowers, chalk-white, light or dark blue, go on for weeks and weeks. Eventually the plants must be sheared to encourage strong new growth, which often flowers again in the autumn.

With so many plants flowering in the early part of the year I always fear there will be nothing left to follow. But somehow room and plants are found. Treasures like *Orchis elata*, now to be called *Dactylorrhiza elata*, and the black-flowered *Fritillaria camtschatcensis* push their way up through the scallop-edged leaves of *Primula sieboldii*, all of which enjoy the damp leaf-mouldy soil at the bottom of the bank.

Several different trilliums are slowly, so slowly, making a new leaf each year. I love each one, but I long to see large comfortable clumps of leaves topped with the three-petalled flowers, in white, burgundy, rose-red, and one that is yellow. I have a few of the double white form, each flower rather like a small *Camellia*. But you can find yourself with a whole family of grandchildren before they have had time to make handsome large clumps.

What a luxury to be able to grow *Phlox stolonifera* when suited, as it seems to be beneath the dappled shade of my old oaks, where it runs about like the proverbial weed. Where I have planted my two forms the soil does occasionally become too dry and I find them wilted but I think the texture is important too: light peat or leaf-mould is what they seek as their trailing stems cover the surface. The large heads of scented lilac-blue or white flowers of *Phlox stolonifera* 'Blue Ridge', and *Phlox* 'Ariene' are a delight in May. *Phlox pilosa* travels underground, sending up suckering stems, every one producing light, dainty heads of pinky-mauve flowers. They begin in late May and continue all summer, another plant I am glad to have found.

The same gales which, several years ago, tore my *Salix matsudana* 'Tortuosa' out of one of the dams across the ponds also blew down the huge old crab apple, part of my original boundary hedge. When the mess was cleared away and the land had settled, I planted *Clematis jouiniana* 'Praecox' and *Hydrangea petiolaris* together to cover the stump and mound of soil. In the spring *Narcissus* 'February Gold' pokes through their entwined stems. Their summer leaves make effective ground-cover, and their delicate flowers, skimmed-milk blue and greenish-white, are very welcome in late summer.

I have planted several hydrangeas, mostly the lace-cap type, which are either blue or white, but never a clear pink because of my acid soil. I was given a cutting of a very lovely pearl-pink lace-cap, but in my soil it is amethyst pink. For *Hydrangea* 'Preziosa' I must provide a special place, well laced with chalk, for it is unrecognizable in acid conditions. That delicious salmon-pink becomes a deep purplish-blue with flushes of crimson while the bronze tinting on the leaves is changed to purple shadows.

I did not expect to find many flowering plants for the late summer and autumn along my Shade Walk, but those I have show up like jewels among several fine foliage plants. I like the leaves of *Tiarella wherryi* which are like emerald velvet, fine contrast for the curious, almost black, strap-like leaves of *Ophiopogon planiscarpus nigrescens*. *Lamium maculatum* 'Beacon Silver' and *L.m.* 'Chequers' have got over their flowering period (when their leaves deteriorate badly) and have begun to make new silvered carpets which will gleam all winter. Standing up among them is *Actaea rubra*, heavy with rich clusters of small scarlet berries. Not far away is *Actaea alba* whose pea-sized white berries are fixed to the stems by crimson stalks, each berry with a black eye. Both these plants make larger and more healthy-looking clusters of fruit when grown in the shade.

In the background are several bushes of *Hydrangea arborescens* 'Grandiflora'. From late summer onwards they are smothered with round heads of small flowers which open green, gradually turning creamy-white, all shades being seen at the same time.

I originally planted a 'bird cage' of *Rubus cockburnianus* at the rough end of the Shady Walk, but it took up too much good soil, too choice a position, so I have planted it elsewhere. In its place I have made a new grouping with, once again, a *Clematis*, the pink *C.* × *vedrariensis* scrambling over a treestump for a background, with *Hydrangea villosa* planted in front. This lovely *Hydrangea* with dark grey-green felted leaves makes rather gaunt branches, which carry large lace-cap heads of violet-blue and pink, quite magnificent when well suited.

In another sheltered place I have planted *Hydrangea sargentiana*, a really noble shrub. The leaves are bright moss-green with a beautiful velvety pile; the large flower heads, like a maid's lace cap, have small blue fertile flowers in the centre surrounded by large white outer florets. Left on the bush they dry in perfect shape.

The foliage of *Polygonatum* × *hybridum*, Solomon's Seal, contributes much to a woodland setting. Much less well known is *Polygonatum verticillatum*. I like to see its delicate stems rising tall and slender in isolation, with a few carpeters at its feet. Each stem is surrounded at intervals with whorls of narrow leaves beneath which hang clusters of small flowers. I find that these, admittedly miserable little flowers, set clusters of berries which the more showy flowered forms rarely seem to manage.

Stiff pokers of scarlet berries (*Arum italicum* 'Pictum'), juicy and large as marbles (but poisonous—beware), appear out of nowhere, their marbled leaves having died down in June, but by November they will be emerging, rolled like cigars, out of the soft soil.

Salvia glutinosa makes a coarse plant for the background. I value its tapering heads of pale yellow flowers when there is little else about. Above it towers *Phytolacca americana* whose many branched candelabra hold upturned clusters of green fruits which finally turn elderberry-black. This Poke Weed has white flowers; the pink-flowered form is called *Phytolacca clavigera*, and comes from China.

A very unusual plant is *Clematis heracleifolia davidiana* which does little until the end of the summer except produce very large, simply divided, dark green leaves. Again, when there are few rivals it produces, over a long period, short sprays of small, scented, blue flowers, rather like thick-petalled hyacinth 'pips'. Sometimes *Lonicera* × *brownii* 'Fuchsioides' planted nearby sends a trailing stem loaded with scarlet tubular blossoms to dangle against the azure-blue.

As we turn to leave the long Shade Walk the late autumn light glints through the drooping flowers of many fuchsias beneath which are little colonies of cyclamens carpeting the ground where the icy snowdrops stood in spring.

4 *Developing the Water Gardens*

Making another Pond

By the summer of 1972 I had become very discontented with the mixed planting of trees and shrubs that continued downstream below the top three pools. Originally the idea had been to cover the steep dry banks of the ditch with shrubs to smother the native weeds. This had been achieved. In summer it looked lush and copsy, but it was far too twiggy in winter, with not enough evergreens. As the Shade Gardens gradually developed on the opposite side of the water from the house garden these shrubs formed a visual barrier, and when one day I was asked if 'the garden opposite belonged to me' I knew what had to be done. But it is always a sad business taking the mattock and axe and destroying years of one's life together with the trees and shrubs. Fortunately I was able to spare the best bit of planting, the fine *Metasequoia*, *Prunus* 'Tai Haku', the Great White Cherry, and *Liquidambar* which became the apex of a revised planting to frame the new pond. I had decided that a mirror of water was needed, to lie between the old and the new Shade Gardens. It would widen the area visually, and reflect the beautiful white trunk and branches of *Betula jacquemontii* which stood alone in a broad grass walk.

On 9 January 1973 I had a small operation. On the morning of the 22nd, from my window, I saw the large crane of the drag-line go lumbering towards the cleared and waiting site. In my diary I wrote that 'I felt shattered and excited—both!' I remember that I felt scared suddenly to make important decisions which I would have to live with, like them or not. However, I pulled myself together and went out to meet my friend, Mr C., to discuss a plan of campaign. Mr C. is one of those eminently capable men who always inspire confidence. But while I was invigorated by his enthusiasm for our project I was worried lest I was not in a fit state to evaluate what he and his vast machine were about to do. For two days the sound of the machine carving up my garden disturbed my peace of mind. From time to time I went to watch. Gradually the steep narrow ditch was opened out. As the shape of the pond gradually emerged the clay was laid across the lower end to form a dam. The digging and building had to be estimated carefully so that the final water level would lie comfortably in the hollow. By four o'clock of the second day the man and machine had done their work. I stood at a distance and surveyed the empty hole, the great heap of piled clay across the far end.

The overflow from the pools above was splashing into the small stretch of ditch, screened by the original planting which now led into this new pond. It would take two or three days to fill. There was remarkably little spoil to be cleared: most of it was built into the dam which, of course, lay high and rough and would need several months to settle. The mown grass that led towards the pond showed very little damage, so carefully had the great machine been manoeuvred round the site.

At that stage, as with the foundations of a new house, the pool seemed too small. But if it were larger, I told myself, that would have created bigger problems removing the spoil. I spent the evening ironing, comforted by the sweet smell of domesticity, and went to bed very tired and slightly confused!

Before the water reached the top of the dam we had to dig a narrow trench in the clay to let it cross over and slither down the slope in a muddy trickle to fall into the last section of ditch which remained at the lowest end of the garden. There was no more we could do then but wait for the dam to settle.

Late summer is the time I prefer for earth-moving jobs. By then the flush of plant and weed growth has slowed up and we feel we can (sometimes) spare time for improvements. One might think that winter would be more suitable, and occasionally it is. But especially where heavy soil is involved, it is best to handle it when it is neither sodden wet nor baked concrete-dry. Another consideration is that I cannot think properly when I am shuddering with cold.

So, near the end of July 1973, we turned our attention once more to the pile of clay which had now settled, and grown quite a crop of weeds, intermingled with surviving plants which had been swept up by the crane bucket. These included the gigantic *Polygonum sachalinense* which had looked positively tropical towering out of the ditch, but must now be banished elsewhere.

There were two major decisions to make. I wanted to change the point where the water would leave the pond so that it did not remain a pond with a ditch entering and leaving in a straight line. What worried me was how it would descend from the dam into the lower ditch. I did not like the muddy trickle which was already showing signs of wearing away the clay. Andrew decided that what we needed were two more small pools, made of concrete, to hold up the water and let it spill gradually down to the lower level. This seemed a marvellous idea, and we sited them to one side of the dam so that it almost appeared that the flow of water was taking a natural curve. Before they could be made, or the pipe laid across the dam, the continual flow of water had to be diverted. Harry made a new channel for it to run outside the area where all the work would be taking place. Then a trench was dug across the dam, sufficiently deep to bury the concrete pipes, plus enough soil above on which grass could grow. Only rarely now do we see the tell-tale sign across the mown grass.

Next the little artificial pools were marked out, and their levels staked. It was not easy to make a good base in the soft buttery clay, but between them Andrew and Harry laid down all the broken rubble and stone they could find, held in position by angle irons well driven home. Pig-netting was laid on top of this, and finally concrete, smoothed and shaped into two shallow basins with a slipway between. When it was sufficiently set the water was redirected through the pipe, and by the next morning the two little pools were spilling over and joining the ditch.

Before long Harry had levelled the dam, and finally brought topsoil to spread over the clay before he sowed it with grass. Within a few days a film of green was to be seen. By the autumn it had merged with the wide grass walks on both sides and the new pond looked as though it had always been there.

Before I could think of planting I knew we had to do a lot more to the soil. We had originally made a small water garden along one side of the ditch. Here I had learnt that the ornamental rhubarb, *Rheum palmatum*, and several other plants, will rot if the soil is waterlogged. Too soon native weeds had overtaken my exotic plant introductions which had never really been happy in the solid, sticky clay. So, for more than a year we had emptied our wheelbarrows of weeds onto the land on both sides of the lower ditch. We had also carted out spare compost from the great heaps stacked to rot, and all the waste pot soil from the nursery which is spent peat and sand. All this helped to make a new topsoil, so that when I came to plant I had a good texture in which to work, and in which my plants could establish themselves before their roots reached the wet clay beneath.

The final stage before planting was to make the hollow block edging which was so successful round the first ponds. When Harry came to edge the lower ditch he widened it and set his blocks so that the water curved round from the little pools into a final stretch which sweeps under a little wooden bridge. We can now stand here and listen to the gentle splashing of water among a lush planting of water-loving plants.

This final straight stretch of water was the reason for the name the Canal Bed, the wide area of damp, low-lying land on either side. To maintain the correct water level, about 2 in./50 mm below the top of the blocks, Harry built another little dam at the very end of our ditch where it disappears under a great willow bush into our neighbour's reservoir.

Now our water levels are constant throughout the year. However many weeks of drought we may have had, the underground water keeps all the pools topped up. Occasionally, after very heavy rain, the levels may rise an inch or two, but never enough to flood the surrounding land. We do have to watch carefully, especially in winter, that the exit pipes are not blocked by sticks and fallen leaves.

The Canal Bed

Although it does not have a very attractive name I sometimes think that this is the most popular bed in the garden, possibly because it is such an unaccustomed oasis of lush planting to be found in our dry Essex farmland. The sound and movement of water and perhaps the sight of a mother duck with her brood of ducklings sailing along the 'Canal' help to suggest that 'God's in his Heaven and all's right with the world', in spite of the mess that we seem to be making of it.

The area planted is about 30 yd/28 m long, 15 yd/14 m across, with the raised water level of the ditch widened to about 4–5 ft/1.5 m across running through its length. There are two trees giving light dappled shade, more or less in the centre: one of the original oaks, *Quercus robur*, and the other we planted, *Quercus palustris*, which has now made a fine young tree. Beneath this I planted an *Acer palmatum*, and two or three *Viburnum plicatum* 'Mariesii' to make eventually a bosky centre and background.

I have already remarked that there seem to be few evergreens, either woody or herbaceous, for the water-side. *Phormium* seemed the obvious choice for a dramatic evergreen, and plants are sited near the dam as exposed features. Certainly they have become irreplaceable in this import-ant bed. I have planted *Phormium tenax* 'Purpureum' with wide purplish-brown leaves which makes a most handsome clump almost 5 ft/1.5 m high in my garden, but can be more in softer climates. The variegated forms of *Phormium tenax* vary, the hardiest I think is not the brightest coloured, but the new young leaves are very attractive, and for the rest of the year they retain creamy-white margins. *Phormium cookianum* makes a smaller plant, still a useful feature in the small garden, and useful to me in this bed, in another grouping. There are many beautiful variegated and purple forms of *Phormium* available which have been introduced from New Zealand.

Most winters they survive, but the occasional bad winter, when altern-ate wetting and freezing, accompanied by wind frosts out of the North, finds them shriven to the base in the spring. With luck they recover, but it takes two or three years before they regain their former splendour. So, we wrap ours up with bundles of straw surrounded by sheets of polythene to protect the greater part of the leaves and leaf-bases from the searing winds. It takes two of us to run round them with long lengths of twine—usually our last job before Christmas. I cannot say that I like the look of our efforts, rather like untidy old crinolined ladies all winter, but it is worth the trouble, and the unsightliness, to preserve these magnificent garden ornaments. Just occa-sionally I am defeated to find that a family of water voles has spent the winter in such cosy comfort and has eaten away a large part of a fine clump!

I was anxious to conceal the edges of the little concrete pools, but not at all sure how dry, or moist, the soil would be. It is, of course, useless to put bog-loving plants in bone dry soil alongside any kind of artificial pool if you have not made proper provision for some kind of underground watering. I think, however, that we were lucky, or perhaps I should say inefficient, as our cement layers for the little pools are not watertight. (With a little more experience I think I can say we would have been lucky if they *had* held water—we have had the experience of waking and seeing the large pools opposite our house windows almost emptied, once by burrowing water voles, and again by an insufficiently rammed dam.)

The small pools ooze water gently into their surrounding banks, which is, of course, ideal. The water level is easily maintained by the constant flow throughout the entire water course. I tried several plants as cover, but those which have lasted and saved me endless weeding are *Polygonum affine* and

Cotula potentillina. I would not have dreamt that this little plant would have liked such a position. It is recommended for crevices in paving, but fortunately my bank is to its liking, and it has crept all along the concrete edges of the pools, hiding them completely.

As an alternative feature to the phormiums I planted a sprawling bush of *Salix repens argentea*. Sprawling sounds awkward and untidy; I don't think this plant is either. It is a low, gracefully spreading bush on the rim of the small upper pool, breaking the curved grass edge of the dam. For weeks in early spring it delights me. There is a wealth of long thin branches studded with silken pearl-sized buds which slowly swell until the bush becomes alight with silvery-white. Suddenly the buds burst into round fluffy catkins, beautiful as mimosa. When they have faded I prune the bush quite hard, taking most of the strong stems back to the base, leaving just enough to keep a reduced shape. The strong rootstock soon replaces them with fresh long branches covered with glistening silver leaves. They add grace to the corner for the rest of the season, and do not impede the cover of *Polygonum* and *Vinca minor* 'Bowles' Variety' which clothe the bank beneath it. The white-flowered form of *Colchicum autumnale* pushes up near the drier grass edge with narrow polished leaves in spring, and crowded clumps of small goblets on tall stems in autumn.

March finds *Lysichitum* just emerging along the water's edge. I have planted several, both the yellow *L. americanum* and the white *L. camtschatcense*, whose leaf clusters are slightly smaller, and whose first surprising flower makes me think that a white duck has just flown in—but the resemblance is only fleeting as the flower opens into a perfect spathe of purest ivory. One clump was not enough. Beneath *Prunus* 'Tai Haku' I planted several of my seedlings, hoping to see their reflections and those of the great showy clusters of cherry together as I looked down into the water from the edge of the Middle Dam. Some seasons it comes just right, on a day of blue skies, with little puffs of white cloud. For me such a performance is as stirring as a great stage production, takes far longer to produce and is never repeated quite the same again.

The drumhead primulas, *Primula denticulata*, like the heavy soil of the Canal Bed, but do not need to take up precious space at the water's edge. Showing colour there with the lysichitums are several forms of *Caltha*. Our own native *Caltha palustris* is as beautiful as any, luxuriating in the black, soggy soil, surrounded by little lilac drifts of the double Lady's Smock, *Cardamine pratensis* 'Flore Pleno', both original inhabitants of this marshy piece of land long before we came. (The single form of *Cardamine* is native.) Lasting longer but making almost too solid clumps of colour for my liking is the double Marsh Marigold, *C. palustris* 'Plena'. They are prettiest, I think, partly opened when they show green centres. Both flop usefully over the hard block edge which prevents all the carefully accumulated topsoil from sliding down into the water. More block-smotherers are the Water Forget-me-not, *Myosotis palustris*, which floats yards of flowering stem out in the water, and several kinds of musk. The most robust of these with me are

Mimulus guttatus, the Monkey Musk, and *M. cupreus* 'Hose in Hose'. This latter has soft copper-coloured flowers, one sitting inside the other.

To conceal my edgings still more I encourage *Caltha polypetala* to float out into the water, and add *Iris laevigata* and several clumps of *Zantedeschia*, the Arum Lily, to break up the straight stretch of the 'Canal'.

Beneath the oaks on either side of the water where it is less moist, I let white foxgloves seed among huge-leafed forms of *Hosta sieboldiana*. I am never sure if it is my soil, or if I have perhaps an extra-good form, but certainly some of the *Hosta* clumps are elephantine. They mingle with *Rodgersia*, which likes moist but not waterlogged soil. I also think it likes a little shade in the hottest hours of the day. Certainly the beautiful *Rodgersia tabularis* needs a sheltered site to retain the perfect symmetry of its huge, dimpled, round leaves.

Sadly, once these great plants begin to spread, a large bed quickly becomes a small one, and you wish you had half an acre of these special, precious conditions. It always amazes me how small and few are the areas I have for really specialized conditions, whether cool, shady, moist *and* well-drained—or, elsewhere, warm and sunny with *deep* fed soil! As time goes by we gradually create new situations by growing shelter and improving soil conditions, but by then the first ones often need re-making too. That is the pattern of growth. Nothing remains the same, there is always change, part is improvement, part deterioration.

Big clumps of *Lysimachia* rise above the bulky foliage plants. *Lysimachia punctata*, common though it may be, is a joyful sight with its stiff spires of bright yellow, and here it usefully colonizes a poor piece of soil beneath the original oak, drifting into *Luzula maxima* 'Marginata' which can also make bad soil look positively luxuriant. It looks so pretty too in May with its sprays of little brown and yellow tassels and finally, and not least, it is still fresh and green all winter.

I learnt from reading Gertrude Jekyll to put *Thalictrum speciosissimum* and *Veratrum* near the water-side. The *Thalictrum*'s fluffy heads of pale greenish-yellow flowers are held high on grey stems which carry stiff fan-like sprays of bluish leaves, wonderful contrast for the stiff, pleated green leaves of *Veratrum*. Around the garden I have all three flowering forms of *Veratrum*—white, acid-green and maroon-purple.

Ligularia przewalskii 'The Rocket' makes another lofty plant—6 ft/2 m spikes of smallish yellow flowers set along purplish-black stems. These giant herbs grow up to take the place of the many candelabra primulas and water irises which have decorated the water's edge in the early summer, and do not really mind being overshadowed later in the season.

Large, round leaves are provided by *Senecio clivorum*. Although its roots may be in water, wilting can occur temporarily with sudden heat in early June. But this is one of the few plants, I think, that has superb foliage *and* superb flowers, especially in the form *Senecio clivorum* 'Desdemona'. As they emerge in spring the newborn leaves are small and purplish-red with a shiny wet look, but they quickly expand, smooth and large as saucers, bronzed-green above, shining mahogany-red beneath, poised on red stalks. Add to this colour scheme large heads of thick petalled daisies the colour of orange peel standing 4 ft/1.2 m above the foliage, and you will agree that this either deserves the most special place in the garden, or cannot be accommodated at all!

A large daisy-plant that is, I believe, quite rare and is certainly very unusual was given to me by Eric Smith, but although it is called *Senecio smithii*, he tells me it was named afore his time. It was introduced as early as 1895 from southern Chile and the Falkland Islands. It must have really wet soil, anything less and it will be a poor thing. Well-grown it makes nice-looking clumps of large puckered green leaves with pale backs. The thick flower stem, about 4 ft/1.2 m high, supports a close-set, roundish head of medium-sized white daisies with greenish-yellow centres. It is not an obviously showy plant, but the shape of the flower head intrigues me. The fluffy seed head which follows is attractive too.

There is planting that I remember all year, and anticipate all spring. After the prostrate Silver Willow has lost its catkins, and the *Lysichitum* spathes are dragging in the mud, the yellow-leafed form of our native *Iris pseudacorus* is at its best. Last year's leaves lie curled like pale wood shavings round the base of the new leaves which are a most delicate harmony of butter and cream. (By midsummer they will be scarcely distinguishable from the green-leafed form.) Nestling among them is *Cardamine latifolia* which seems to be a perfect complementary harmony with its large trusses of cool lilac flowers.

Just opposite, across the little pools which now look quite natural with their softened edges of *Cotula* and a few moss-covered stones, is a little 'field' of cotton grass in full flower, and dancing among it is a *corps de ballet* of *Primula pulverulenta* 'Bartley Strain', the palest pink version, with slender stems all powdered white. Further downstream is the lovely old wine-coloured form which I should not like to be without, *Primula pulverulenta* itself.

The running fern *Onoclea sensibilis* joins in this reckless party, and I know that before long it will be out of hand, if it is not so already. But for a brief while I can stand on my little bridge looking up the 'Canal' towards the small brimming pools which spill and splash among these exquisite plants— the great phormiums, both dark and light making strong accent in the middle ground between the Canal Bed and the Bog Gardens above—all framed in the background by the great oak, weeping willows and Swamp Cypress and finally calmed and united by the New Pool and wide mown grass walks. For a brief moment in time there is complete harmony.

In our first garden, where we struggled with chalky boulder clay and destructive droughts, our enthusiasm for gardening was declining by the middle of July, and sank lower and lower until we were rescued by the autumn (sometimes delayed till winter) rains. As the summer days went pitilessly by, often drearily overcast, the grass withered to nothingness, few flowers were worth looking at, and only my drought-resisting foliage plants provided relief from the weary scene.

I have since learnt how to cope more efficiently with drought and dry soil, as I still have plenty of both, but although my Damp Garden has problems just as severe—probably more so—the great advantage is that plants can be found and grown without hindrance to prolong the flowering season from earliest spring to the back end of autumn, without a break. But please do not think that the garden is a perpetual blaze of colour. That would be dreadful, surrounded as we are by cornfields and orchards. There is a time, in midsummer, when everything does seem to be in flower at the same time but, mercifully, that does not last. The quieter seasons always seem to me to be the best, when it is possible to be pleasantly surprised by colour rather than satiated by it.

Astilbes are coveted, understandably, by almost everyone who sees them. Everything about them is good. Beautiful foliage, often warmly tinted, often delicately divided into fernlike fronds, is topped with tapering spires of tiny fluffy flowers in many shades from creamy-white through pastel pinks to rich dark reds or purply-puce. It is not likely you will care for all of them—certainly will not plant them all together. To make a choice among the many fine hybrids is bewildering, but I find I prefer the slender open spires rather than the short dense heads which look rather like upturned dish mops. Almost always I go back to the species, or near species. They really prefer part shade combined with moist conditions and I have not yet a sufficiently suitable area to show off many of these beautiful plants. Of the large forms I have only planted two white ones. *Astilbe rivularis* attracts me because of its noble form, with impressive foliage and 6 ft/2 m stems of arching plumes made up of small greenish-white flowers developing into an interesting seed head; but it does demand a lot of space. 'Professor van der Wielen' is a little smaller, and more generous with its flowers, but they still make large, gracefully arching sprays.

Two small astilbes are my favourites for the edges of my cool damp borders. The first is a hybrid of *Astilbe simplicifolia*, of which there are several delightful garden forms, some with bronze-green leaves and short but light open heads of rosy-pink flowers. *Astilbe* 'Sprite' is possibly the best known and loved of these dwarf astilbes; given moist soil and not too much scorching sun it flowers for weeks in the late summer with pale, almost flesh-pink flowers set in an airy spire, about 1 ft/300 mm high. With soft clumps of finely cut bronze leaves the season carries on until the frosts, when the flowers are replaced gradually by the warm chestnut-brown seed heads.

Astilbe chinensis 'Pumila' is, I think, an under-rated plant. Its foliage is flatter and broader and the little shoots spread around to make very competent ground-cover. They send up barely branched flower spikes, about 9 in./230 mm high, which continue to elongate and provide light mauve-pink tapers for weeks—I could say months—into the late autumn. I find the regimented ranks of seed heads equally attractive, remaining so all winter, until they are cut down.

Another unusual *Astilbe* is *Astilbe taquetii* 'Superba'. It flowers late in the warm Indian summer we often have as autumn in East Anglia, when *Astilbe chinensis* is still looking its best along the grass edge of the border. This elegant plant lifts slender spires of vivid cyclamen-purple on 4 ft/1.2 m stems, very welcome when there is little risk of other colours clashing. There are usually a few flowers nearby on *Lysimachia ciliata*, another uncommon plant but one that gives excellent value from the moment it pushes its milk-chocolate-coloured leaves through the ground in spring. It makes running clumps of fine stems moderately set with leaves which are topped for months with loose heads, not spikes, of little dangling pale yellow flowers.

I must not leave out two foliage plants which dominate the bridge end of the Canal Bed. *Physocarpus opulifolius* 'Luteus' used to be called *Spirea opulifolia*, which may help you to recognize that it is a shrub. Each year it sends up tall, elegant, 6–8 ft/2–2.5 m branching stems, clothed with prettily shaped leaves of a really clear yellow which remain throughout the growing season. As soon as its rather inconspicuous flowers have shown themselves I prune the strong stems back to within 1 yd/1 m or so of the ground, keeping a reduced shape for effect. If you neglect this pruning the bush becomes a shapeless tangle, and the foliage is not nearly so clear and brilliant. It stands on one side of the Canal like a great arching bower while opposite, repeating the colour, is a fountain of golden grass-like leaves made by *Carex stricta*, 'Bowles' Golden'. How fortunate for us that Mr Bowles went to the Norfolk Broads and kept his perceptive eyes to the ground. When all the colour has gone from the flowers, and only the seed pods of *Primula*, *Iris* and *Veratrum* remain, then these two plants dominate the scene.

Late autumn is the time of the grasses. The great ones, all the different *Miscanthus*, add grandeur to the centre of the bog beds, while *Molinia caerulea* 'Variegata' has also outstayed any flowering plant as a feature. Throughout autumn it declines gracefully into a small ivory shower as its flower stems and leaves gradually whiten.

On the opposite side, also placed against the mown grass edge, are low tuffets of *Carex morrowii* 'Aureo-Variegata', which have been brilliant all summer but will be more appreciated throughout the winter. With every narrow leaf of this green and yellow grass-like plant curved and outlined against the bare earth, it is one of the very few plants that will remain of all this rich summer glory.

Two more small willows at this bridge end of the bed are *Salix lanata*, and *Salix hastata* 'Wehrhahnii'. *Salix lanata* takes a long time to be even as big as a gooseberry bush; I have to be careful that it is not smothered by its neighbours. It is a willow from the far north. During the great drought of 1975 I was fortunate to be able to go to Norway, and was very excited to see this willow just opening its catkins beside melting pools of snow, in mid July. With us, of course, it produces them in spring, exceptionally large and woolly pale yellow catkins. The leaves are unusual too, being broadly round covered with silky hairs. *S. hastata* 'Wehrhahnii' is about the size and shape of a good blackcurrant bush. It has attractive polished purple-brown young shoots which carry round white catkins, woolly and snow-white as those cotton wool 'buds' you can buy at the chemist.

At the base of it is *Verbena corymbosa*, an eccentric member of a family most of which will only survive in my hot, dry, gravelly garden. This one runs about in moist soil, producing small heads of violet-mauve flowers endlessly throughout the summer, and is no deterrent to the clumps of *Trollius ledebouri* which grow up through it. But I think the time is not far off when it will have to be removed, as it is rather too exuberant for this limited space.

I have only allowed myself one *Iris kaempferi*, apart from the form which has variegated leaves and not unsightly purple flowers. Considering the struggle the leaves must have to resist the virus which is causing the variegation I think the flowers are rather fine, certainly a good violet-purple. But my white-flowering form is one I have grown from seed. To an expert it may have it faults, but as I am not yet acquainted with any that may have romantic-sounding Japanese names, and long pedigrees, I look upon mine with fond ignorance and admiration. I think it is beautiful. Large, pure white, floating petals—for a brief while it lights the scene.

At the end of the summer I can often find flowers on *Caltha palustris* 'Alba'. It is the first Marsh Marigold to appear in spring. In early March my clumps are tightly packed with buds, like small white eggs, or perhaps marbles, at ground level. They push up quite quickly, regardless of icy conditions, until each plant is a tidy mound of round green leaves, studded with shallow china-white saucers. These first flowers drop their petals to form round green seed heads filled with shining jet black seeds, but new flowers still continue to come for weeks and weeks. There seems to be hardly a day in the summer when I cannot find a flower tucked away somewhere on one of my plants. I have one plant of *Caltha leptosepala*, which is not nearly so generous. Perhaps I have not taken sufficient notice of it; I do admire it, a beautiful large-flowered white, but I have not given enough thought to propagating it.

By midsummer there is little room for weeds in the Canal Bed. The problem is usually to find the time to see that the strong do not subdue the weak, in this overloaded bed.

The Taxodium Bed

A few treasures have slipped across the bridge into a little continuation bed made around a Swamp Cypress, *Taxodium distichum*, which now stands about 25 ft/8 m high. Here one of the many springs that travel beneath the surface of my Shade Beds and grass walks has been dug out and runs across the surface as a shallow ditch, at right angles to the 'Canal'. On either side of this little ditch I have planted *Matteuccia struthiopteris*, where its beautiful shuttlecocks of fern fronds catch the light in early summer making a tender green background for the first Blue Poppies, *Meconopsis betonicifolia*. In the background are two more great ferns, outlined against a huge bamboo, *Arundinaria japonica*, which shields the whole bed from the south.

Osmunda regalis, the Royal Fern, is well known, loves to be planted at the water's edge, and cannot have too many helpings of well-rotted leaf-mould or compost. I think perhaps they take many years to show their best for mine are still not nearly as impressive as illustrations I have seen.

Blechnum chilense, which I have long called, wrongly of course, *Blechnum tabulare* (and how difficult I find it to unlearn old names!) is one of those rare treasures, a really magnificent evergreen for the bog garden, as well as being a very distinctive and unusual fern. It does need a sheltered situation to preserve its great leaves through a bad winter, and probably makes far more imposing plants in the warm, wet West Country than we can manage in East Anglia. But I enjoy my plants, which are slowly increasing, producing each year a few more of those broad, dark green leaves which look as though they had been stamped out of leather.

Thinking back to the Blue Poppies, this little sheltered corner seems to have suited them fairly well, although they are but a token to the drifts of them as they can and should be grown in open glades in moist and sheltering woodland. It is the dry air as much as dry roots which kills them in many gardens.

Sometimes I have a few plants of another poppy. Making great rosettes, so heavily coated with silky golden hairs that the leaves appear almost gilded, is *Meconopsis regia*. I watch these rosettes expand with mixed feelings, knowing that once they have decided to flower this marvellous pattern and texture of foliage will deteriorate. All its strength is used up to produce a stout stem as tall as I am from which hang, like a great candelabra lamp, shallow saucers of pale lemon petals. These are followed by large, round, felted seed pods which altogether must contain, and shed, millions of seeds. Then the plant dies. But I never see young seedlings around as I do the proliferation of foxgloves. Maybe one or two, in my seed boxes, if I am lucky.

Two or three musks are treasured here. *Mimulus lewisii* is quite distinct, growing in much less wet soil than the rest, making upright plants which are covered with soft rosy-mauve flowers. Beside it I have planted a charming dwarf *Lythrum*, *L. virgatum*, only about 2 ft/600 mm high, whose slender branching spikes are crowded with bright magenta-pink flowers, and the minimum of narrow leaves to detract from the flame of colour.

The flowers of *Mimulus ochrid* could sound identical to *Mimulus guttatus* for both have a yellow base, variously spotted and splashed with brownish-crimson. But to see *Mimulus ochrid*, with its tone of yellow that is just right for the blood-red markings which are in correct proportion, is to see that it is in a class of its own. To compensate, perhaps, the more commonly seen Monkey Musk, *M. guttatus*, is much more vigorous, making large shawls of flower-smothered stems which float out into the water alongside airy blue masses of Water Forget-me-not, *Myosotis palustris*. Incidentally, the spelling is *Mimulus ochrid*, not *M. orchid* (I think it is the name of a lake in Albania).

I treasure a fine but uncommon *Polygonum* in this bed of specialities. I have not yet found enough of just the right conditions for it to flourish really well. It is one more of my plants which lays claim to the water's edge but where, if I do not watch continuously, plants can be overlaid and smothered by their more successful neighbours, such as the vigorous musks. This plant is *Polygonum miletii* which thrives best with its roots thrust deep into continuously wet soil where it makes slowly increasing clusters of narrow dark green leaves. Tall slender stems carry thick short heads of flowers the colour of ripe loganberries, and about the same shape. These flowers are produced from late summer until the frosts, not in great quantities, but each flower remaining fresh for weeks. When I am searching for seed I can only tell, as one does with a ripe loganberry, by the slight darkening of the crimson bloom, that the seeds may be formed and ready for collection. Often I am surprised to rub an almost perfect-looking flower head in the palm of my hand and see, with delight, the shining chestnut-coloured seeds.

I have two more polygonums which are similar in habit but less demanding of situation. Both will grow in full sun, provided the soil does not dry out. A fairly stiff soil with enough humus suits them well. The first is *Polygonum carneum* which is a really worthwhile border plant, being tidy of habit and flowering for weeks throughout the summer. Produced in abundance, the flower heads are bright, but a much lighter colour than *P. miletii*, on the salmon side of pink. *Polygonum sphaerostachyum* (*P. macrophyllum*) also makes similar clumps of neat narrow leaves, but has flowers that veer towards the purple side of pink. Like the old fashioned roses, and some of the border *Phlox*, it is a colour impossible to describe, of such a beautiful luminous tone you remark on it immediately.

Beside *Polygonum miletii* I have planted *Carex grayi*. This is a plant that might be enjoyed by many flower arrangers. Above its grass-like leaves it holds tall sprays of curious seed heads, round clusters of inflated capsules, interesting and unusual, both green and when dried brown.

Diphylleia cymosa, the Umbrella Leaf, sends up a few of its large double-lobed round leaves. I wonder how long that splendid clump has grown with its back to a great bluff of stone in the rock garden at Kew. Must I be patient, or shall I need to move my plant to a more suitable position where its constitution will be more suited? Then perhaps it will also produce heads of insignificant flowers to be followed by bold blue berries on crimson stalks. Mr Graham Thomas calls it 'most unusual and dignified'—I think so too, but where shall I find a position to match?

Absurdly different, but very lovable, are the wee species of *Trollius*. They are a charming excuse to sit down on the grass and peer into their glistening faces. *Trollius pumilus* makes little clumps of bright green finely cut leaves above which stand enamelled yellow cups on thin branching stems. *Trollius yunnanensis* is similar, but taller.

In the shade of the Blue Poppies, *Primula secundiflora* droops its plum-purple flowers, slightly dusted with greenish-white meal, while a group of *Dodecatheon* seedlings produce variation in their dart-like flowers which are sometimes called 'Shooting Stars'.

Around the base of the Swamp Cypress, *Taxodium distichum*, which forms the centre of this small bed, I have planted five or six clumps of *Kirengeshoma palmata*. Every year I look forward to this unusual and beautiful plant. Its fresh leafy stems are arched over by the heavy sprays of creamy-yellow shuttlecock-shaped flowers which are produced from late August to the end of September. Nearby I have planted *Rodgersia tabularis* for its unique effect. The light green leaves are almost perfectly round, slightly frilled at the edges, while the tall leaf stalks are attached to the centre of the leaves causing an indented 'dimple' on each upper surface which can be as much as 3 ft/1 m across, but never so far in my garden. But a pile of these beautifully shaped leaves (even 18 in./460 mm across) looks very spectacular and scarcely needs the drooping heads of creamy-white flowers which tower above them, handsome as they may be. Where there is not enough room for *Gunnera*, this plant might be considered, provided there is adequate protection from sun and wind, and the soil is perpetually moist. It creates both drama and tranquillity among more fussy-leafed plants.

5 *The North-facing Clay Bank*

This piece of land lies just inside the southern boundary of the garden. Originally there was no bank, but a second spring-fed ditch ran from west to east to join the main ditch at a right angle. About thirty years ago my husband decided to excavate a small reservoir on the tongue of land which these two streams entered, to irrigate his fruit farm. The clay bank was made then—it was spoil from the reservoir, laid along our side of the ditch which still flows along the base of the south side of my bank and forms the boundary between our land and our neighbour's farm. For many years this clay bank lay undisturbed. Three or four fine elms backed it, standing on the headland of the farm. At the lower end of the bank, on the edge of the reservoir, we planted a golden Weeping Willow, *Salix* 'Chrysocoma', and the stately Silver Willow, *Salix alba*. Both these were put in as substantial cuttings about twenty years ago, and are now mature trees. An alder was placed, visually about the middle of the bank. It produces quantities of catkins in spring and is a fine feature. But with the loss of the elms through disease, much character has gone, and I am, slowly, recreating a leafy, shady atmosphere.

Three or four years ago I decided that this north-facing bank was too good to waste. Although not nearly as leafy as I would like it to be throughout its length, there was part shade at one end, created by the mature willows, combined with a water-retentive soil. Surely, I thought, plants which value heavy soil and a north aspect could be accommodated here. For many years we had piled our weeds and garden rubbish all over this bank, using it as a compost heap—not very beautiful, but it was out of the way and available. One of the problems with above-average-sized gardens can be the long trek with trolleys and barrows to either the bonfire site or compost heap; I am finding it necessary to screen suitable sites with quick-growing shrubs. These valuable sources of combined topsoil and composted plant waste are then at hand to be put back into the beds from which they were originally taken.

In recent years our neighbour bought and enlarged the reservoir, so large tools were again working on my boundary. As my bank was nothing but sticky plasticine-like clay with a small accumulation of decomposed weed waste spread over it, I arranged for the drag-line to scoop on a few bucketsful of field soil. This was easily done, several hundredweights at a time, I should think, dumped as easily as teaspoonsful of sugar, while the machine stood on the farm headland.

Harry had by now been joined by Keith, and together they tackled the job of making a new garden from this unprepossessing site. I do not care for steeply sloping banks, they are awkward to work and walk on, and rain tends to run off, rather than soak in. A slippery, slithery bank does not offer comfortable resting places for plants or people, or suggest individual groupings.

We had plenty of good logs so we decided to terrace the bank to make three gently sloping levels. As the work progressed the new levels were top-dressed with plenty of rotted compost and grit, for the soil that had been added was of a close, heavy texture, usefully water-retentive but cold and sticky in winter, liable to cake if it was allowed to dry out in summer. Before planting began these top-dressings were forked into the soil below, and I hope the worms will have helped to integrate the whole.

Creating More Shade

To create shade I have planted on the edge of my neighbour's headland fast-growing trees which will, eventually, I hope, compensate for the loss of the elms. *Populus trichocarpa* × *balsamea,* the Balsam Poplar, I have had before. It shot up, 6 ft/2 m a year, to a great height, filling the air with its resinous scent on memorably warm days in early spring. I hope it will grow as fast here to help take the place of the elms. I always grieve to see really big trees disappear from the landscape, knowing that it takes more than one lifetime to grow such fine specimens.

Populus serotina 'Aurea', the quivering golden-leafed poplar, takes a few years to make its mark, but it is a beautiful companion for the tall Silver Willow which also shoots up 5 or 6 ft/2 m a year once it is established. *Salix matsudana* 'Tortuosa' I have added to the group. All these trees stand on the farm side of my bank, separated from it by the little stream. Eventually I hope they will create a large screen to filter the sun but from where their roots will not greedily invade my bank.

On the south-facing farm side of my bank, at the base, I have planted *Betula pendula* 'Dalecarlica', the Swedish Birch, and *Cotoneaster* × *watereri* 'Cornubia', both of which already make good features.

Idesia polycarpa I have long admired with its huge poplar-like leaves on bright red stalks. I have placed my young tree in the corner by both my boundaries, and it is growing fast in the heavy soil. I look forward to its strings of little green flowers. Long clusters of pea-sized shining red berries will only follow if you plant both male and female trees.

This group of leaf-losing trees needed some evergreens to create interest and solidarity in winter, so I added *Picea omorika*, my favourite slender spruce, and several interesting hollies. *Ilex* × *altaclarensis* 'Camelliifolia' has beautiful leaves with scarcely a prickle, large and shining, of a dark purplish-green in winter. When mature it will make a fine pyramidal shape to lead the eye up into the alder and poplar beyond it.

To one side of the dark green holly I have placed *Ilex aquifolium* 'Flavescens' to make strong contrast. The young leaves are totally butter-yellow and, as the old leaves mature, the pale tint remains only at the tips of the leaves. But the effect of the bush is softly yellow, all the year round.

Eucryphia 'Nymansay' is growing very well, already making a stately column of foliage and producing its clusters of cupped white flowers for weeks in late summer.

Two shrubs of *Pieris* have also taken well, flowering abundantly even while young plants. *Pieris taiwanensis* carries large clusters of waxen white Lily-of-the-Valley-like flowers. They are closely 'threaded' onto drooping stems set in pale olive-coloured bracts, the whole delicate colour scheme contrasting with the rich green of the narrow leathery leaves. There will be a second display in late spring when the new young shoots unfold rich bronze-red. These shoots can be seen from the farm, causing great interest when they first appeared above the bank. Some years we are lucky and these tender flower-like shoots are not damaged, but our treacherous spring frosts can, and often do, harm them. I am always astonished how quickly they produce new shoots, less vividly coloured but still attractive. The other *Pieris* is, I think, *P. japonica*, in its pink form. The shrub has smaller leaves and deep rose-pink buds which open palest pink. They are held by dark copper-coloured bracts, attached to dark stems. Both these beautiful early flowers need to be brought into the house to admire their unique quality, their very sumptuousness, so early in the year. It is not easy to appreciate them being hurried along by the cold east wind, nor in the garden will you detect the strange faint scent which is released by the warmth of a room.

Lower down the bank, nearer the path, is a planting of another early flowering shrub, *Ribes laurifolium*. This relation of the Flowering Currant has long racemes of hellebore-green flowers. Each little pale flower has a darker green centre. The old leaves have a very matt, almost silk-like finish, while the younger ones have red stems, with red veins and shading on their backs. It is a quiet little shrub, but valued because of the pallid tones of its flowers and their early appearance. Elsewhere I have planted it at the foot of a north-facing wall with the winter-black ivy, *Hedera helix* 'Atropurpurea', for a background. In summer it looks very like the common hedge ivy, of which it is a form, being then dark green, but in winter the leaves turn dark purplish-black, each well-shaped leaf highlighted with emerald veins.

Finally, to create more immediate but light shade on my cool terraces, I have planted *Acer negundo*, the Box Elder. This makes a small light tree with smooth green twigs and leaves delicately variegated, giving almost the impression of sunlight. *Acer negundo* 'Variegatum' has irregular white edges to its leaves, *A.n.* 'Elegans' has yellow.

Apart from the need to create shade I am still endeavouring to mask the top of the bank. When you stand on the grass walk and look up, the top level of the bank is well above head height, disappearing as it were into the sky. It still looks to me too much like an ancient burial mound. Some of my trees and shrubs screen this effect, especially in summer, but the spaces in between still bother me. I have planted clumps of *Iris foetidissima* 'Citrina', *Mahonia repens* and *Vinca minor*, all to cover the bare clay. Eventually I hope the skirts of my shrubs will completely screen the top edge in summer, if not in winter. I have recently planted bush willows, such as *Salix gracilistyla*, and *S. daphnoides*, whose smooth purple stems are overlaid with white bloom, on the rear side of the bank to emerge over the top in fine fan-like shapes as another background feature, interesting in winter, lush and leafy in summer.

On the top terrace of the north-facing garden side I have planted a few more shrubs to mingle among my plants. *Aronia melanocarpa* 'Brilliant' caught my eye on Messrs Hillier's stand at the RHS Great Autumn Show a few years ago, and very pleased I am to have it, especially in autumn when every little leaf changes gradually to brilliant red. It has small clusters of white flowers in spring, rather like hawthorn, followed by shining black fruits.

Not all the plants that I have added to this bed are necessarily the ones that will stay there. With most new beds I find myself adding far too many things which I hope will do there, but which are also experiments. Or they may merely be temporary residents, put there to grow and increase a little while I am finding, or making, a better situation for them.

Plants Which Tolerate Heavy Soil

I have not given the measurements of this bank which is now the home of many plants which would not thrive easily elsewhere in my garden. It is 125 yd/120 m long, and about 12 yd/10 m deep, that is from the grass walk edge to the top of the bank, and as much again from the top of the bank, dropping to the ditch on the south side. The soil, you will remember, is heavy, intermixed with vegetable waste, fine grit and a little peat.

I had a pressing need to find somewhere for my collection of double primroses—so they were the first plants to arrive here. They have flourished exceedingly well, quite unlike anywhere else in the garden; even the miffy double white has made most healthy-looking clumps of rich green leaves on almost solid clay at the top of the bank between the shrubs. Why there, you may be thinking, and not on a more favourable site lower down on the prepared terraces? I ask that myself, until I remember that I had many more unfamiliar plants to accommodate, and I knew that primroses love clay, nor were they short of leaf-mould.

Now my stocks are increasing I am not certain that I like the look of too many together. (How hard we are to please!) Fortunately the best time to divide them is during flowering, if you can bring yourself to tear them to pieces when you have waited all year to see them. But that is what I do to get young pieces established before we have any real heat to wilt them. We reduce the leaf surface by half at least, pot the special ones, that is those we have least of, and shelter them in a shaded tunnel.

If I find too many blossoms being picked off by mischievous birds I push a few short twigs into the soil and weave a web of black cotton over the plants, which is effective without being unsightly.

We do not, as yet, have many genuine old fashioned varieties of double forms. I have mentioned the double white, *Primula vulgaris* 'Plena Alba'. We also have *P.v.* 'Lilacina' whose massed stems of rosette-shaped blossoms bury the light green leaves. The colour is a delicious cool lilac. *P.v.* 'Marie Crousse' makes an excellent contrast, with light claret-coloured flowers edged with silver. In between these colours I have another pinky-mauve double which I think came originally from Mrs Fish. All these forms have rather lax flower stems with perfectly formed rosettes which open well.

For several years now we have assiduously sown seed of Barnhaven origin, and have acquired a few fairly good doubles. I cannot say they are *really* good because I have seen the amazing ones that Mr Jared Sinclair has at his fascinating nursery in Cumbria, and I judge mine by his. But each spring we hover optimistically over the last year's batch of seedlings, looking for the buds, knowing that only the fat ones will produce a double flower, and that rarely a good full double. So you can see why it is they are rare, and if ever you are offered one you might wonder whether money can buy the years of care that have produced it, not only the nursery's care but the breeders whose patience is legendary.

As with laced polyanthus primulas it is essential to divide the double primulas at least every two or three years. If they have been neglected the leaves become smaller and smaller, sprouting from a crowded ugly-looking knobby base. These knobs must be cut away as completely as possible. Each new shoot is usually attempting to produce clean white roots at its base, but those that do not can be boxed, or potted up and kept moist and sheltered until they have done so.

Although I am, I confess, ensnared by the double primroses (and double forms of *Primula auricula* too) I do on the whole prefer single flowers. I have two single-flowered primulas that look well at the base of my bank, near some especially large-flowered seedlings of a purple *Helleborus orientalis*. One is *Primula* 'Cowichan' with garnet-red velvety petals, the other *Primula* 'Garryarde Guinevere' which in spring has crinkly purplish leaves which set off large heads of pale mauve-pink flowers held in purple calyces. These are separated by a large patch of sombre-coloured spidery plants of *Ophiopogon planiscarpus nigrescens*. This impossible name is well suited to an impossible-cannot-be-real looking plant. 'Whatever is that?' is how it is inevitably addressed by anyone meeting it for the first time. Related to *Liriope*, this strangely attractive plant from Japan spreads flat clusters of smooth, strap-shaped leaves of the darkest purple shade—indeed they are almost black. They send up short clusters of little violet-coloured flowers which set sprays of shiny black berries in autumn.

To make sharp contrast with these strange plants I have chosen *Bergenia* 'Abendglut'. (Both are evergreen.) I love the *Bergenia* family. Although they do look tatty for a brief while in late winter–early spring when the old leaves are deteriorating, the new ones come so quickly, are so fresh, so well shaped and always provide interesting balance and change of shape and texture, so often needed in a new planting. Not only do they remain evergreen, many of them assume rich tints of bronze, russet-red and carmine throughout the winter. Here, on this bank, with the dusky hellebores, primulas and strap-leafed *Ophiopogon* they add large rosettes of crinkle-edged round leaves, and double flowers of vivid rose-pink.

As spring grows more confident, green cut-leafed carpets of *Viola gracilis* will be smothered with rich violet-purple flowers. From reading I am not certain if this is the true form. It has delicately twisting petals which give the flower a butterfly appearance.

Around and through the mats of *Viola* appear the erythroniums. So quickly they come and go I look each day to make the most of them. First comes *Erythronium dens-canis*. Folded oval leaves push a firm tip through the soil and expand to soft sage-green, heavily mottled and spotted with chocolate-brown. The large flowers hang folded on cold dull days, but immediately the sun warms them they flare back like cyclamen petals to show off the blue powdered anthers. They are generally cyclamen-pink in colour but seedlings do vary; some are almost white. I like to plant *Corydalis solida* nearby with low trusses of little amethyst-blue flowers out at the same time, which disappear as quickly. Fleeting as these little treasures are, they are some of my most valued plants, coming at the end of winter when spring still seems very reluctant, except for the mating birds which sing all day long, oblivious of the cold winds and snow showers that are part of March.

Erythronium revolutum comes a little later. It has narrower leaves and slightly taller stems of rose-pink flowers, while *Erythronium tuolumnense* has large shining green leaves and branching flower stems which carry several small turkscap flowers of rich yellow.

Two or three big patches of *Primula denticulata*, in shades of lilac, reddish-purple and white start opening their round balls of flowers at ground level, gradually lengthening their stems and expanding their leaves over several weeks. I like their great rosettes of pale green leaves which remain handsome for the rest of the summer.

I have tucked a few species paeonies onto the middle terrace, including *Paeonia cambessedesii*. It has increased in size from a seedling so the soil does not seem to displease it. None the less, I read that it needs well baking in sunshine to flower well, so I may have to move it.

I have just planted seed of *Paeonia wittmanniana*. If and when it germinates I am sure it will be raised on this terrace where I can watch it until it is large enough to be moved, if it should be necessary. Immature beds often provide a haven for plants that need to be watched until they are big enough to be increased, either by seed, division or cuttings.

The variegated form of Solomon's Seal, *Polygonatum falcatum* 'Variegatum' is slowly increasing in a pocket all to itself. It has smaller leaves than the familiar *Polygonatum* × *hybridum*. The fat buds emerging through the soil are pink, and so too are the leaf stems, while the leaves are narrowly outlined with white. I have elsewhere a very small amount of *Polygonatum* × *hybridum* 'Variegatum'. This plant is very heavily varie-gated, each leaf slightly twisted and strongly striped with cream and green. It makes a much smaller plant, both in height and leaf size, because it is so variegated. It is keenly sought but increases very slowly, having so little chlorophyll. I think it is more interesting than beautiful, but I thought it worthwhile to mention the difference between the two.

Among the plants that were new to me was *Dentaria digitata*. Apparently it is more than three hundred years since this plant was first described, occurring in mountain woods of west and central Europe. I have been slow to catch up with it. Flower buds and folded leaves emerge together, both tinted purple and almost invisible against the leaf-mould, but as each unrolls the finely cut leaves become green while the flowers open soft rosy-lilac. Lovely as these are I was perhaps even more impressed by the curious clusters of scaly white roots which produce this delicate structure.

Looking at the purplish-pink buds of the variegated Solomon's Seal, thrusting up taller every day, smooth and streamlined as icicles, my eye was caught by two or three large plants of *Euphorbia amygdaloides* 'Rubra' growing beside them. This coloured form of our native Wood Spurge varies considerably from seed; we have selected an extra-dark form. In the March sunlight the colour was enhanced by the yellow-green curtain of the Weeping Willow, *Salix* 'Chrysocoma', which makes a backcloth to this end of the bank. All winter the tip shoots of the *Euphorbia* are a rich purplish-red but in late March, as the tip arches over, the young leaves stand up like a turkey's crest and as the light shines through them the colour brightens almost to brick-red. Over the weeks the heads will gradually expand into large clusters of emerald-green 'eyes' and the colour will drain from the mature leaves, which become dark blue-green. But after the seed has set, new shoots with red leaves will appear to make interest for the autumn and winter.

Among the low carpeting plants along the edge of the grass walk are different coloured forms of *Prunella*. This plant enjoys full sun and relatively dry soil, but it prefers a heavy meadow-type soil and will easily shrivel and die in poor light soils without adequate rainfall. *Prunella* has strong purplish-blue flowers in the wild, but the form called *Prunella grandiflora* 'Loveliness', which has light lavender-blue flowers, is more often grown in gardens. There is a good white form, and also very attractive is the one which makes a glowing carpet of raspberry-pink flowers.

Another low-growing plant I enjoy in spring I obtained as *Geranium dahurica* (of gardens). As the leaves emerge through the soil in neat, round clumps each one is a combination of pink, apricot and cream, with no green at all, making a pastel patch of colour against the dark soil. As they mature the finely cut leaves turn light green. The flowers are soft lilac. Dahuria is a region of south-east Siberia and north-east Mongolia, so this little plant can stand intense cold. Like most geraniums it requires a well-drained soil but is not a drought-loving plant.

Some of the mossy saxifrages make tidy cushions studded with rose or white flowers in early summer. Two I grow more for their leaves than their flowers, which are white. *Saxifraga* 'Bob Hawkins' makes quite large rosettes of leaves edged with white in summer, flecked with touches of crimson in winter. *Saxifraga moschata* 'Cloth of Gold' makes much smaller rosettes in a lovely cool shade of yellow.

I would like to make another raised bed for these small plants, and others like them which need to be looked at closely in a cool and partly shaded situation. I already have such a bed for drought-loving plants, made against a west-facing wall which now provides a home for many small things. They revel in this well-drained sunny bed which lifts them to a height that is closer to the eye for viewing and easily to hand for weeding.

Although well-kept rock gardens can be all-absorbing, I am not drawn to make one in my present garden. It is set in countryside that can only be called flat, composed of sedimentary clay, sand and gravel. Eruptions of weathered limestone would look quite out of place. There are more suitable rocks to choose and sometimes I think it would be a challenge to attempt a rock garden, but I know that my garden has become too large to allow me such flights of fancy. At the beginning of our gardening life together Andrew and I made a small alpine garden, and it gave us great pleasure. For rock we used the large pieces of ragstone, or ironstone, that were subsoiled out of the fields. These rock-like lumps are formed where water has lain in the soil. A pocket of clay lies beneath the gravel holding up the water which deposits iron among the gravel, cementing it into a rock-like layer. Roots of crops such as fruit trees seeking water cannot penetrate this layer and the trees show signs of distress, with poor growth and small fruit. This hard layer must be broken up. Drainage channels are dug and rock-like pieces of ragstone are pulled to the surface. I still have a few of these pieces which have a pleasant reddy-brown colour. I have set them in my wall bed where they help to break up the long length and create little mini-scenes for the really small alpines.

The opposite side of this wall faces east, providing me with every temptation to make a collection of small, cool-loving plants—more saxifrages, small ferns and two or three suitable slow-growing shrubs which would form bastions to break up the straight length and perhaps create little micro-climates around them.

Linnaea borealis, which now threads its way among *Primula polyneura* on the edge of a shady walk, could be persuaded to hang down over the edge of my cool raised bed. I already have a pot of *Fuchsia procumbens* put on one side, waiting for my thought to become a fact. This extraordinary little *Fuchsia* is not entirely hardy; it has overwintered outside in mild winters, but I always keep a few cuttings safely in a frost-free greenhouse. It produces completely prostrate trailing stems covered with small heart-shaped leaves. Among them, if you look carefully, you will find tiny upturned tubular flowers, bizarrely coloured in orange, purple and green. Weeks later you will find cherry-sized plum-red fruits nestling among the leaves looking as though someone had dropped them there by mistake.

Fuchsia thymifolia (or a hybrid thereof) will certainly be in my new bed. Again, I cannot say it is reliably hardy, but it is worth keeping a young plant on a windowsill through the winter. Like *Fuchsia procumbens* it is so different from the well-known hybrid fuschsias that you would not be blamed for failing to recognize it as a member of that family. It makes a small dainty bush which can hardly wait to produce new shoots before they are set at every leaf joint with pairs of tiny flowers. Continuously throughout the summer come cascades of tiny bright rose-pink flowers, and if you have taken a few cuttings just as a precaution they will continue to flower in a frost-free greenhouse all winter.

We shall probably make the front wall of the raised bed of old railway sleepers which started life here as the fronts and backs of my potting frames. I think they will make a more sympathetic wall for woodland plants than the harsh concrete block wall which reflects the heat on the other side. (When I see properly made raised beds, with good rock work and plenty of deep crevices for alpine treasures, I feel a stab of envy, but quickly swallow it down, hoping I may be showing others as well as myself what we can do with our plants in areas which cannot come by natural building material.)

The yellow-leafed Barberry, *Berberis thunbergii* 'Aurea', I have tried elsewhere and lost. I think it might be suitable on my cool raised bed as I do not imagine it will easily grow too large. Its thin-textured leaves do not like to be sun-scorched.

Among the small plants that are lodging temporarily on my bank but need to be lifted closer to hand and eye to observe them closely is *Potentilla tabernaemontani* (*P. verna*) 'Goldrausch'. I was given this plant by the Countess von Stein Zeppelin when I visited her nursery in southern Germany. It is a delightful memento of a very happy occasion. The Countess has been a dedicated plantswoman for fifty years and has an amazing collection of good plants. *P.t.* 'Goldrausch' makes prostrate clusters of small scallop-edged leaves which produce abundant short sprays of rich orange-yellow flowers. It seems hardly ever without a flower, from spring until severe winter weather.

Calceolaria tenella runs about on the lowest terrace, sending up little stems carrying pouched 'lady's slippers'. I think it would be too invasive for my raised wall bed. Certainly *Coptis trifolia* will be there with its neat mats of fresh green divided leaves all the year round, and such delicate shallow cup-shaped flowers so early in the year, snow white in colour.

But I shall achieve neither book nor garden if I spend so much time dreaming of what I might do. But when this bed is built I shall discover, I know, another range of plants that will be new to me, which I have never troubled to learn because I did not have the right place to suit them.

The *Phlox* family provides something for almost every type of garden. The drought-tolerant forms, such as *Phlox douglasii* and *Phlox subulata*, flourish in the well-drained upper garden, but the cool soil of the bank suits *Phlox adsurgens* much better. Low tangled mats of small leaves are lost beneath quantities of round salmon-pink flowers. *Phlox* 'Wagon Wheels' is a selected clone of this popular plant, with flowers less rounded and petals slightly separated, producing a more star-like effect. It is different, but I would not say it was better.

I have planted *Phlox* 'Chattahoochee' in several parts of the garden to see which suits it best. I have decided that the sunny gravel is too exposed and starved in times of drought. I suspect that it may not like sticky clay. My plants look best so far where the bank soil has been lightened with plenty of grit and garden compost. The first winter I was shocked to see them wither and die with the frosts—or so I thought. But in early spring I was relieved and delighted to see many new purple-tinted shoots pushing up through the old stems. They grow to about 10 in./250 mm long, clothed with narrow, dark green leaves and every branch carries large heads of beautiful violet-blue flowers, each intensified with a purple eye.

I am trying another fascinating but tantalizing *Phlox* at the sunniest end of the lower terrace. It is called *Phlox bifida*. It seemed to me to be a plant for the open sunny garden, so I planted it in my Mediterranean Garden. Some years I have quite a large cushion-mound, studded with uniquely shaped white flowers, but suddenly it dies, I never know why. I am hoping that a heavier diet will suit it, but its hard stiff foliage makes me think it must be an exposed mountain plant, certainly not one from damp woodlands.

Tucked into two crevices made by adjoining logs are two prestigious plants, as yet little more than leaf clusters and famous names to me. One is *Ranunculus lyallii*, the large white New Zealand Buttercup. Mr Alfred Evans, in his tantalizing book *The Peat Garden*, describes it as having semi-double flowers with saucer-shaped leaves 12 in./300 mm across. My plant has survived for two years, but with leaves no more than 2 in./50 mm across! However, I am thankful to see them still there, and the hope that it might improve and flower one day draws me to its well-marked spot to check that its very special resident is still at home.

Notholirion bulbiferum is another plant that is slowly rewarding my innocence of its waywardness rather than any acquired knowledge or skill. From a thin wisp of a leaf, rather like a seedling leek, it has developed over two or three years a sturdy-looking fat cluster of leaves. This year it was strong enough to send up a single flower stem which stopped at about 2½ ft/760 mm: every day I rushed to see what was happening next. Slowly, over several weeks, a head of drooping deep lilac bells was produced. Best of all Graham Stuart Thomas arrived just before the last flower had faded. I must have read his thoughts on this plant, recorded in my much-thumbed copy of *Perennial Garden Plants*, a dozen times while waiting for my plant to flower. He reminded me that the bulb dies after flowering so today, thinking about it, we have just dug around and found two small bulbils which we replanted with a little additional compost. Although I have been delighted to see my bulb flower, and hope we may keep it, it is probably better suited to warmer and damper parts of the country.

Another small plant that has found a congenial home on the lowest level of my bank bed is *Gentiana farreri*. In the autumn, from among close-packed mats of narrow, bright green leaves, emerge large upturned trumpets of a most startling blue, unlike any other gentian blue, with the colour intensified by the sharp white throat. Reginald Farrer found this unique plant forming high alpine ground-cover in northern Kansu-Tibet.

A handsome Japanese grass provides brilliant contrast and is equally demanding of attention for far longer, from the time its fresh leaves unfold in spring until the late autumn frost. *Hakonechloa macra* 'Albo-aurea' is a tiresomely awkward name for this gem among grasses, whose leaves arranged in soft arching clumps remind me of coloured ribbons, vividly variegated gold and buff with warm touches of bronze.

I have spent a long while finding a suitable place for *Chiastophyllum oppositifolium*. You would think with its rather succulent rosettes of leaves that a dry place would suit it, but it comes from steep rocky foothills in the Caucasus, which suggests that it is probably happiest with its roots tucked into some humus-filled crevice, preferably facing north. That is where its charming catkin-like sprays of bright yellow flowers would best be displayed. Lacking rocky crevices, at least I now have healthy-looking clumps on the edge of my cool border.

Iris setosa is making good contrast. I have two forms. Among the larger plants I have put *I. setosa* itself. It makes clumps of soft green leaves and in May–June produces quantities of light purple flowers on not too leggy stems, about 2 ft/600 mm long. These are followed by round, pale, greyish-brown seed pods, good for picking. The dwarf form, with flower stems of less than 12 in./300 mm, looks charming among the mat-forming plants.

Japanese anemones have always seemed to me to thrive enviably better at other people's garden gates than wherever I have tried to suit them, but now they too are revelling in some of the deep pockets of old composted weeds that suggested the start of this new border.

Two unusual hydrangeas are already making bulky features without any sign of fainting in warm weather. One is the curious *Hydrangea* 'Ayesha' which I originally grew as a cutting given to me many years ago by the late Mr Norman Hadden. The wide, rather flat heads are packed with thick-petalled, seemingly half-closed buds, which look not unlike lilac blossom. Each thick petal is deeply cupped and slightly crinkled which helps to create this effect. On the bank my shrub has greenish-white buds which open pink, probably because of the fresh soil lifted over from the farm, which must be neutral. Elsewhere in the garden, where the soil is acid, the flowers are slightly grey-blue. Here too, on this north-facing bank, I have also planted *Hydrangea sargentiana* with its large leaves of almost shining velvety texture. I find that all my lace-cap hydrangeas look and do best in deep, rich soil in partial shade. Some I have sheltered beneath the ancient oaks where they have grown well, though a prolonged autumn drought sometimes shortens the length of flowering, withering the beautiful gentian-blue florets of *Hydrangea* 'Blue Wave' before its time. But other possible sites, where the soil remains moist, in the hollow of the garden, can become frost pockets in winter as the cold air sinks into the lowest-lying land, killing the tender flower buds.

It has taken several years for me to appreciate another unusual shrub,

Xanthorrhiza simplicissima. In early spring, as the leaves unfold, drooping sprays of small dark maroon-coloured flowers appear. I am always glad not to have missed them, but I could do so easily. Not until autumn do I stop to stare again, and then with pleasure. A quite uncommon colour harmony of rich purple and bronze, lit with light yellow, is flooding the deeply cut leaves that clothe the suckering shoots standing about 3 ft/1 m high. This shrub thrives in moist or clay soil. I am thinking of planting a few suckers of *Xanthorrhiza* near to *Callicarpa giraldiana* 'Profusion' to add to the colour scheme which will be dominated by the clusters of small bright violet berries that belong to *Callicarpa*.

The lowest end of the north facing bank is the dampest, and is almost completely shaded from the south by a tall Silver Willow, *Salix alba*, and the more spreading Weeping Willow, *Salix* 'Chrysocoma', which are planted behind the bank. Just before we reach the shade we are stopped by a plant that disturbs more people than it pleases. It is *Carex buchananii*, without even a touch of green. It makes a small fountain of stiff buff and pinkish-copper stems which erupt into arching sprays of flowers and filaments. Standing isolated, every wisp and line reflecting the light, I find it beautiful, but some people think it looks dead. I had been racking my brains to know what to put under it—something very flat like a carpet—when suddenly I thought of *Acaena microphylla* and planted a few pieces round the base. They settled in immediately, in time to show me that their rosy burrs might be just what was needed to harmonize with the *Carex* and to weld several other unusual plants nearby into an interesting group. *Ophiopogon nigrescens* is just below the *Carex*. The tiny bronze-green leaves of *Acaena*, shaped like minute rose leaves, can thread harmlessly among those black strap leaves, and will not detract from another neighbour, a pansy we call *Viola* 'Penny Black'. This has larger flowers than *Viola* 'Bowles' Black', about the size of an old fashioned penny, velvety sooty-black with the smallest golden eye. I do not find it very robust; certainly it needs a choice cool position.

Like a waterfall dripping into the deep reservoir behind them, the willows create a background for a collection of ferns. (I seem to have little collections of ferns wherever I can find both shelter from sun and wind, and where the soil does not become too dry in midsummer.) None of the ferns I have planted here will stand waterlogged soil in winter, nor will the rest of the plants I have put with them.

I was given a plant of *Dryopteris erythrosora* by Mr Reginald Perry when my husband and I visited him at his nursery and had the unforgettable experience of being shown every rarity he possessed. Do jewellers have the same joy running fine stones through their fingers as plantsmen do sharing their love of good plants? They cannot have more, of that I am sure.

We associate ferns with particularly tender shades of green. *Dryopteris erythrosora* catches your breath in spring when the young leaves are warm bronzy-red, especially beautiful caught in the low rays of the evening sun. As they mature they become a rich glossy green. Another *Dryopteris* is *D.*

goldieana. When I first had this fern I could see nothing gold about it, but after it had settled down I found that the young fronds are pleasantly tinted yellow and carry on growing to make a fine feature over 3 ft/1 m in height.

I have put *Hypolepis millefolia* on the very edge of the little path that leads to the back of the bank. I am confused between this and *Dennstaedtia punctilobula*. There is a difference, I believe, but perhaps not enough to worry about in the garden. Both are very pretty with finely divided leaves like low and dainty bracken, but both are vigorous underground travellers and will ruthlessly march through anything. *Dennstaedtia*, for all its fragile appearance, obliterated a bed of variegated Lily-of-the-Valley. I think they are ideal where there is plenty of room, in shade or part shade, and where they will not menace choice plants. If you do plant them unwisely they are not difficult to eradicate—sorting out your treasures from among them is more bothersome.

I have also planted *Polystichum aculeatum*, the Hard Shield Fern. It is a British native and one of the best we can grow, making tall distinguished-looking clumps of firm fine-cut and shining leaves which remain throughout the winter.

Polystichum munitum is from western North America, and is sometimes called the Christmas Fern. How difficult to describe ferns—they are so beautiful, each so distinctive, yet I find myself struggling for the right words to capture what I see. *Polystichum munitum* is similar in texture to *P. aculeatum*: they both have hard, smooth and leathery leaves. But the sickle-shaped leaflets attached to the central stem of *P. munitum* are not divided, they are entire, like the flattened teeth of a comb with slightly serrated edges. Each frond, standing waist high, makes an impressively strong feature winter and summer.

Rather like a scaled-down version of *P. munitum* is *P. lonchitis*, the Holly Fern. Although at a casual glance this fern looks similar it is but half the size, and looking more closely you notice that each leaflet is edged with tiny curving prickles, hence its name. Another curious feature with both these ferns is that at the base of each leaflet, on the upper edge, close to the main stem, is a small upstanding point, like a little thumb. Each fern makes a beautiful simple design as you hold a frond against the light, so very different from the intricate, lacy structure of *Polystichum setiferum* which is fuzzily complicated.

The simplest fern shape must be *Asplenium scolopendrium*, best known and loved as the Hart's Tongue Fern. There are many forms, some quite horrible, I think, with curly crested tips. I have one or two plants, but I cannot admire them. The great charm of this fern, for most people I am sure, lies in the wide, slightly undulating, ribbon-like leaves. I have a form which seems to make particularly long and elegant 'tongues'. I have had, and lost, the rare form called 'Crispum' in which the side margins look as though they had been scalloped with a small goffering iron (used in Victorian times to iron starched frills on babies' pillow-cases and maids' caps. My Victorian mother possessed one.) The reason for such inexcusable failure was setting

out a young plant before I had found the right position for it. The hedge
bottoms of the West Country are often crowded with the common form of
Hart's Tongue Fern—they are not difficult to grow, when conditions are
right—but they would never survive hedge bottoms in dry and windy East
Anglia. As with many other plants it has something to do with a humid
atmosphere, as well as sufficient moisture at the roots.

Snowdrops look just right among the winter-green ferns. I split up my
clumps to spread them around, immediately after flowering, sometimes in
full flower. They do not resent this, but flower the next year most reward-
ingly. I am always glad to move plants when I can see that it would be nice to
have this or that transferred to another place. To wait until a plant has died
down (bulbs especially), often means that I forget it until it is too late, and
then I cannot find it, when all the leaves have gone. Fortunately it is ideal to
move snowdrops in green leaf.

I have planted two elegant shade-loving plants among my fernery. The
first to flower is the white form of Lady's Locket, *Dicentra spectabilis* 'Alba'.
This lovely plant has delicate-looking pale green leaves which are just right
for the pendulous lockets of ivory. As they open, the big round leaves of
Brunnera macrophylla 'Hadspen Cream' will be slowly developing and will
continue to produce new leaves until the arrival of autumn frosts. This is yet
another plant which we owe to Eric Smith who first selected it and then made
it possible for us to treasure it in our gardens. It differs from *Brunnera
macrophylla* 'Variegata' in having a much gentler degree of variegation. The
leaves are not startlingly green and white, but have a much lighter green
background, irregularly bordered with primrose-yellow.

Cimicifuga simplex 'Elstead Variety' pushes through the soil very finely
divided purplish-tinted leaves which mature to dark green with purplish
branching stems. Not until autumn do we see the spires of purple-tinted buds
which open into tiny fluffy cream flowers.

To eventually hide the clay bank behind my ferns I have planted a
young scion from my beautiful Golden Yew. It will take time, but is worth
the wait. For more immediate effect, and directly beneath the willow
branches, I have planted various ivies, not variegated, all green leafed, but
some are curled, others heavily veined or cut, all busily sending out long
runners to hold and drape the clay with a living shawl. Among them I have
planted a very unusual arborescent type called *Hedera helix poetica*
'Arborea'. It slowly makes a dome-shaped bush covered throughout the
winter with clusters of developing fruit which, by spring, will have become
not black, but orange. I have been surprised and pleased how well the ivies
have grown in this sticky, solid clay at the back of the bank. Admittedly I
gave them a hand by chipping out holes of a reasonable size and filling them
up with compost. This compost could have resulted in a rash of chickweed
and other nuisances which would have swamped the ivies, but I made use of
a chemical aid, which in such circumstances is a blessing. After I had dotted
my plants over the shaded and particularly steep part of the bank I had it
sprayed with a pre-emergence weedkiller. This substance is most useful

where you are waiting for ground-cover to grow and it is not practical to do a lot of hand-weeding. But you have to be certain that the plants you are spraying over will not be affected. Some, including hairy-leafed plants like pulmonarias, could be killed. It is best to experiment first to be certain. Also, it only kills emerging seedlings, and does not affect established weeds. They must be dug out or spot treated with something else.

A pretty little single white primrose, which I call 'White Wanda' because it has something of the crinkled dark leaves of *Primula* 'Wanda' is scattered among the ferns to follow the snowdrops, while several large clumps of *Carex morrowii* 'Aureo-Variegata' are a joy all the year round. The *Carex* is in the sunshine, next to *Carex buchananii*, which I should have said is not reliably hardy. I always keep a few plants in a plastic tunnel protected with a few handfuls of dry straw. This is perfectly adequate, and we pull the plants to pieces to make more in the spring. Enjoying the same mollycoddling is a beautiful but definitely not hardy grass, *Pennisetum villosum*. I plant it out on the sunny edge of the bed, where the light can catch every silvered hair of its drooping flower heads. Like the other members of this family the flowers can be likened to furry caterpillars, but that does less than justice to this extraordinary grass. In late summer and autumn they appear, large, soft to touch, a tassel of fine white hairs with an intricate lyre-shaped pattern within. On a still autumn morning, bejewelled with dewdrops, every finest hair is outlined, the tassel looking twice as big as you thought it was. You try to pick it, the dew pearls are scattered—and the magic is gone.

The more unusual hostas are gathering strength in this favoured place. Already many years have gone into their making, many years from the life of Eric Smith and others who are specializing in this king of foliage plants. Once hostas were considered coarse plants, to be tucked into the back of the shrubbery. They *are* fine among shrubs and will, in my experience, do much better there than exposed to full sun on poor soil. The yellow-leafed forms particularly must be protected from scorching, and I am finding that the glaucous blue-leafed ones both look and do much better with a little shade. A small group which took my fancy for several weeks during the summer was made with *Meconopsis betonicifolia*, *Primula bulleyana* and a small blue-leafed *Hosta*, one of Eric Smith's *Hosta tardiana* crosses. Unbelievably, the blue of the poppy petals did not kill the extraordinary wax-blue of the *Hosta* which grew beneath it, while the brilliant orange of the individual *Primula* flowers, set in whorls around slim stalks, was threaded among the poppies, making a perfect complementary harmony.

Hosta sieboldiana can flourish in more open situations provided it is well fed and mulched, but the most enormous leaves are produced in partial shade with ample moisture. It is part of my spring routine to go round with canisters of slug bait and sprinkle it among the newly unfolding *Hosta* leaves, and those of *Veratrum* too, both of which are ruined when riddled with holes.

The golden bamboo, *Arundinaria viridistriata*, adds to the fresh, almost spring-like tones of yellow and light green that remain as features all summer on my cool bank. If I remember to cut down the old foliage in early spring the new canes come springing up, tall and unhampered, looking much brighter and fresher without last year's tattered remnants.

Into deep, deep pockets of pure leaf-mould and garden compost I planted *Lilium giganteum*, or *Cardiocrinum giganteum*, as it is correctly· called. Each year the shiny heart-shaped leaves grow more numerous and larger, so the bulbs must be building up strength. What a thrill it will be when a flower spike emerges, after so many seasons of looking and checking to see that they still survive. After flowering, after that immense effort when the stout stem may have been 10 ft/3 m tall from which dangled long greenish-white trumpet flowers followed by huge, equally handsome seed pods—after all that, the bulb will die and we shall start again to watch the offsets build their way up.

I am reminded of a story about Gertrude Jekyll, whose patience was being sorely tried one day by a less practised visitor who repeatedly told the great gardener how lucky she was to have such marvellous soil. They were passing a pit a little way in from the edge of the woodland path along which they were walking. Just then a donkey appeared, its side panniers loaded with garden refuse—cut down plants, weeds and fallen leaves. All were tipped into the hole and a layer of the fine sandy soil was forked into the pit before another load arrived. 'That,' observed the great lady tartly, 'is my marvellous soil.' And I've no doubt she explained that it would be a year or two yet before the mixture became sweetly decomposed and fit for a new planting of *Cardiocrinum*.

Another lily which likes rich, damp soil is *Lilium pardalinum*, the Leopard Lily, from California. I have a fine form called *L.p.* 'Giganteum'. It hangs its scarlet spotted flowers from stems over 6 ft/2 m high, above all the plants on the bank bed. The bulbs are curious, not individual bulbs like all other lilies I know, but clustered masses of scaly clumps which can be broken up. I see that the Royal Horticultural Society *Dictionary* says 'Bulb rhizomatous'—that's just right, in two words, but it would not prepare me for the surprise I had when I first dug up one of those curious clusters. *Lilium superbum* sounds not unlike *L. pardalinum*. I do not know it yet, but I read that it can be grown in very wet, even boggy conditions.

When I first thought of planting this north-facing bank, I was tempted to make a peat garden. But on consideration two things were against the idea. The first was the cost of bringing peat blocks hundreds of miles to this unlikely area. The second was the weather. Once dried out, peat is next to impossible to wet. It was against my principles to create something so artificial as an irrigated peat garden, so I have not, and cannot write about many of those plants that can only grow where peat, humidity and moisture at the roots are all combined. If you have those conditions you will find all you need in *The Peat Garden and its Plants* by Alfred Evans. You could not be in better hands, for Mr Evans is responsible for the famous peat garden at the Edinburgh Botanic Gardens.

6 *Large-scale Water Gardening*

Not many people have the privilege of planting around the edges of a large stretch of water and those who have may perhaps find it to be more of a burden than a privilege, which is a pity. By the careful choice of comparatively few plants, a really magnificent piece of landscaping can be achieved with the minimum of upkeep. I think it is largely because owners do not know what to plant that many opportunities for improvement are overlooked.

Water gardening on the landscaping scale is a quite different affair from the marginal plantings I have considered in a garden setting. I am not sure if I have stressed sufficiently the amount of work involved in maintaining marginal planting, unless it be on a very small scale. When conditions are warm and moist weeds and plants all ramp away merrily if not kept strictly under supervision. But with care, and knowledge, in planting and management, choice subjects can be preserved together in some of the most beautiful plant combinations in gardening.

The owner of a lake-side or farm reservoir starts from quite a different angle. On a large scale there is neither room nor time for delicate plants that need protection from giants and invaders. These in fact can become desirable in the right circumstances, that is, where there is ample room.

In large-scale planning it is, I think, well understood that whatever you decide the end result must fit harmoniously into the natural environment. Groups of native trees will, on the whole, look best and be more likely to survive long after our time than too many exotics which can create an unnatural look. That does not mean that we should shut our eyes to those hosts of suitable trees and shrubs that occur in similar situations elsewhere in the world. Although rhododendrons have been planted successfully around artificial (and natural) lakes, where the soil is not waterlogged, they are not what I have in mind in East Anglia and would certainly be a disaster around an exposed reservoir. But if you are surrounded by sheltering stands of birch and pine in the west or the northern counties, they would fit as harmoniously as do hollies and laurels with us. Evergreens are particularly needed in winter to contrast with the bare stems of deciduous trees.

Simple, but devastatingly invasive plants like the Common Reed, *Phragmites communis*, and the Reed Mace, *Typha latifolia*, commonly but erroneously called Bulrush, can be used with great effect in natural surroundings where there is ample room and depth. Avoid at all costs planting such things where the water is shallow overall for they will completely colonize it, and the water will vanish.

The same applies to floating plants. When considering water-lilies—which surely could be seen more often on stretches of still water—you have to remember that there are varieties suited to varying depths of water. If the water is shallow and you plant a lily which prefers greater depth it will pile itself up into a great huddle of leaves with no room for flowers to float to the surface.

Thinking of surfaces and depths reminds me of farm reservoirs, which are not all that uncommon these days. Few farmers have time or inclination for much ornamental planting, but many are planting trees on odd corners of their land to prevent the 'prairie' look, to conserve birds, native plants (so-called weeds) and the creatures that feed on them. We are learning that we must pay attention to our own native ecology, to try to understand the relationship of soils, climate, plant and animal life, with us as part of it, not striving against it. It is not so easy to pay attention to all this and try to make a living out of the soil as well, but neither can we afford to ignore it indefinitely.

The farm reservoir is a business interest, part of the farm economy, used to provide water for crops. So there will be the likelihood of the water level being reduced by several feet and remaining there for some weeks at a time. Then, not only is it an unsightly feature, as a gaping muddy hole, but anything planted around the rim that is shallow rooted may be left high and dry in cracked and parched soil.

In my experience that has rarely been the case. For the last few years I have been planting around the farm reservoir which ends my garden. It was originally begun by my husband, about thirty years ago, at the far end of the soggy wasteland which has now become my Damp Garden. The underground springs keep the water level constant in my five pools, even in severe drought. The water splashes quietly from one pool to the next, in gentle gradient, to flow quietly through the Canal Bed and under a Weeping Willow, where it merges with the reservoir. The springs are derived from rain water which seeps down through porous soil until it reaches the practically impervious clay beneath. Here it must travel sideways over the surface of the clay towards the lowest point, small trickles of water meeting up with others, so that if you could skim off the porous soil you would see a system of small tributaries leading to the main ditches (see diagram, p. 17). This precious water travels through the lower garden and is led to the reservoir to be stored for use in time of drought. There is a large outlet pipe at the far end to take the surplus away downstream through an alder wood.

In 1976, the year of the Great Drought, our neighbour enlarged the reservoir to provide irrigation for his fruit farm. For months in the early part of the year the drag-line and bulldozer crawled about the vast muddy hole looking like toys in a scene of huge desolation. A few oaks and hollies were spared, but such is the damage done by compacting the clay soil with heavy machines that within two years they were all dead and had to be cut down.

In making a large hole you create a mountain of spoil. Some of it was used to make a wide dam, the rest had to be distributed over the farm and some on to my land. About 2 ft/600 mm of plasticine-like yellow clay was spread over about an acre or so of my poorest gravel, which lay parallel to the reservoir. It has been an interesting experience to develop a new garden on this extraordinary mixture, and it is teaching me a lot about gardening on clay (see pp. 121–6). However, three or four years is not very long to gain experience; it may become another story one day but just now it does not really come into the Damp Garden—it lies above it. From the Clay Garden you can see the reservoir in the hollow and look across to the neatly marshalled lines of fruit trees which rise beyond it.

The long summer drought was broken by an exceptionally wet autumn. After several months the new reservoir was filled to overflowing by the revitalized springs. Now, in the autumn of 1976, it was my ambition to cover the raw clay and fringe the naked perimeter around the empty stretch of water with trees, shrubs and robust plants.

Some Trees and Shrubs

Willows are the obvious choice for sticky, wet soil. It was not until I had room to experiment that I began to appreciate them. Apart from the well-known Weeping Willow I had tended to dismiss them as having long, narrow, green leaves—nothing really very striking. But with closer acquaintance I have learnt to value them, not only because they thrive in soil that few other trees stand, but also because of their variety and grace.

In Hillier's *Manual of Trees and Shrubs* there are nine pages of willows to choose from, with the sizes ranging from creeping dwarfs (charming in the rock garden) to noble trees and bulky shrubs, which were what I needed. We already had the fine *Salix alba* and several mature specimens of the Weeping Willow, *Salix* 'Chrysocoma'. We allowed to remain an ancient *Salix fragilis*, or Crack Willow, well named because it has weak joints. After strong winds we have to pick up the litter of branches scattered over the grass walk. This willow grows on a steep bank overhanging the water. Years ago an ivy berry must have been dropped by a roosting bird for now there is a dark, heavy mass around the base and halfway up the great trunk. The ivy roots cannot become waterlogged, but the willow can delve deep into wet soil beneath the reservoir. Together they make a mature feature which I am reluctant to remove, despite the advice of the man on the bulldozer to get it out the way before it fell down! It shows no sign of doing that and, in spite of the mess it occasionally makes, I shall continue to admire its great head against an empty Essex sky while I wait for my own plantings to balance it.

With this large empty landscape there was room for repetition. In the spring I cut several straight branches from my original *Salix alba*, trimmed them and stuck them in the ground like pea-sticks. (Not in a row, but singly where I needed a tall feature!) They soon sprouted new leaves, and are now fine young trees making several feet of growth a year.

Another form of *Salix alba*, *S.a.* 'Sericea' ('Argentea'), the Silver Willow, has quite the most striking foliage of all my willows; it is less vigorous

E. Several kinds of willow catkins: *Salix melanostachys* (left),
S. sachalinensis 'Sekka' (centre) and *S. gracilistyla* (right)

than *Salix alba*, which is one of the loveliest sights for the water-side being of such noble proportions with graceful branches which sweep down over the surface of the water. My Silver Willows are still no more than large shrubs, about 8 ft/2.5 m high and across, but will eventually make small trees. Their long, narrow leaves are the whitest, shining silver, so they stand out brilliantly all summer long from among the other shrubs, making lovely reflections in the dark water.

One of the first willows we planted for its catkins was *Salix aegyptica* (*S. medemii*). It quickly shot up strong wands, 10–15 ft/3–4.5 m, and was always the first to be wreathed with large, bright yellow egg-shaped catkins, often in February. It was originally planted in the garden to provide height while we were waiting for the Swamp Cypresses, *Taxus distichum*, to make their way more slowly into the important features they are today. Recently the *Salix* had to be removed as it detracted from the cypresses and was beginning to damage one of them, competing for air space. It is hard to destroy a tree you have planted, but it was less painful than it might have been because in recent years the catkins were never so fine as when it was a smaller and more vigorous sapling. Cuttings rooted easily and made over 6 ft/2 m in the first year, so fresh young saplings have been planted out and I shall hope to keep them pruned as shrubs where we can easily see the handsome catkins, rather than let them develop into rather lanky trees.

Quite a different-shaped bush, the very opposite in fact, is *Salix sachalinensis* 'Sekka'. This willow causes great interest among flower arrangers, quite understandably, because occasional stems become fasciated, that is, they look as though several stems have been stuck together halfway along their length and then squashed flat under a heavy weight. This induces the free ends, studded with catkin buds, to splay out into an irregular curved outline which can be a complete arrangement in itself. Dropped into a jug of hot water and glycerine it will, on removal, remain perfect, complete with half-opened 'pussy flowers' for ever, until you grow tired of it. But unless you have plenty of room to spare there are many more useful shrubs for flower arrangers—and the fasciated branches are few and far between, even on my shrubs which must be 12 ft/4 m across but not more than about 6 ft/2 m high. The great majority are straight and are strongly grown shoots which give me more pleasure for several weeks in the early spring. The dark purplish stems hold round, polished buds which open first to white then pinky-grey before they suddenly expand into long and narrow yellow catkins, a lovely sight when the whole bush is covered. Because of its spreading shape I value this willow in summer for the amount of bare ground it covers and have planted it at the water's edge, where the banks of the reservoir shelve down steeply and the intensive root system binds the soil and prevents subsidence.

Another splendid form of *Salix alba* is 'Chermesina', which we used to call 'Britzensis'. I think it produces the most vividly coloured stems of all. Orange-tinted at the beginning of winter they gradually deepen to startling shades of orange and scarlet-red, illuminating the water's edge as they are caught in welcome winter sunshine, perhaps on a frosty day or, better still, when a layer of snow covers the ground. Such a day is good for the more subtle-coloured stems which are needed for contrast, for the various 'Violet' willows. I have *Salix daphnoides and S. acutifolia* 'Blue Streak', both of whose young blackish-purple stems are coated with a fine waxy bloom.

More willows, for height as well as bulk, include the Twisty Willow, *Salix matsudana* 'Tortuosa'. I think this tree is enchanting in spring, when its new leaves are emerging, but in high summer I cannot really admire the twisted leaves close to. I really enjoy these trees in winter, when they catch the light along their polished, buff-coloured corkscrew branches. The 'Twisty Willow' makes a large tree in my wet soil, but I have noticed them growing much smaller in London, near to Marble Arch I think, where they rise above island beds of other shrubs. Obviously this is a less advantageous site, but the result so far is very attractive as they have grown tighter, smaller in scale, like elegant narrow fans of pale spiralling twigs.

I have recently acquired *Salix × erythroflexuosa*, which is a cross between *S.* 'Chrysocoma' and *S.m.* 'Tortuosa'. Although only in its second year from a cutting it has already made a stout little trunk of a warm ochre-yellow colour, while the spiralling branches are a rich chestnut.

Two more willows please me because they quickly make large shrubs, invaluable for masking the bare reservoir banks. The first is *Salix elaeagnos* (*S. rosmarinifolia*); I think that might be its name, but apparently *S. rosmarinifolia* is surrounded by confusion. The definition in Hillier's *Manual* sounds like my shrub, which is large but graceful, its wand-like branches tinted purple and densely set with long, very narrow leaves of a dull leathery green above, and white beneath, which look very pretty as a gust of wind ruffles them.

Even more delicate in leaf is *Salix gracilistyla*. Pale translucent leaves crowd polished olive-green stems. Yet despite its tender appearance this willow stands out conspicuously on the edge of the water, being one of the most vigorous, and quickly forming a tidy, rounded shrub. In winter pairs of pointed buds show up as soon as the leaves have dropped, while in spring they are among the first to swell into small, neat, furry grey catkins flushed with pink.

From among the smaller willows I have included several bushes of *Salix hastata* 'Wehrhahnii' and *Salix repens argentea*, which I have described in Chapter 4. I have planted groups of them on the curve of the grass walk that edges the wide slope leading down to the water's edge. It may be, in years to come, that we shall catch only glimpses of the water between the trees and shrubs, when they are full of leaf in summer time, but I am thinking that the level must drop when the water is pumped for irrigation and then we will be glad of the screen. Fortunately there seems to be ample water, and thus far it has not dropped much more than 2–3 ft/600 mm–1 m. This kind of fluctuation does no harm to strong-growing trees and shrubs, as their roots will have penetrated deep into the wet clay beneath.

Another possibility, which can make an interesting feature where space is limited, is *Salix purpurea* 'Gracilis'. It makes a small bush, roughly 3 × 3 ft/1 × 1 m, consisting of very thin, dark purplish-black shoots. They are smooth and inviting to touch, with masses of fine shoots growing straight upwards to make a neat, tidy shape. The leaves are in scale, small and narrow, dark grey-green above, light beneath. One bush alone can be used as a feature. I have massed several on the edge of the reservoir where their dense but tidy shapes please me in winter. They are sometimes recommended for making a low hedge in damp soil. This sounds a good idea, for they do not need cutting as frequently as other coloured-stem willows. However, it is a pity to neglect them entirely; they do slowly grow larger. Mine are now head high, time they were pruned to a basic shape, to encourage bright new shoots.

I knew it would be difficult to tear myself away from the willows, which once I passed by. I cannot describe all those I grow now, but will mention finally one which always fascinates visitors with its very unusual catkins. It is *Salix melanostachys*; you will remember the name if you think of the dark mood, melancholy. Before the leaves appear, matt, sooty-black catkins slowly swell to show a glimpse of red before they burst into yellow fluff.

Although we are already beginning to enjoy a bosky, leafy look around the reservoir in summer, winter and spring are inviting too, with many different coloured stems, curious twisted shapes, and the seared remains of sedges and grasses. The wide expanse of water is alive too, with mallard duck in winter plumage.

On the higher, drier slopes I have planted Silver birches, alders and hollies. The Balsam Poplar, *Populus trichocarpa*, is growing at a tremendous rate to take the place of the stately elms, and fills the air with its special sweet fragrance when there are still few signs of spring. I hope its searching roots can do no harm here, with only the farm headland to invade. My original tree became a menace in the garden, throwing up suckers along the edge of a border far removed from its trunk, where its roots had been cut by the edging tool.

Populus × *candicans* 'Aurora' also had to be ejected from the garden because it has the same greedy habits. There is room for it around the reservoir, and its large, oval, creamy-white leaves, tinged with pink, make good contrast with the narrow green leaves of many of the willows. It needs to be hard pruned every few years to encourage the variegation; this can be attended to at the same time as the willows are pruned. Those we value for their vigorous, whip-like growths should be cut every other year in early spring, before the buds begin to break. If they are left indefinitely they become a criss-cross of old and new stems, which are not only short, but poorly coloured.

I must not forget *Populus serotina* 'Aurea', the beautiful Golden-leafed Poplar. This tree is not quite so vigorous initially but does in time make a very large tree, a perfect companion for *Salix alba*, the White Willow. I know of a mature planting of these two beside a railway viaduct which spans the road, with low-lying land on either side. Together they create a scene which is very satisfying. The fine trees tower high above the elevated railway, their straight trunks complementing the pillars of the arches while their graceful branches, fluttering with silver and golden leaves, soften the good brickwork.

One of the most beautiful trees you can plant in damp soil is *Alnus incana* 'Laciniata', the Cut-leafed Alder. Not many miles from my garden is a famous tree and shrub garden planted by Sir Charles Eley roughly eighty years ago. It is opened for two Sundays in May and June when we can see many rare and well-grown specimens. One of the most outstanding is *Cornus florida* 'Rubra', its leafless branches smothered with pink and white blossoms that resemble nothing else. High above our heads *Davidia involucrata* hangs out its dainty linen—large, oval-shaped white bracts that have given the tree its common name, the Handkerchief Tree. *Magnolia sinensis* catches eyes and noses, spilling fresh fragrance from downturned, shallow, creamy cups. It is wonderful to be able to see these things—and many more—long established and magnificently grown, so many years after the idea was first conceived of making this sheltered valley garden.

But despite the many beautiful things in flower I was impressed above all by several specimens of the Cut-leafed Alder. Their columnar trunks soared high above us to support a canopy of delicate, lace-like leaves which swept down to enclose us and make a setting that needed no flowers to adorn it. If you have room go out quickly and plant a little grove of them. You will be enchanted now when they are only a few feet tall—for someone's grandchildren you will have endowed a magic circle.

Only gardens wisely planted with trees are lasting and not, of course, for ever. I find it awesome sometimes to try to look up to the top of a really huge and ancient tree, standing close against the trunk. There are some in Kew Gardens where I am made dizzy, not only by the immense size and complicated structure of wood above me, but by the thought of the long centuries that have elapsed since it was planted by one man with a spade.

Dogwoods are planted for their coloured stems. The most vivid enamelled red stems are made by *Cornus alba* 'Sibirica', better known perhaps as 'Westonbirt'. I like its clusters of grey-blue berries which show up against the plum-red autumn leaves. *Cornus stolonifera* 'Flaviramea' makes similar terminal clusters, but they are pearl-white. I picked a few branches and put them into a jar with the cupped white blossoms of *Anemone × hybrida* 'Honorine Jobert' and the double white form of *Saponaria officinalis* which grows round its feet. All three looked good together, so unexpectedly fresh in late autumn. *Cornus alba* 'Flaviramea' needs regular hard pruning to produce the straightest and brightest yellow-green shoots, but if you like to have the berries you must let it go for a year or two. By planting several, and pruning them alternately, you can have both.

Two 'ghost' brambles look good in the 'wild garden', but like all wild gardening must not be neglected if you wish for the best effects. *Rubus cockburnianus* makes the largest bush in my garden. I cut the old stems to ground level each year just as the new canes are emerging. *Rubus thibetanus* is similar but daintier. Its leaves are even more fern-like, so heavily coated with silky hairs that they appear soft grey above, almost white beneath.

I have a third bramble, not often seen but always admired when sprays of its flowers are put in a vase, where they will last for days. *Rubus ulmifolius* 'Bellidiflorus' looks very like our common blackberry, except that its long flowering shoots are covered with double flowers. Pale grey buds open to tightly packed, lilac-coloured rosettes. My bushes are planted in the Clay Garden above the reservoir. Each spring I trim them to leave a tidy, compact shape which will produce the coming season's flowering shoots. I cut off the long trailers which were made the previous summer because they are tip-rooting and would soon take over the entire Clay Garden.

I should, at this stage, explain that while some of my plantings may make the Reservoir Garden look as though it were all too easy, that was not quite the case in the beginning. In fact I suspect I almost lost Harry, in more ways than one, in those early days of planting. It had slipped my mind that he cannot swim, so it was not the state of the soil alone which caused dark silences and stiff lips. There we were, especially on the farm side opposite our garden, slithering up and down the wet clay with nothing to stop us going into 17 ft/5 m of icy water below. The old tractor with its buck loaded with gritty compost stood above us on the farm headland. We dug holes as best we could in the wet clay, so solid and sticky we had to stop and cut it off our spades with a knife. Drainage slits had to be dug beneath the holes, else they filled up like wells with water whenever it rained. The gritty soil was carted to the holes by the bucketful—we could not use a barrow. It was very slow, very dirty work, with little to show at the end of a long day but small twigs lost in the dusk and a lot of dirty tools to clean, not to mention clothes and boots. The first year there was a poor response for all our efforts, but I reminded myself that it was asking a lot for anything to grow in heavily compacted clay. I could be thankful most things were still alive. The next year was better, and I was encouraged to go on, to plant a few more things each year, until now I marvel that so few years have passed since we began the Reservoir Garden. Once a year, usually about July, the coarse grasses, rushes and buttercups which have also colonized the banks are scythed and we sprinkle a handful of base fertilizer around the trees and shrubs. It would be better if it were done earlier no doubt but, like the farmer, we have no time to spare earlier. Before long I think they will not need that small assistance, but will themselves smother the native weeds.

On my side of the reservoir I have allowed a much wider area for planting, and used a few more exotics to blend with the garden. I could not resist planting two more Swamp Cypresses, *Taxodium distichum*. Although they lose their leaves in winter their tall, narrowly pyramidal shapes will eventually pierce the skyline, as they do in the garden. I have also repeated *Thuja plicata*. The tree we planted twenty years ago dominates a mixed group summer and winter, but is especially valuable in winter. I tend to stress the importance of evergreens in the garden. They are not planted as solid and continuous barricades, but where the planting is most successful they form the basic core of the main groups. Some deciduous trees and shrubs make very attractive outlines when planted as specimens, but many others, especially if herded together, can produce a dull shapeless tangle in winter. I have not found it easy to find evergreens that both look well and do well around the exposed reservoir. On the drier banks I think hollies will finally be the most successful and long lasting, always good with Silver birches. There are many to choose from; a careful study of the Holly Walk at Kew is very helpful. The variegated ones look better, I think, in more formal settings, but in natural landscaping those with rich glossy foliage and good berries are preferable. Among these *Ilex* × *altaclarensis* 'J.C. Van Tol' is one of the best, but there are others I would like!

In a more sheltered corner I have planted bamboos. *Arundinaria japonica* forms lush masses of dark glossy green leaves and makes imposing thickets many feet high and across. Much more elegant is *Arundinaria nitida*. It does not sucker so freely, but extends slowly as a compact circular clump. I have a clump, planted about fifteen years ago, where the canes now stand 12 ft/4 m high, and it is 9 ft/3 m across. Bamboos can be restrained by digging out the suckers which transgress beyond their allotted territory, but it is tough digging. I tend to associate them with large gardens, but not long ago I visited a garden on the outskirts of London, originally a long, very narrow sloping site about 25 ft/8 m across. The previous owner had planted predominantly foliage plants most brilliantly. The enclosing high, and rather unsightly, walls had vanished behind magnificent stands of fine-leafed bamboos, alternating with wall shrubs and climbers. Every inch beneath was full of plants, hostas and ferns predominating, surrounding little pools. The step-ways (no space was wasted by making a definite path), consisting of laid blocks or rocks, veered from one side to the other, instead of making two narrow boring borders down each side. On consideration I wonder if the construction of the little pools was designed to keep the roots of the bamboos in their place. Nothing seemed to be suffering while the natural effect of dappled shade created by the lacy bamboos overhead was quite astonishing. Such a situation would prevent the scorching of their foliage by extra-severe frosts, which we sometimes have in the open.

Arundinaria murieliae is very similar to *A. nitida*. The most obvious difference is the colour of the mature canes, which are stained dark purple on *A. nitida*, and whose leaves are slightly narrower, altogether creating a very dainty yet distinctive appearance. The stems of *A. murieliae* remain green, and the leaves too have a rather softer effect, being light pea-green in colour. Both these bamboos can be grown very successfully in large tubs, provided you do not neglect to water them adequately and feed them occasionally.

Another bamboo which had to be banished to the outer garden is *Sasa veitchii*. This invasive plant is successfully colonizing the steep clay banks where it forms thickets about 2½–3 ft/600 mm–1 m high. The dull purplish canes carry wide, stiffly held leaves. They are 1½ in./37 mm across and 6 in./150 mm long, forming plain green ground-cover all summer. But in autumn the colour is withdrawn from their edges, leaving a pale straw-coloured border which gives a bold variegated effect lasting all winter. In the right place, where there is ample room and it cannot force strong shoots through herbaceous plants, it is both admirable and useful.

Another low-growing but extremely invasive bamboo which must be avoided in the wrong place is *Arundinaria vagans*. It provides plenty of fresh green leaves and is excellent where strong ground-cover is needed in difficult places, such as heavy clay soils. It will also flourish in dense shade, provided it is not bone dry.

I have already written elsewhere of the bad habits and bean-pole like structure of *Aralia elata*. It has now found its home in the heavy clay soil around the reservoir where it is giving far less trouble, obviously finding it more of an effort to thrust up too many suckering shoots. Instead the main rods have shot up above the surrounding bamboos where they now display their huge elegant leaves, creating an almost tropical effect, backed by the falling curtains of weeping willows. In early autumn they are topped with large fluffy heads of tiny creamy flowers, adding to an already exotic picture. The flowers can be seen more easily on a smaller specimen of *Aralia elata* 'Variegata', which I have placed on the opposite side of the grass walk that runs along the reservoir border. Close to you can see the pretty pink stems which support the elderflower-like mass of creamy flowers, but I doubt if I shall see many of the small purple-black berries which are sometimes set on the plain-leafed form. But they are not the main reason for growing this shrub. It is the magnificent foliage, quite the most dramatic and beautiful (provided you like variegated plants) of any variegated shrub. I imagine that, because it is partially stunted by variegation, the habit is less gawky, the thick prickly stems branch much nearer the ground, and eventually create quite a low broadheaded tree. The leaves are enormous, almost 3 ft/1 m long and half as much across, handsomely divided and irregularly bordered and splashed with creamy-white. They are not easily obtainable, except from a few specialist nurseries, having to be taken as young shoots and grafted onto the plain form. As they are frustratingly economical in the number of branches they make there never seem to be enough shoots to take, unless you have a plantation of stock plants. If you are fortunate enough to obtain one remember that the suckers which will come up from the base are from the plain stock and must be removed. If you are more fortunate than I you might find the golden variegated form. I should not be so greedy. I am nearing the boundaries of my land (tucked close up against them in most places!) but there are still vast quantities of trees, shrubs and plants that I do not know and cannot hope to grow because I have not the space. Three hundred acres would scarce suffice, and I have twelve! Time too becomes more precious and each year is noticeably shorter. So I am beginning to learn to be more selective. It is tempting, and sometimes sensible, to repeat plants which have been successful elsewhere, but one needs new ideas from other people, other gardens, other countries sometimes, to bring a fresh look to the garden.

Berries provide highlights in autumn, and some of the best are produced by the Guelder Rose family, also called Water Elder. *Viburnum opulus* can be found wild in Britain on the edge of woody places or in hedgerows, usually not far from a running ditch or marshy place and more commonly, I think, on chalky soils where the rich green leaves turn to brilliant pink and crimson autumn tints. I see but a ghost of that colour on my wet clay, but the berries are lovely. I grow two selected forms. One is 'Notcutt's Variety' which is more vigorous in every way than the wild form, with stronger growth and larger clusters of luscious-looking transparent red berries. The other form has yellow berries and must, I think, be 'Xanthocarpum'. It has large pea-sized berries, which start green and slowly change to a pale and opaque creamy butter-yellow. These marble-textured berries are quite exquisite, hanging over the rim of a container, when arranged with something else that may be stiff and upright. But that is not all. As they ripen the colour deepens to translucent amber and, as the leaves fall, may still be seen hanging in heavy clusters. Some years the birds have ravaged them but my little half-Siamese cat, Emma (short for Emacia, she was brought to me, skin and bone) has such a restless, busybody nature that I suspect she has become something of a deterrent. I have tried spraying some of my berried trees and shrubs, and others, like cherries and *Forsythia*, which have their buds systematically stripped by bullfinches, but the birds usually win in the end. I cannot blame them. When the ground is iron-hard and icy blasts sweep the garden I like to think there is some food and shelter available.

To return to the wild Guelder Rose. There is a well-known form called the 'Snowball Tree', because it makes round balls of greenish-white sterile flowers which gradually become cream-coloured. They hang like pom-poms from the branches of what can become a tall, rather gaunt shrub which is usefully placed behind others, perhaps behind the other two viburnums I have described for their berries. In June these two provide another spectacle when they are covered with flat heads of tiny fertile flowers surrounded by showy white sterile florets, looking much like a lace-cap *Hydrangea*, except they are smaller.

I have described elsewhere the Japanese *Viburnum plicatum* 'Mariesii'. There are several forms, all extremely beautiful, their horizontal branches simply loaded with creamy lace caps, sometimes all sterile, sometimes just larger. One I have called 'Pink Beauty' has flowers which turn pink as they age, but which also continue to produce new flowers, for months it seems, until the autumn.

I would not put any of these forms of *Viburnum plicatum* into such wet soil as our English *V. opulus*, but they all need deep rich soil. A *Viburnum* which so far has defeated me is *V. betulifolium*. When properly suited it is one of the most amazing sights in autumn, with infinitely more grace and elegance when in fruit than our rather heavy *V. opulus*. Imagine a large open shrub, more than 10 ft/3 m high and across, much branched and so loaded with dainty sprays of small glassy red berries that you can see it from afar, glowing red in the distance. I remember seeing it like that in the Valley Gardens at Windsor, but although I have grown bushes easily that size and introduced others planted alongside to encourage fertilization, only the meanest little clusters of berries have appeared, sometimes one branch only. Why, I wonder? My original planting was scrapped when we made the last pond, and new ones have been planted, hopefully, beside the reservoir, but I still wait to be dazzled by their splendour. Meanwhile I quite enjoy their shape and their leaves which are small and oval, like birch leaves.

Giant Herbs

As some trees and shrubs proved too large, or invasive, for the garden, so some of my more vigorous herbaceous plants have also gravitated to this outer garden. They *must* be vigorous to thrive in the heavy soil, with the minimum of attention. Those that certainly would prove a menace elsewhere will probably, eventually, be overcome here, squeezed out by invading trees and shrubs. However, nuisance value has not been the criterion for selecting plants for this outer garden. Large-scale planting needs large and imposing plants, so naturally several groups of *Gunnera scabra* were among the first to be planted. We placed them just above the water's edge, making extra-large holes and filling them up with barrowloads of garden compost. Every other year we heap farmyard manure among them to encourage the production of spectacular leaves. They take several years to establish a starchy base and strong root system to support their magnificent superstructure.

Further away from the water, where the soil is not waterlogged, are groups of ornamental rhubarb. I have a clone of *Rheum palmatum*, which has larger, redder leaves then *R.p.* 'Atrosanguineum' itself, but instead of producing fluffy spires of crimson-pink flowers, they are creamy-white. On looking it up in Graham Stuart Thomas's *Perennial Garden Plants* (what would we do without that mine of information?) I think my plant might be a good form of *R.p. tanguticum*, which he says produces white, pink or crimson flowers on different clones. I find one can get very muddled with rheums! I saw a form I much admired in the Munich Botanic Gardens. Its leaves were still richly suffused red in July, while the leaf shape was not so palmate, but had far more indentations, scallop-shaped, along the edges. It was labelled *R.p. tanguticum*. I have since been sent something called *R.p. tanguticum* (not from Munich) which so far is a boring thing, with no red colouring at all and nothing like the plant I saw in Munich. One that I covet especially since seeing Roy Lancaster's slides of Nepal, where he showed it growing in its natural habitat, is *Rheum australe* (*R. emodi*). It looks not unlike *Rodgersia tabularis* in shape, a huge circular green leaf like a giant navelwort, most desirable I thought.

The ornamental rheums look their best from spring until about August, when they begin to look rather untidy and their colour fades. But by then other large herbaceous plants hide them from view. One which does this most successfully is *Inula afghanica*. A coarse great plant that stands easily

10 ft/3 m tall, it makes large piles of long, dock-like leaves. From them emerge stout stems topped with a spire of knobby green buds which open to smallish, yellow daisy flowers. The colour and size of the flowers are not really important, but the outline of the whole plant, from tipmost buds down the leafy stem to the lush pile on the ground, catches the eye and looks good in the setting.

It is amusing to remember that the ligularias belong to the *Senecio* family, and one of their relations is the ubiquitous groundsel, *Senecio vulgaris*, which cowers like a mouse among its elephantine relations. *Ligularia przewalskii* 'The Rocket' enjoys the wet clay, its black stems and narrow spires of clear yellow flowers outlined against the water. The shorter and bulkier *Ligularia dentata (L. clivorum)* spreads its mahogany-backed leaves in the shade of *Salix elaeagnos*, where the huge heads of vivid orange daisies contrast with the fluttering grey and white leaves. Another 'groundsel' which produces quite sumptuous flowers is *Ligularia × hessei* 'Gregynog Gold' (*L. dentata × L. wilsoniana × L. veitchiana*). I like the large, heart-shaped green leaves which make fine weed-smothering clumps. The inherited characteristics from its parents have produced a spire-like habit combined with large flowers, so the result is tall stems, 6 ft/2 m, set with large cone-shaped heads of bright yellow daisy flowers which have quite long drooping petals.

There are other interesting members of this varied family—some I have, some I covet. With them all it is vital to remember that slugs and snails dote on them, so make sure bait is laid immediately the leaves emerge in spring. It is miserable to face, for the rest of the year, those large prominent leaves riddled with holes.

Heracleum mantegazzianum, which can be dangerous (it causes nasty blisters on the skin) looks, on first encounter, like something out of a pantomime. In my Wild Garden it looks fine and can hurt no one. I have shaken seeds in the bare spaces between young shrubs where they have built up strong crowns to support the 12 ft/4 m plus hollow stems which carry branching heads of huge cow parsley-like flowers. These gigantic plants die when they have flowered.

Angelica archangelica behaves in the same way, but is not quite so large, and has only benign characteristics, one of which is its delicious flavour when candied. I love to see its pale green heads supported well above its own foliage and the surrounding plants. When you scatter seed of huge plants haphazardly it is advisable to walk regularly among young trees and shrubs to remove anything (including seedling blackberries, which I dig up by the bucketful, since my neighbour has a blackberry plantation) which would, when mature, flop against the permanent plantings and spoil their shape.

Kniphofias, or Red Hot Pokers, are also useful to break the comfortable monotony of too many rounded shapes. I grow them from seed and have selected those which make the tallest and biggest flowers, in shades of vivid red and orange, to group along the grass edge, where it is not too wet in winter. For a background they have arching clumps of Pampas Grass.

It is interesting as you travel around to notice how variable are the flower heads of Pampas Grass. I have seen some so thin and skinny as to be worthless to my mind, especially when seen growing from a matted tangle of half-dead foliage. Neither can I say that I like the pink ones very much, in spite of seeing some magnificently grown specimens recently, the flower stems at least 12 ft/4 m, possibly 15 ft/5 m high. They had a dark, almost maroon-like depth of colouring, heavily overlaid with silky hairs which veiled and softened it. In the right place, with a light background, possibly a building, it might have looked very unusual and handsome.

I have a picture in my mind of Pampas Grass in November, on a silvery frosty morning, all colour gone, the reservoir sheeted with ice, the sky broken with horizontal bands of low cloud. A silver and white morning would be a dreamlike setting for the elegant plumes of the most beautiful of all Pampas grasses, *Cortaderia selloana* 'Sunningdale Silver'. The plumes of this grass are not solid dust mops but are open silky, feathery pennants, fluttering high on tall stems, sometimes 10 ft/3 m tall.

I have also planted *C.s.* 'Pumila'. It has close, compact and creamy-coloured heads on shorter stems about 5 ft/1.5 m high. I especially like its foliage, which makes a very attractive shimmering shape nearer the edge of the border. And I am glad to have discovered *C.s.* 'Aureo-lineata', whose leaves are yellow striped, making the plant a very light and important feature. It needs to be planted in an exposed position, either as a specimen in mown grass or as a focal point on the edge of a border.

Other great grasses for large water-sides must include the *Miscanthus* family, especially *M. sacchariflorus*, which can easily top 12 ft/4 m. But the others, *Miscanthus sinensis* 'Zebrinus' and *M.s.* 'Silver Feather' grow almost as tall. All thrive with the minimum of attention once they have become established; merely cut down the tall canes before the new ones emerge in spring, preferably before winter gales have blown them into battered heaps.

I would like to grow *Arundo donax*, the Giant Reed from southern Europe, really well. I think it must be the tallest, most imposing, grass-like plant that we can grow. (I have a small plant which is, I hope, established.) From a great height it produces cascades of soft blue-grey ribbon-like leaves on tall, strong stems which shoot up from ground level each season. It deserves a choice situation in deep, rich soil.

My plants of the rare and lovely variegated form will always remind me of my visit to the nursery of the Countess von Stein Zeppelin in southern Germany. Her plant was growing in a large tub which could be carried to a sheltered place in winter. She showed me the little side shoots which grow in the axils of the leaves, and kindly gave me some. I brought them home, set them in pans and kept them in my frostproof but cool greenhouse where they rooted easily. Unfortunately this lovely plant is not reliably hardy in Great Britain, surviving outside in only the most favoured warm sites. I plant mine out in the summer, after the risk of late spring frosts has passed. By the autumn they have made large exotic-looking features planted among such treasures as *Cimicifuga simplex* 'White Pearl', *Salvia uliginosa* and the lovely

Japanese anemones. This year we are experimenting, leaving some outside, covered with straw. They will lose their tops, but we hope the basal buds and roots will still be alive in the spring, and so make an earlier start. As insurance we keep others boxed up and covered with straw in a plastic tunnel, and still a few more in the frostproof greenhouse. Once planted they grow well and are so outstandingly good-looking that it is worth the trouble to keep them.

The Giant Reed Mace, *Typha latifolia*, is colonizing a shallow shelf where we had a little landslip. It cannot travel further into the deep water that shelves steeply beyond it. I prefer *Typha angustifolia* which has more slender velvety-brown heads, but in clearing it from my shallow garden ponds, where it was becoming a menace, I somehow lost it through carelessness.

The yellow-flowered native water iris, *Iris pseudacorus* 'Variegata', makes huge clumps of handsome foliage which, together with its roots, protect the edge of the banks. I found that the wind-driven waves beat against the bare edges and started to wear them away. *Glyceria maxima* 'Variegata' has helped with this problem, being one of the few plants that can quickly colonize raw clay. It could be too invasive and is practically ineradicable, but I am counting on the natural development of large smothering shrubs, like the willows, to control it. Meanwhile its patches of green and white striped leaves look attractive from across the water. The Water Forget-me-not was brought in with the *Glyceria* and here and there floats out rafts of tiny blue flowers which are anchored among the grass roots.

A dramatic plant which could be bitterly regretted in the wrong place is *Polygonum cuspidatum* 'Spectabile'. In early spring, when the rheums are unfolding their crumpled crimson-backed leaves, thick jointed stems emerge topped with bright cherry-pink buds. Rapidly the stems lengthen and the buds unfold leaves marbled in a startling combination of red, buff, cream and green. Eventually the mass of branching stems tops 6 ft/2 m while the red tints slowly fade; but the leaves continue to be softly variegated, some of them totally cream, or buff, or butter-yellow. I have planted this extraordinary plant on the farm side of the reservoir, where we can admire it from across the water, but where I do not think it will be able to invade the farm!

Near to it is another powerful invader, *Petasites japonicus giganteus*, the Giant Butter Burr, with huge round leaves that almost rival *Gunnera* when it is well established, more than 3 ft/1 m across. They look magnificent reflected in the water and I cannot help admiring their wickedly wandering shoots, thick as my thumb, which push through the clay like butter. We go there to prise them out when we need to make new plants. The leaves disappear in winter revealing the bare clay, where no weed can survive beneath their dense shade. In February this bare soil is suddenly decorated with Victorian posies. Round buds, large as tennis balls, open to layers of delicate green bracts which turn back to form an encircling frill for the centre, packed with tiny creamy-white flowers, faintly scented. So pretty they look, so desirable, especially to the flower arranger. We have, by tactful inquiry, saved several small rock gardens from being obliterated by this invasive giant because their owners fancied it on an early spring visit.

There are a few more great plants which provide flowers in late summer and autumn. Perhaps the finest is *Eupatorium purpureum*. We have a form which has extra-dark purple stems and deep coloured heads of cinnamon-pink fluffy flowers. They take several years to make imposing clumps, with dozens of flowering shoots which associate loftily with the large grasses at about 8 ft/2.5 m. They are so strong they can push through rough grass, running buttercups and anything else that may have colonized the banks.

Fagopyrum cymosum is a seldom-seen plant which has its place in the autumn scene. It is the American buckwheat. I wonder if it is the plant whose seeds are ground to make buckwheat flour. It is related to the polygonums, and sends up quantities of elegant branched stems furnished with pretty leaves, triangular shaped, with veins and stems stained red. From late summer to November they are topped with lacy clusters of small creamy-white flowers.

In a rough corner, at one end of the reservoir, *Polygonum sachalinense* creates a scene like a tropical jungle. Thick, jointed, bamboo-like canes rush up each year to about 15 ft/5.5 m, carrying huge oval green leaves. In late summer strings of little white flowers dangle from the leaf axils. In winter we cut them off at ground level and lug them to the bonfire of apple prunings which is burning conveniently near.

Maintenance of Large, Damp Areas

At the start of this chapter I spoke lightly of maintenance with the minimum of upkeep. You may be wondering how it is done. At the beginning I started with clean ground because it was a newly re-made stretch of water. That was an initial advantage. But the moment we started bringing in our garden compost we introduced weed seeds, and even the churned-up clay was not sterile; grasses, rushes, creeping buttercups and marsh thistles all appeared the first year.

We treat the farm side and the garden side of the reservoir differently. Eventually the farm side will be a continuous rim of trees and bushes which will look after themselves apart from a bit of pruning. And if that were not possible it would not be a disaster. The bank is too steep and awkward to use a mulch of straw so we have allowed the natural weeds to cover it; they have also helped to bind it and prevent erosion by rainfall. The weeds are scythed down once a year, usually in July. This is not ideal for maximum growth and development but it is the best we can do and is probably as much as most people considering planting such a situation could manage. Satisfactory progress has been made, after a slow start, with this low level of maintenance because, I think, only the toughest colonizers have been chosen.

Root competition from tight packed weeds could be relieved by the careful use of a suitable weedkiller, but great care must be taken to see that it does not come in contact with the green bark of young trees. Weeds closest to the young stems should be removed by hand. A few forkfuls of farmyard manure would be more advantageous, and the invigorated weeds kept down a little more frequently, preferably by an earlier cut in the spring.

If you are thinking of adding some interesting trees and shrubs to already established scrub or marshland then I would advise you to use a total weedkiller several weeks before planting around each individual site that you propose to plant. Ideally, of course, you could scythe the brushwood and dig out a sufficiently large space for a newcomer to find breathing space, but for most people today that would mean the job would never get done. There is either not enough time or enough muscle to do the job.

I do not like using weedkillers, but there are times and situations where they are the practical best. Provided they are used infrequently, that the right ones are chosen and used with great care, then I find that I am able to reclothe and care for my soil and plants most of the time by natural means.

I have already said that the reservoir border on the garden side is much wider. It is also less steep and meets a broad grass walk which runs alongside it. It has become the mixed planting of trees, shrubs and large herbaceous plants which I have just been describing. Originally I promised myself that this garden must not demand any fussy handwork, and so it has remained, apart from pruning and cutting down.

From the beginning of planting it has been mulched with straw. I buy several trailerloads of straw bales from a nearby farm every autumn. (It is possible for anyone, and not extremely expensive, to lift the 'phone and order it from a local contractor.) Straw saves months of work, helping to feed the soil as well as protect it. We put it down thickly, all over, like a great eiderdown, usually before Christmas. It is a good job for raw cold weather. If, as I usually do, I have afterthoughts and wish either to remove or add something, it is no trouble to push aside the straw, dig a hole, add gritty compost and then tidy the straw back around the new introduction. We do not necessarily add straw every year. It depends how much is left at the end of the season. In the spring we lightly sprinkle, over newly laid straw, a straight nitrogenous fertilizer such as sulphate of ammonia to help break it down. It is necessary to do this otherwise the micro-organisms which actually do the work take nitrogen out of the soil and so, temporarily at least, the plants are losing nitrogen rather than gaining it.

The straw is inviting to walk on, to inspect plantings without clay-covered boots, and the strong-growing herbaceous plants push up through it with no difficulty. Hardly a weed appears. Initially there were several docks which were easily forked out; they could have been hand-painted with a systemic weedkiller if no one was around to dig down deep enough, to get out the strong roots.

Sometimes, when I am planting a large area and there is no time to put down a mulch, or we may have run out of mulching material, we make sure that it is totally weed-free when I have finished planting by hand-weeding the inevitable annuals which appear within days of digging. Then we spray the whole area, even over the foliage of plants, with a pre-emergence weedkiller. This poisons the soil surface so that delicate germinating weed seedlings are killed as they emerge. It does not kill your plants as well. Some plants, however, especially those with felty leaves such as pulmonarias, will not tolerate it. But it must be said in fairness that quite a lot of plants, particularly woody things like roses, and many trees and shrubs, are quite unharmed by pre-emergence weedkillers.

Although pre-emergence weedkillers are widely used in commercial practice, where it is too expensive to do a lot of manual work, I personally do not recommend their use in gardens as a general rule, only as an expedient when other methods, for the time being, are not practicable.

We are using mulches more and more, rather than weedkillers. Both cost money, but with a mulch the results are *all* bonuses. The soil surface is protected from compaction, hardcapping in dry weather, erosion when it is too wet—as well as the germination of weeds. Beneath the surface moisture is conserved and over the years a good soil texture is gradually built up. With a mulch plants are not shocked—they do not have to pull themselves together as they do after even a mild dose of poison—but grow away well and themselves cover the ground more efficiently.

I use straw among our trees, shrubs and areas of coarse planting, along the edges of borders, where plants are smaller, or anywhere. Where the straw would look unsightly I use pulverized bark. Peat would be just as good; use whichever is closer to hand and, therefore, likely to be cheaper. As with the straw mulch a light dressing of nitrogenous fertilizer applied before the peat or bark is spread is beneficial, although there have been seasons when I have omitted to provide it.

It is not cheap gardening to use mulches. But a crushed bark or peat mulch looks so good, and is beneficial in every way. It enables me to grow thousands of plants which I could not possibly do if the same acreage had to be carefully hand-weeded many times a year. There is some hand-weeding to be done, especially in the early part of the year when really determined weed seedlings manage to struggle through the mulch. But it is a much quicker and more pleasant job than niggling fine grasses and weed seedlings out of every bare square foot.

Annual meadow grass, once my worst weed, is of no consequence now. Those odd ones that appear are almost a pleasure to pull out, which they do so easily. Fat Hen and chickweed still tend to be too much in evidence the first year after the ground has been heavily mucked or I have rotavated in last year's compost heap. But once we have pulled out these nuisances, and in some places have had to top up with a little more bark, the rest of the season remains fairly clean, the major part of our time in the garden being taken up with general tidying, such as cutting down finished plants and cutting grass edges, with only the odd bucketful of weeds to pick up as we pass by.

I am often asked how much bark to put on, how deep should it be. Not less than 1 in./25 mm, more if you can afford it. It is not an economy to put it on too thin. The soil must be well covered and sufficiently deep so that strong-hearted seedlings cannot struggle to the light. Sometimes, with new plantings of small things, we have to make two attempts to cover the soil, otherwise the small plants are buried. I find too that I have to make sure that scratching blackbirds searching for worms do not bury tiny treasures.

7 *Garden Management*

Soil Improvement and Border Renovation

Please do not skip this chapter. It is bound to be tempting to do so—all that boring stuff about soil structure and double digging. Besides, it usually takes all one's time to get new plants into the ground as quickly as possible before they have dried out and died. So one cannot take too long preparing the site. I know, I have thought and behaved in exactly the same way. But for the last twenty years I have been involved almost daily with land that had been considered unusable by anyone within living memory, where I have a most varied range of soil conditions. There is raw red gravel which would ideally make driveways or building material; elsewhere there is our moist sour silt and beyond that solid brick-making clay. I have been forced again and again to study my soils, to see how I could improve them and maintain that improvement.

Soil is our most valuable commodity, however bad it may, at times, appear to be. Oil and precious elements we could live without, but we were born originally out of the soil and must respect it. As a child I loved the feel and smell of soil and no doubt exasperated my mother by frequently being covered with it. Even today I am sometimes guilty of traipsing it over newly washed tiles, when it is understandably called 'dirt'. But I cannot bear to hear people speak of soil as dirt, although I believe that in America it is the generally accepted word. Perhaps there it is not so generally used in a derogatory sense.

I have spent a lot of time in this book describing plants and plant groupings which are suited to specialized conditions, primarily damp ones. In my book *The Dry Garden*, which describes that area of my garden which is on gravel soil, I selected plants that are adapted to stand drought conditions. But the right choice of plants for our soil is not the whole answer to problems in gardening. We must start, and end, with the soil.

I admit that I have become obsessed with my soils, with the challenge that has surrounded me in my varying types of land, situated in close proximity, in a comparatively small area (twelve acres) of land. Nothing gives me more pleasure than being able to push my hand into the soil with scarcely the need for a fork. Of course, I am far from achieving this everywhere and frankly will never do so, but it is the goal for which I aim. Like most of you reading this book, I had neither the experience nor the facilities at the beginning to cosset my soil as I am able to do now, but then, neither was Rome built in a day. I began as an innocent amateur, not having seen or touched such land before. So I shall describe in this chapter how I have dealt with my silt and clay soils.

The silt. Initially the silt seemed wonderful. Black and practically stoneless, it was so easy to dig, a great joy after years of sticky boulder clay in our previous garden, and then the stony gravelly soil we also have here. In places where there had been tall stands of bracken rising and falling for scores of years, the soil was soft and full of humus, and surely would grow anything. For several years, at the very beginning, we had little help in the garden. We often lined out our plants in temporary resting places while we cleared and marked out new beds. I enjoyed digging the soft, damp soil. It was most satisfying to dig out the rope-like roots of bracken, long underground thongs of wild hop and remaining stumps of sloes and blackberries. (The mountainous tangles of blackberry bushes, wild sloe, elderberry and sapling willows had already been swept away by the bulldozer.)

The fine soil felt good in my hands and smelt sweet most of the time. But here and there as I was digging it smelt sour. I knew that meant bad drainage somewhere but I did not stop to consider what we should do about it. I pressed on, impatient to have the beds ready for planting as soon as possible. 'Plant in haste, repent at leisure' is an old saying, but like many wise words they are always more meaningful to me after I have burnt my fingers.

For the first year or two most of the plants did well in the virgin soil. The pleasurable digging had fluffed it up, making a nice crumbly texture for them to root about in. The dormant weed seedlings welcomed the improved conditions, and they shot up too. Before long we were continually weeding, carting off load upon load of topsoil attached to the weed roots. Then we had a typical long period without rain. There was no protecting layer of plant growth, whether weeds or accumulated leaf-litter. (I soon found that the autumn leaves are all blown away when there are not enough plants established to trap them.) Although there was moisture available, derived from springs not far below, the top spit became dry and the surface caked. When the rain eventually came it could not penetrate the dried silt but lay on the surface rather like mercury, or where there was a slope it ran off. In some places, at the end of winter, I could still dig and find dry, powdery soil. We used to wish in those days for a fall of snow, to lie like melting sugar on the surface and slowly soak into the parched soil beneath.

I found that shallow-rooting plants like *Tiarella*, *Tellima* and *Heuchera* spread their soft little roots like a web over the surface of the silt. Once it became panned, by treading or by rainfall, these carpeting plants could be lifted off the surface, clinging to a few soil particles, unable to penetrate the compacted soil.

Something had to be done to improve the soil structure. We realized that although it had appeared to be laced with humus (we were largely taken in by the rich, dark colour) that, in fact, was not the case in most places. So I began my policy of carting back the vast piles of rotting weeds, cut-down remains of summer and anything else I could find to improve the texture of the soil. We had noticed that where Percy, with his bulldozer had made an enormous bonfire at the very beginning of the garden the plants always looked well, where the ashes had been spread. I am sure that it was not only the potash and other nutrients that may have been provided by the ash, but also the opening of the soil by those sticks and particles of charcoal which were not consumed by the fire, and which probably took several years finally to break down.

About seven years after we had begun the garden I decided to start my plant nursery. Slowly the two projects grew side by side. The growth of the nursery helped the development of the garden, not only by providing some help with maintenance, but by forcing me to consider better methods and management.

I discovered the importance of using various mulches (see pages 52–3 and 115–16), which I value for weed control and moisture conservation. Also when they eventually rot down and become incorporated with the soil they help to improve the soil texture.

Quite recently I have discovered another material to improve close-textured soil—fine grit. I found that the addition of humus was not enough. Perhaps it would be more accurate to say that despite occasionally being able to buy muck to add to the compost, these dressings were not enough to prevent the soil settling down too firmly, making it difficult for fine roots to penetrate, too cold and sticky in spring when I wanted to plant. What could I do to open the soil? Well, we were buying fine grit, ⅜ in./10 mm gravel, from our local sandpits, to mulch the tops of the nursery pots, to guard against excess evaporation. We used a similar grit in the peat/sand mix which was inside the pot. Why not rotavate some of this into the stone-free soil?

The Shade Beds which I have described in Chapter 3 were going downhill. Only the most strongly rooted plants, such as *Hosta*, *Eupatorium* and *Ligularia*, were giving their best. Even *Trollius* and the astilbes were dwindling. This was maddening because there was moisture, not too far below them, but there was no capillary action, no natural sucking up of water between the soil particles.

We decided to re-make these beds, to dig everything out except the trees, shrubs and those plants not distressed. Keith did this, carefully lining out everything worth preserving in a reserve border. He also dug out pernicious weeds, such as running buttercup, Hedge Woundwort, *Stachys sylvatica*, which is easily recognized by its pungent, unpleasant smell, and plenty of 'Codlins and Cream', a kind of Willow-herb commonly found in damp soil. These and others were weeds which had invaded the beds and penetrated plants, undetected over the last few years. As much garden refuse as was available was spread over the beds, including nursery waste which is mostly peat and sand from discarded pots. Then a thick layer of grit, enough to make complete cover, was flung across the soil. All of this was rotavated to make an even mix. We used pick tines, sharp pointed rotavator blades which cut through the soil, thinking this would be less likely to create a hard pan underneath where the normal rotary blades scrape the under surface. The work was done in the autumn, when the soil was not wet and everything could be incorporated evenly and lightly.

The following spring I started replanting. What a difference there was in the soil! In April, often using only a hand fork to make the holes, I found it light and open, not wet, but damp enough to provide plenty of loose crumbs to press round the roots of the plants. In the same area, where such preparations had not been made, the soil came up solid and wet, and had to be beaten with a border fork to break the slabs into lumps, not fit for fresh plantings at all. As the soil slowly dried out it broke down quite finely—but that was at least six weeks, possibly two months later and I like my major planting done before June. But because of the quality of the soil, and the presence of underground springs, I do continue to add a few plants throughout the summer to these beds which remain damp, something I cannot possibly do in the dry gravel areas of my garden.

The clay. I find the clay in my garden the most difficult, next-to-impossible stuff to deal with. I am not referring to heavy clay-based soil, which is bad enough, but to the dense plasticine-like substance which is my subsoil in the Damp Garden, and with which I only come into close contact in two very different situations.

The first is by the water-side. I have mentioned the problem briefly elsewhere, but as it is a problem that never goes away, it needs to be looked at, and dealt with, repetitively.

My original borders around the first ponds near the house were not very well prepared. It was partly impatience, partly that we had not enough additional good material to add—and, I must confess, we did not feel up to prising out any more of the wickedly heavy clay than we were obliged to do. Over the years the more vigorous plants—*Miscanthus*, *Gunnera*, *Iris* and *Phormium*—waxed bigger and taller in the solid clay, but the more delicate plants, like primulas and astilbes, waned. They hung on but did not flourish; neither were there the sheets of seedlings I had hoped for. The thin layer of vegetable waste which we had originally applied was soon used up, and several years of weeding, in the pre-mulching era, removed much of the heavy meadow silt. In places we were down to the solid substratum.

One tends to lose interest in beds which are not functioning properly. I knew that something drastic would have to be done when I could make time to stop and think what that should be. Suddenly it came to me. The two narrow beds must go. A time comes when I realize that I must cut down the work, especially when I have been busy making new and better beds elsewhere. So these rather fussy beds disappeared, and it was good to see the mown grass right to the water's edge, with just a few leafy plants like *Zantedeschia aethiopica*, Arum Lily, *Carex stricta*, Bowles' lovely Golden Sedge, and several forms of *Iris laevigata* planted in the water, against the block edging, to break the hard edge.

Now I was left with two water-side beds each about 30 yd/28 m long and 3 yd/3 m wide; this is wide enough to plant balanced groups of medium-sized plants, like *Iris*, *Astilbe* and *Primula*; or just wide enough to fit a *Gunnera*, or a big group of *Rodgersia* or *Ligularia*. The soil is not saturated 10 ft/3 m away from the water's edge, but the water-table is not far below. I thought that if I could improve the quality of the top spit of soil, some of that moisture would rise through capillarity, and could be used by plants which needed damp conditions but would not tolerate drowning.

Once again the smaller plants were removed and heeled-in. The beds were virtually emptied—only the great gunneras were left with their lofty companions, *Miscanthus sacchariflorus* and *Miscanthus sinensis* 'Zebrinus'. (And, of course, the framework of Swamp Cypress, *Taxodium distichum*, *Metasequoia glyptostroboides*, and a few water-loving shrubs.) *Carex riparia* 'Variegata' was painstakingly removed, every wiry thong that could be seen. It is one of the most lovely water-side sedges, with its long, thin arching leaves which are striped white, many of them in spring being totally white. However, it does run about much too invasively if planted without fore-knowledge. In small tidy areas it should either be avoided altogether, or perhaps planted in an interred bucket with only the smallest of drainage holes. By lake-sides, or pond-sides, among coarse plantings of large bog-side plants, it will probably be subdued by other inhabitants just as demanding.

We have made another discovery which has proved a boon where invasive plants have been difficult to eradicate. We paint their leaves in summer with a systemic weedkiller. There are several of these on the market, and new ones continually being introduced. Whatever you choose, read the directions carefully before you begin, and then experiment on a small scale. Some chemicals, I have found, are translocated, that is the chemical passes through contact from the roots of the treated plant to others around it, causing distortion if not death. Having decided which chemical to use great care must be taken to avoid *any* drops falling onto the leaves of other plants. We have been using 'Round Up', which contains N-phosphonomethyl glycerine and it has been most successful, both as a total weedkiller, and when used for spot treatment. A similar weedkiller is also marketed under the label 'Tumbleweed'.

A weed problem which had been bothering me was a running grass which appeared in the periwinkle border (*Vinca minor*, in various forms) which edges my drive shrubbery. The vincas had proved a blessing as ground-cover, despatching all earlier nuisances such as chickweed and annual meadow grass, but this wretched Red Fescue was making its presence disquietingly obvious, spoiling the tidy effect of the low evergreen carpet. So, wearing rubber gloves of course, my weedkilling girl soaked a piece of old towelling in the diluted mixture, squeezed it out and carefully wiped handfuls of the grass. It takes several weeks before you can be sure of the results, but then we were delighted to see withered remains of the untidy grass—all were dead and the periwinkle unharmed. You could use a brush, which we do on many weeds, but be careful the weedkiller does not run down into the mat of plants. There is a weedkilling glove; we have bought one, but tend as yet to find our own methods preferable—probably a matter of habit!

A day, or several days, spent spot treating weeds that are difficult or impossible to remove in any other way is so well worthwhile, saving weeks of work later on when whole plants, if not large parts of borders, may have to be removed to tackle the intruders by conventional spade and fork. I am thinking particularly of occasions when weeds such as nettles, perennial grass, brambles, docks and dandelions are locked firmly into one's choice plants or shrubs. If you can reach them before they have engulfed the plant there is less risk of damage with the chemical. By that time I would choose to dig up my plant and carefully separate it from the weed.

That digression has taken us too far from the water garden, as most of these weeds do not flourish in soggy soil, but you *will* have a weed problem among your bog plants, some of the weeds probably turning out to be certain of your selected plants which have themselves become too invasive. Before I leave the subject a word of warning: I must stress that the greatest care should be taken not to let weedkiller drop into the water. It could do great damage to all pond life.

After twenty years there are now two things vital to improving the soil in my bog beds. One is to have plenty of lightening material to add, the other is to have a strong and willing helper to do the adding. I am not so good now at heaving heavy weights. Thankfully, Harry is still going strong, and enjoys tackling such jobs. After all his hard work clearing out the bed it is comforting to think that if a few pieces of the Variegated Sedge, *Carex riparia* 'Variegata', do reappear through a newly planted batch of *Trollius*, they can be safely treated, to dispose of them finally.

I have come to the conclusion that, wherever possible, we must leave the pure clay alone and try to build a soil on top of it. Several layers had already been removed, over the years, on the roots of weeds, so the level of the pond-side borders was below the level of the mown grass walks. I needed a large amount of gravelly soil to put onto them as a basic layer.

What is waste at one end of my property is a valuable commodity at the other. The nursery is sited on very stony soil. From time to time some of this is dug out to make way for plunging beds or covered tunnels. The top spit, although gravelly, is not worthless, having had generous dressings of some kind of vegetable waste over the years, and is piled into heaps until we need it. It is a lovely feeling to have plenty of the right material to hand. The old tractor, with its large three-sided metal box on the back, which we call a 'buck', made many trips to bring a fresh spit of topsoil. (One of these days I hope to buy a small tipper-truck. We hired a large one recently to help us with some building work, and I can see that it would be an ideal tool for many jobs. Lighter than the tractor, easily manoeuvrable, it would save time with so many jobs—weeding, spreading bark and straw—and there would be far fewer journeys than with wheelbarrows, and it would be much nippier than our Merry tiller trailer. There are several baby tractors available for gardens. No doubt some are more than pretty toys but all are costly, and in a big garden you must have something reliable and strong enough to do really heavy work sometimes.) The next ingredient for my pond-side beds was a large heap of nursery and garden waste consisting of spent potting soil (peat and sand) and rotted vegetable matter. This was spread all over the gravelly soil. Finally a layer of grit was spread over this, and the whole rotavated as deeply as we could.

This work was done in the autumn. Today, a cold but sparklingly sunny New Year's Day, I have just been out to examine these beds. With a long pronged fork I have dug into the mixture and found a most satisfying depth, almost two spits deep, above the clay, and several wriggly pink worms in each hole I dug. These will have been introduced no doubt with the additional soil which has included good topsoil saved when plants have been dug up to be divided. The soil which falls from the roots onto the pack-house floor is always the best, including leaf-mould and decomposing bark from earlier dressings. All this good material is a bonus derived from the routine work of the garden and nursery. Whenever I feel a little anxious about the time we spend weeding, cutting down and tidying up, which is little enough, I remind myself that the large piles of waste will, in a year or two's time, be worth more than loads of muck to me. Rotted down they will be readily available to the plants whereas muck, unless very old, has to be broken down by soil organisms before it is available.

On the whole I tend to use farmyard manure as an additional mulch, where I think such plants as hostas and hellebores, both greedy feeders, need it, and keep it on top of heavy soil, letting the birds pull it about in winter, and then the worms drag it down. Some years it produces a crop of Fat Hen, a typical farm weed which probably seeded over it as it lay in the farmer's yard, but that is easily pulled out. Otherwise I dig in muck, or rotavate it into my light land over a three-year rotation, if I can manage that.

The second area where I have had to come into close contact with clay has been my new Reservoir Garden. This is such a strange situation, and it is unlikely that many readers will have anything quite so bizarre to deal with, but my experiment so far is worth recording, I think. It is an area about an acre in size, originally a very light gravel soil sloping gently south into the hollow where, thirty years previously, we had begun to make a small reservoir. Before it was finished exceptionally high tides and flooding occurred along the East Coast. Much damage was done, and all earth-moving equipment was rushed to the distressed areas, including those working to complete our reservoir. Somehow they never returned. As a result, mountains of clay which had been scooped up from a depth of about 15 ft/4.5 m were left piled along the bottom of the gravel slope. In 1976, the year of the Great Drought, with my neighbour busily enlarging the reservoir, it seemed a good opportunity for me to hire these huge earth-moving tools for a few days, to level out the clay hills, so that we could see the new reservoir behind and beyond them. Clearing and burning had to be done first, as in the intervening twenty years a large Crack Willow had seeded, making a solid block of willow saplings perched up on the rough mounds.

Fortunately, some of the clay could be lost building a wider dam, but the rest had to be disposed of somehow. I suggested it be spread all over my gravel slope, which let water through like a colander, and was quite the driest and poorest piece of land I had. So the bulldozer crawled up and down, smearing the orange-coloured clay ahead of it. Because the mounds had lain so long, affected by weather and the root action of the vegetation that had germinated over them, and because of the long drought, the close-textured clay was dry like caked face powder and so could be evenly spread. There was not much for me to do but walk around, suggesting a bit of levelling here or banking there. The area was not large enough to create anything but the gentlest change of gradient. I was more bothered about the problems ahead. Although I was hoping that somehow I could amalgamate the clay with the gravel beneath to make a more retentive soil, I knew it would not occur overnight. Meanwhile I was wondering what would happen when the rains came and this stuff got wet.

Can you imagine anything as silly as two women carrying a wheel-barrowful of compost and sand, their wellington boots sticking and slithering ankle deep in liquid clay? That was how it was one day the following spring. During the autumn we had managed to mark out large, irregular beds, and plant a basic framework of trees and shrubs. Every hole was a struggle, cleaning the clay off our tools and trapped boots. I found that the clay layer varied in depth—about 1 ft/300 mm deep where it was shallowest, about 2 ft/600 mm deep overall. I hoped that the newly made holes would not fill up with rain water like mini waterbutts, but we had made them as shallow as we dared, realizing that we must try to build up a soil on top of the clay. So far we have seen nothing die of waterlogging on this site. In those holes where we were able to penetrate the clay layer there was, of course, no risk.

I had ordered a lot of *Eremurus*, thinking how splendid they would look, their lofty spikes seen in profile against the reservoir which lay below them. So that spring morning, one of my girls and I set off to plant them. Before we knew what was happening the heavy barrows had sunk up to their axles in the greasy clay. I suppose we should have given up. But I hate putting things off. By the time the clay would be dry enough to do the job in a proper manner the *Eremurus* would, or should, be showing 3 ft/1 m of growth. We looked at the sunken wheels, then at each other, and without a word, but a lot of laughter, manhandled those barrows to where we wanted the gritty soil. Prising out just enough clay to make a shallow bed, we tipped in a layer of compost, spread out the brittle starfish shaped roots, and then put another generous layer over the top. Finally we covered them with straw, to protect the soil—the plants did not need it. In the years that have followed our *Eremurus robustus* have stood more than 10 ft/3 m tall with gigantic columnar heads of close-packed, shell-pink, starry flowers followed by green, cherry-plum-sized seed pods. I have seen pictures of these statuesque plants growing wild in the western Tienshan in Central Asia, and in Afghanistan, in steppe-land on the lower slopes of the mountains. They can stand intense cold in winter, great heat in summer as their clumps of strap-shaped leaves shoot up quickly in spring to make use of the early moisture, but have usually withered by the time the flowers open. They should not rightly be appearing in *The Damp Garden*—indeed they will rot in perpetually moist soil—but they do not object to clay, and I think they relish it to support those tremendously heavy heads. During the last four or five years I have tried to add something to these beds every year. From the beginning they were deeply smothered with straw. As the straw disintegrated huge heaps of bonfire remains were scattered over, including quite a lot of burnt soil as well as ash and charcoal. We have not tried deliberately burning clay ourselves, but I had a friend whose garden soil drove him to the conclusion that it was better to garden on top of it than in it, and he showed me his bonfires heaped with clay which baked into a reddish crumbly biscuit. As it cooked slowly he added more. Finally, when it was cold, he crushed it up and spread it over the soil together with leaf-mould, pine needle litter and sand.

We spread any spare stony soil from our gravel area over our clay garden. The results, after all this effort, amaze and delight us. I shall not describe the groupings in this book—they are so far largely experimental and I've no doubt some will change over the next few years—but we have lost scarcely a tree or shrub. On the contrary, the growth and vigour have been a joy to see. Already the top spit of added soil is, I am sure, becoming incorporated with the top few inches of clay beneath. I am encouraging this by constantly digging about to add new plants. Although I swore I would not add plants, that this was to be strictly an area of trees and shrubs, with no maintenance by hand, I am beginning to plant what I call coarse herbaceous plants around the edges as ground-cover, to make interest and contrast. Great drifts of *Colchicum* are not difficult to maintain, for example, nor the colourful bergenias which create such a warm, live look in winter. All the plants push strongly through the straw cover, and apart from the time spent actually planting there is very little handwork done here. The few days in the year spent eradicating the odd weed, pruning the shrubs to ensure good shapes, or carting away the heavy seed heads of *Eremurus* are nothing compared to the weekly routine of grass cutting.

It still has a long way to go, but the birds, worms, soil bacteria and, I think, the plants themselves, are all helping to mix the raw clay with the varied materials we are adding, and all of this will eventually, I hope, begin to be incorporated into the gravel beneath.

Conclusions on Damp Soil and its Texture

Books have been written, and more could be written, on the vast subject of soil and the ways we should treat it. Every practising gardener has something useful to say about his soil and the way he deals with it. I have dealt primarily with my own types of soil, hoping that some of my experiences may be helpful to others faced with such extreme types.

Some readers may live in counties where heavy clay stretches from one parish boundary to the next, where there is no possibility of carting lighter soil from one end of the garden to the other. But it is possible to buy fine grit, and if you are able to treat only a few square yards at a time, you will be thankful for the improvement.

I have not mentioned soils on chalk or limestone because I have no experience of them, but I am sure the same principles, aimed to improve the soil texture, will apply.

Finally, I have scarcely mentioned the use of concentrated fertilizers. That is not because I disapprove of them. In my own garden I have, from time to time, had the soil tested to see whether it were short of one particular mineral—magnesium perhaps, or potash. Then I would add what was needed.

Sometimes, when the soil is too acid, or out of balance for any other reason, plant nutrients become locked up and no amount of concentrated fertilizer poured onto it will be effective. Clay soils which have been farmed or gardened over a long period with only concentrates, with no bulky organic matter returned to feed the soil organisms (which play such a part in the health of plant life), become lifeless and eventually barren. Fertilizers can only work well when there is a proper balance, a good soil structure, organic matter and a healthy soil population. I personally look upon fertilizers as vitamin tablets, which are useful when necessary but do not take the place of the good square meal which is what humus is to plants and the soil population. When that is present you rarely need concentrates.

For those who cannot make or obtain enough vegetable waste, a combination of peat, or well-pulverized bark, plus a little organic concentrate would be the next best thing. I use chemical concentrates rarely and sparingly when tell-tale signs of deficiency are seen.

Soil Treatment Summary

1 Check drainage

(a) Dig a trench through waterlogged soil to see the profile of soil beneath the surface. Sometimes you find a block of clay which is causing the trouble.

(b) Digging a trench is not as bad as it sounds. Use as narrow a spade as you can find to keep the trench narrow.

(c) Fill the trench three parts with coarse stone, cover it with a sheet of polythene, then fill the remainder of the trench with soil.

(d) For those with large areas to drain, there are firms who specialize in laying perforated plastic pipes. They use quite a small machine which makes a narrow slit trench. See that the pipe is laid on a bed of coarse stone, with more laid over it so that water can trickle to find the slits in the pipes and be carried away. With big drainage schemes on farms, earthenware pipes, laid end to end, are used.

2   Digging

(a) Deep digging is helpful if soil has become very compacted, but try not to bring clay subsoil to the surface.

(b) A heavy soil left rough-dug in winter will fall into a crumbly tilth in spring, if you catch it just right.

(c) Fine grit, about ⅜ in./10 mm, spread generously and forked in the top spit is worth as much as humus for its lightening effect. Sharp sand could be used as well.

(d) Dig as little as is necessary. Make holes deep enough to take trees and shrubs, trenches for celery and runner beans which can be filled up with a mixture of some of these—compost, well-rotted muck, kitchen waste, well-wetted peat, plus a little fertilizer.

(e) For general purposes, once shrubs and herbaceous plants have been planted on heavy land, add your improving materials to the surface. Most feeding roots are in the top few inches of soil, so it is there they will be searching for organic matter. Too much forking about will break them.

3   Mulching

A mulch will protect those feeding roots. It will protect the surface of the soil from drying out, and check the germination of weed seeds. Once established many of the plants themselves will do all this.

(a) *Fine material* to be used among small shrubs and plants, and where the appearance is important:

Peat—the coarse grade lasts longer and is not so easily blown away.

Forest bark is more efficient if finely crushed. If the pieces are not sufficiently crushed sturdy seedlings jostle their way among them, as the pieces slide on each other, rather like tiddlywinks. The bark needs to be shredded to a fibrous texture when it is more stifling. Untreated bark, obtainable in bulk, or smaller amounts from the source of supply (usually the Forestry Commission—or else they will advise) is usually fairly well pulverized. If the bark has been freshly pulverized it is best to let it lie in a heap for several months so that it becomes partially decomposed.

Spent hops from breweries; available in some places.

Grit—useful as a mulch on top of pots, sink gardens and raised beds of alpines.

Cobble-like stones I have seen used as a mulch and weed-deterrent on a bed of dwarf conifers. Worth considering in the right district where stone and rock are available. Soil always seems to be moist under stones.

(b) *Coarse material*—for use in large areas, chiefly among trees and shrubs:

Straw—obtainable ready baled from farms or contractors. Not expensive—a good dressing lasts two years. Remember to add a little nitrogen.

Bracken is laboursome, but I would cut and use it if I could get nothing else.

1 Part of the long walk beneath the ancient boundary oaks at White Barn House

2 *Iris laevigata*

3 *Phormium* plants guard the entrance to the Canal Bed

4 *Thalictrum aquilegifolium* (left) and *Rheum palmatum* (centre)

5 *Bergenia* 'Silberlicht'

6 *Lunaria biennis* 'Variegata'

7 View showing great contrast of foliage and form in the Canal Bed

8 *Heuchera americana*

9 *Polemonium caeruleum* (left), *Aquilegia vulgaris* hybrid (right) and
Euphorbia griffithii 'Fireglow' (background)

10 *Sambucus racemosa* 'Plumosa Aurea' (left background), *Pieris formosa*
(right background) and *Hosta sieboldiana* (foreground)

11 *Senecio smithii*

12 *Primula* 'Silver Lace'

Mushroom compost—I have used this in the past. It was pleasant and easy to handle, but at that time it contained rather a lot of chalk. I stopped using it as I did not want too great a build-up of chalk, which could be washed down onto soils where I had acid-loving plants.

Polythene. Black polythene can be obtained in strips or sheets from horticultural suppliers. It is useful primarily in the vegetable garden or where plants are in rows. I have bought some for experiment, but have not yet used it! But I should, to compare efficiency and costs with other materials and methods.

Management of Grass on Silt and Clay Soils

I have come rather belatedly in my story to the consideration of lawns and grass walks in damp gardens. Among the various branches of gardening I consider myself to be least expert in the art of maintaining good grass. Much of the mystery, I suspect, lies in giving the kind of care and attention which I try to give to my plants, of which I give, I must admit, but a fraction to the grass. But the best-planned borders can be degraded by poorly kept or neglected grass.

Grass is not just a hard-wearing border-to-border carpeting material to be rolled out and then left to fend for itself, apart from savage attacks with a lawn mower. Given soil conditions that are ideal for healthy growth, perfectly adequate lawns can be achieved with only a little more attention. But, as with our garden plants, there are many different kinds of grass, and they all have their likes and dislikes.

The suppliers of grass seed blend into their mixtures several varieties which together help to make the kind of sward you are hoping for, whether it be tough and hard-wearing for a playing field, or fine and velvety to set off a well-tended garden. You will need to tell your seedsman the kind of soil you have, so that he can help you select those grasses which thrive in your conditions.

I am ashamed to say that I have mislaid the analysis which was recommended for my soils, but there is nothing secret about these formulas. Provided you have the right type of grass for your soil and climate and, as in my case, state firmly what you do not want, that is, not one blade of the coarser perennial rye grass, then you have only the problem of sowing and maintenance to bother about.

I have great respect for the skilled and knowledgeable people who devote their lives to the problem of maintenance, which I have mentioned rather flippantly. Consider a football pitch in winter, often soaked with rain or snow, with twenty-two hefty men skidding up and down at least twice a week. Or the bowling club, where the woods click gently on still summer evenings, on a green firm and smooth as a billiard table covered with velvet. Or the grounds at Wimbledon! I have none of that expertise. I can only tell you how, so far, I have managed my grass on both clay and wet silt.

Grass on moist silt. As with almost everything else that has happened here, I have discovered what knowledge I have largely by stumbling over the solution. The problems are there from the beginning, but one does not immediately recognize them to be problems.

After many years in our previous garden, watching our lawn burn up to dust in long periods of drought, we were so thrilled to have perpetually damp silt that we never imagined there could be any problems. Making a seed bed was easy, the grass germinated freely, tillered and made up well that first season. But after the winter rains, with all the underground springs running full tilt beneath the green carpet, we found that we could not use the mower in some places till well into June, because it sank into soft, wet soil.

This was no good. We had to start thinking about drainage which, of course, we should have done in the first place—before the grass was sown. Now we had to make drainage trenches based on a herringbone system to pick up the surplus water and lead it into the ponds. First the turf was carefully lifted and narrow trenches were dug, about 1½–2 ft/460–600 mm deep. They were filled three parts with coarse gravel, then infilled with soil and the turves relaid. This performance has been carried out from time to time over the years, wherever drainage problems have become evident, that is, when in winter you stand on the grass and the water squelches up between your boots.

With hindsight I think that not only should we have done this at the beginning, but we should also have spread fine grit thickly over the silt before sowing and lightly worked it into the surface layer to improve the soil texture, to give each grass plant aeration as well as moisture. But we were not in a position to have help with such tasks so the knowledge would not have been of much comfort. For several years now I have said that *this* autumn we will dress all the lawns on the damp silt with fine grit, but other matters more to my heart have had precedence and this experiment has not yet taken place. When it has I am hoping that it will help with our moss problem.

Mercifully, because of the ever-present moisture, the Damp Garden lawns look pretty good all summer, no matter how dry the weather. However, in spring the bright green colour is largely caused by soaking mats of moss. I marvel that the grass is not choked completely, but with drying winds in March, often followed by rainless weeks, the moss retreats and the grass takes over. We have made some effort to get rid of the moss. In spring we spray it with a dilution of iron ferrous sulphate, which blackens it, and we blithely presume it has been killed. We then laboriously rake out the matted remains, including old dead grass which is, I do not doubt, very beneficial (for stomach muscles as well as the health of the grass!). But next spring the situation appears to be very much the same—disheartening.

Even if I bought a decent machine to do the unpleasant scraping it would still be a tedious, repetitive job, taking too much precious time. It may have to come to that one day, but I think that if I could really improve the surface drainage by scattering plenty of grit, allowing the grass to grow through, and then adding more, perhaps making several applications over a period of time, that it might discourage the moss. But I tell myself that damp soils are the natural home for moss. And in East Anglia we can rely on drying weather to subdue it. My Damp Garden lawns appear an oasis of green to our visitors in dry times, and while I know they are a lot less than perfect, I am grateful that they look and act as well as they do.

Grass on raw clay. When it came to thinking about the grass walks around the new Clay Garden I knew I had problems, the 'soil' being plasticine-like clay dredged up from the bottom of the reservoir. The first difficulty was trying to make some kind of tilth into which we could sow the seed. (This was before I had thought of using grit.) We watched the state of the clay throughout the late winter and spring. By early April we found that the March winds had dried out the top few inches enough for us to use the disc harrows just to break up the solid bed of clay. Then there was another period of waiting and watching daily for the stirred-up clods to reach just the right state of crumbliness for us to attempt a seed bed. Then early one Saturday morning it seemed just right, at least, as nearly right as it could ever be. Harry jumped to it, and worked throughout the day to get the seed in while the light lasted. Thank goodness he made it—the next day it rained all day, and for the rest of that summer the soil was either pastry wet or biscuit dry. It would have been impossible to sow the seed again during that season.

For weeks, it seemed, after it was sown, I lay on my stomach trying to detect the first signs of life as germinating seeds by the million thrust up their first probing spears. The conditions were bad. Cold March winds chilled the soil, capped the crust, and did their best to dehydrate the delicate-looking shoots. At their other end the tiny grass plants had to force little roots into a harsh and horrible substance which could not be called soil. What nutrients could they possibly be finding to give them strength, I wondered. But plants get on with their lives as best they can while we fret ourselves uselessly. Eventually it came, slowly, so slowly, that pale haze of green over the raw clay. I relaxed momentarily, with relief.

By the autumn most of the area was covered with little plants sufficiently developed to take up an application of a peat-based grass fertilizer. This gave them a little impetus but I considered that more than a tonic was needed. We had the year's accumulation of nursery waste standing by. Instead of spreading it over the latest planting scheme it was all carted out and scattered over the young grass. We walked over it and raked up anything that might be too smothering for the young plants to push through. The response was astonishing. Almost immediately the green became richer and darker; those areas which had lost out because there were not quite enough rations to go round looked pale and anaemic by comparison. Now we started making a separate heap of our pot waste especially for the grass, until the whole area had received a dressing of this worn-out peat and grit mixture (worn-out for potted plants, but obviously offering something substantial to the grass).

One autumn, two or three years after we had sown the grass, I found myself with the remains of a very well-rotted muck heap, enough, I thought, to spread all over the grass. I admit that it did look extraordinary, young groups of trees and shrubs standing in a landscape carpeted with old cow manure. 'Was I going to plough it all up and make a new garden there?' I was asked several times by visitors who, not a bit put off, picked their way around it. I replied, no, but I thought the grass needed feeding as well as the borders and this was one way of doing it. We borrowed a set of harrows (which is like a huge rake) to pull behind the tractor, finally to distribute and break up any smothering pieces. But I think we need not have bothered. The grass, which had been almost obliterated by the generosity of our dressing, simply shot through and absorbed it greedily. Now, after six years, it is some of my best grass. Never, with all the compost I could muster, would I have made such a sward on the raw gravel which is beneath the layer of clay. Recently I have been enlarging the beds, to cut down the amount of mowing. As I cut the turf with my edging tool to mark the new edge I pick up a piece to see what has been happening. The grass is densely tufted, a rich dark green. Immediately below it is a black spongy layer, a good inch thick, while below that is the wedge of yellow clay. Some of the spongy layer will be the remains of peat and manure which we have added previously, but that would be very thin and compressed now if nothing else had happened. Much of what I can see has been formed by the grass itself, the successional growth and decay of roots and shoots which, over the years, is building a layer of humus on top of the clay. Not only that, the roots which penetrate the once structureless clay are making passages through which air and water can penetrate. As they die they too break down, and eventually make nutrients for new exploring roots. Holding this quiet success story in my hand I feel almost guilty to be ripping up these survivors whose tough beginnings I watched only a few years ago. But effort need never go to waste in the garden. Some of these turves will be laid elsewhere. The rest will be stacked in a neat pile, so that the tufty grass, the peaty layer and the thin slice of clay beneath will become integrated into a heavy soil. It will be there, a fine heap, the very thing I need, one of these days.

I have not mentioned the use of fertilizers, weedkillers, or a score more things that would fill the several chapters needed to do justice to the story of grass. . . . But that is another writer's story.

8 *Garden Plans*

I have listed and shown the plants in separate groups within each plan, hoping it will help in visualizing the effect. In small-scale planting these individual combinations might well be ample, or could even be reduced again. They are not the only or the best combinations that could be made; neither need they be kept in watertight compartments. Plants of similar habit could be selected from the other groups and all would look harmonious provided you are careful to blend the *shapes*. It is as important to have plant shapes contributing to the design as it is to take care with colour blending. For myself it is more important. Naturally one avoids horrible clashes of colour, but that rarely occurs when plants are grown with their natural associates.

Plan for the Swamp Garden

The majority of plants used *must* have perpetually wet soil; those indicated around the edge will grow in a few inches of water. *Gunnera* is one of the few which could be harmed by being waterlogged in winter. I like to plant the crown of *Gunnera scabra* slightly above water level on a raised mound or bank. Its roots quickly find boggy soil but the resting buds are not drowned in winter if the level should rise.

The same applies to *Phormium*. We make a good job of protecting our spectacular clumps of *Phormium*, both the green-leafed *Phormium tenax* and the purple and variegated leaf forms (see page 72).

It is worth repeating that the ornamental rhubarb, *Rheum palmatum* will rot if it is planted in waterlogged soil. It needs deep soil, well laced with well-rotted vegetable waste, soil that does not dry out. Well suited it will stand full sun, but also looks well in dappled shade. Savage winds can damage such huge and tender leaves, whereas the leaves of *Gunnera* are hard and horny. *Rheum alexandrae* will tolerate wetter conditions, as it grows wild in mountain meadows with candelabra primulas, but it will not tolerate waterlogged soil.

I would hesitate to use so many different plants all together unless the planting were on a very large scale. But I have made groups of plants which I consider look well together. There are, of course, endless permutations within this range, conditioned largely by the scale of planting.

I tend to think of natural pools with clay-based bottoms as I have had little experience with lined pools. The main problems with man-made pools are usually overall size—usually lack of size!—and depth of soil. However,

F. Plants for the Swamp Garden

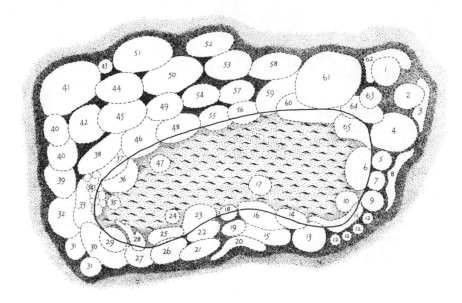

Key to plan:

1. *Phormium tenax*
2. *Phormium tenax* 'Variegatum'
3. *Houttuynia cordata*
4. *Salix repens argentea*
5. *Senecio smithii*
6. *Zantedeschia aethiopica* 'Green Goddess'
7. *Iris versicolor*
8. *Lysimachia nummularia* 'Aurea'
9. *Lythrum salicaria*
10. *Scirpus tabernae-montanus* 'Zebrinus'
11. *Myosotis palustris*
12. *Primula bulleyana*
13. *Ligularia dentata*
14. *Lysichitum camtschatcense*

15. *Verbena corymbosa*
16. *Peltiphyllum peltatum*
17. *Aponogeton distachyum*
18. *Caltha palustris* 'Alba'
19. *Luzula sylvatica*
20. *Mimulus guttatus*
21. *Primula pulverulenta*
22. *Lythrum virgatum*
23. *Pontederia cordata*
24. *Butomus umbellatus*
25. *Iris laevigata*
26. *Polygonum mileti*
27. *Lysimachia ciliata*
28. *Calla palustris*
29. *Eriophorum angustifolium*
30. *Euphorbia palustris*
31. *Carex morrowii* 'Variegata'
32. *Iris kaempferi*
33. *Aruncus dioicus* (*A. sylvester*)

34. *Primula florindae*
35. *Typha angustifolia*
36. *Iris pseudacorus* 'Variegata'
37. *Cardamine latifolia*
38. *Astilbe* hybrids
39. *Rudbeckia fulgida* (*R. speciosa*)
40. *Rodgersia podophylla*
41. *Cornus alba* 'Spaethii'
42. *Rheum palmatum*
43. *Taxodium distichum*
44. *Miscanthus sinensis* 'Variegatus'

45. *Veratrum album*
46. *Osmunda regalis*
47. *Zantedeschia aethiopica*
48. *Onoclea sensibilis*
49. *Polygonum amplexicaule*
50. *Miscanthus sinensis* 'Zebrinus'
51. *Salix elaeagnos* (*S. rosmarinifolius*)
52. *Miscanthus sinensis* 'Silver Feather'

53. *Eupatorium purpureum*
54. *Polygonum bistorta* 'Superbum'
55. *Caltha palustris* 'Flore Pleno'
56. *Carex stricta* 'Bowles' Golden'
57. *Trollius europaeus*
58. *Ligularia* 'The Rocket'
59. *Polygonum campanulatum*
60. *Menyanthes trifoliata*
61. *Gunnera scabra*
62. *Glyceria maxima* 'Variegata'
63. *Inula magnifica*
64. *Hemerocallis* 'Kwanso Flore Pleno'
65. *Caltha polypetala*

small pools well maintained look infinitely more attractive than large, neglected, muddy pools. A few well-displayed plants are much more effective than the confused tangle that can result when there is no shortage of room and enthusiasm but insufficient discipline meted out to plants and planters.

In designing my groups, whether large or small, I try to keep in mind the image of a main vertical line connected to the earth with strong and interesting foliage. This basic shape is emphasized and decorated throughout the growing season with a succession of flowering plants, until finally all together contribute to the warm glow of autumn with seed pods and flowering grasses, while the lush foliage, over many weeks, turns to rich shades of brown, copper and gold.

For the creation of an artificial pool, deciding on depths and suitable materials to use, including containers for aquatics, you should read the Wisley Handbook No.29, *Water Gardens*, by Ken Aslet. It is full of good practical ideas clearly set out and temptingly illustrated.

One last warning when making an artificial pool. Unless you can arrange for irrigation, or some other artificial way to moisten the soil *outside* your pool, the natural state of the soil will probably be very dry, at least it will be when damp-loving plants are most in need of moisture. Possibly the best way to overcome this without irrigation is having the pool surrounded by paving and perhaps a rock garden, so leading naturally into plants associated with dry gardening.

Plans for Sunny Damp Beds

There are so many plants that could be selected for these beds, most of our garden plants in fact, excluding those that could be called drought-resisting plants. However, I have chosen from among hundreds—if not thousands—about one hundred which would certainly suffer if planted in poor soil with low rainfall. They need a good moisture-retentive soil and adequate rainfall, but the soil must also be well drained, and in no case may it be waterlogged.

Travelling westwards and north, from Essex, I sometimes think the rainfall goes up by the inch about every fifty miles, so there will be many gardens where most of the plants will flourish. But we have to remember that if we hope to have flowers in the autumn good foliage must be maintained during the summer months.

Because I needed to clarify my own mind, having so many plants to choose from, I decided, as I never do in my own garden, to divide the year in half and design two beds, one to flower from spring to midsummer, the other from midsummer until late autumn. By glancing down the groups listed you will see many of the plants which I have found look well together, and which incidentally, as individual groups, continue to provide flowers and foliage over several months. But to create a bed that is interesting for most of the year you can select groups from either plan, to your own choice, and match them together.

G. Plants for the Sunny Damp Bed Flowering from Spring to Midsummer

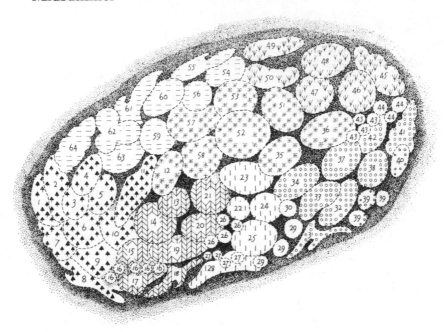

Group 1:
1. *Campanula* 'Burghaltii'
2. *Aconitum × bicolor* 'Ivorine'
3. *Aquilegia formosa*
4. *Valeriana phu* 'Aurea'
5. *Gentiana lutea*
6. *Achillea decolorans* 'W.B. Child'
7. *Veronica gentianoides*
8. *Prunella* 'Loveliness'
9. *Phlox pilosa*
10. *Monarda didyma* 'Beauty of Cobham'
11. *Dracocephalum sibiricum*

Group 2:
13. *Thalictrum speciosissimum (T. flavum glaucum)*
14. *Hemerocallis flava*
15. *Physostegia virginiana* 'Summer Snow'
16. *Zigadenus elegans*
17. *Primula denticulata*
18. *Ajuga reptans* 'Burgundy Glow'
19. *Polygonum carneum*
20. *Geranium* 'Johnson's Blue'
21. *Aruncus dioicus*

Group 3:
22. *Camassia leichtlinii*
23. *Filipendula purpurea (F. palmata)*
24. *Delphinium* 'Alice Artindale'
25. *Morina longifolia*
26. *Lilium croceum*
27. *Fritillaria meleagris*
28. *Erigeron* 'Dimity'
29. *Geum rivale* 'Lionel Cox'
30. *Leucojum aestivum*

Group 4:
31. *Viola cornuta* 'Alba'
32. *Aster yunnanensis* 'Napsbury'
33. *Heucherella ×* 'Bridget Bloom'

34. *Geranium rectum album* 'Kashmir White'
37. *Heuchera cylindrica* 'Greenfinch'
38. *Iris setosa*
39. *Bergenia* 'Abendglut'
40. *Dodecatheon meadia*
41. *Waldsteinia ternata*
42. *Astrantia maxima*
43. *Lilium szovitzianum*
44. *Filipendula hexapetala* 'Plena'

Group 5:
45. *Geranium sanguineum* 'Album'
46. *Stachys macrantha* 'Robusta'
47. *Chrysanthemum maximum*
48. *Iris chrysographes*
49. *Alopecurus pratensis* 'Aureus'
50. *Campanula latifolia* 'Alba'

Group 6:
35. *Campanula lactiflora*
36. *Cephalaria gigantea*
51. *Centaurea macrocephala*
52. *Phormium tenax* 'Variegata'
53. *Miscanthus sinensis* 'Zebrinus'
57. *Euphorbia palustris*
58. *Rheum palmatum*
12. *Ligularia* 'The Rocket'

Group 7:
54. *Symphytum × uplandicum* 'Variegatum'
55. *Ajuga reptans* 'Purpurea'
56. *Ligularia* 'Gregynog Gold'
59. *Hemerocallis* 'Kwanso Flore Pleno'
60. *Trollius ledebouri* (of gardens)
61. *Verbena corymbosa*
62. *Rheum alexandrae*
63. *Geranium pratense* 'Striatum'
64. *Geranium himalayense (G. grandiflorum)*

H. Plants for the Sunny Damp Bed Flowering from Midsummer to late Autumn

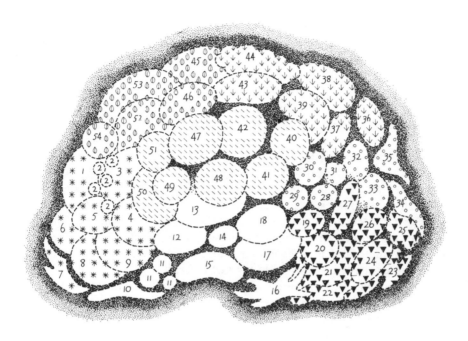

Group 1:
1. *Liriope muscari*
2. *Lilium speciosum*
3. *Polygonum amplexicaule*
4. *Chrysanthemum uliginosum*
5. *Aconitum carmichaelii* 'Arendsii'
6. *Schizostylis coccinea*
7. *Viola cornuta* 'Lilacina'
8. *Stokesia laevis*
9. *Astrantia major* 'Margery Fish'

Group 2:
10. *Polygonum affine*
11. *Molinia coerulea* 'Variegata'
12. *Aster* × *frikartii* 'Mönch'
13. *Euphorbia sikkimensis*
14. *Artemisia lactiflora*
15. *Solidago* 'Golden Thumb'
16. *Gentiana septemfida*
17. *Hosta ventricosa*
18. *Echinacea purpurea*

Group 3:
19. *Salvia uliginosa*
20. *Stipa arundinacea*
21. *Epilobium glabellum*
22. *Ophiopogon planiscarpus nigrescens*
23. *Nierembergia rivularis*
24. *Hosta undulata univittata*
25. *Mimulus* 'Wisley Red'
26. *Symphytum rubrum*
27. *Gentiana asclepiadea* 'Knightshayes'

Group 4:
28. *Phlox*, border variety
29. *Veronica virginica* 'Alba'
30. *Lythrum salicaria* 'Firecandle'
31. *Phlox*, border variety
32. *Lysimachia ephemerum*
33. *Lobelia cardinalis* 'Queen Victoria'
34. *Polygonum affine*
35. *Pratia treadwellii*

Group 5:
36. *Astilbe* 'Sprite'
37. *Chelone obliqua*
38. *Hemerocallis* 'Golden Chimes'
39. *Lysimachia ciliata*
43. *Astilbe taquetii* 'Superba'
44. *Astilbe chinensis* 'Pumila'

Group 6:
40. *Scrophularia aquatica* 'Variegata'
41. *Eupatorium purpureum*
42. *Phormium tenax* 'Purpureum'
47. *Miscanthus sinensis* 'Silver Feather'
48. *Arundinaria viridistriata*
49. *Inula magnifica*
50. *Molinia caerulea altissima*
51. *Vernonia crinita*

Group 7:
45. *Alopecurus pratensis* 'Aureus'
46. *Astilbe* 'Professor van der Wielen'
52. *Inula hookeri*
53. *Rudbeckia fulgida deamii*
54. *Lobelia vedrariensis*

There are endless possibilities for grouping plants. Sometimes it is enough to find just three or four which, put together, create a little scene, an atmosphere, a melodic line perhaps; these things I feel when my planting comes right—which is not always.

There must be a theme, which you state firmly. It may be a shady corner where you will intensify the feeling of cool tranquillity, or it may be a sun-warmed backyard where bright colours and aromatic foliage will evoke memories of a carefree holiday in the far south. With an informed choice of plants, and perhaps a fine seat or earthenware pot, you will decorate your theme with many variations throughout the year, not forgetting that a quiet background will sometimes be needed to show off a star performer.

To be more practical: I may have chosen some plants which are not reliably hardy in some other parts of the country, although it would be hard to find anywhere colder than Essex when the winds come straight out of the north-east. We have less snow but not lower temperatures, I think, than most of the rest of the British Isles. There are days when some of my visitors think we definitely *are* the coldest part of the country. A plant I had in mind is *Salvia uliginosa*, whose tall nodding heads of bright Cambridge-blue flowers are such a delight for weeks in autumn. It has survived here nine out of ten winters covered with some kind of litter, but we always keep a few roots potted and tucked under cover, usually half a bale of straw, in a covered plastic tunnel. In theory the same procedure goes for *Lobelia cardinalis*, but I must confess it has survived many years unprotected. However, it would be wiser to cover it.

The very large plants in the centres of the beds would probably be far too bulky for many people, but I would not ignore them altogether unless I had the tiniest of gardens. One of my daughters has one of those, where I am sometimes used in a consultative role as every spare inch counts.

I would not recommend *Cephalaria gigantea* anywhere but in a large garden where, for much of the season, its displays of pale lemon scabious-like flowers perched on top of tall gawky stems can make unusual and interesting contrast, say on the edge of a shrubbery, or the back of a large border. I like to plant it with *Campanula lactiflora* because they are found growing wild together in well-watered and sheltered gullies at the head of mountain valleys where the forest ends, in the Caucasus. But *C. lactiflora* is one of the glories of the garden. Each plant sends up several strong stems 5 ft/1.5 m tall, each topped with a wide, airy bouquet packed with pale blue bells. Sometimes a white form occurs, sometimes a deeper blue. All are desirable, creating an atmosphere of lavish abundance which should not be lacking in any garden. Just one or two good large plants can do that for you and remove any pinched feelings about having a small garden. I should not forget to tell you that if you cut off the main flower heads of the *Campanula* as soon as they have faded you will have a new crop almost as spectacular in the autumn.

In Plan H I have used a grass, *Molinia caerulea altissima*, the purple-headed Moor Grass. All summer you hardly notice it among its colourful neighbours, where it eventually reaches about 6 ft/2 m. An upright column of stiffly held stems is topped in August with dark, purplish-green flower heads well worth looking at, but you still might not be very impressed—until late October and November, when almost all the flowers have gone and the leaves of the garden are having a ball, all to themselves, decked out in the final and most fiery colour scheme of the whole year. Then you can almost feel a glow from my clumps of *M.c. altissima*. Every tall stem, thick and round as a knitting needle, every pennant-like leaf from tip to ground level, is ablaze with colour—making ripe corn look dull by comparison. I remember a cold, frosty day in November when I called the girls who work with me to come and stand among the glowing grasses, to see the light reflected from them—and there we stood, elated by the golden sheaves as tall as ourselves.

In less sentimental mood, I do think we could use grasses much more imaginatively than we do in this country—and not always buried in among other plants. Used as specimens, where you can enjoy their shape as every leaf and curving stem catches the light, they can be as pleasurable and much longer lasting than most flowers. In Germany I saw, in an hotel garden alongside a motorway, a planting of grasses in an enclosed space set with cobbles and paving. I thought it was very beautiful, in contrast to the hard outlines of the building and the dark mirror-like surfaces of the large windows. I would not have thought myself of planting ornamental cabbages among them, but although I laughed to see them they were not displeasing, for they repeated the shape of the rounded cobbles.

Plans for Shady Damp Beds

In making these plans I have tried to imagine gardens where light shade and damp conditions are constant. The shade could be provided by buildings, or there may be overhead shade cast by trees. In all cases I am presuming there will be reasonable rainfall during the summer months as the plants I have chosen will not stand competition from the greedy roots of trees and shrubs close planted in the drier parts of the country. Neither am I imagining deep, dark shade.

In my own garden I have had to grow extra shelter, apart from my existing ancient oaks, to protect tender foliage not only from the glare of the sun but also to shield it from desiccating winds. I rarely imagine plants without trees and shrubs to provide a setting which will remain in winter, so I have indicated a few which I have used myself. If you already have a background established you could ignore my selection.

The plans I have made started off as one border, but I decided it was becoming rather complicated to fit into a book, so it has become two plans which could be placed side by side, with perhaps a little modification at the seam, if you have room to expand and could manage them both.

They are not intended as plans to be reproduced faithfully, but to suggest groups of plants which I have found grow and look well together in

I. Plants for Shady Damp Bed (1)

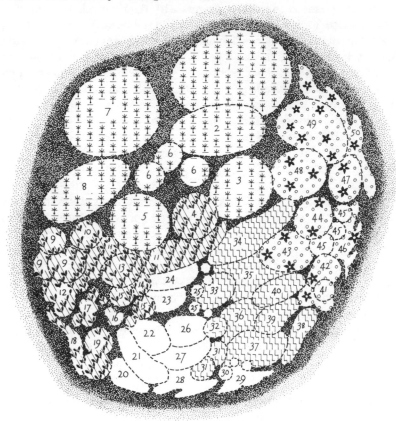

Group 1: 4. *Polygonatum verticillatum*
9. *Hosta* 'Thomas Hogg'
10. *Iris foetidissima* 'Variegata'
11. *Geranium macrorrhizum*
12. *Alchemilla mollis*
13. *Digitalis ciliata*, or *D. grandiflora*
14. *Iris foetidissima* 'Citrina'
15. *Polystichum setiferum* 'Acutilobum'
16. *Digitalis parviflora*
17. *Primula calderiana*
18. *Viola cucullata* 'Freckles'
19. *Pulmonaria saccharata*

Group 2: 20. *Arisaema candidissimum*
21. *Mertensia virginica*
22. *Dicentra spectabilis*
23. *Selinum tenuifolium*
24. *Cimicifuga simplex* 'White Pearl'
25. *Lilium speciosum*
26. *Aconitum × bicolor* 'Ivorine'
27. *Actaea rubra*
28. *Viola septentrionalis*
29. *Veronica prostrata* 'Trehane'
30. *Gentiana asclepiadea* 'Knightshayes'

Group 3: 31. *Liriope muscari*
32. *Valeriana phu* 'Aurea'
33. *Tovara virginiana* 'Variegata'

34. *Polygonatum × hybridum*
35. *Geranium endressii*
36. *Anemone × hybrida* 'Honorine Jobert'
37. *Hosta undulata univittata*
38. *Hakonechloa macra* 'Albo-aurea'
39. *Geranium maculatum*
40. *Astrantia major* 'Sunningdale Variegated'

Group 4: 41. *Pulmonaria longifolia*
42. *Heuchera cylindrica* 'Greenfinch'
43. *Hosta fortunei* 'Albo-picta'
44. *Scrophularia aquatica* 'Variegata'
45. *Smilacina racemosa*
46. *Mitella breweri*
47. *Brunnera macrophylla*
48. *Aruncus dioicus*
49. *Rodgersia podophylla*
50. *Tiarella cordifolia*

Group 5: background shrubs and large plants
1. *Salix* 'Chrysocoma'
2. *Arundinaria japonica*
3. *Hydrangea paniculata* or *H. macrophylla* lace-cap varieti
5. *Weigela* 'Looymansii Aurea'
6. *Angelica archangelica*
7. *Salix alba* 'Sericea'
8. *Arundinaria nitida*

J. Plants for Shady Damp Bed (2)

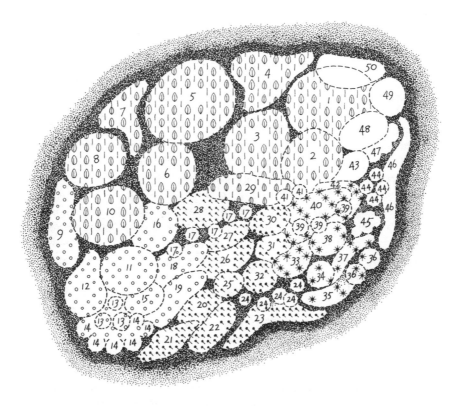

Group 1: 9. *Epimedium × versicolor* 'Sulphureum'
11. *Aconitum carmichaelii* 'Arendsii'
12. *Phlox paniculata*
13. *Milium effusum* 'Aureum'
14. *Primula vulgaris* 'Lilacina'
15. *Paeonia mlokosewitschii*
16. *Hosta sieboldiana*
17. *Lilium speciosum*
18. *Anemone tomentosa*
19. *Geranium macrorrhizum* 'Variegatum'

Group 2: 20. *Dentaria digitata*
21. *Blechnum penna-marina*
22. *Hosta lancifolia*
23. *Phlox stolonifera*
24. *Erythronium* 'Pagoda'
25. *Digitalis ferruginea*
26. *Fuchsia magellanica* 'Versicolor'
27. *Geranium phaeum*
28. *Euphorbia sikkimensis*

Group 3: 30. *Gillenia trifoliata*
31. *Tricyrtis formosana*
32. *Brunnera macrophylla* 'Langtrees'
33. *Trillium grandiflorum*
34. *Lathyrus variegatus* 'Albo Roseus'
35. *Hepatica triloba*
36. *Hosta fortunei* 'Aurea'

37. *Uvularia grandiflora*
38. *Euphorbia amygdaloides* 'Rubra'
39. *Meconopsis betonicifolia*

Group 4: 40. *Kirengeshoma palmata*
41. *Thalictrum dipterocarpum*
42. *Tiarella cordifolia*
43. *Aconitum vulparia*
44. *Disporum sessile* 'Variegatum'
45. *Saxifraga fortunei* 'Rubra'
46. *Ajuga reptans*
47. *Tellima grandiflora* 'Purpurea'
48. *Helleborus orientalis*
49. *Polystichum munitum*
50. *Eomecon chionantha*

Group 5: background trees, shrubs and large plants
1. *Acer negundo* 'Elegans'
2. *Rheum palmatum*—for grand effect
3. *Eucryphia* 'Nymansay'
4. *Trachystemon orientalis*—for ground-cover
5. *Liquidambar styraciflua*
6. *Mahonia japonica*
7. *Geranium nodosum*—for ground-cover
8. *Ilex × altaclarensis* 'Camelliifolia'
10. *Physocarpus opulifolius* 'Luteus'
29. *Arundinaria viridistriata*

cool conditions. Quite a few of the plants I have chosen can, in the cooler northern and damp western counties, be grown without shade. Others, like the *Rheum* which I have chosen for dramatic effect, do not often need shade but certainly need shelter from damaging winds, and sometimes from sun scorch.

Primarily I hope my plans will be helpful to guide you as to approximately where in the border the plants could be put, whether for practical or aesthetic reasons. For example, plants which can be a menace, such as the lovely *Eomecon chionantha*, or the modest *Geranium nodosum*, have been relegated to lonely positions under light trees, where their underground runners need not be for ever regretted.

Other plants, like *Aconitum* × *bicolor* 'Ivorine', *Astrantia major* and heucheras, can be grown in sunny situations provided they are given deep, rich soil. But they harmonize with the real shade-demanders and add immeasurably to the design, as well as flowering satisfactorily in part shade.

It would take too much space to describe all the desirable plants that can be grown in cool, damp shade. I cannot leave the subject, however, without mentioning a few more treasures which we can grow with ease when the conditions are right.

Among the multi-coloured carpets of *Ajuga reptans* and soft green *Tiarella cordifolia* I plant *Anemone apennina* and forms of our own native Wood Anemone, *Anemone nemorosa*. As well as the double white there are several named forms, both pink and shades of blue. Simply breathtaking I find is a planting I have of a large lavender form placed to face the light so you can see inside its deeper stamen-filled heart—I think it may be *A. nemorosa* 'Allenii'. The blue is intensified by an under-planting of *Viola labradorica* which has small dark purple leaves and quantities of lighter purple flowers. Groups of *Fritillaria camtschatcensis*, with their bloomy black petals with mahogany corrugated linings, add great style to this planting.

Of the many variations of snowdrop (*Galanthus*) I have a few of the more distinct. I have not yet become an addict so cannot boast of many variations on this perfect, simple theme. Those I have are enhanced by other early spring flowers among which I value several different *Cordyalis*, and these, especially the pink and blue ones, make perfect companions for *Erythronium dens-canis*, the European Dog's Tooth Violet. These last two flowers can be scattered among the more solid furnishing of the Shade Garden floor: they make the loveliest ornament among the fallen leaves and bare spaces of late winter, but they disappear almost as quickly as they have come and seem quite content to lie quietly among the roots of their summer companions.

A very useful lesson that was brought home to me by my old and much esteemed friend, Sir Cedric Morris, is the fact that we can use space in the soil both ways. Not only do we plant side by side, but also, in different depths, we can plant one plant on top of another, provided their seasons for leafing and flowering do not overlap too much. This applies particularly to combinations of plants and bulbs, but can also apply with plants which die down early in the year to be followed by those that are backward in making an appearance.

Arum italicum 'Pictum' will grow in comparatively dry shade provided large holes, at least as big as a bucket, are dug and refilled with plenty of good compost, but both it and *Arisaema proboscidium*, the Mouse-tailed Arum, I use in my damp shady borders. Other distinguished relatives include *Arisaema triphyllum* and *A. consanguineum*, both of which I am growing but not as they can be seen in some West Country gardens.

Ferns I have scarcely mentioned. They merit a book to themselves and fortunately several have been written by people who have devoted their life's work to the subject. In my descriptive list at the end of Chapter 9 are those I have been able to grow reasonably well (and a few badly) in East Anglia, the least suited part of the country for ferns.

As we all sometimes think that the grass on the other side of the fence is the greenest, so we in the dry areas tend to look towards the moist West Country, to wet Wales and the cool northern counties and feel envious of the plants that grow there so well, which often we cannot grow and should not attempt. I am lucky to be able to grow some of them, but there are far, far more to be found, and endless permutations for grouping them within the basic structure of design; that is, you take account of scale, shape and season, so that not everything is in bloom at once and that quiet seasons are well furnished with good foliage.

9   *Alphabetical List of Plants*

Although this list will include some bog-loving plants, the majority of them can be grown in any good moisture-retentive soil. Where such conditions exist or can be contrived there need scarcely be a dull week from early spring until late autumn, as new growth and fresh flowers can be relied on without the interruption of damaging droughts.

It is in no way intended to be a comprehensive list of all the good garden plants which one could grow given damp conditions. There are bound to be favourite plants missing. Neither do I include aquatics. The following are the plants which I grow, and have come to know in my own garden with its rather special conditions.

ACHILLEA, Compositae. Most achilleas do not qualify for entry in these lists. Some of the larger species, ideally suited for filling large gaps in the herbaceous border, do prefer a retentive soil, but can hang on in something less than ideal. One which deserves deep rich soil in sun is:

decolorans 'W. B. Child' (*A. serrata*), said to be of Swiss origin. In spring it forms neat, tidy, non-running clumps of fresh green finely cut leaves. By June it is a white bouquet swaying elegantly on the edge of a border. Each wide lace-like head is made of many flowers held in a flat loose cluster, poised on thin stalks, furnished with finely fretted leaves. Each composite flower has a dark green eye which slowly turns to greenish-white, surrounded by chalk-white ray florets. There is nothing daintier or more prolific for picking in armsful for a June wedding or enjoying as it stands. If cut down when faded there will be a second crop. (2½ ft/760 mm.)

ptarmica is from the water-meadows of Eurasia. 'The Pearl', a garden form, is also good for picking, and lasts well in the garden. Pure white, double, button-shaped flowers on 2 ft/600 mm branching stems in mid summer. It is invasive, but will grow in any good retentive border soil.

ACONITUM, Ranunculaceae. Monkshood or Wolf's Bane. The flower shape strongly resembles a monk's cowled hood, but the tuberous roots are deadly poisonous if eaten. It does no harm to divide the crowded clumps occasionally, to encourage the production of strong flower stems.

× **bicolor.** A number of named garden plants shelter under this name, probably hybrids between *A. napellus* and *A variegatum*. *A. napellus* (Eurasia) covers a number of allied species, including *A. napellus* itself, with finely cut leaves and almost unbranched spikes. *A. variegatum* (Eastern Alps and Central Europe) has tall branching spikes and large flowers. Both are found in partially shaded damp places. Hybrids include 'Blue Sceptre' and 'Bressingham Spire': stiff straight spires of almost 3 ft/1 m carry deep violet-blue flowers in July–August. 'Spark's Variety', another hybrid, grows tall, 5 ft/1.5 m with open branching heads carrying darkest violet-blue flowers.

carmichaelii (*A. fischeri* of gardens) is found in stands of large herbs on the borders of damp meadows and woods with *Filipendula*, *Veratrum* and huge umbellifers in Kamchatka and Amuria. 'Arendsii' is a fine garden form of *A. carmichaelii*, superb in late September and October with large shadowed blue flowers on 5 ft/1.5 m stems. Close inspection shows kinship with the buttercup family. If you lift the top petal, which looks like a hooded cowl, you will find it is sheltering the stigma while the rest of the petals form the familiar innocent face of the buttercup surrounding the central boss.

vulparia (*A. lycoctonum*) is from woods and damp shady places in the mountains of Europe and north Asia to China. I have seen it massed in a grassy gulley in the Pyrenees, with mauvy-rose fluffy heads of *Thalictrum aquilegifolium*. Tall, about 5 ft/1.5 m, the slender branching stems carry yellowish-green flowers, not unlike little delphiniums. It flowers for weeks in late summer.

ACORUS, Araceae. The 'Sweet Flag' from east Asia and eastern North America; naturalized in Europe.

calamus grows in bog or shallow water, with long narrow blade-like leaves attached to rhizomes, very like an *Iris*. The roots and leaves are spicily scented, valued when earth floors were strewn with sweet-scented rushes. They have been used medicinally and for their perfume and restorative qualities. Dried they are still used as flavouring, among other things in toothpaste, gargles and gin.

— **'Variegatus'** makes a striking water-side plant: the handsome sword-like leaves are boldly variegated green and ivory-white, with rose-pink bases in spring. (3–4 ft/1–1.2 m.)

gramineus grows in wet places round ponds and along streams from India to China and Japan. It is much smaller and makes neat grass-like tufts, ideally suited for small ponds, sink gardens if kept moist, or even an aquarium. (5 in./130 mm.)

— **'Variegatus'** has leaves brightly variegated cream and green.

ACTAEA, Ranunculaceae. These woodland plants are admired for their graceful habit, delicately cut foliage and clusters of berries which are poisonous, hence the name Baneberry.

alba. From the forests of north-east America, this is a most extraordinary and beautiful plant when well grown. Elegant clumps of stiff slender stems are furnished with light green divided leaves. Spires of fluffy white flowers become spikes of pea-sized white berries in late summer. Each is fastened to the main stem by short stalks which are thick and crimson-red. On the side opposite to the stem each white berry has a conspicuous black dot. (2½–3 ft/760 mm–1 m.)

erythrocarpa, found in conifer woods, from east Russia to Japan, has clusters of small maroon-coloured berries.

rubra, from the woods of north-east America, makes far better plants and berries, in gardens, if grown in part shade when it is the most showy *Actaea*, with large clusters of smallish berries. They are attractive in July when jade-green, and gradually turn to gleaming scarlet, remaining handsome for weeks into early autumn. (2½ ft/760 mm.)

spicata. The British and European form, from cool conifer forests, has clusters of small black berries at the tip of 18 in./460 mm leafy stems.

ADONIS, Ranunculaceae. Choice plants for the early spring garden, with very superior buttercup-like flowers. Likes retentive soil in sun.

amurensis, from Manchuria and Amuria to Japan.

— 'Fukujukai'. The bent necks of this flower can be seen emerging in mild weather early in the New Year. The finely cut foliage and stems are purplish-brown at first but are green by the time the flower has opened its glistening yellow cup during February–March. (10 in./250 mm.)

— 'Plena', among nests of ferny foliage crouch double shining flowers with green centres. (6–10 in./150–250 mm.)

vernalis. Found in the meadow steppes of Russia, with cowslips, the shining single saucer-like flowers are ruffed with fretted leaves. (9–12 in./230–300 mm.)

AJUGA, Labiatae. Bugle. Sometimes classed as a rampant weed when well suited among the wrong companions, it needs damp soil to show its best. The dark-leafed forms colour best in an open situation.

pyramidalis. From mountain meadows and open woods in central Europe to the Altai and China. It does not run invasively but makes dense, slowly spreading clumps of dark green smooth leaves. Spikes of small vivid gentian-blue flowers are held in whorls of navy-blue bracts, looking like little pagodas in spring. (6 in./150 mm.)

reptans. Found in water-meadows, damp spots in woods (mostly oak) in Europe and west Asia.

— 'Atropurpurea' makes rosettes and runners of shining beetroot-coloured leaves with short spikes of blue flowers in spring. (5 in./130 mm.)

— **'Burgundy Glow'.** The beautiful foliage is suffused rose and magenta, edged with cream. The light blue spikes of flowers are a bonus. (4 in./100 mm.)

— **'Multicolor':** bronze foliage curiously splashed with pink and cream; only looks good when well suited in rich leaf-mould soil in semi-shade. (4 in./100 mm.)

— **'Variegata'.** The least strong-growing, best in shade or on north-facing borders. Grey-green leaves are boldly edged with cream. (2 in./50 mm.)

ALCHEMILLA, Rosaceae. Found in France, Switzerland and a few spots in Scotland. Both *A. conjuncta* and *A. erythropoda* will grow in full sun if the soil remains damp. (6 in./150 mm.)

conjuncta is closely related to *A. alpina*. It differs in that the individual leaflets, which compose the little parasol-shaped leaves, appear to be seamed halfway to the centre. The top side of each leaf is smooth dark green, the back appears to be lined with shimmering silk which just shows as a silver edge. Both leaves and small sprays of tiny green flowers are valued by flower arrangers, particularly for pressed flower pictures. In the garden the plant makes a neat low cushion, valued for its attractive foliage.

erythropoda was discovered in a piece of mountain turf brought home from Turkey by J. R. Mar. Small scallop-shell leaves of soft blue-green are set off by sprays of tiny lime-green stars which turn coral-red as they age; a pretty foliage plant by the edge of a cool walk.

mollis. Lady's Mantle is found in east European mountain meadows, making a far larger plant than the other two. The downy, rounded leaves may be 4–5 in./100–130 mm across, the radiating veins prolonged into gentle scallops whose finely serrated edges exude pearls of moisture on still humid mornings. All June and into July long sprays of frothy lime-green stars cool the wealth of colour that comes with mid summer. The flower stems are 18 in.–2 ft/460–600 mm.

ALISMA, Alismataceae.

plantago-aquatica. The Water Plantain. From shallow water and mud in the ponds and quiet streams of temperate Eurasia and North America. This plant forms clumps of smooth oval leaves standing out of the water on long stalks, from which rise stems up to 3 ft/1 m high, bearing big, open and airy pyramids of many tiny white flowers.

ALLIUM, Liliaceae.

ursinum. Ramsons. Comes from the moist woods of temperate Europe and far into Asia, often in wide drifts. This wild onion, the bulbs of which used to be eaten by the gypsies, sends up flat heads of white, starry flowers, about 10 in./250 mm high, above two broad, shiny leaves, rather like those of Lily-of-the-Valley. As they seed and multiply so readily, they soon form a carpet, and can be a nuisance in the garden, but are attractive in open woodland.

AMSONIA, Apocynaceae.

tabernaemontana (*A. salicifolia*), from north-east America. Will grow in half shade, or in full sun in moist soil. The charm of this plant lies in the curious colour of the flowers. At the top of many slender wands, set with narrow, willow-like leaves, sit dark-stemmed clusters of thin green and dark blue pointed buds which open small slate-blue stars. The effect of greenish-blue in these modest heads is appealing. They flower from June to early July. (2 ft/600 mm.)

ANAPHALIS, Compositae. It comes as a surprise to learn that these grey-leafed plants come from damp places, but by experience I have found that they wilt and deteriorate where true drought lovers, like artemisias, flourish. They need a retentive soil to keep their foliage healthy until late summer when they produce their display of tiny white everlasting daisies. All these *Anaphalis* must be picked fresh for drying before the centres have browned. When dried they are lovely, massed alone, or used as filling material among other 'drieds'.

cinnamomea (*A. yedoensis*) (also known by Japanese botanists as *A. margaritacea var. yedoensis*). *A. cinnamomea* itself is a plant of warmer climates. I am familiar with the name *Anaphalis yedoensis* which belongs to the form from Japan, where it is found in sunny places along rivers. Thin branched white-felted stems stand 2½–3 ft/760 mm–1 m, bearing broad oval dark grey leaves with pale backs and white edges, topped with loose clusters of small chalk-white everlasting daisies. Stripped of leaves, hung upside down to dry they make excellent 'drieds'. *Anaphalis margaritacea*, in its other varieties from eastern North America and north-east Asia, is similar in habit with narrower green leaves. They both flower from August to October.

triplinervis is found by rocky stream-sides in the Himalayas, sometimes with mats of pink *Polygonum*. Ideal for the edge of the border, it makes low, neat mounds of very white felted leaves which are buried beneath wide sprays of crisp white daisies, slightly larger than those of *A. yedoensis*. Flowers July to October. (12 in./300 mm.)

— **'Summer Snow'** is a selected form, slightly smaller, which flowers a little earlier. (10 in./250 mm.)

ANEMONE, Ranunculaceae. There are many anemones, spring and autumn flowering, for dry and damp soils. I shall consider first the largest and stateliest, those known as Japanese anemones. This title includes some species and many cultivars, all providing long displays throughout late summer and early autumn. They thrive in heavy soils, in sun or part shade, making colonizing clumps when ideally suited. In light soil they must have sufficient moisture throughout the growing season. The following are the species from which the garden hybrids have been developed.

hupehensis. This name is generally accepted as covering several varieties of *Anemone* as well as the type. The type is a rare species from central and west China, with rounded pink petals, darker on the reverse; the leaves are divided into three deeply toothed leaflets, producing flowers in late summer. (2 ft/600 mm.)

— japonica, naturalized in Japan from China for hundreds of years. It differs from *A. hupehensis* in having many narrow, slightly quilled petals of uniform, soft magenta-pink. (2 ft/600 mm.)

tomentosa (*A. vitifolia* of gardens). The great plant collector, E. H. Wilson, mentions *A. vitifolia* as growing with *Artemisia lactiflora*, *Astilbe rivularis*, *Aruncus* and others in openings among woods in west Sichuan. This appears to be *A. tomentosa*. It is extremely vigorous, producing sheaves of shallow saucers, pale pink inside, with deeper reverse, and flowering earlier than garden hybrids. (4 ft/1.2 m.)

vitifolia. From the Himalayas. Although this name is usually applied to *A. tomentosa*, this rare plant is smaller and more compact. The flowers are usually white. (2 ft/600 mm.)

There seems to be confusion in the naming of the above tall, closely related anemones which, in their various forms, are widespread in the Chinese mountains, extending to the Himalayas and growing in moist stony soil at the edges of woodlands and among bushes.

× **hybrida.** I take refuge under this title with the many beautiful cultivars which have been produced from among these species. Some are larger, paler in colour, or deeper. Some are double. Personally I prefer the single forms with perfectly formed round cupped petals. 'Honorine Jobert' is the unsurpassed old fashioned white, flowering for weeks in the autumn, elegant on tall stems up to 5 ft/1.5 m. There is a rose-pink form equally well shaped. For smaller gardens or border edges there are dwarfer forms, including 'September Charm'. (18 in./460 mm.)

narcissiflora. From damp mountain meadow slopes to the lowland Arctic meadows of Europe, to the Himalayas and Japan, and North America. The stems of this *Anemone* rise to a height of 8 in.–2 ft/200–600 mm, according to where it grows, from a clump of much cut leaves. At the top, each bears a cluster of white flowers, usually with rosy backs, above a green ruff of leaves.

nemorosa. Wood Anemone, of moist forests of Europe and north-west Asia. A very closely related plant is found in North America. They grow almost anywhere, preferably in part shade under trees or shrubs, in light or heavy soil but are best left undisturbed to colonize the floor of shrubbery or wood. There are several good named forms which include 'Allenii', 'Blue Bonnet' and 'Robinsoniana'. They open to the sun large shallow saucers of breath-taking blue, centred with yellow stamens, exquisite among the dark purple leaves of *Viola labradorica*. The double white is a treasure. (6 in./150 mm)

ranunculoides. From damp open woods of Europe to the Caucasus. Has smaller flowers but creates a pretty effect with yellow pointed starry petals. (4 in./100 mm.) There are paler versions, and a double form. All the wood anemones disappear by mid summer.

rivularis. From the damp, rocky subalpine meadows of the Himalayas to the mountains of west China; a close relative of *A. narcissiflora*. The white petals are backed with metallic-blue which is repeated in the blue anthers. (2 ft/600 mm.)

sylvestris. From open woods and stony hillsides of central Europe to the northern meadow-like steppes of Russia, west Siberia and the Caucasus. This spring flowering *Anemone* runs freely in light soil, is more restricted in heavy soils. Drooping white flowers of good size are followed by large clusters of creamy cotton wool which contain the seeds. (12 in./300 mm.)

ANEMONOPSIS, Ranunculaceae.

macrophylla. From mountain woods in central Japan only, and rare even there. This beautiful plant has leaves twice cut into threes, and its stems grow some 2–2½ ft/600–760 mm tall. They bear open heads of quite large, nodding, waxy flowers like those of an *Anemone*, purple outside and lilac within. I have grown this plant but lost it before I saw its full beauty, a victim of our cruel winds. I shall try again, in true woodland conditions of moist humus-rich soil in semi-shade, and *shelter from wind*.

ANGELICA, Umbelliferae.

archangelica. From damp bushland of north and Arctic Europe and Green-land. A handsome Cow Parsley, whose smooth and tender stems are boiled and candied to make cake decorations. It needs deep moist soil to produce a large leafy plant with branching stems holding several large, domed heads of light green flowers. It looks very statuesque in the bog garden, overtopping most things. The seed heads should be removed before they have seeded into everything. Not a perennial, it may take two or three years to flower, seed and die. (6 ft/2 m.)

AQUILEGIA, Ranunculaceae. There are multitudes of aquilegias, both species and hybrids. Some enjoy sun, others prefer cool shade; most relish well-drained but not dried-out soil.

alpina. From the Alps and north Italian mountains, in rocky bushy places. Deep blue, sometimes blue and white. (2–3 ft/600 mm–1 m.)

— × vulgaris. Found in woods and thickets in the Alps, Europe, Siberia and the Himalayas. These crosses include many shades of blue, rich plum, soft pink and white. The blue-green foliage is as handsome as the flowers, especially late in the year when tinted with shades of purple. Excellent in shade or semi-shade, to follow spring bulbs. May–June. (2½ ft/760 mm.)

canadensis, from the north-eastern United States and Canada in rocky woods, this plant is similarly coloured to *A. formosa truncata* but smaller, and with a larger central yellow bell of petals. (2 ft/600 mm.)

chrysantha, from the open woods of the southern Rockies. All soft yellow with long spurs, it is one of the species from which the long-spurred hybrids were raised, and is a vigorous plant, growing up to 3 ft/1 m high.

coerulea, from grassy openings in spruce woods and in aspen copses of the central Rocky Mountains. Blue and white flowers, long-spurred. (12–15 in./300–380 mm.)

flabellata 'Pumila', from alpine rocky turfs of north Japan, north Korea and Sakhalin.

— **'Akitensis'** is a larger cultivated form. Beautiful leaves, rounded and blue-green, make a setting for short-stemmed rounded flowers which are blue and white, distinctive and charming. (10–12 in./250–300 mm.)

— **'Nana Alba'.** A white form with thick petalled creamy-white flowers. (10 in./250 mm.)

formosa truncata grows in the shade or part shade of wood openings in the Californian mountains and the Rockies south from Alaska. One of the daintiest, with multitudes of nodding flowers, brilliant scarlet and yellow on much-branched stems. The pistil and stamens extend well below the pointed scarlet sepals giving a sharp dart-like effect as the long spurs end in a very short circle of petals. May–August. (2½–3 ft/760 mm–1 m.)

longissima, from partially shady rocky slopes on the last spur of the Rockies in west Texas. The flowers are almost white, with very long spurs. July–October. (2 ft/760 mm.)

HYBRID STRAINS

The long-spurred garden aquilegias are hybrids of the western American species. It is difficult to keep a particular strain pure from seed, as they cross very freely, but the progeny are nearly all beautiful. A few named hybrids have been inbred recently, and are more reliably true from seed, for example 'Crimson Star' and the McKana hybrids.

ARISAEMA, Araceae. Members of the Arum family, valued for foliage, flowers and berries. Most of them need plenty of humus in semi-shaded retentive soil.

candidissimum. From rocky slopes and cliff ledges in west China. The great plant collector, G. Forrest, first found it on the sides of the upper Yangtze gorge in Yunnan. One of the latest plants to appear through the soil. Not

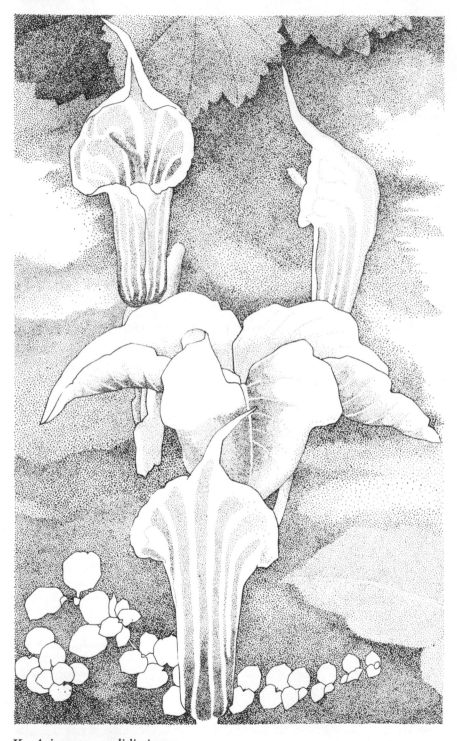

K. *Arisaema candidissimum*

until June do the bare pink stems appear, opening into the narrow spathe which is white-veined and shadowed with pink and green on the outside, pink and white candy striped inside. The pointed tip overhangs the white spadix, sheltering it from the rain. Neatly wrapped round the base of the stem is a single leaf which unfolds surprisingly large, three-lobed, like a great clover leaf. A mound of them is very handsome, especially in autumn when they turn the colour of chamois leather. This plant will grow in an open situation, provided it is planted in good retentive soil, but is best sheltered from wind. (Flowers 6 in./150 mm; leaves 3–9 in./80–230 mm long and wide.)

consanguineum. Found in moist wood openings and among bushes, from the Himalayas to the west and central Chinese mountains. Like a very elegant umbrella, supported on 18 in./460 mm long slender stems mottled green and brown. The green hooded flower, striped with brown, extends a long thin brown tail from the tip of the spathe to hang down in front. Does better in the moist and warm gardens of the West Country.

triphyllum. Jack in the Pulpit. From rich woods in the eastern United States north to Nova Scotia. For cool shady places. The markings on the spathe vary in intensity. Basically green, the stripes inside are light or dark purplish-brown, lit with palest green. Intensifying the colour is the dark spadix protected beneath the overhanging spathe tip. Orange-red berries seed themselves in favourable sites. June–July. (1 ft/300 mm.)

ARISARUM, Araceae.

proboscideum, from shady moist slopes in the Apennines. The Mouse-tailed Arum is well named: tiny tubers increase readily beneath humus-rich soil, sending up dense clusters of small shining green leaves. Hidden among them are tiny flowers, white inside with brown backs, the spathe tips extended into long thin tails which poke out among the leaves as though tiny mice had dived in, head first, to hide. Best in shade, near the edge of a path where you can stoop to see them. May. (4 in./100 mm.)

ARNICA, Compositae.

montana. From alpine and subalpine turf in the mountains of central Europe and northern Asia, this plant produces handsome orange daisy flowers, long petalled and strangely scented. A distillation produces Tincture of Arnica, used to soothe bruises. June. (1 ft/300 mm.)

ARTEMISIA, Compositae.

lactiflora. Grows in moist meadows and forest clearings in the mountains of western China, often with tall anemones, *Aruncus, Astilbe rivularis* and others. It is the odd man out in a family, most of whom are adapted to drought conditions. Tall stems up to 5 ft/1.5 m carry jagged green leaves topped with large loose heads of small creamy-white flowers, effective among the autumn aconites or Japanese anemones.

ARUM, Araceae.

italicum. Found in woods and among bushes on rich soil, from Spain to the Caucasus and Morocco to Tunisia.

— **'Pictum'** (of gardens). Narrow, spear-shaped, glossy and dark green leaves are vividly veined and marbled with creamy-green, edged with an undulating narrow green border. Unrivalled winter foliage lasting until late May when large pale green spathes can be found hidden among the leaves. By June all has vanished. Large spikes of juicy scarlet berries emerge from the bare soil in September–October. (18 in./460 mm.)

I have another similar *Arum* which is, I think, called *A.* 'Marmoratum' by gardeners, although I have had that name disputed. It has much larger and broader leaves of brighter green with only the main veins narrowly picked out with cream. It increases more slowly but when established makes important-looking piles of leaves so needed in late winter and spring as contrast to many small things.

ARUNCUS, Rosaceae.

dioicus (*A. sylvester*). Goat's Beard. Grows in mountain woods and along shady stream-sides from central Europe to China and Japan; also in North America. Makes a superb garden plant from the moment its elegant sprays of light green pinnate leaves emerge in spring. I like it best just as the flowers are opening. Long tapering spires of tiny green buds become cream seed pearls, finally bursting into a plume of creamy frothy blossom, towards the end of June. Male plants make superior flowers, but females produce graceful chestnut-brown seed heads. (5–6 ft/1.5–2 m.)

— **'Kneiffii'.** Flowers similar to *A. dioicus* but daintier, as is the whole plant. The leaves look as though they have been eaten to the veins by some creature but perversely (perhaps because it is the natural state) these thread-like segments appear delicately attractive. Flowers slightly later. (2–2½ ft/600–760 mm.)

ASARUM, Aristolochiaceae. Mostly hardy plants for shady places in leaf-mould soil, grown primarily for their foliage.

caudatum. Grows in deep conifer woods, often along streams, in the coastal mountains from central California to British Columbia. The leaves are somewhat heart-shaped and matt green, while curious reddish-brown flowers with three tail-like tips lie flat on the ground, hidden among the leaves. (3–4 in./80–100 mm.)

europaeum. Covers the floor of central European, Scandinavian, Russian and west Siberian woods, as ivy does in British woods. Round kidney-shaped leaves of rich glossy green on slowly creeping surface shoots eventually make almost evergreen carpets. Dull brown flowers crouch unseen except by fertilizing flies and beetles. (3–4 in./80–100 mm.)

ASTER, Compositae. An enormous genus of daisy-like flowers, including many large and small perennial plants, including alpines. Michaelmas Daisies are included among the large perennials. They can only look their best in good deep soil with adequate moisture throughout the growing season. Some of the old fashioned hybrids remain the healthiest, less prone to disease, with less floppy stems. Garden hybrids have been evolved from among the following species:

amellus. From rather dry open woods and rocky grasslands of central Europe to Asia Minor and the northern meadow-like steppes of Russia. The wild form is scarcely known, but many named selected forms exist, very varied in quality. The general habit is low growing with rough leaves and clusters of large flowers in many shades from lavender to violet, including various pinks. Some stand well, others flop untidily. A familiar named form is 'King George'. It is also one of the parents of the hybrid *A.* × *frikartii* 'Mönch'. (2 ft/600 mm.)

divaricatus (*A. corymbosus*), found in open woodlands and thickets. Standing drier conditions than many other asters, this plant comes from southern Canada and the eastern United States. It has taken me some time and several plantings to appreciate this, one of the first Michaelmas Daisy-like plants to flower. It produces quantities of very thin, rather floppy branching stems which are almost black and make good contrast with clouds of tiny, white star-like flowers. But initially the flowers look just too small to be effective. However, gradually they expand a little more, and as they age they flush lilac-mauve, starting at their pointed tips until they are suffused to their central darkened hearts. I learnt from Gertrude Jekyll to group them among bergenias which they soften with pretty disarray, from mid August and into September. (2 ft/600 mm.)

ericoides (*A. multiflorus*). This *Aster* grows in dry but rich soil in the eastern United States and Canada, and is also common in the prairies. *A. ericoides* and *A. multiflorus* are sometimes separated into two species, *A. multiflorus* growing further south and west. There are many varieties, with almost no disadvantages. They make compact clumps of fine wiry stems covered with tiny leaves, branching into airy heads smothered with tiny starry flowers. They rarely need staking, and are seldom affected by disease. They come both short- and tall-flowering, late into the autumn. (3–4 ft/1–1.2 m.)

× **frikartii 'Mönch'** (*A. amellus* × *A. thomsonii*) (*A. thomsonii* is from the west Himalayas). Each individual stem (3 ft/1 m) produces seven or eight side branches starting from the base, all carrying further branching heads of flowers. An established clump will send up many such stems resulting in a wide-spreading elegant bouquet of flowers which lasts for months (August–October), somehow never looking untidy with dead flowers. Individual flowers are 2½ in./60 mm across, warm lavender-blue with yellowish-green centres. Absolutely the best Michaelmas Daisy, for long display and sheer beauty: does not need staking, and is not affected by mildew. Deserves the best soil and position in the garden.

lateriflorus is found in damp or dry but rich meadows and prairies of the eastern and central United States and Canada.

— 'Horizontalis' is so stiffly twiggy it appears almost like a small shrub, covered all summer with small dark green leaves, the whole smothered by October with tiny starry flowers, silver-lilac petals centred with large bosses of clover-pink stamens. Good near autumn-flowering colchicums. (2 ft/600 mm.)

novae-angliae. From damp sunny meadows and along swamp edges in the north-eastern and north-central United States and Canada. This is the hairy parent of many garden hybrids, needing sunlight to open its incurved petals, but producing healthy disease-free offspring with tall stiff sturdy stems, up to 6 ft/2 m. The type has mauve flowers, but good clear pink shades include 'Harrington's Pink'. 'Alma Potschke' is more recent, compact and low growing (2½ ft/760 mm) with startling cherry-pink flowers.

novi-belgii. From swampy places where it is frequent near the Atlantic from Newfoundland to Georgia. It has smooth green leaves on slender elegant stems (4 ft/1.2 m) topped with large pyramidal sprays of cool blue flowers. Self-sown seedlings vary; some are rather wishy-washy. Modern named varieties tend to have developed the flower at the expense of the plant—too large, too double flowers proving overweighty for the stems which have to be supported. But the colours are often lovely, from white through shades of pink to lavenders and blue. Among the trouble-free old varieties are 'Climax' (5–6 ft/1.5–2 m) with single mid-blue flowers, and 'Blue Gown' which flowers a little later.

tradescantii (of gardens) (*A. paniculatus*). The wild plant is *A. paniculatus*, growing in moist meadows in the eastern USA and Canada. It is very similar to *A. ericoides* but although larger overall (4 ft/1.25 m) the flowers and leaves are even smaller, large sprays of tiny white flowers lasting until the frosts.

There are many different alpine asters. I select one of the best for general purposes, ideal to edge a border.

yunnanensis, from alpine grasslands of the south-west Chinese mountains. Tufts of hairy leaves produce many erect stems (9 in./230 mm), each bearing a solitary blue daisy flower.

— 'Napsbury'. This garden form achieves great effect: large blue flowers are lit with warm orange centres.

ASTILBE, Saxifragaceae. Astilbes must have rich garden soil which remains moist (not waterlogged). Most look well and do better in partial shade. The species provides dwarfs as well as tall plants, so there is great choice among the many hybrids, for size as well as shades. Their rusty-brown seed heads in late summer and autumn are almost as effective as their tapering panicles of tiny flowers. The following are the few species I grow:

chinensis. From moist rocky slopes among woods in the northern Chinese mountains, north to Amuria, Manchuria and Korea.

— **'Pumila'** is a selected garden form, ideal for moist edges. Narrow branched spikes of densely set, rose flowers with blue anthers produce a mauve-pink effect. I like the narrow, stiffly upright silhouettes which continue until winter as buff seed heads. Carpets of broadly spreading foliage make useful ground-cover. (15–18 in./380–460 mm.)

davidii. Found in moist, shady places in Sichuan with *Geranium napuligerum*, *Ligularia dentata*, *Adenophora*, etc. It is similar to *A. taquetii*, but has slimmer spires of flower.

rivularis. Growing in lush valley meadows and wood edges from the Himalayas to the west Chinese mountains, this giant *Astilbe* is for the wild garden, or for large-scale water-side planting (not in the bog). Great stems of broad divided leaves, glossy above, bristly beneath, are so heavily veined they produce a quilted effect. In August it is overtopped with huge arching plumes of small greenish-white flowers which last long as nut-brown seed heads. Underground shoots could be a nuisance in a restricted area. (6 ft/2 m.)

taquetii. From eastern China.

— **'Superba'** is the garden form. It flowers when other astilbes have finished. This *Astilbe*, and *A. davidii*, can do with less moisture (but not drought) and will take more sun than the others, but they will also flower and look superb in partial shade. *A.t.* 'Superba' has smallish crinkled leaves tinged with bronze. The flower head, supported on a dark mahogany stem, held well above the leaves, elongates into a dense compound spire made up of thousands of deep mauve fluffy flowers. (4 ft/1.2 m.)

HYBRIDS

× **arendsii.** This group name, commemorating Georg Arends of Ronsdorf, covers many garden hybrids raised since 1907 between four species. These are the Chinese *A. davidii*, and three Japanese species, *A. astilboides*, *A. japonica* and *A. thunbergii*. Through these four, the differing characteristics have been introduced. Some, especially the dark red-flowered varieties, have beautiful, translucent, mahogany-tinted foliage which adds colour to the garden immediately it appears, remaining dark-tinted all summer. The flower colours range from white, through shell-pink, rose-pink and salmon to red and magenta. The shapes of the spires vary as well—some are short and stocky, some tall slender pyramids, others make graceful recurving panicles. The following hybrid is less frequently seen but suits my garden:

'Professor van der Wielen'. This large graceful plant is well provided with handsome leaves, topped with arching sprays of creamy-white flowers. August. (4 ft/1.2 m.)

A group of dwarf hybrids has *A. simplicifolia* among several parents. *A. simplicifolia* comes from central Pacific Japan where it is rare. The group includes the following very popular plants:

'Bronze Elegance'. Very attractive bronze-tinted, shining green leaves are topped with short arching sprays which open creamy-salmon flowers, fading to deep rose. (12 in./300 mm.)

'Sprite'. Much-divided leaves, chocolate-bronze when young, slowly changing to very dark green, the setting for wide triangular sprays of pale, shell-pink, fluffy flowers. They last for weeks, imperceptibly deepening to chestnut and finally reddish-brown seed heads—most welcome in the autumn border. August–November. (15–18 in./380–460 mm.)

ASTRANTIA, Umbelliferae. Masterwort. The flowers of *Astrantia* are modestly charming at a distance, quite entrancing close to: branching stems are topped with a continuous display of posy flowers, each consisting of a dry-textured ruff of petal-like bracts, the centre filled with tiny quivering fertile flowers. If you press your thumb into the centre it lies flat like the spokes of a wheel, making a perfect flat shape for dried pictures, not messily squashed. They will grow in part shade or open borders provided there is adequate moisture.

carniolica. From subalpine turfs of the eastern Alps.

— 'Rubra' is the form grown in gardens. Smaller than other astrantias, about 18 in./460 mm high, sometimes I think it a dull plant until I look more closely. The flowers are a sombre burgundy-red with tufts of stamens the same shade tipping the jade-green seed cases which fill the centre. My plants often look best in autumn when moister soil and a little shade encourage a fresh crop of flowers, perfectly formed, the buds glowing ruby-red, and a low sun shining through the opened 'petals' like stained glass.

major. From subalpine meadows and open woods of the central European mountains.

— 'Alba'. I collected my form from a roadside ditch in the Auvergne. Similar to 'Shaggy', with petals not quite so long or narrow, but larger than 'Margery Fish'. It starts flowering in midsummer, continues until late autumn. (2½ ft/760 mm.)

— involucrata 'Shaggy' can produce flowers more than 2 in./50 mm across with long narrow white 'petals', more widely separated with green pointed tips. (2½ ft/760 mm.)

— 'Margery Fish'. A specially good selected form which flowers for months throughout the summer and autumn. Rose-pink buds open to show white 'petals' with sharp green tips surrounding the central boss of tiny fertile flowers which remain as little pink tufts on top of the fat green seeds developing beneath them. Creates a fresh country look, in the garden or picked. (2½ ft/760 mm.)

— **'Sunningdale Variegated'**. One of the most handsome of variegated foliage plants: leaves shaped like deeply cut sycamore leaves. In spring, deep green floods the centres, washing out towards the edges and tips which are vividly pale green and cream, a striking feature for several weeks. Then, as the flower stems mature, in June, the leaves darken to green all over. Flowers similar to 'Margery Fish' are produced continuously until late autumn, making two seasons of interest from this fine feature plant. (2½ ft/760 mm.)

maxima. From rich moist subalpine meadows and wood edges of the Caucasus, found in well-watered rocky gullies with giant *Heracleum*, *Cephalaria*, etc., or in open meadows with *Scabiosa caucasica*, *Veronica gentianoides* and others. This plant has broader and fewer 'petals' of even rose-pink inside, bitter-green on reverse, filled with rose-pink fertile tufts. The leaves are smaller and rounder, divided into three parts. It increases by thin white underground shoots so making slowly invasive clumps in the right soil and conditions; hopeless in poor sandy soil. A very choice and beautiful plant. (2½ ft/760 mm.)

BERGENIA, Saxifragaceae. Megasea or Saxifrage. Although bergenias will tolerate drier conditions than hostas, the damp garden would be deprived without them. It is interesting to note where they come from, which indicates, I think, that they are not meant for the really hot spots. Apart from the species there are many hybrids. The flowers are handsome but it is primarily the foliage, large, rounded and evergreen, that I value most. With the new hybrids much emphasis is on those which colour well in winter. For the best colouring they need full exposure and soil not over-rich in humus. While the crimson tones are superb on my light soils, they are also rich, but darker, in the clay garden. Regretfully the display of flower we should have in April from some species is sometimes spoilt by late frost. When undamaged massed blossoms of *Bergenia* are a beautiful and long-lasting sight.

ciliata. Comes from Nepal, Kashmir and west Pakistan, where it is found on damp rocky slopes among woods. The large rounded leaves are densely covered on both sides with short fine hairs, softly furry to touch, matt dark green to look at. Well placed against a wall or warm corner they are distinctively good-looking all summer. But the first sharp frost destroys them, although the stout rhizomes are unharmed. Palest pink flowers are set off by cherry-red calyces, but too often are reduced to brown pulp by the cold of our 'blackthorn winter'. (1 ft/300 mm.)

— **ligulata** is found filling wet side-gorges in the lower forest zone of the

Himalayas in the open or part shade. I do not possess this but, while similar to *B. ciliata*, its leaves have a hairy margin, the flowers are slightly flushed pink, and all are susceptible to frost.

cordifolia. Comes from Siberia. One of the largest leafed species: large, rounded, leathery green leaves, slightly puckered with crinkled edges, and large heavy sprays of light pink flowers in April. (18 in./460 mm.)

— **'Purpurea'.** Large smooth leaves, with wavy edges, are green all summer, except for the odd ones which turn bright red or yellow, usually in late summer, before they decide to die. The rest remain, to assume warm bronze and magenta tones as the weather grows colder. The tall flower stems (18 in./460 mm) looking like sticks of rhubarb are topped in May with close-set heads of vivid magenta flowers which some find shocking and are, if scarlet tulips are nearby. Not so free flowering as some, but odd blooms appear again in late summer.

crassifolia. From moist openings in larch-pine forests, up to the subalpine meadows of the Altai and Trans-Baikal mountains of Siberia. Large oval or spoon-shaped leaves produce even brighter winter colour. I have just picked leaves with surfaces ranging from cherry-red to rich plum, with reverse sides a glowing carmine-red, a wonderful sight, these vivid patches of colour against emerald winter grass. Flowers in May on slender stems, dainty sprays of pale lavender-pink. (15 in./380 mm.)

purpurascens. From moist rocky, bushy slopes in the Himalayas to the mountains of the China-Tibet borderlands. Most bergenias tend to hold their leaves horizontally in large rosettes which, closely packed, make useful ground-cover. In summer *B. purpurascens* has dark green, narrow tapering leaves held straight upright, quite useless as ground-cover, but perfectly designed to show off their superb winter colour. A slight twist to the leaves further aids the display, deep beetroot, almost liver-red on the polished surface, with lighter carmine-tinted backs for contrast. The flower stems are slender, cherry-red, topped with drooping clusters of brownish-pink flowers. (18 in./460 mm.)

I have a seedling given to me by Eric Smith, with *B. purpurascens* and *B. cordifolia* 'Purpurea' as parents. It has the colour of the former and the generous curvaceous shape of the latter. In a bed of many new hybrids it stands out easily as the best foliage form.

stracheyi. From grassy, bouldery slopes, often among dwarf rhododendrons, on the Himalayas. This is a little thing by comparison. Small rounded leaves about 3 in./80 mm long make neat rosettes. Pure white flowers with green eyes and calyces crouch low in tight clusters among the leaves. Appearing in March they are too often caught by frost.

HYBRIDS

Well-known hybrids include:

'Abendglut', 'Evening Glow', which makes smallish, flattened rosettes of rounded slightly crinkled leaves, very dark-toned in winter. Flowers appear intermittently in spring and early summer (a few more in autumn), arching sprays of wide open crimson-pink flowers.

'Beethoven' is another Eric Smith plant. Leaves and flower clusters are twice the size, a really first-rate pure white form, when the weather permits.

× **schmidtii,** possibly the most generally known hybrid—not the most interesting. Flowers very early, often in February if the weather is right, tucked deep among the leaves, gradually emerging with quite large sprays of soft pink flowers if undamaged. It has rather flat oval green leaves which never change colour. (12 in./300 mm.)

'Silberlicht', 'Silver Light'. I think this plant varies from year to year. The flowers open white, enhanced by soft chocolate-brown calyces. As they age they become suffused with pink—sometimes. But other years the pink tinge comes much sooner. I suspect it may be caused by cold weather. The flat smooth leaves remain green in winter. (12 in./300 mm.)

BRUNNERA, Boraginaceae (*Anchusa myosotidiflora*).

macrophylla. A woodland plant from the summer-green forest of the Caucasus mountains facing the Black Sea, and along its coast. In spring wide sprays of tiny forget-me-not-sized blue flowers are held above the heart-shaped leaves developing beneath them. As the flowers fade the leaves become a feature, large as tea plates, matt and dark green. Although they will do in comparatively dry shade they are finest where the soil does not dry out.

— **'Hadspen Cream'.** Another good plant from Eric Smith. Light green leaves are irregularly bordered with deep cream which dissolves partly into the central zone. Easier to produce perfect leaves, and gentler in colouring than *B.m.* 'Variegata', but does need part shade and good soil. (18 in./460 mm.)

— **'Langtrees'** was given to me by Dr Tony Rogerson; the name commemorates his garden in Devon. Large dark green leaves are evenly marked with a border of silvery-white spots which look as if they had been applied with a brushful of metallic paint. (18 in./460 mm.)

— **'Variegata'.** The central zone is marbled greyish-dark green, irregularly bordered with ivory-white; sometimes almost the whole leaf is white. It must have a sheltered shaded site with sufficient moisture. The variegation is delicate and browns easily. (18 in./460 mm.)

BUPHTHALMUM, Compositae (*B. cordifolium, Telekia speciosa*).

speciosum. Common in moist woods and along streams in south-east Europe to the Caucasus. A grand plant for large-scale planting, creating wide mounds of large, heart-shaped, aromatic leaves. Large fine-rayed yellow daisies are displayed for weeks in mid summer. It is handsome as a feature plant in rough-cut grass. (5 ft/1.5 m.)

BUTOMUS umbellatus, Butomaceae. Flowering Rush, of Europe and temperate western Asia. It prefers a free root run in shallow water, but is best confined in a large pot in a small pool. But then it must be replanted annually or it will give up flowering. Above narrow sword-shaped leaves stand tall (3–4 ft/1–1.2 m) flower stems. Shaped much like an *Allium* flower head, the green and maroon-stained buds open pale pink flowers, with dark centres, held upwards on irregular-length stems. They make good seed heads with upturned red-brown capsules.

CALLA palustris, Araceae. Found around and in ponds and quiet water in northern Europe, Siberia, eastern Canada and the north-east USA. Long rhizome-like stems float at the water's edge, anchoring themselves in the mud or bank-side by string-like roots which dangle from the undersides. Small, shiny, heart-shaped leaves clothe the stems which do not flower until the second year. Small greenish-white arum-like flowers in May are followed sometimes by small round clusters of red berries. A useful plant to mask the pond edge. (3–4 in./80–100 mm.)

CALTHA, Ranunculaceae. Buttercup-like plants for very wet soil.

leptosepala, from wet subalpine and alpine stream-sides in the Rocky mountains—Alberta and Oregon to Arizona. Slow-growing and comparatively rare, it has white flowers and dark stems. (9–12 in./230–300 mm.)

minor (*C. palustris minor, C. radicans*). A mountain plant from Scotland and northern England, useful because, although a little smaller, it flowers when the others have finished. (12 in./300 mm.)

palustris. The King Cup or Marsh Marigold, common in marshy meadows and sometimes wet woods throughout Europe, northern and central Asia and North America. One of our best native plants, it is still to be found along river banks, stream-sides through open woods or low-lying wet meadows. Best suited perhaps for the larger garden pond, it makes a large graceful mound of shining rounded leaves, with brownish branching stems covered with single flowers filled with rich yellow stamens. (18 in./460 mm.)

— **'Alba'.** From the Himalayas, this plant looks and behaves so differently one could imagine it belonged to a separate species. Early in February the first rounded buds are pushed through the mud to open green-centred white flowers of appealing purity. Whatever the weather the flowers keep coming, creating a dome of white blossoms by the water-side. By April seeds are already formed but there are still fresh flowers and many more buds to come, tucked down in the damp shadowed clumps of neat round leaves. (15 in./380 mm.)

— **'Flore Pleno',** the very popular double form. I like to look closely at the individual flowers: five broad yellow sepals support a packed heart of crimped petals, green-centred when young. Although very compact, and much more suitable for small areas, it is almost too packed with colour for my taste, but the shining mounds of foliage make good ground-cover for the rest of the year. (12 in./300 mm.)

polypetala. Found along brooks and by springs in the Caucasus mountains. A joy for large soggy areas, or by lake-sides where it will soon fling out large rafts of round, saucer-sized leaves from the bank-sides. It never makes a brassy display, but individual stems hold out larger-than-usual flowers for your inspection, continuing this pleasing habit for many weeks, in spring and early summer. (2 ft/600 mm.)

CAMASSIA, Liliaceae. Bulbous plants which make handsome vertical features in early summer, either naturalized or in a border to create effect. They will not thrive in poor dry land.

cusickii. From damp meadows in Oregon. Very large bulbs produce long wavy leaves about 1 in./25 mm wide and 15 in./380 mm long. Smooth flower stems grow up to 3 ft/1 m, topped with spires of ice-blue narrow-petalled star-shaped flowers.

esculenta (*C. quamash*). Grows in wet meadows and along stream banks in colonies, on the Rockies and mountains from British Columbia to Utah and central California. It has blue flowers varying in intensity, as has *C. cusickii*, and there is some confusion in gardens concerning the two. But the bulb of *C. quamash* is a staple article of diet for the Northern Indians. The bulbs, about 1 in./25 mm in diameter, are placed in baskets in a kind of 'Dutch Oven' in which the leaves of *Lysichitum* are included. There they are cooked slowly in hot steam and left to cool, when they will have dissolved into a kind of flour from which bread is made. When boiled in water the bulbs also yield a kind of molasses. (12 in./300 mm.)

leichtlinii. Common in damp or rather sandy meadows near the coast of British Columbia, it seeds itself readily in rich damp soil. Tall slender spires of cream-coloured, almost waxen flowers can be allowed to raise themselves in gaps among low shrubs or rounded mounds of plants. It apparently comes in blue forms, but I have not met them. I do have:

— **'Plena',** where every single blossom has become a packed rosette of creamy-yellow, longer lasting than the single form, less delicate, but very impressive. They increase slowly, which makes them doubly desirable, being choice and beautiful. (2½–3 ft/760 mm–1 m.)

CAMPANULA, Campanulaceae. Another huge genus containing species for moist conditions. The following are a few which wilt in my dry garden, but do well where the soil does not dry out.

'Burghaltii', a hybrid, related to *C. punctata*. A tangle of underground shoots send up slender stems hung with long pale-washed grey-blue bells,

2–3 in./50–80 mm long which have unfolded themselves from dark purple-pleated buds. The gradations of subtle colour, together with the size of blooms, draw attention to this lovely plant. It will grow in sun, in well-fed soil. First flowers in early summer, often a second crop in autumn. (2 ft/600 mm.)

lactiflora. From well-watered gullies between the upper forests on the Caucasus, with *Heracleum*, *Cephalaria*, *Buphthalmum* and other large plants. Glorious in good soil, the stout leafy stems each support a huge bouquet of hundreds of open bell flowers, to be found in several shades of blue, including a white form. Plants stopped in May will flower later, so the season can last from July to the end of September. For full sun or part shade. (4–5 ft/1.2–1.5 m.)

latifolia. Grows in moist woods in northern Europe to central Siberia, and in damp mountain gullies further south to the Caucasus. Strong basal clumps produce stiff upright stems with large, rather nettle-like leaves. They are smaller in the top half where long tubular flowers almost 3 in./80 mm long, in good forms, are set in the axils of the leaves. Variable from seed, there are selected forms, shades from violet-blue to palest mauve. My favourite is white with extra large bells, placed against dark background, or in cool shade. (3–4 ft/1–1.2 m.)

latiloba is found in central Siberia in moist open or part-shaded places. It makes mats of rosettes on the ground of which the strongest send up flower spikes. The only form I have is 'Percy Piper', close set for more than half the length of stem, with rich blue, flat, saucer-shaped flowers, each containing a blue ovary, like a jewel, from which protrudes a three-branched blue stigma. (2–2½ ft/600–760 mm.) There is a pale pink form too, but the one I covet is 'Alba'.

punctata. Of grassy slopes in the hills and mountains of Japan and north China. I include this plant because, although seldom seen, it is thought to be a parent of *C*. 'Burghaltii'. It has large tubular flowers of creamy-white or mauve, spotted with red. (12 in./300 mm.)

trachelium. Nettle-leafed Bellflower or Coventry Bells. A spreading plant, valued in the wild or where there is ample room for its leafy stems which carry wide bells in the top half. Double forms are good, in white and lilac—in summer—up to 3 ft/1 m.

CARDAMINE, Cruciferae. Cuckoo Flowers, Lady's Smock, also Cress.

latifolia. From wet meadows and brook-sides in the Pyrenees and northern Spain. A larger plant than *C. pratensis*. Rich green foliage makes spreading mats in wet soil by the water-side. In spring long shaped heads of light mauve flowers (about the size and shape of Honesty) make cool contrast with pale spring foliage. (12–24 in./300–600 mm.)

pratensis. Common in wet meadows and other damp places of temperate and cold Eurasia and North America, it is usually found in gardens as the double form.

— **'Flore Pleno'.** Small, pinnate (cress-like) leaves form a flat rosette rather like a green paper doily. In May delicate stems carry a shower of tiny double pale lilac flowers, about 12 in./300 mm high. It does not set seed, but leaves lying on the wet surface sprout roots and tiny shoots which form new plants.

trifolia. From moist woods on the lower Alps and other southern mountains. A tiny charmer for the edge of a damp shady path, a damp raised bed or a cool spot in the rock garden. Roundish, three-part leaves are evergreen, becoming purple-tinted with winter cold. In early spring naked stems carrying heads of small chalk-white flowers stand above the slow spreading mat. (6 in./150 mm.)

CARDIOCRINUM, Liliaceae. Used to be called *Lilium giganteum*, but deserves to be put in a class of its own.

giganteum. Found wild in open or part-shaded glades in woods in the Himalayas and south-west Chinese mountains. It must be the event of a lifetime to see these magnificent plants in flower. It takes several years for the bulbs to reach maturity and then hollow flower stems, as much as 3 in./80 mm across at the base shoot up to about 10 ft/3 m or more. The base and lower part are clothed with large bright green glossy leaves, much like Arum Lily leaves, but heart-shaped. In July the upper half of the stem is hung with many greenish-white, trumpet-shaped flowers, some 10 in./250 mm long. When the flowers are over the leaves remain fresh until autumn, supporting the large and handsome seed cases. Finally all collapses. The bulbs which have expended this tremendous effort are exhausted and waste away, but offsets are to be found, and must be planted out in deeply prepared pits, filled with rich vegetable waste and good topsoil.

CAUTLEYA, Zingiberaceae. Related to *Canna* and *Roscoea*.

spicata. From the Himalayas.

— **'Robusta'.** For deep rich soil, in sun, but sheltered from wind. In late summer spikes of light orange flowers make bold contrast with maroon-red bracts. They are held just above the long pointed leaves, set upright against stout red-tinted stems. The black seeds which follow are enclosed in almost white cases, on erect stems. (2 ft/600 mm.)

CENTAUREA, Compositae. Most knapweeds are valued for their ability to thrive in poor soil. The following prefers something better.

macrocephala. From subalpine meadows of the Caucasus. It makes robust clumps of coarse, tongue-shaped leaves. In July the stiff flower stems are topped with large, yellow knapweed flowers which emerge from shining-brown scaly buds. Strong enough for the wild garden, it is effective as a background for something lighter in a border. (3–4 ft/1–1.2 m.)

CEPHALARIA gigantea, Dipsacaceae (*C. tatarica* of gardens). Widespread in rich, moist, subalpine meadows of the Caucasus, this is a great gawky plant but intriguing where room can be found for it. Stout enough for rough-cut grass, a tough rootstock produces a base of large, handsomely divided leaves. Branched stems are flung well above the final leaves ending in primrose-coloured, scabious-like flowers with green centres, occurring on and off until autumn. (6–7 ft/2–2.25 m.)

CHELONE, Scrophulariaceae. The name is derived from the Greek for turtle.

obliqua. From marshy places in eastern North America, sometimes in part shade. It adds rich colour—a warm cyclamen-pink—and an unusual shape to the autumn garden, provided the soil remains moist. Dark green leafy stems are topped with a tapering cluster of buds which, as they swell and open, resemble the wide gaping head of a turtle. When the terminal flowers have faded new buds open down the stem to prolong the season from mid August to October. By then the spikes of fat green seed pods remain, interesting in the garden or picked. (2½–3 ft/760 mm–1 m.)

CHIASTOPHYLLUM, Crassulaceae.

oppositifolium (*Cotyledon simplicifolia*). In crevices of limestone cliffs, sometimes part shady, of the basal slopes of the Caucasus facing the Black Sea; often with ferns and *Sedum stoloniferum*. It is very attractive in a cool crevice on the rock garden, or a shaded raised bed which does not dry out in summer. Rounded fleshy leaves, scallop-edged, look healthy all the year round: 4–6 in./100–150 mm stems carry drooping sprays of bright yellow flowers in June.

CHRYSANTHEMUM, Compositae.

coccineum. From the mountain meadows of the Caucasus and north Iran, this plant is widely cultivated and improved, grown under the name *Pyrethrum roseum*. In the wild its large, yellow-disced, single daisies vary from nearly white to rose, above clumps of ferny leaves, but it may be carmine in garden forms. It grows 1–2 ft/300–600 mm tall.

maximum. The Shasta Daisy, from the Pyrenees. I dare not get involved with the many named garden forms which have been evolved from the original, large, single white daisy. They include single forms with either good broad petals or finely shredded ray-like petals, or they can be semi-double with interesting centres, or entirely double like pom-poms. Some are tall-stemmed, some short. Naming can be hazardous. They flower July–August, all thriving in sun, in soil which does not dry out. (2½–3 ft/760 mm–1 m.)

uliginosum, from Hungary. Another plant for damp places in the wild garden, or in the border with Michaelmas daisies and *Aconitum*. Loose clusters of chalk-white, green-eyed daisies, each 2 in./50 mm or more across, are held on top of tall leafy 6 ft/2 m stems. Their freshness is welcome in the short days of October–November, provided they have been placed to face the sun: they will turn their backs to you if the sun is behind them.

CHRYSOGONUM, Compositae.

virginianum. From the USA where it grows in rich soil. It might be ignored if it did not flower so persistently. It makes a low-growing modest plant with slightly bristly, tooth-edged leaves on reddish stems which carry star-like five-petalled flowers of bright canary-yellow with brown dots of stamens, for weeks, all summer—a modest edge to a border. (6 in./150 mm.)

CIMICIFUGA, Ranunculaceae. Bugbane. In my garden these are choosy plants, only thriving in precious areas of moist shade. Moist soil in full sun will not do; the leaves, especially of *C. simplex*, scorch horribly. Well grown they are among the most elegant and beautiful of late summer-autumn plants.

cordifolia (*C. americana*). From the woods of eastern North America. One of the first to flower, with broad cut leaves, rather like the Japanese Anemone, but lighter green. Tall stiff stems carry tapering spires of brown buds which open pale cream fluffy flowers in August. (5 ft/1.5 m.)

racemosa. Grows in rich woods in the north-eastern USA. With fresh green divided leaves and very long wands of pure white flowers, this is the first to flower, in July. (5 ft/1.5 m.)

simplex, sometimes listed as *C. foetida intermedia*. From mountain meadows to alpine regions of Japan, also in Sakhalin and Kamchatka. There are two named forms of this found in gardens, both are treasures.

— **'Elstead Variety'** has finely divided dark green leaves. In September tall thin stems stained purple divide and carry spires of purplish-brown buds opening pure white flowers which are fixed close to the stem with tiny pink stalks giving just that touch of warmth which is missing in the icy purity of *C.s.* 'White Pearl'. (4 ft/1.2 m.)

— **ramosa 'Purpurea'.** I do not have *C.s. ramosa* itself, but like many who see it in my garden I am very impressed by this unusual form, given to me by Herr Heinz Klose, a remarkable plantsman from Kassel, in Germany. Every part, except the foaming spire of flower, is deeply stained with dark purple. The upper surface of the large, handsome, divided leaves, the 6 ft/2 m column of slender branching stems and the round close-set buds all make a dramatic contrast to the narrow bottle-brushes of sweetly scented fluffy white flowers. This is a noble plant, of much greater substance than 'Elstead Variety', flowering in late August–September. It has only been introduced recently, and will be available before long in limited quantities.

— **'White Pearl'.** Above a base of finely cut, light green leaves are held stiffly branching stems. In October each wand is set with seed-pearl buds of ivory tinted palest green. These burst open to form an elegant pure white bottle-brush carried on arching stems. The pale green seed pods, which form quickly once the flowers have gone, are attractive too. (4 ft/1.2 m.)

CLINTONIA, Liliaceae.

andrewsiana. From the deep shade of conifer forests of the north Californian coast ranges. My knowledge of this plant is confined to the fresh green leaves, rather like Lily-of-the-Valley, which emerge from a basal crown. I am waiting, not only for the flower stem which could be 2 ft/600 mm topped with pinkish-purple, bell-shaped flowers, but also for the bluish-purple berries which should follow in autumn. It does best in sandy peat, in a damp shady position.

CODONOPSIS, Campanulaceae.

clematidea. From rocky, stream-side mountain meadows in the central Asian Tien Shan to the western Himalayas. This beautiful bellflower can grow in quite dry situations, when it is short, but perhaps is best planted to scramble over rocks or tall plants in moist soil, when its rather weak stems, clothed in small leaves, may reach a length of 3 ft/1 m to reach the sun. Its large hanging bells are palest blue, but marked inside with a most fanciful pattern of deep purple and orange.

COLCHICUM, Liliaceae. Most make large bulbs so need a good diet to produce them. They will grow in full sun, but although some are found in moist meadows, most of mine do best in well-drained soil that has been heavily enriched. A wet climate would not hurt the bulbs but waterlogged soil does not suit. They look right in rough-cut grass, or in drifts among shrubs coming up through a suitable ground-cover. There are many different species and forms. These are just a few:

agrippinum—see under *C. variegatum*.

autumnale. Wild in Europe in mountain meadows, rarely seen in Britain. Misleadingly called Autumn Crocus and Meadow Saffron: it is neither. (*Crocus sativus* produces saffron.) *C. autumnale* has flowers of rosy-lilac, about 2 in./50 mm long, on perianth tubes of 4–8 in./100–200 mm, appearing in the autumn without leaves (so they are also called Naked Ladies) which do not emerge until late winter to become a feature in spring.

— **'Alboplenum'** increases slowly, seldom seen. Double white flowers with pointed petals are held close to the soil on short stems. Flowers late in the autumn.

— **'Album'** produces clusters of small white goblets on long white stems. Very attractive, increases well.

cilicicum. Wild in central Turkey, in the Taurus Mountains; probably related to *C. autumnale*. Free flowering, on shorter stems than most, so stands up well, opening a month before *C. speciosum*. Leaves appear soon after the flowers have finished. (Flower segments 2–3 in./50–70 mm on short perianth tubes.)

speciosum. Wild in northern Turkey, northern Iran and the Caucasus, on mountain slopes up to 6000 ft/2000 m. Under this name are found some of the best and largest flowered forms found in gardens. Beautiful large goblet-shaped flowers have broad segments up to 1¼ in./30 mm broad, 3½ in./90 mm long, on sturdy perianth tubes. They range in colour through pinkish-lilac to strong reddish-purple. Some have a deep white throat. They are at their best in October.

— **'Album'** is a treasure; large, pure, rounded petals form an almost closed goblet.

— **'Waterlily'** is the popular double form. They are all best grown through some kind of low ground-cover which supports their stems and keeps their petals free from rain-splashed mud. Their large glossy leaves are handsome in spring, dying away in mid summer.

variegatum grows wild in the eastern Aegean Islands and western Turkey, but is unknown to me and rare in cultivation. Similar to it is *C. agrippinum*, which may be a hybrid of *C. variegatum*. The dark bluish-green leaves are short, with wavy edges, making a flattish rosette against the bare soil in spring. The flowers are not rounded but funnel-shaped, opening flat when the sun warms them. The very pointed segments, 1½–2 in./40–50 mm long and about 1 in./25 mm broad create a flower up to 3 in./80 mm across, on short perianth tubes. The flowers are pinkish-lilac in colour, chequered with a darker shade. In good soil they make well, one bulb increasing to a dozen or more, all producing several flowers, so that an individual clump will carry a fine cluster of flowers. In poor thin soil the offsets will be too small to flower.

CONVALLARIA, Liliaceae.

majalis. Native in the woods of Europe, from the Mediterranean to the Arctic Circle and across temperate Siberia. A well-prepared bed under a north- or east-facing wall is probably the best situation. Good drainage, plenty of humus, cool conditions and patience to see if they will settle where you have chosen are what they need. They can become a menace so think several times before choosing your site. (6–9 in./150–230 mm.) There are different forms apart from the commonly grown native, including a double white, a rather indifferent pink, and a larger flowered form called 'Fortin's Giant'.

— **'Variegata'** produces leaves with narrow gold stripes. It tends to revert; I have read that it needs more light to prevent this, so I have moved my plants. So far they are sulking. (6 in./150 mm.)

COPTIS, Ranunculaceae. 'Gold Thread'.

trifolia. From damp conifer woods and bogs of the colder parts of the northern hemisphere, a tiny plant for a choice cool place. Low mats of shiny green, deeply cut leaves are starred in March with single saucer-shaped flowers on 3 in./80 mm stems. The yellow roots produce a dye, and a valuable tonic medicine.

CORNUS, Cornaceae.

canadensis. From the conifer forests of Canada, the northern USA and north-east Asia including Japan. (The latest name for this plant is *Chamaepericlymenum canadense*, but I cannot bring myself to use it.) Underground shoots revel in cool leaf-mould soil and send up whorls of rounded shiny leaves which form a low carpet in partial shade. Just above them, in June, stand the flowers, looking rather like large greenish-white buttercups, but in reality the 'petals' are four large bracts. The centres are supposed to set small scarlet berries; mine never do. But the leaves and stems change to lovely wine shades in autumn. (6 in./150 mm.)

CORYDALIS, Papaveraceae. Most have fragile-looking flowers and leaves, but some will stand surprisingly dry conditions. The following look and last better in partial shade with soft damp soil in the growing season:

bulbosa (*C. cava*). Widespread from northern Europe to the Balkans, in rich woods. There is confusion between this and *C. solida*, but the tuber of *C. bulbosa* is often hollow on the upper surface and makes a larger plant, 6–8 in./150–200 mm, with soft spires of plum-purple flowers, and grey-green leaves, much dissected. They appear unaffected by the cold days and nights of early spring. I particularly like the creamy-white form, *C.b.* 'Albiflora'.

cashmeriana. Found wild in the Himalayas from Kashmir to Bhutan and southern Tibet, up to 19,000 ft/6000 m on bouldery slopes, often in sheets. North Country gardens do best with this exquisite plant. Further south, cool peaty soil in a north-facing situation must be found. Neat clusters of finely dissected light green leaves show off short dense clusters of vivid sky-blue flowers in early summer. (6 in./150 mm.)

cheilanthifolia. From China. It remains a feature almost all the year round with its pretty fern-like foliage of soft olive-green and long display of light yellow flowers. It will seed itself among primroses in partial shade. (10–12 in./250–300 mm.)

solida. Widespread in Europe from Scandinavia to the Balkans, in open woods and bushy places. The unsuitable-sounding name refers to the tubers which are like little new potatoes, slightly flattened and yellow in colour. This pretty little plant suddenly appears among early spring flowers. Much-dissected pewter-coloured leaves are topped with soft clusters of bluish-lilac flowers which look so well with the purple-flowered *Erythronium* and snow-drops. When they have set seed their fine foliage quickly disintegrates and they disappear without trace. (3–4 in./80–100 mm.)

CREPIS, Compositae.

aurea. Found in subalpine meadows from the Carpathians to the Alps and Apennines. This plant has rosettes of leaves much like the common dandelion, but more refined. The flowers are burnt-orange, lovely beside something blue.

CROCOSMIA, Iridaceae. Montbretia. I listed some of these plants in *The Dry Garden* and said that they would grow in any soil except heavy untreated clay or bog. They thrive best in humus-enriched soil that does not dry out, where their bulbous roots will increase and flower freely unless overcrowded. They may be divided in spring and replanted in refreshed soil, in full sun or part shade. Their flowering season is August–September. The tough and indestructible *Montbretia*, now called *Crocosmia × crocosmiiflora*, has been superseded by some very beautiful hybrids which are becoming more widely known and enjoyed. Most are bred from two species, *C. aurea* and *C. pottsii*, found wild in South Africa.

aurea. *Tritonia aurea* is tender, and probably not in cultivation in the British Isles. But its clear light colouring and wide nodding flowers have contributed to some fine hybrids. Unfortunately it follows that some of the large-flowered varieties are less hardy than those with smaller flowers. (3 ft/1 m.)

masonorum differs from the other species I list in holding its brilliant orange-red flowers upright on the top side of its arching flower stem which stands about 2½ ft/760 mm tall. The knobby seed heads which follow are a delight for flower arrangers, as are the dark green blade-shaped leaves which make beautiful curved shapes when dying to a soft warm beige colour.

pottsii is the hardy parent of *C. × crocosmiiflora*. Its vivid vermilion-red flowers are smaller than those of the other two species, and are borne on erect, not arching, 3 ft/1 m stems. This plant and *C. aurea* have produced many hybrids, bred early in this century, varying considerably in size of flower and hardiness. Many have been lost, but some have survived and been revived from old gardens in the milder and damper West Country. I grow the following:

'Citrinum'. I suspect this name, but as such I obtained it. It is much admired for the cool contrast between its light green leaves above which stand upright spires of soft orange-yellow flowers. (2 ft/600 mm.)

'Emily McKenzie'. This is the only really large-flowered variety that I possess. Flowering later than the others, the large, widely expanded flowers are dark orange, strongly contrasted with dark maroon-red calyces and, as if that were not enough, there is a ring of blood-red around the pale throat from which flare out light orange stamens. (2 ft/600 mm.)

'George Davison'. This name commemorates the head gardener at Westwick Hall, near Norwich, who was one of the first hybridizers of these plants. I like to have this plant of his, raised not so far away from me, in East

Anglia. It flowers earlier than *C.* 'Citrinum', with warmer flowers of soft orange, on slightly arching stems. (18 in./460 mm.)

'Solfatare'. I do not do well with this strangely lovely hybrid. Neither cold nor too dry conditions suit it, so it belongs more happily to warmer, wetter counties. There its sheaves of bronze-tinted leaves will not look as though they were on the point of dying, but only make you marvel how right they are to set off the soft apricot-yellow flowers in late August–September. (18–24 in./460–600 mm.)

rosea see *Tritonia rosea*.

CROCOSMIA × **CURTONUS.** Alan Bloom has raised very fine hybrids between these two. The most dramatic is perhaps 'Lucifer', which has the important architectural quality of *Curtonus* but is topped in August with wide purple-stemmed sprays of brilliant tomato-red trumpet-shaped flowers. (4 ft/1.2 m.)

There are others, varying in height and intensity of flower colour. 'Spitfire' forms a closer head of more widely opened brilliant orange-red flowers, the colour heightened by a yellow throat and protruding yellow stamens. Not so tall as 'Lucifer', it stands about 2½ ft/760 mm and the blade-like foliage is also reduced in scale.

CURTONUS, Iridaceae.

paniculatus. *Antholyza paniculata* is related to *Crocosmia*. It is valued in garden design for its imposing sheaves of stiff, sword-like, pleated leaves which make strong contrast in mixed borders, and are particularly lovely in the autumn, when they turn to coppery shades. The flowers are less impressive, being rather small orange-red trumpets, but they are held in wide arching sprays and followed with an attractive seed head that adds interest to dried arrangements. (3–4 ft/1–1.2 m.)

CYCLAMEN, Primulaceae. I was uncertain whether to include cyclamens in this book as some will do in comparatively dry shade, and a few in full sun. However, where I have seen them naturalized, the rainfall has been heavy compared with East Anglia. They will not tolerate poor drainage, but as they are found wild in the shelter of low bushes in woods or among broken rocks and stones, watered by mountain storms, so in the garden they need open gritty soil well enriched with humus, sheltered from drying winds. The following are the hardy forms most generally grown.

coum has a wide distribution through eastern Europe, the Caucasus, Asia Minor and into Iran. The name covers a group of slightly varying forms. Some have leaves entirely green, others have silver marbling on green; sometimes they are round, or can be kidney-shaped. The flowers appear in winter to spring with short petals, ranging from white to rich carmine. All have a red stain at the base of the petals. (2 in./50 mm.)

europaeum (*C. purpurascens*). Wild in the southern Alps, from Italy to

Yugoslavia and Czechoslovakia. It flowers in autumn, all shades from white to pink, and is sweetly scented; best in semi-shade, not too dried out when dormant. The leaves remain for most of the year, rounded and varying from green to mottled silver. (2 in./50 mm.)

hederifolium, best known as *C. neapolitanum.* The Ivy-leafed Cyclamen grows wild from Italy to western Turkey. This is the easiest *Cyclamen* to grow and makes large corms if left undisturbed. I recently moved some in my garden almost 12 in./300 mm across; they looked rather like dried cowpats. They have beautiful large leaves of varying patterns of silver and green, and are free flowering, in shades of pink and a fine pure white. We look for seedlings in September, and collect and box them up to give them a good start. But in more favoured sites, undisturbed under trees, they increase freely. (4 in./100 mm.)

repandum is found wild from Italy to the Greek Islands. It does better in the warmer and damper south-west where I have seen it naturalized like bluebells under rhododendrons. The flowers are variable in shades of pink to white, and are scented. The leaves vary also, some dark marbled with pale green, others heavily silvered. (3–4 in./80–100 mm.)

CYPRIPEDIUM, Orchidaceae. These are not easy plants but because of their unusual beauty they are much desired. They are comparatively rare plants in the wild so it is a debatable point whether we should leave them in peace in their native home, or try to preserve them in our gardens. Certainly we should not attempt them unless we have the right conditions. There have been more than a dozen different kinds introduced from northern countries around the temperate world. Here are two of the best known:

calceolus. Lady's Slipper. Found in rocky woods and clearings from central and northern Europe to Siberia; also in the Pyrenees and the Caucasus. It will grow in either chalk or acid conditions, though usually in limestone districts, provided there is good drainage combined with moisture-holding humus, in a cool sheltered position. Plants need to be left undisturbed for several years to produce many stems of slippered flowers. In spring one flower appears, sometimes two, consisting of a large pouch or slipper of yellow, netted with dark veins, balanced by twisted chocolate-brown 'petals'. (1–2 ft/300–600 m.)

reginae (*C. spectabile*). Moccasin Flower. Grows in open boggy woods, moist meadows and peaty bogs in the northern United States and Canada, widely distributed from Manitoba to Georgia. This is the largest and most beautiful of them all, 15–30 in./380–760 mm. It must be planted in deep, rich peaty soil, with a little grit added. It will also do in turfy loam provided there is a moist bottom. Deep planting is necessary to keep the roots cool and moist in summer, safe from frost in winter. The whole plant is handsome. Deeply pleated leaves sprinkled with short white downy hairs are held upright on stiff stems. At the top are one or two flowers: each proudly held large pouch, about 1½ in./40 mm long, is rich rose-pink. The 'petals' are not twisted but are broad and snow-white, sometimes flushed rose.

DACTYLORRHIZA, Orchidaceae. Under this name are now found the following plants which formerly we called *Orchis*.

elata. Native in southern France, Spain and Algeria. This is one of the most striking terrestial orchids we can grow in gardens. They need deeply cultivated soil with plenty of humus. Heavy clay, dry sand or pure chalk will not do. They will grow in sun or part shade where their savage colour is enhanced by a dim background. Stout stems, growing up to 2½ ft/760 mm, are encircled towards the base with long fresh green leaves and topped with dense clustered heads of rich lilac-purple flowers. The flower head itself can be up to 9 in./230 mm. long.

foliosa. The Madeira Orchid is often confused with *D. elata*, but the flower spike is less tall, more pyramidal in shape. Th colour is redder, a rosy-purple, while the rich foliage is spotted with dark blotches. (18 in./460 mm.)

latifolia. This is our well-known Marsh Orchid, native to Britain and Europe. It has narrow leaves, often with maroon spots, and slender spikes of lilac and rosy-lilac flowers, with paler throats. Grown well, in deeply cultivated moist soil, it is well worth growing. (18 in./460 mm.)

maculata. This old name for the Spotted Orchid has been discarded as it seems to have covered more than one species. I cultivate one which I have not identified but which used to grow wild in the small wet meadow that is now my garden. Its leaves are covered with large maroon spots and it sends up spikes of white flowers faintly washed lilac, pencilled all over with darker lavender. (12–15 in./300–380 mm.)

DELPHINIUM, Ranunculaceae. I make but brief mention of hybrid delphiniums, as I grow only one. The following species include those which are parents of modern garden hybrids. They vary from dwarf plants which will stand fairly dry and sunny positions to tall forms which must have moisture throughout the growing season and shelter from damaging wind. Garden hybrids need well-prepared holes, using well-rotted farmyard manure, or vegetable compost, plus a mulch to keep the soil cool and moist.

cardinale is found among chaparral bushes or on stony stream-sides in sandy soil in mountains of southern California. It is not suitable for really damp soils in Britain, as they are too cold for it. It has long spikes of red flowers with yellowish inner petals, and is being used as a parent to introduce pink shades. Rarely seen in England, it needs full sun (and rich moist soil). (4 ft/1.2 m.)

cheilanthum (*D. formosum* of gardens). Parent of many hybrids, this makes a dainty plant with wiry stems. (3 ft/1 m.)

elatum. From well-watered rocky subalpine slopes in the mountains of central Europe, north and east to the Caucasus and Altai, and the flood-plain meadows of the Ob and Yenesei in Siberia, reaching the Arctic. This is a tall blue species which has been the main parent of tall garden hybrids. (6 ft/2 m.)

grandiflorum (*D. sinense*). From lower mountain meadow-steppes to alpine turfs from Lake Baikal to north China. Also responsible for dwarf and dainty forms. (2 ft/600 mm.)

nudicaule. From the cool canyons of the coastal mountains of northern California. This is another Californian with soft orange-red blooms; not a good perennial as a garden plant, but being used for breeding.

HYBRIDS

The hybrid delphiniums fall into two main groups. The tall, large-flowered hybrids (4–8 ft/1.2–2.5 m) need the richest soil, staking and every other care including slug bait. The others are the Belladonna hybrids which are smaller (3–5 ft/1–1.5 m), seldom need staking, are less heavy in effect, but still tasty to slugs. The only one which has survived the changes in my garden, resting now among the old fashioned roses, is 'Alice Artindale'. In deep enriched soil she makes a good 6 ft/2 m, and needs staking, I regret to say. The tapering spires are close set with tightly double flowers which are remarkable. Not a formless muddle as you might expect, but even petals, tightly packed, of rich blue edged with green towards the centre, make perfect rosettes.

DENTARIA, Cruciferae. Toothwort. Closely related to Cardamine. There are several of these spring-flowering plants worth growing in half shade among shrubs, cool peaty beds or borders. They like best a light soil well enriched.

digitata (*Cardamine pentaphyllos*). From beechwoods of the Alps and Pyrenees. In early spring it unfolds fine-cut, purple-tinted leaves together with the bowed flower buds. As they expand the leaves become fresh green and the flowers open into showy heads of soft lilac-pink cuckoo flowers. The roots are curious—clusters of white scale or tooth-like shaped pieces—best divided in spring. (12–15 in./300–380 mm.)

DICENTRA, Papaveraceae. These are fragile-looking spring flowers which are easy to grow in cool part shade with plenty of leaf-mould. All dicentras have a long flowering season, from late spring to mid summer.

eximia. From the woods of the USA. The type is similar to *D. formosa*, not well known in gardens.

formosa. From forests and forest glades in the coast ranges and Sierra Nevada from central California to British Columbia. This I find the toughest, standing drier conditions than the others and making quite good ground-cover. Fern-like foliage, which remains good, is pewter-grey tinged with maroon, good contrast with bold leaves like *Hosta* or *Brunnera*. Nodding sprays of flowers, small rosy-red lockets, stand above the leaves. Named forms include 'Adrian Bloom' which has almost raspberry-red flowers, and 'Spring Morning', whose flowers are palest pink. (15–18 in./380–460 mm.)

— **'Alba'** is much better known and rightly so with its low-growing much divided fresh green leaves and clusters of small greenish-white heart-shaped lockets held on jade-green stems. I have in the past incorrectly called this plant *D. eximea* 'Alba'. (12 in./300 mm.)

oregona. From Oregon, is closely related, but has blue-grey foliage with cream coloured flowers.

— **'Langtrees'.** I was given this form, which varies slightly, by Dr Tony Rogerson. The foliage forms dense colonies of an outstanding blue-green colour, as much commented upon as the cream- and pink-tinted flowers. It is a help to know that this plant runs vigorously in rich light soil, but in the right place that is no disadvantage. (18 in./460 mm.)

spectabilis. Bleeding Heart, Dutchman's Breeches and Lady's Locket: all these nicknames have been given to this well-loved plant. It comes from cool sheltered places in Korea, Manchuria and China. From top to toe it is good to look at. Standing about 2 ft/600 mm an established clump sends up many graceful stems, lightly set with greyish-green leaves. Sprays of comparatively large, heart-shaped lockets dangle beyond the foliage on rose-tinted stems, each flower a rich rose colour. If you are indiscreet and turn the heart upside down and open the petals you will see, sitting inside, the little white shape which suggests the name 'Lady in the Bath'.

— **'Alba'.** Not so well known—this exquisite plant has light green leaves with almost transparent green stems from which dangle ivory-white lockets. (2 ft/600 mm.)

DIERAMA, Iridaceae.

pulcherrimum. Angel's Fishing Rod. From mountain-sides in rich moist soil, often part shaded, in eastern Cape Province, South Africa. These bulbous plants produce tall, grasslike clumps of tough broad leaves which erupt like a fountain. High above them cascade sprays of large delicately formed bells which fall in showers from the tips of fine wire-like stems. They vary in colour from silvery-pink through deep rose to plum-purple. Attractive too are the bead-like seed cases, strings of small chestnut seeds enclosed in silvery paper cases. (5 ft/1.5 m.)

pumilum. This dwarf species, about 2½ ft/760 mm, flowers freely, with 'rods' more upright, their lines not cast so wide, taking up less space. The flowers are soft rose-pink. Hybrids between the two occur readily. Both these species of *Dierama* like full sun in a deep, retentive, but not wet, soil.

DIGITALIS, Scrophulariaceae. Our native purple Foxglove, *Digitalis* *purpurea*, a biennial, seems to grow in open dry places as well as in cooler situations. Foxgloves often germinate by the thousand in a newly cleared piece of woodland, standing like soldiers in ranks, in full sun. There are several perennial foxgloves which I grow in semi-shade with leaf-mould soil. Those I have seen in the Alps were always on dampish north-facing slopes on grassy verges or among low bushes. The following have a long flowering period during July and August:

ferruginea. From subalpine and woodland meadows of the Caucasus, this plant is quietly distinctive. It has dark green leaves and tall slender spires of round buds which open short, rounded, bronze-coloured flowers. (4 ft/1.2 m.)

grandiflora (*D. ambigua*). From open mountain woods and rocky slopes of Europe to Siberia. This plant has broader, slightly hairy leaves. The good-sized flowers, 1½–2 in./40–50 mm long are primrose-yellow, netted inside with brown. (2 ft/600 mm.)

lutea has smooth green leaves and tall stems which branch a little, carrying one-sided racemes of very narrow creamy-yellow flowers. (3–4 ft/1–1.2 m.)

parviflora. On stonefalls and steep rocky grassland from hills to subalpine zone of the north Spanish mountains. I find this plant very distinctive; dingy from a distance, fascinating when seen close to. Its leaves are distinguished from the others by purplish-mauve shading at the base of the leaf stalk and a fine white rim which edges the leaves. The stout flower stem is short, about 2 ft/600 mm, crowded for the top two-thirds of its length with narrow copper-coloured flowers set all round the stem, which is unbranched. Close-set chestnut-coloured seed cases prolong the season of interest.

There are others, but foxgloves have no scruples about intermarriage, so I am not at all certain of the purity of some of my plants. Most of them are attractive. One we call *D. ciliata*, from the subalpine glades of the western Caucasus, but of which I can find no reference in gardening books, is especially likeable. Taller than *D. ambigua*, it has narrow, slightly hairy leaves and large graceful branching heads of pale primrose-yellow flowers. (3–4 ft/1–1.2 m.)

DIPHYLLEIA, Podophyllaceae.

cymosa. Umbrella Leaf. From rich woods in the Appalachian mountains of the eastern USA. This is a woodland plant, to grow with blue *Meconopsis* in damp cool shade. Round, two-lobed leaves attract attention because they are large, almost 12 in./300 mm across when well grown. Clustered heads of unremarkable flowers are followed by deep indigo berries held well above the leaves. (2½ ft/760 mm.)

DISPORUM, Liliaceae. These are related to *Polygonatum* and *Tricyrtis*. They like moist peaty or woodland soil in partial shade.

sessile. From woods in hills of Japan, Sakhalin and Ryuku islands.

— **'Variegatum'**. A very attractive foliage plant, like a dainty Solomon's Seal, about 18 in./460 mm high with oval leaves conspicuously striped pale green and white. The flowers in spring are creamy-green bells.

smithii. From the northern conifer forests of the west coast of North America. This is a dubious name for a plant which makes low hummocks of rather wiry stems covered with shining green leaves. Hidden among them are small ivory bells which later turn into bright orange fruits. It must have moisture and shade. (12 in./300 mm.)

DODECATHEON, Primulaceae. These are North American plants of damp places ranging from moist valleys in the Prairies to high mountain meadows of the Rockies and western ranges, one extending to the Arctic. There are about thirty different species, much resembling one another, except that some are taller, such as *D. meadia* (about 2 ft/600 mm), while others are shorter. The colour range is from white to rose and purple. They are very beautiful on account of their downturned, dart-like flowers poised on short arching stalks which spring from the top of each stem. They make basal clumps of broad-bladed leaves, rather like primroses, but smooth and some-times brownish-green. They like moist but well-drained soil with plenty of humus, and shelter from the sun.

ECHINACEA, Compositae (*Rudbeckia purpurea*). Wild in rich moist meadows of the eastern and south-eastern USA, this is a dignified late summer daisy of unusual colouring. Several large daisy flowers produced at the top of stiff branching stems have widely separated clover-red petals. In startling contrast the hard central cone glistens orange-brown. There is a lighter, more cerise-pink form called 'Abendsonne'. The best dark-toned form is 'Robert Bloom', which continues to flower into October. It needs a sunny situation in deep retentive soil enriched with humus. (2½–3 ft/ 760 mm–1 m.)

EOMECON, Papaveraceae. The Dawn Poppy.

chionanthum. From turfy glades and river banks in the woods of east China to Sichuan. Round waxed grey leaves, slightly crinkle-edged and veined, are a setting for naked stems which hold short-lived drooping white flowers filled with gold stamens, in spring. Both leaves and flowers have charm; but best grown in light dampish soil under trees, where the wandering shoots cannot overwhelm smaller plants. (18 in./460 mm.)

EPILOBIUM, Onagraceae.

angustifolium. Found in moist open woods and banks of Northern Europe and Asia to Japan, and North America from east to west, spreading quickly after forest fires. The well-known Rosebay Willowherb is much too invasive for the garden but I was given a white form some years ago and it has not become a nuisance. It has not had the best of conditions, but it certainly deserves a good spot in the wild garden which it graces in late summer with tall spires of cool white flowers with green calyces. (4 ft/1.2 m.)

glabellum. From wet, rocky subalpine and alpine mountain slopes in New Zealand. Tumbled masses of cream-coloured funnel-shaped flowers seem to continue from mid to late summer, followed by fluffy seed heads but no troublesome seedlings. Clumps of small shining light green leaves expand slowly but are never a nuisance. It grows easily in retentive soil, in sun or part shade. (12–15in./300–460 mm.)

EPIMEDIUM, Berberidaceae. This group of plants is on my shortlist of indispensables in the garden. From slowly creeping rootstocks they produce low mounds of exquisite leaves held on fine wiry stems. Some are evergreen, but many of those which are not truly evergreen retain their leaves all winter in rich shades of russet-brown. All except the evergreen should have their leaves trimmed off about February–March, just before the flower stems emerge, otherwise these are lost among the copious foliage. Quantities of fine stems carry sprays of small fragile columbine-like flowers. The leaves are invaluable, both for their colour and shape, to pick, or to use as a feature as well as excellent ground-cover. They are woodland plants, and will grow in shade or part shade in almost any open soil, provided it is enriched with humus.

grandiflorum (*E. macranthum*). From the woods of central and south-western Japan and Manchuria. The young spring foliage is almost beige-brown, above which are held sprays of mauve-pink flowers, a lovely combination (10 in./250 mm.)

—**'Rose Queen'** has larger but fewer flowers, of rich rose-pink with long white-tipped spurs. There is a lovely white form called 'White Queen', and 'Violaceum' is dark lilac. These are the largest flowering forms and deserve a choice position in cool leaf-mould soil. (10 in./250 mm.)

× **perralchicum.** A handsome evergreen hybrid between *E. perralderanum* and *E. pinnatum colchicum*, raised at Wisley. It has good leaves and large bright yellow flowers without spurs. (18 in./460 mm.)

perralderanum. From the evergreen oak forests of Algeria. Large, glossy, toothed leaves and long sprays of bright lemon-yellow flowers are held well above the leaves, which are an asset all the year round. (12–15 in./ 300–460 mm.)

— **'Fronleiten'.** I was given this plant in Germany, where it is very popular. It is low growing and compact with reddish tints both in the young leaves and in winter, making very attractive ground-cover. The bright yellow flowers are pretty in April–May. (4 in./100 mm.)

pinnatum colchicum is almost evergreen, turning to bright tints in winter, with yellow flowers in spring (12 in./300 mm). It comes from the forests of the western Caucasus and the Black Sea coastal plain.

pubigerum. Found in woods from the Balkans to Asia Minor. This has the least showy flowers, small and cream coloured, but attractive because they are held on tall sprays well above the pale green, more rounded leaves. (18 in./460 mm.)

× **rubrum** (*E. grandiflorum* × *E. alpinum*). Over several weeks in spring this plant produces the strongest leaf colour. The new leaves unfold almost transparently pale green, washed with coral. This quickly deepens and the whole plant becomes warm brick-red, standing out among the cool yellow-greens of other spring foliage. The flowers are crimson with white spurs. Finally the leaves quieten to green. (9 in./230 mm.)

× **versicolor** (*E. grandiflorum* × *E. pinnatum colchicum*). There are several clones of this cross, all tending to have pale yellow flowers. The form I know and grow is 'Sulphureum', which I find makes the toughest ground-cover, combined with good leaf colour and most freely produced flowers, 10 in./250 mm, sprays of palest primrose in April.

× **warleyense.** A hybrid raised in Miss Willmott's garden, it makes less dense clusters of leaves. The flowers are surprisingly orange, caused by a mixture of pink and yellow. (12 in./300 mm.)

× **youngianum 'Niveum'.** A hybrid between *E. grandiflorum* and the ever-green southern Japanese *E. diphyllum*. This choice *Epimedium* is compact and low growing, about 6–10 in./150–250 mm high. In spring the small, pale, brown-washed leaves form a base for myriads of tiny, white, snowflake-like blossoms. When they have gone the leaves have changed to light green. It takes time to establish sizeable clumps.

EPIPACTIS, Orchidaceae. Helleborine. Quiet unusual plants for damp, not saturated, soil in part shade, valued for their shape as much as their subtly coloured flowers.

gigantea. The Brook Orchid. Found on the banks and streams and around springs along the Californian coast, east to Montana and Texas; sometimes called 'False Lady's Slipper'. It is related to the *Cypripedium*, and resembles it in the leafy stems although they are taller and more graceful, making an interesting vertical shape. The tip curves gracefully with the weight of several curiously formed, smallish flowers of sombre green and brown. The lower lip is not pouched but open and inviting, like a treacherous trap, lined with orange-red and leading to a dark purplish-crimson heart. (1–4 ft/ 300 mm–1.2 m.)

palustris. The Marsh Helleborine. From wet woods and marshy stream-banks of Europe and temperate Asia, except in the extreme north. (8–20 in./ 200–500 mm.) I do not have this plant but it looks attractive in a photograph I have of a piece of wet fenland, growing with the Marsh Fern, *Thelypteris palustris*, and *Lysimachia vulgaris*. Narrow leaves, ribbed and lance-shaped, stand upright on stems which grow 1–2 ft/300–600 mm. The slightly drooping flowers held in a loose spike have three pale greenish-purple sepals with three white petals tinged with pink at the base.

ERANTHIS, Ranunculaceae.

hyemalis. The Winter Aconite. From woods and shady places of south-eastern Europe, and widely naturalized elsewhere. This little plant will grow in the open, as its cut parasol leaves and yellow buttercup flowers in their green frill appear and disappear again—so early in the year. It grows larger and finer in moist shady places. (4–5 in./100–130 mm.)

ERIGERON, Compositae. A very large genus, including some North American species, which together have resulted in many named garden hybrids. They are sun-loving but will not give their best in thin starved soils. Reasonably retentive soil means a longer lasting display. Of the many hybrids my favourite is 'Dimity'. Tidy clumps of evergreen leaves produce a succession of pinky-mauve daisies with orange eyes and buds, a lovely combination throughout June and July. Short stems, 12–15 in./300–380 mm, prevent the plants becoming untidily floppy.

ERYTHRONIUM, Liliaceae. Dog's Tooth Violet, Adder's Tongue, Glacier Lily. All these names describe different parts of the plants or their habitat. They are choice and spring flowering, needing cool peaty or leaf-mould soil in light shade. There are about twenty different species, all but one from America.

californicum. Found wild in California from sea level to 3000 ft/1000 m under pines, redwoods and maples in humus-rich soil. Creamy-white lily-shaped flowers show orange-brown markings ringed round the base. Dark green leaves are strongly mottled with brown. (12 in./300 mm.)

dens-canis. Dog's Tooth Violet. Grows wild in woods and grassy glades, sometimes in colonies in mountain meadows, as in the Pyrenees; widespread in Europe across Russia to Korea and Japan. Small corms, smooth, ivory-white and pointed are shaped like the canine teeth of a dog. The colour of the flowers varies from almost white through rose to deep cyclamen. Long petals on short (3–4 in./80–100 mm) stalks hang folded on dull days, but flare back like cyclamen petals when the sun warms them. The leaves are oval and matt, blotched with brown on bluish-green. High in the Pyrenees you can find them everywhere in short turf, but thunderstorms wet them most days while their leaves are up. They soon disappear after the flowers have faded. (6 in./150 mm.)

oregonum. Found wild in northern Oregon, Washington and Vancouver Island in fir woods. This is an easy species, with white or cream flowers with yellowish centres outlined with zig-zag markings of deep orange brown. (15 in./380 mm.)

revolutum. Widely distributed from central California north to southern

Canada and Vancouver Island, near streams, swamps and in woods up to 3000 ft/1000 m. Its large drooping flowers are clear rose-pink, two or three to a 10 in./250 mm stem, held well above brown-tinted leaves. Among named forms is 'Pink Beauty'. (10–12 in./250–300 mm.)

tuolumnense. Grows wild in California, in Tuolumnense County, at 1500 ft/500 m in gritty clay soil, rich in humus, beneath oak and Yellow Pine. Its rather more upright leaves are shining yellow-green. Tallish stems, 15–18 in./380–460 mm carry several bright yellow flowers held well above the leaves.

HYBRIDS

The following hybrids look well coming through low ground cover such as *Dicentra formosa* 'Alba' or *Viola labradorica*, protected from savage cold winds which can damage the delicate lily-like blooms.

'Pagoda'. A cross with *E. tuolumnense*, it stands a little taller than 'White Beauty' with butter-yellow flowers, and stems and leaves a little more strongly tinted brown.

'White Beauty' may be a form of *E. oregonum* or a hybrid. The flower stems, 6–9 in./150–230 mm carry large pale cream flowers which reflex back to show creamy stamens and a ring of reddish stain at their base. Broad wavy shining leaves are slightly marbled.

EUPATORIUM, Compositae.

ageratoides. Also known as *E. urticifolium.* It has nettle-shaped leaves but does not sting. It is well liked by those who know it and grow it well, but needs moisture-retentive soil to keep health and vigour into September when the leafy stems are topped with loose flat heads of fuzzy creamy-white flowers. It is not spectacular, but unusual and attractive. It does need a bit of support. (2½–3 ft/760 mm–1 m.)

purpureum resembles our own Hemp Agrimony, but is bigger and brighter coloured. It is found in damp water-sides in south-east Canada and the eastern USA. This plant is handsome in a big way, standing 6–8 ft/2–2.5 m tall. Many stout purple-tinted stems are furnished from top to bottom with whorls of dark green pointed leaves. Large flat heads, more than 1 ft/300 mm across of mauve-pink upturned fluffy flowers on dark purple stalks are repeated on a dozen or so smaller side branches. There is a form with extra dark purple stems and purplish-rose coloured flowers. It is a magnificent structural plant seen from a distance, impressive close-to and has a long flowering season in autumn.

EUPHORBIA, Euphorbiaceae. Spurge or Milkweed. There are many species. Care needs to be taken with the milky white sap which can blister skin. The following prefer cool conditions and moisture-retentive soil.

amygdaloides. From the woods of central and southern Europe and western Asia to the Caucasus. Our native Wood Spurge is a relative of *E. robbiae*. It grows best in leaf-mould soil in part shade. The splendid form with young foliage and stems of rich mahogany-red, *E.a.* 'Purpurea', can be ruined by mildew, which is aggravated by drought conditions. The plants recover, but the display is spoilt. There is also a variegated form. I have yet to grow this really well—perhaps it never does, or perhaps I have not given it just the right place. Flowers in spring. (18 in./460 mm.)

griffithii. From the Himalayas. The selected form 'Fireglow' has almost tomato-red flowers, light olive-green foliage with red veins, and orange-brown stems. It will grow in full sun but likes heavy retentive soil. I have a form with darker flowers, stems and foliage which originated with Miss Hilda Davenport-Jones. The backs of the young leaves and veins are coral red, the flower stem intensifying in colour leading to flowers which are brilliant orange-red. The chaplet of leaflets beneath the clustered flowers are also stained and shaded with this fiery colour. Gives a long display—early to late summer. (3–4 ft/1–1.2 m.)

palustris. Found in marshy places from France to the Balkans and western Asia. This plant does for the damp garden what *E. wulfenii* does for the dry garden. It makes a spectacular feature plant with many leafy stems, 3–4 ft/ 1–1.2 m high, creating a bushy shape that can be several feet across, topped for weeks in spring and early summer with wide flat heads of soft greenish-yellow flowers. Odd fresh flowers are produced later in the year, and in the autumn the dying foliage sometimes turns to brilliant shades of cream, orange and crimson.

robbiae. Found in woods, sometimes with *Hypericum calycinum*, from the southern Balkans to Turkey. It would be a shame to leave this one out, as although it will grow in dry shade, gardens with damper conditions would be deprived without it. It is invasive, so is not suitable for very small gardens, but is invaluable where there is room, in sun or shade. The dense colonies of large rosettes, darkest green lit by long heads of yellowish-green flowers which start in spring, continue through the summer and can look well, bronze-tinted, in autumn. It makes handsome evergreen ground-cover. (2–2½ ft/600–760 mm.)

sikkimensis. From the Himalayas. In February and March, among pink and purple hellebores, the new low rosettes of leaves and stems are tinted glass-red. They elongate into tall willowy stems, 4–5 ft/1.2–1.5 m, when the leaves have become light green with a white vein and noticeable red leaf stalks, creating a very fresh effect at the end of July and on into September. The flowers, in wide flat clusters, commence in early July. By August the round blue-green seed capsules continue to be set off by yellowish-green collars. The central head is surrounded by two or three side branches which carry fresh flowers in autumn.

FAGOPYRUM, Polygonaceae. The annual *Fagopyrum sagittatum* is culti-vated for its seeds, to make poultry food, and buckwheat flour for human consumption. Another of my mystery plants was given to me as *F. cymosum*. I am not certain that this is the correct name, but whatever it may be it makes an elegant leafy perennial for the wilder parts of the garden. A slowly increasing rootstock sends up 5–6 ft/1.5–2 m tall branching stems which carry large ivy-shaped leaves marked with red veins. Large panicles of small white polygonum-like flowers appear by the end of August, continuing into October.

FILIPENDULA, Rosaceae. Sometimes confused with *Astilbe*, having simi-lar tiny fluffy flowers, but the meadowsweets are held in flattish heads instead of narrow spires. They are damp meadow plants so must have retentive soil. Some are tolerant of part shade, which prolongs the flowering. Their woody rootstocks are not far beneath the surface so a mulch is very beneficial. These plants used to be called *Spiraea*, and there is still some confusion in my mind over their exact identification.

palmata. From flood-meadows of eastern Siberia to Japan. (The garden plant may be a hybrid.) I think this is the plant I grow. It does not run, but forms tall (4–5 ft/1.2–1.5 m) elegant clumps of light green foliage topped with wide flat heads composed of hundreds of tiny pale pink flowers. I also have *F.p.* 'Elegans' and *F.p.* 'Elegantissima' which have rather darker, more finely cut leaves with brighter and darker pink flowers and glowing heads of bronze-red seed heads, as effective as the flowers. I have seen these two listed under *F. purpurea* (Japan) which is similar to *F. palmata* but flowers a fortnight earlier. The three I grow I value highly. My only regret is their susceptibility to mildew. Where I have planted them in wetter soil this has not been such a problem.

rubra. Queen of the Prairies. From damp meadows of the north-eastern USA. We grew this originally as *Spiraea venusta* 'Magnifica'. It is magnifi-cent where there is room. It sends out exploring roots and shoots seeking fresh soil, but being shallow-rooted is not difficult to dig up and replant. Tall, 6–8 ft/2–2.5 m stems carry dark, green, vine-like leaves and are topped with wide feathery masses of deep rose flowers about 12 in./300 mm across.

ulmaria. Our native Meadowsweet; of wet meadows and water-sides in Europe and temperate western Siberia. There are two cultivated forms of this in gardens.

— **'Aurea'** can be one of the choicest foliage plants, if you can grow it well. It needs enough light to produce rich yellow leaves but not direct sunlight which scorches them. It must have continuously damp soil. The quality of leaf deteriorates a little when the white flowers are freely produced, but I usually cut them off to encourage new foliage, which remains yellow throughout the entire season. (12–15 in./300–380 mm.)

— **'Variegata'** can look well if it is regularly divided and planted in refreshed soil. The dark green vine-shaped leaves are centred with vivid yellow. It is inclined to revert, and is prone to mildew. (2½ ft/760 mm.)

FRAGARIA, Rosaceae.

× **ananassa 'Variegata'.** This is a variegated form of the cultivated strawberry. It needs retentive soil when it will make handsome clusters of leaves broadly splashed with creamy-white. Young plants are produced at the end of runners so it will weave itself between other plants preferably in part shade. A few fruits are produced, usually malformed, but they taste like the real thing. (3–4 in./80–100 mm.)

indica (*Duchesnea indica*). Found in woods and along stream-banks in ravines from India to China and Japan. This can be a rampageous weed in unsuitable places, but among shrubs, under trees, where there is nice leafy soil, not too dry, this strawberry-like plant makes rapid ground-cover with long trailers of dark green leaves. Bright yellow flowers from May–October set round red fruits which look attractive but are tasteless. (2 in./50 mm.)

vesca 'Semperflorens'. These are the alpine strawberries which flower and fruit from May to November, including named forms such as 'Baron Solemacher'. Part shade, a humus rich soil and a regular supply of moisture is what they need. (6–10 in./150–250 mm.)

FRANCOA, Saxifragaceae. Bridal Wreath. From Chile. This plant makes large multiple rosettes of softly hairy, turnip-shaped leaves, crinkle-surfaced and rich green. They are often grown in greenhouses, or stood about in pots for the sake of their tall bare stems which carry branched wands of pale pink or white flowers, rather like extra large *Heuchera* flowers. The entire spike remains fresh for a long time, and the seed heads which follow are attractive. These plants retain their leaves in winter, looking too tender to stand very severe weather. I obtained my seed from the Harlow Car Gardens in Yorkshire, and the plants have survived several winters, but seed is saved as a precaution.

appendiculata. Tall, 3 ft/1 m branching stems with long tapers of pale pink-flushed flowers with each petal eyed deep carmine-red in late summer.

sonchifolia has white flowers flushed with pink, and is a little later. (2½ ft/760 mm.)

FRITILLARIA, Liliaceae. There are many species of these strangely attractive bulbs in cultivation. I described a few in *The Dry Garden*. Here are a few more which need rather moister conditions, in humus-rich soil, with good drainage.

camtschatcensis. In damp peaty meadows, sometimes in part shade, all round the north Pacific, from Washington to Alaska and Kamchatka to north Japan. This extraordinary fritillary likes a rich open soil in part shade where it will do well, making its curious bulb which looks rather like a small spoonful of cooked rice squeezed into a round ball. The bulblets can be pulled apart and grown for several years before they can make a flowering stem. Fresh green, glossy leaves are set in whorls around the stems which can be from 12–15 in./300–380 mm high. The flowers are open pendent bells, up to 1¼ in./30 mm long. They are almost black, smooth outside, heavily corrugated inside where the colour is slightly lighter, dark chocolate-maroon. There is some colour variation: some bulbs produce less fine not such dark-coloured flowers. There is also a green form, I am told. They flower in May.

meleagris. Snake's Head Fritillary. Our native species, also found wild in most of central Europe to Scandinavia, in damp meadows. This lovely plant can still be seen in Britain, in a few protected water-meadows. It is easily grown provided the soil never becomes too dry. Standing 10–12 in./250–300 mm, the stems are lightly set with narrow blue-green leaves. The tapering chequered bells with angular 'shoulders' can be found in many shades. The white and palest pink ones are usually shaded and faintly chequered with green. The warm plum and sombre purple shades have darker chequering, and are sometimes overlaid with a greyish bloom. April–May.

pallidiflora is found wild in the central Siberian mountains, up to 9000 ft/3000 m. This is a treasure for the garden. On short thick stems, 12–18 in./300–460 mm, broad, lance-shaped, grey-green leaves diminish in size towards the tip. The lovely flowers, several to a stem, are large and pale citron-yellow, overlaid with green and faint tan veining. They will grow in sun but need deep enriched soil. April–May.

verticillata. Found wild in central Siberia and east to China, in grassy openings in woods. All shades of green are displayed in this modest plant. Slender stems, up to 2 ft/600 mm long, are set with whorls of narrow blue-green leaves which become slimmer towards the top of the stem when their tips become tendrils, perhaps to ensure that in the wild the flowers are held well up among surrounding grasses. They are exasperating to grow, making many bulbs but only a few flower at a time. The angular seed cases surrounded by dried tendrils are works of art themselves and rare enough to be treasured among dried flowers.

GALANTHUS, Amaryllidaceae. I do not have the knowledge to write about the many forms, hybrids and species of snowdrops, or even of the variations of the Common Snowdrop, *G. nivalis*. In general it helps to know that most do best in heavier soils and semi-shade, and that their bulbs should not be dried out or sun-baked. Most of them are woodland or mountain meadow plants of central and especially south-east Europe and west Asia to the Caucasus and north Iran, though a few (from the eastern Mediterranean lands), and not commonly grown, prefer drier, scrubby places, sometimes in full sun. Some fine, very large-flowered forms have been raised, and some have been collected, especially local varieties of *G. nivalis* that flower in the autumn before their leaves have developed. A few of the wild species, for instance *G. elwesii* and *G. caucasicus*, have broad grey leaves which are decorative.

I have in my garden a small stock of an impressive snowdrop which may be a late-flowering form of *G. byzantinus*. It appears after most have faded, is still fresh in mid March, with much larger, more globular flowers than any others.

GALAX, Diapensiaceae.

urceolata (*G. aphylla*). Grows wild in open woodland in mountainous districts from Virginia to Kentucky. A beautiful foliage plant for cool moist conditions, the rounded heart-shaped leaves are of a leathery texture on fine wirelike stems. They are rich green and glossy with marked veins radiating from the centre. In winter they are edged and sometimes flushed with reddish tints. The size of the leaf varies according to the amount of moisture. Rarely 3 in./80 mm across in my garden, I have seen it described as twice that size in favourable circumstances. Slender spires of tiny white flowers are produced in early summer. A lovely plant for a cool peaty garden.

GENTIANA, Gentianaceae. It comes as a shock to learn that there are about four hundred species of *Gentiana*, including some which are yellow and scarlet as well as blue, purple, violet or mauve. Those we are concerned with are moisture-loving plants from high mountains where they are fully exposed to sun but have a continuous supply of underground water in summer. I can only describe those I grow, which must be the least difficult.

acaulis (of gardens). The well-informed know of the myths and mystery surrounding this plant. Most of us are content to think of it as the large intensely blue trumpet which sits close to the ground on absurdly small clusters of tiny leaves. It likes full sun in heavy soil that does not dry out. In some gardens it produces sheets of flower, in others green mats with no flowers. One is advised to move it, yard by yard, until, with luck, it arrives at the right place. (2–4 in./50–100 mm.)

asclepiadea. Grows in woods and damp meadows and rockfalls in the mountains of central Europe to the Caucasus. The Willow Gentian is so called because of its narrow leaves on long graceful stems which bow beneath the sheaves of rich blue flowers arranged around the upper half of the stem. Planted in deep moist soil (including chalky soils), well enriched with humus, in shade or part shade and left undisturbed, these plants grow larger and more impressive. The white form, 'Alba', has slightly smaller flowers but, well placed, perhaps near *Euphorbia sikkimensis*, its arching stems crowded with green-throated white trumpets are very unusual in September. (1–2 ft/300–600 mm.)

— **'Knightshayes'** is distinguished by deep blue trumpets which have conspicuous white throats. (2–3 ft/600 mm–1 m.)

farreri. Discovered by Reginald Farrer, in alpine turfs in Kansu, north-west China. The plant we now grow may not be the original introduction but it is of a blue unlike any other, a light, glowing Cambridge blue, on narrow trumpets which have white throats, striped and spotted with green. They sit on low small-leafed cushions of fresh green. A sunny site that does not dry out, in lime-free soil, is what they need. (4 in./100 mm.)

lutea. Grows in subalpine and alpine stony grasslands of central and southern Europe to Asia Minor. It is a splendid sight to see great clumps of this unusual-looking gentian in sunny mountain meadows where the cows graze, leaving them isolated in short turf. It is easy to mistake them for *Veratrum*, which sometimes grow with them. Tall stout stems, 2½–3 ft/ 760 mm–1 m, are set with wide upstanding ribbed leaves and topped with whorls of pale yellow trumpets. The pale fawn-coloured clusters of pointed seed cases are also worth having. Patience is needed to achieve several flowering stems as large plants cannot be transplanted, only young seedlings, preferably pot grown. July–August.

sino-ornata. From high alpine turfs in south-west China or the borders of Tibet. These plants make wide-spreading mats of grassy foliage and will produce sheets of upturned blue trumpets streaked with green if your soil is lime-free and has remained moist (but not stagnant) throughout the summer until the end of September–October. A good mulch of peat or crushed bark aids this, and also helps to ensure that you have a bed of gentians and not annual meadow grass, which surreptitiously germinates among them and is a great fiddle to weed out. (4 in./100 mm.)

GERANIUM, Geraniaceae. Cranesbills. These hardy plants are among my most valued for furnishing the garden. They both mark and provide cover for bulbs such as lilies and *Camassia*. Their pretty foliage makes contrast between strong-leafed plants like *Hosta* or *Hemerocallis*, as well as providing modest charm between more spectacular subjects best separated. They quickly make practically weed-proof ground-cover. It is hard to imagine gardening without them. There are many which will grow in almost any soil, ranging in size from those suited to small gardens or the rock garden, to larger plants ideal for borders and shrubberies. I wrote about those that will tolerate dry conditions in *The Dry Garden*. A few of those will creep into this book since they respond well to something better, together with others I consider too choice to risk in my really dry areas.

endressii. From the Pyrenees. In its several tonal shades, this is one of the best: light silvery-pink, salmon-pink and deeper rose-pink forms can be found, together with finely cut parasols of apple-green leaves which cover the soil in weed-proof mounds. 'Wargrave Pink' is the name of the salmon-pink form, while 'Claridge Druce' is a very vigorous hybrid, making larger mounds, 2–3 ft/600 mm–1 m high, with darker grey-green leaves and magenta-pink flowers. These plants produce flowers throughout summer and autumn.

himalayense (*G. grandiflorum*). From the Himalayas. Under this title shelter several good plants. *G.h.* 'Alpinum' makes low, 1 ft/300 mm dense clumps of finely cut leaves which are tinted with bright shades of orange and scarlet in the autumn. The large single flowers are violet-blue with a warm reddish centre. It flowers throughout June and early July and increases well in any reasonable soil, in full sun. The one I take a little extra care with is:

— **'Flore-pleno'**. The colour and shape of these flowers remind me of some old fashioned roses. Fully double, the petals are ruched and puckered in shades of pinky-mauve, deepening to violet in the centre. They stand about 9–12in./230–300 mm, and flower from mid June to August.

'Johnson's Blue'. This outstandingly good garden plant is similar in habit to *G. himalayense*, but without the reddish centre the blue of the petals seems more intense. (12 in./300 mm.)

macrorrhizum. From shady rocky slopes of southern Europe. This *Geranium* will stand fairly dry conditions in sun or shade, but it is so useful in any area provided there is good drainage that I cannot leave it out. Its scented, scallop-edged leaves provide dense weed-proof cover about 12 in./300 mm high. Small unrooted pieces of woody stem with just a tuft of leaves can be broken off and struck in cool soil in spring. They will root quickly, and are invaluable where large areas need to be covered. Pale shell-pink flowers held in deep coral-coloured swollen calyces have long protruding stamens while thrust beyond them is the rapier-like pistil, the 'Cranesbill'. (In many members of this family the pistil is attached at the base to the seed case and when they are ripe the 'rapier' splits and projects the seeds far away from the parent plant.) There is also a form with magenta-pink flowers. They flower in May–June.

— **'Variegatum'**. The slightly felted leaves are splashed with cream and gold, sometimes with a dash of cherry-red around the scalloped edges. The flowers are magenta-pink, held just above the leaves. A cooler situation, in part shade, suits this plant best. (9–12 in./230–300 mm.)

maculatum. From rich woods of eastern and midwestern USA and southern Canada. This makes a choice feature plant, one of the earliest to flower in May. Clustered heads of soft lilac-blue flowers with pale centres stand on 2 ft/600 mm stems, pushed through a dome of large parasol-shaped leaves with frilly edges. They will stand full sun in an enriched retentive soil, but also look well in part shade with *Dicentra* and *Tellima*. The leaves are beautiful in autumn, suffused with fawn, orange and red.

phaeum. From damp meadows and open woods of south-central Europe. Silk-textured flowers of blackish-maroon float on slender branching stems (2–2½ ft/600–760 mm) in shade or part shade over light green foliage freckled with dark brown spots. The clumps divide easily, and seedlings occur, all making useful cover. Flowers of seedlings will vary; some will be light plum-coloured. There is also a white form.

pratense. The Meadow Cranesbill. In moist meadows from the Pyrenees and Britain to north China. The single-flowered forms have two faults. They seed too freely, and they tend to flop. But for many people these faults are redeemed by the sheaves of beautiful clear blue flowers. Among the best is *G. pratense* 'Striatum', whose flowers are striped blue and white. There is also a pink form. Where there is ample room, or in the wilder parts of the garden, or in thin woodland, they are delightful. (2½–3 ft/760 mm–1 m.)

The old fashioned double forms do well in a sunny or part-shaded border in a retentive soil, and remain in flower over a long period throughout June and July.

— **'Plenum Album'** has greenish-white double flowers, rather smaller than the others.

— **'Plenum Caeruleum'.** Light violet-blue flowers, making a fine display for weeks.

— **'Plenum Violaceum'.** This, I think, is the best of the three double forms. Rich deep violet-blue flowers, well shaped, make a fine display for weeks. It appears that the plant we have called *G. rectum album*, from Kashmir, comes into this group. It is a beautiful plant, making spreading clumps of fretted leaves above which rise 2 ft/600 mm branching stems crowded with saucer-shaped flowers more than 1 in./25 mm across. They are white, finely veined and capillaried with lilac. It is now called 'Kashmir White'.

psilostemon. Formerly known as *G. armenum*. From the mountain meadows of north-east Turkey and the minor Caucasus. Although it enjoys full sun, I have found that this grand plant does altogether better when not starved or allowed to get dry. It needs good drainage, but a little extra moisture means more luxurious plants which retain their flowers longer. From that moment in spring when pointed crimson-red buds appear at soil level, immediately identifying it, it calls for your attention. Gradually a handsome mound of wide, deeply cut parasol-shaped leaves is formed. Above them, in mid summer, comes a long succession of intense magenta-carmine flowers, dramatized by black centres. Lovely autumn tints in the foliage provide a final display. (2½–3 ft/760 mm–1 m.)

sylvaticum. From mountain meadows and open woods of Europe to Siberia, reaching the Arctic. Another early feature plant, making a good companion for *G. maculatum*. The flowers are darker, violet-blue with a white eye, standing up to 3 ft/1 m tall over clumps of dark green divided foliage. I am ashamed to say I have lost my '*May Flower*', one of several named forms, which include pink, plum and white, none of which I yet possess.

wallichianum. From the Himalayas in damp valley meadows and wood edges. 'Buxton's Variety' is the selected form. It is a treasure among many good cranesbills, and since it saves itself for the late summer it needs and deserves a good retentive soil. It makes lax sprawling stems radiating from the centre of the clump. The pretty wedge-shaped leaves are deeply toothed and speckled, light on dark green. The perfect saucer-shaped flowers are blue streaked with fine red veins which run into a cool white centre filled with purple-black stamens set around the carmine stigma. It is just breathtaking, from August to the end of October. It looks wonderful draped like a shawl over a low wall, but on the edge of a border it is a joy to look down upon and its neighbours are not too smothered by the continually lengthening flower stems. (12 in./300 mm.)

GEUM, Rosaceae. The following are all single-flowered types which are ideal as border edging plants. They like sun, but will not stand drought at the root. A reasonably heavy soil with plenty of humus and adequate rainfall will suit them.

'Borisii' (of gardens) (*G. bulgaricum* × *G. reptans*). *G. reptans* grows in high gravelly places and on shaded rocks in central Europe; *G. bulgaricum* is from the Balkans. The neat clumps of dark green leaves make a perfect setting for bright tomato-coloured flowers about the size of a tenpenny piece, on short stems (about 12 in./300 mm). They flower throughout May and June.

× **intermedium** (*G. urbanum* × *G. rivale*). *G. urbanum* 'Herb Bennet' has small yellow flowers and grows in open woods and wood edges of Europe to central Asia. This hybrid makes large ground-covering clumps of admirable green foliage, topped with interlacing thin brown stems each carrying rich yellow single flowers. The reddish-brown sepals and hairy centres remain a feature for some time after the petals have dropped. (12 in./300 mm.)

— **'Coppertone'.** This seedling occurred in my garden. It makes a rather more refined plant than its parent, with slightly nodding flowers whose petals are the softest apricot-pink, or newly polished copper. (10 in./250 mm.)

montanum. From mountain meadows and stony slopes or open woods of south-central Europe. This plant is a gem which, in cool soil, produces large cupped yellow flowers, mostly in early summer, but a few more later in the year. Just as attractive are the feathery globular seed heads in warm rusty-brown. (6–9 in./150–230 mm.)

rivale. Water Avens. From the wet meadows and marshes of the lowlands and mountains of northern and central Europe and Asia, and most of North America to the Arctic. The following are attractive garden forms which have arisen from *G. rivale*. They all need damp soil.

— **'Leonard's Variety'.** Above strong clumps of green divided foliage stand hairy red stems holding clusters of almost bell-shaped flowers. Mahogany-red calyces enclose coppery-pink petals with yellow stamens peeping below. (12–15 in./300–380 mm.)

— **'Lionel Cox'** has soft red-brown stems and dark calyces which hold greenish-yellow petals, sometimes flecked with red. It starts flowering in

May, and where there is plenty of moisture will continue almost all summer, often giving a good display in August–September. (12–15 in./300–380 mm.)

GILLENIA, Rosaceae.

trifoliata. Of rich woods in the Appalachian mountains of the eastern USA. Seen as a single stem of flower I do not think this plant would turn many heads, but growing as a well-behaved clump in a suitable setting, in part shade, it is rarely passed by. Massed stems, 3–4 ft/1–1.2 m high, are clothed with widely spaced trifoliate leaves. The colour of the russet stems intensifies towards the tips of the branchlets which are set with almost red buds from which flare ribbon-like white petals. The flowers are small but the general effect is distinctive and dainty. When the flowers have gone sprays of reddish-brown calyces remain.

GLAUCIDIUM, Glaucidiaceae.

palmatum. This beautiful Japanese semi-woodland plant is native to the islands of Honshu and Hokkaido, and is part of the woodland flora on the high mountain slopes. Regrettably I have not yet established a plant. More has to be done to create just the right micro-climate. Gardens where the air is moist as well as the soil, combined with plenty of rich leaf-mould, may perhaps see plants as described by Mr Alfred Evans in his good book *The Peat Garden*. Many stout shoots, some up to 4 ft/1.2 m in height carry two large palmate leaves just below the large, four-petalled, pinkish-mauve flowers.

GUNNERA, Haloragidaceae. There are two species of these gigantic plants grown in gardens, and they both produce the largest leaves we can grow in the temperate zone. They can be grown without access to a pond or lake, but then a huge hole, 6 × 4 ft/2 × 1.2 m must be dug out, drainage material put in the bottom, and the hole filled up with a rich mixture of loam, manure and vegetable waste. In summer ample water must be given. By natural water a good hole must still be prepared, although not quite so large. It is a waste of a good plant to press the roots into a slit in raw clay. Once established generous dressings of manure need to be given every spring if you wish for the largest leaves which have been recorded at 9 ft/2.75 m in diameter on stems 8 ft/2.5 m high. That is possible in the warm counties of the south-west, and no doubt in Ireland, but a foot or two less is still pretty impressive while leaves 4–5 ft/1.2–1.5 m across are adequate. The plants need to be sited where they are not tattered and torn by strong winds. In winter some protection must be given to the resting crowns.

chilensis (*G. scabra*) is found further south than *G. manicata* (as far as the colder regions of Patagonia and Chile) so it is rather hardier. Its rounded leaves are rather more puckered and scalloped, but the stout stems never grow quite so tall.

L. *Gunnera scabra*

manicata inhabits deep valleys and gulleys full of rich alluvial earth and decayed leaves in southern Brazil. It is the more tender of the two. It makes the largest leaves and is also distinguished by its fruiting body. It is rather absurd to talk of the flowering stem of these gunneras. They thrust up enormously heavy club-shaped stems covered with pointed knobs, or in the case of *G. manicata*, the knobs are more widely separated, are longer, and more flexible, like fingers. The whole thing is brownish-green to start with; one never sees anything that could be called a flower, but something must go on because minute round seed capsules are formed which turn orange when ripe.

HACQUETIA, Umbelliferae.

epipactis (*Dondia epipactis*). From bushy places in the eastern Alps. With its first flowers opening in late January or early February this curious little plant eventually makes low cushions packed with yellowish-green flowers. In fact each 'flower' consists of six large, frilly, petal-like bracts which are olive-green, while the centre is packed with many tiny, fluffy, yellow flowers. Division of the black bootlace-like roots should be done just before growth commences in early spring. They prefer to be left undisturbed, in part shade, when they will reappear as reliably as winter aconites. (5 in./130 mm.)

HELIONAS, Liliaceae.

bullata. The Swamp Pink. This grows in moist areas in eastern North America and flowers in May. I lost my plant before it became established. It makes an overwintering crown of strap-shaped leaves; from the centre a 12 in./300 mm stem emerges, topped with a tightly-packed head of small, pink, starry flowers.

HELLEBORUS, Ranunculaceae. These plants will grow in almost any soil and situation but do best in a retentive yet well-drained soil, in part shade or sun. They do not object to lime. Shading the roots with a mulch or dressing of manure helps to preserve moisture, and feed them; they are greedy feeders. Their large evergreen leaves are both ornamental and make good ground-cover.

Watch your plants for aphis attack in early summer when the leaves are tender and juicy; it is wise to cut off the leaves of the Christmas Rose and Lenten Roses in late winter to lessen damage by leaf spot, which shows black or brown blotches on the leaves. This can be a nuisance in warm damp weather and if left spreads to the flowering shoots and destroys them. An insecticide copes with the aphis. A fungicide, such as Captan, protects the newly emerging flower stems and young leaves.

There is a very useful booklet called *Gardener's Guide to Hellebores* by Brian Mathew, which will tell you a great deal more about this fascinating genus. The following are familiar to me:

corsicus, from Corsica, Sardinia and the Balearic Islands. It is quite hardy, but the flowers can be damaged by severe wind and frost. It makes many stout stems, usually a dozen or more, although I have stopped counting at fifty on old, well-nourished plants. They form compact, shrub-like mounds all summer of handsome grey-green leaves, markedly veined. Some people deplore their winter habit, which is to drop their stems so they radiate like the spokes of a wheel, making way for new shoots in the centre. I find that the great flower heads, made up of many pale green cups, turn upwards in spring and practically fill this gap. Staking them produces a stiff and unnatural look. They will grow in full sun provided they are not starved, or in moderate but not deep shade. They stand approximately 2–2½ ft/600–760 mm.

foetidus is found wild in Britain, and in Europe from Spain to Italy. It prefers damp woods and coppices on limestone or chalk. In the garden it grows perfectly well without chalk, in sun or shade, where not too dry. It is quite different from *H. corsicus*, although it has a similar dramatic colour scheme: drooping clusters of palest green bells stand above delicate mounds of holly-green leaves, fan-shaped and finely divided. It has a strange pungent winter smell. (18 in.–2 ft/460–600 mm.) The flowers of both *H. corsicus* and *H. foetidus* start to open early in January if the weather is not too severe, and remain in flower for four to five months.

lividus, from Majorca, is similar to *H. corsicus* but is tender, and only suitable for really sheltered gardens in southern counties. It makes a smaller plant. The beautiful leaves are dark glossy green with conspicuous cream veins, giving a marbled effect. The backs of the young leaves and the leaf stems are plum coloured. In March–April large clusters of pale green cupped flowers heavily flushed with rosy-purple almost smother the plant. I have a plant in a little courtyard facing south, sheltered from the north and east. As I write it has fifteen flowering stems, standing about 18 in./460 mm high.

I have hybrids from these two where the vigour and hardiness of *H. corsicus* are combined with the light plum tints of *H. lividus*. They vary in intensity of colouring, but none are pure green, and some have particularly good foliage in spring. This is the cross known as *H. × sternii*.

niger. The Christmas Rose. Found wild in woods and coppices on limestone in southern Europe, from Germany to Yugoslavia and Italy. My plants rarely seem to flower before the end of January. They like a fairly heavy, preferably alkaline, well-drained soil with ample humus, and then to be left undisturbed apart from a mulch and the occasional gift of farmyard manure. Seedlings seem to vary slightly. There are named clones which include 'Potter's Wheel', supposed to be the largest. All are beautiful with large flat-faced flowers held stiffly on short pink stems; some turn to quite deep shades of salmon-pink as they age. (Up to 12 in./300 mm.)

HELLEBORUS ORIENTALIS HYBRIDS

This group contains the most sumptuously beautiful of late-winter/early-spring flowers. Grown from seed few can be discarded, with colours which will include greenish-white, bronze-white, pale pink washed with green, soft reddish-plum, or deep smoky purple. In shape and size they will vary too—there will be round prim cups, dark purple outside, cool green inside; others will droop like round ripe plums; and some will hold open their large petals to show pale cream stamens in startling contrast.

These are the plants known familiarly as 'Lenten Roses'. They are all easier to grow, and generally flower more prolifically, than the Christmas Rose. They like cool conditions, so under north walls, or semi-shade from trees and shrubs, in good retentive soil, will suit them well. Their flower buds appear at the end of January if the weather is favourable, and the display of fine blooms lasts into April.

The blood of several different species has contributed to these very mixed hybrids. They include:

— **abchasicus** is from the Caucasus along the Black Sea coast. It has drooping flowers of deep red-purple, the intense colour often tinting the nectaries and leaves at the top of the stems. (12 in./300 mm.)

orientalis (*H. cyclophyllus*), creamy-green; from west to north-east Turkey, the Black Sea area, preferring damp shade at low levels, but higher it can be found in open alpine meadows.

— **guttatus,** is from Russian Georgia. It means spotted or freckled, and among the hybrids there are both white and deep pink flowers heavily spotted inside with dark red, while some of the plum shades are peppered with very fine dark dust-like markings. (12–15 in./300–380 mm.)

purpurascens, from eastern Europe, has shorter stems with smaller, very neatly cupped flowers, in shades of muddy-purple, sometimes very dark purple, with pale green inside. (12 in./300 mm.) *H. torquatus* (of gardens) belongs here, it is a hybrid. Among the best is one of Eric Smith's hybrids, 'Pluto'.

viridis. Growing wild in central and southern Europe, in coppices on limestone, this is a quiet plant with deciduous leaves. The saucer-shaped flowers have a distinctly bluish-green tone. (12 in./300 mm.)

— **occidentalis.** This seems to be the north European version of *H. viridis*, growing in similar situations, including Britain. Even among our native plants there is some variation. The flowers are smaller, but more cupped, and plain green without the bluish tinge.

HEMEROCALLIS, Liliaceae. These plants are related to *Hosta* and *Phormium*. Tough and enduring, they will grow in sun or part shade in any good border soil, provided it is not too dry, in grass in moist soils, or by the water-side. They have long been grown in gardens, admired for their lily-shaped and sometimes fragrant flowers which, individually, last only one day, but are produced in long succession. The Chinese have considered them a delicacy in salads for some thousands of years. Their new foliage, pale yellowish-green, is welcome in early spring while later the large fountain-shaped clumps make contrast, or ground-cover, or trouble, if they are in the wrong place, and flop over something more precious.

The species are not generally seen in gardens, but they have contributed to the amazing range of hybrids that can now be found, both in colour and form. There are some lovely greenish shades, many yellows, orange, soft apricot, shades of rose and deep mahogany-red. The larger-sized plants, with tall flowering stems, tend to be in less demand now but are still magnificent massed where room can be found. The small ones, some scarcely 2 ft/600 mm high, give the owner of the smaller garden a chance to look down the throats of these exotic plants. Specialist catalogues can be found giving details of many hybrids. The following are a few of the species which have contributed to the great variety:

aurantiaca. From China. It may be a garden form or hybrid; the flowers are intense orange. (3 ft/1 m.)

citrina. Of uncertain origin. In gardens it is called *H. citrina* 'Baroni'. This plant opens in the evening scented, pale greenish-yellow flowers, rather stiff and narrow. August. (3 ft/1 m.)

dumortieri. From mountain meadows of east Siberia, Manchuria, Korea and northern Japan. Early flowering, in May–June, the plant has deep yellow flowers with dark brown buds, and is very free flowering and scented. (2 ft/600 mm.)

flava. From moist meadows and steppes of south-eastern Europe to far eastern Asia. This is a very old garden plant, with clear yellow, perfectly shaped lily flowers, deliciously scented. Flowers in June. (2½ ft/760 mm.)

fulva. From southern Europe to eastern Asia, found in moist meadows and along stream-banks. This plant introduces the tan shades: the flowers have a zone of brown around the throat, and an apricot line down the centre of each 'petal'. (4 ft/1.2 m.)

— **'Kwanso Flore Pleno'.** From Japan comes this very old plant, making large clumps of broad leaves. The flowers are large, of a rich orange colour, with a strong central V of deeper orange-red. Within it is another, smaller, slightly malformed flower. This lacks the purity of form to be seen in the single flowers, but the 'petals' do not shrivel so quickly, so providing effective colour in landscape planting. July–August. (4 ft/1.2 m.)

— **'Kwanso Flore Pleno Variegata'.** The leaves are boldly striped with green and white, very handsome when it is good. The plants need to be watched, and only the best pieces replanted as it is inclined to revert. (2½–3 ft/ 760 mm–1 m.)

— **'Rosea'.** A natural variant from Kuling, China. It is soft coppery-rose, a forerunner of the pink varieties. (3 ft/1 m.)

middendorfiana. From high mountain meadows of Sakhalin, Amuria, Korea, Manchuria, north China and north Japan. Similar to *H. dumortieri*, flowering a little later. Makes a low compact plant topped with branching stems of bright orange-yellow flowers with brown buds; scented. (2 ft/600 mm.)

minor. This Day Lily produces dense clumps of narrow grassy leaves, and flower stems about 10 in./250 mm high. The large sweetly scented flowers are rather few, and lemon-yellow, opening wide from brownish buds borne well above the leaves. This species and others have been used to create dwarf hybrids for small gardens.

multiflora. From the mountains of central China. The last to flower, possibly a parent with *H. dumortieri* of one of the very best Day Lilies, *Hemerocallis* 'Golden Chimes'. Standing well above neat clumps of foliage, the flowers are soft orange-yellow with contrasting brown buds. *H.* 'Corky' is similar, with flowers of soft yellow. These two have a delicacy combined with wealth of blossom that makes them very desirable. They flower in mid summer, at 2½–3 ft/760 mm–1 m. *H. multiflora* itself grows up to 4 ft/1.2 m.

HERACLEUM, Umbelliferae.

mantegazzianum. From damp subalpine wood-edges in the Caucasus. In deep, rich, moist soil, this gigantic Cow Parsley can stand up to 10 ft/3 m, more generally 6–10 ft/2–3 m, with several flat white heads up to 2 ft/600 mm across. At the base of thick hollow stems a pile of rough dissected leaves will be several feet across. The seed head is as decorative as the flower, but should be removed before hundreds of large flat seeds have been scattered wide. It looks good broken off short, the hollow stem thrust onto a nail driven into a wall, so that the radiating spokes form a wheel-like pattern. The seeds can be left on, or removed; either way the design is complete in itself. June–July.

I must give a word of warning. The sap from this plant is very toxic, to some skins more than others. Do not plant it where children may brush against it. Every part of it is covered with fine bristles containing a virulent substance which causes painful blisters. I would not give up growing this dramatic feature plant, but teach everyone to respect it, and take care.

minimum 'Roseum' is so tiny and produces its flowers so hurriedly as if to say, why bother to compete with such an impressive relative? For those who bother to kneel down, or maybe plant it on a cool raised bed, it is rewarding. Low tuffets of finely cut, dark green leaves, produce almost stemless umbels of deep rose-red Cow Parsley flowers, held just above the leaves. (3–5 in./ 80–130 mm.)

HEUCHERA, Saxifragaceae. The most popular are probably the red and salmon-pink flowering forms which are easily grown in full sun and on any reasonable garden soil. They do not thrive in starved sand or gravel soils. Where the soil tends to be dry plenty of humus and a little part shade will help. If left to themselves they deteriorate, making many woody stems with small leaf clusters. Dug up, and the best pieces replanted into refreshed soil, they will make large handsome clusters of fine foliage, with stronger flower stems. The two I grow for their quieter colouring are:

americana. Satin Leaf. From dry rocky woods of the eastern USA to the Mississippi. This was also called *H. richardsonii*. The young leaves are an exquisite blend of soft orange-tan and brown shades maturing to green with copper-brown shading. The top sides glisten like satin, while the backs are slightly bristly. They are somewhat heart-shaped, scallop-edged and slightly puckered between the radiating veins. The flower stems, 2 ft/600 mm, topped with wide spires of tiny green and brown flowers are of secondary interest in the garden, but can intrigue the flower arranger. A succession of new leaves enhances the edge of the border until autumn, staying in good condition all winter until new ones push them aside in spring. They will thrive in sun or part shade in good retentive soil.

cylindrica. Western North America.

— 'Greenfinch'. There is nothing colourful or really dainty about this plant, but I like it. I would grow it for its foliage alone. In its best form large rosettes of round scalloped leaves are dark green overlaid with a silvery sheen. The dark veins become chocolate-brown in winter. Stiff, uncompromising 3 ft/1 m stems hold small, pale green open bells in darker green calyces. The flowers are held sternly upright. Among billowing masses of *Polemonium carneum* and *Geranium* 'Johnson's Blue' this plant provides welcome contrast in form. From seed the flowers vary in size and the leaves may be plain green.

sanguinea. Coral Bells. Found in northern Mexico and Arizona. Short stems 9–12 in./230–300 mm high carry large bells of brilliant red shades, over dark, sometimes marbled leaves. Alan Bloom has introduced very good named forms, including 'Firebird' (2½ ft/760 mm) and 'Red Spangles' (18 in./460 mm.)

× **HEUCHERELLA** 'Bridget Bloom' (*Heuchera brizoides* × *Tiarella wherryi*). This marriage, also arranged by Alan Bloom, has produced a much appreciated plant. It makes low clusters of pretty scallop-edged leaves, light green in colour, slightly rough and hairy with a dusting of brown spots and blotches along the veins. Spires of tiny pink blossoms in shades of pink, light and dark, are held on dark brownish-pink stems, throughout May and June, often with recurrent blooms. This plant must have good retentive soil, preferably in part shade. (20 in./500 mm.)

HOSTA, Liliaceae. Funkia or Plaintain Lily. Most of the hostas we grow in gardens today are hybrids or sports. Some came originally from Japanese garden clones, some are still being introduced by hybridizers in America and Japan. Eric Smith in Britain has devoted many years to this genus. I have been curious to know just what conditions are like where they are found wild, or whether any are still found in natural surroundings. I was especially pleased to have a letter from a correspondent in Japan (Don Elick) who knows the country and flora well. I quote from him:

> Hostas are amazingly adaptable but in the wild they generally grow in rich, damp, shaded sites. Only a few true bog species grow in the open, and this is mountain sunlight with long days of storms and mists. Our mountains in summer are rainy and dark. Let no one fool you about rarity. Hostas are EVERYWHERE in this country, though the species are very local. Actually they can be grouped roughly by preference to site. A few grow in true bogs or snow-melt meadows, i.e. *Hosta lancifolia*, the smaller species such as

H. *longipes* and the *venusta* group on wet cliffs or shaly slopes, and the big-leafed ones in rich woodland. My local big species are not at all distinguished, with coarse leaves and spacy flowers the colour of dirty dishwater. A nice medium sized species which may be *H. tardiflora* grows about fifteen miles to the north of here on the wet cliffs of Tenryn river gorge. I have never seen a variegated *Hosta* in the wild, the fancy-leafed forms have arisen in cultivation or were collected out of existence years ago.

In my own garden I have found that while some hostas will do fairly well in drier situations provided the soil is well enriched with humus, and covered with a mulch, they all do infinitely better in part shade where the soil remains moist. The yellow-leafed forms particularly need shelter from direct sunlight which scorches their thin leaves, although they need enough indirect light else their leaves will turn green too quickly. The lovely 'blue'-leafed forms, whose dark green leaves are coated with a waxy bloom, thrive and look better in part shade. Eric Smith has produced some lovely 'blue' forms, and new variegated ones also. Once planted in suitable conditions hostas should not be disturbed. It can take several years for a newly acquired *Hosta* to recover completely from the surgery that is necessary to remove it from the named clone. Often the first year or two the leaves are half the size they can be when properly established. Finally it must be remembered that snails and slugs thrive on a diet of *Hosta*, and nothing is more depressing than to see these lovely leaves riddled with holes. Slug bait must be put down as soon as the buds swell preparatory to unrolling the first leaves, and not forgotten later. It is obtainable now in tall drum-like containers making application simple. The following forms are well tried in gardens; most are obtainable. There are many more, but it takes years to build up stock of a new *Hosta*.

crispula. Unfortunately this especially fine *Hosta* is not freely available. It differs from *H.* 'Thomas Hogg' in having much larger leaves, of darker green, with the undulating edges broadly banded with white. It is much better when grown in shade. (2½ ft/760 mm.)

elata. Since variegation is the fashion this plant is not well known. But when something restful is needed I value these matt pale green ribbed leaves, tapering from a broad base to markedly pointed tips, with wavy edges. (2½ ft/760 mm.)

fortunei 'Albo Picta'. A great favourite, handsome when only half suited, but transformed when left undisturbed in deep moist soil in shade. The leaves will then be 9 in./230 mm long not counting the stalk, and 6 in./150 mm across, of a delicate, almost translucent texture, the centre in shades of yellow and cream, the outside border painted with a brushful of wet, dark green paint. By mid summer they will have become green. The leaves are slightly puckered between the wide-spaced veins. (2½ ft/760 mm.)

— 'Aurea'. These delicate leaves are entirely butter-yellow for their first few weeks in spring. Strong sunlight will disfigure them with brown patches. By mid to end of June they will have become light green. (18 in./460 mm.)

— **'Marginato-Alba'.** Grown in open sunlight this can be quite boring, large sage-green leaves with very narrow white margins. This also is the look of newly divided pieces. But, once established in rich soil and shade, the degree of variegation can be dramatic. In the most shaded leaves, often those shaded by others in the clump, half or more of the leaf surface will be ivory-white. In others the broad white margin penetrates from the edge down between the veins making longitudinal patterns of cream on the central green zone. This plant can be either a disappointment or a real delight. The leaves are moderately large and heavily corrugated, on tall stalks. (2½ ft/760 mm.)

— **'Obscura Marginata'.** This unhelpful name stands for *Hosta* 'Gold Edge', which some people know, while others of us call it, erroneously but understandably, *H.f.* 'Marginata Aurea'. Whatever we call it, it is an excellent garden plant, taking more light without detriment provided the soil is not dry. It differs from *Hosta ventricosa* 'Variegata' in having larger leaves, broader at the base and more rounded. The slightly puckered centre is dark green with a broad irregular greenish-yellow edge which lasts through the season. It is vigorous (2 ft/600 mm) and makes well.

'Honeybells' has the blood of *H. plantaginea*, so inherits the perfume, but has very pale lilac flowers instead of white. The leaves look similar, light olive-green and pointed, with undulating edges, but they are stronger, retaining a fresh healthy look when some other hostas are past their best. (3 ft/1 m.)

lancifolia. Although smaller than many and 'penny plain', this *Hosta* deserves to be more widely appreciated. The dark green, shining, narrow leaves make wide overlapping mounds, useful as ground-cover, attractive as a garden feature, or as leaves to pick. The flowers are good—large, deep lilac trumpets on tall slender stems—produced with such generosity as to make a welcome feature in late summer. (3 ft/1 m.)

plantaginea. One of the few hostas which comes from China and not Japan. It is very choice and lovely to look at, but not the easiest to grow well, needing both moisture and warmth well into the autumn. It is then, in October, that the surprisingly large lily-like flowers, marble-white in colour and texture, are usually produced. In cool counties the chill of winter usually overtakes them before the flower spike has had time to unfold. But the leaves are beautiful too, glossy, arching, heart-shaped leaves of a yellowish-green tone. They are as fresh as the spring in late autumn. *H. plantaginea* 'Grandiflora' is similar, but has longer narrower foliage. Both these hostas make good conservatory plants. Or they could be used (as all the hostas) in garden pots or tubs, sheltered from excessive sun, provided they are kept well fed and watered. (2 ft/600 mm.)

rectifolia (*H. longipes* of gardens).

— **'Tall Boy'**. A superior hybrid with much better foliage than the species. Large, heart-shaped and fresh green leaves make impressive clumps while above them on erect stems sometimes more than 4 ft/1.2 m tall hang rich lilac bells throughout August. A spectacular *Hosta* to place in bays among shrubs.

'Royal Standard'. Here is a valued hybrid which, in good conditions, grows easily and robustly. Stout green buds open pure white, sweetly scented trumpet-shaped flowers held well above the strong clumps of deeply veined, fresh green leaves. August–September. (2½ ft/760 mm.)

sieboldiana (*H. glauca*, *Funkia sieboldii*, etc.). This is generally recognized as a wild plant and not a garden cultivar. It grows in the woods on the west side of central Japan which receives much snow. Of all hostas this one produces the largest, most dramatic leaves. Grown from seed there will be slight variations in depth of colouring: some will be light grey-green, some more bluish. They may vary too in the amount of deep veining or puckering. But all, in ideal conditions, can make leaves up to 18 in./460 mm long from tip to base of the leaf, and 12 in./300 mm across. It is usual to buy plants from a good clone which has been selected for division. The flowers, which are very pale lilac, set in rather stumpy heads, stand just above the mounds of leaves. In late autumn the dying of these leaves is breathtaking. Almost overnight, after the first frost, the colour changes to glowing shades of honey as the great piles slowly disintegrate. (2½ ft/760 mm.)

— **elegans**. This selected form has very large leaves with a deeper tone of grey-blue, deeply veined and puckered. (2½ ft/760 mm.)

— **'Frances Williams'**. This *Hosta* has medium-sized deep blue-green leaves, heavily veined and quilted, with a wide butter-yellow margin which runs irregularly towards the centre. There are others which are probably of the same origin which look similar, and to confuse matters are probably called 'Frances Williams' too! They are all interesting but not all are as good. (2–2½ ft/600–760 mm.)

'Thomas Hogg'. I have great affection for this *Hosta*. It is so reliable. Not so glamorous as some maybe, but never untidy or boring. The medium-sized fresh green leaves are not rounded, but narrowish with pointed tips. The wavy white margin extends partly down the leaf stalk, while there is a shading of light and dark green in the centre of the leaf. Fresh leaves continue to be produced until well into the autumn, while the smooth texture prevents dirty drips from overhead trees disfiguring them. (2 ft/600 mm.)

tokudama. Said to be wild in south-west Honshu, Japan, this *Hosta* produces fewer leaves, rather cup-shaped and deep grey-blue. It is a parent of some of the new 'blue' forms. The colour is caused by a heavy wax coating over a firm textured, dark green leaf. This 'blue' colouring is a marvellous foil for orange- and apricot-coloured primulas, and, strange as it may sound, is not killed by the true blue of *Meconopsis betonicifolia*. (12–18 in./300–460 mm.)

undulata. This is a small-growing *Hosta*, very good as edging to shaded borders. The leaves are almost spirally twisted, with centres totally cream and with dark green undulating margins. It is very good in early summer but new leaves with less marked variegation are produced later in the year. The leaves stand scarcely 12 in./300 mm high, the lilac flowers on 18 in./460 mm stems, are produced in late summer.

— **erromena.** Here, thankfully, is another good, fresh green leaf. I love the variegated ones, but do need a variety of green ones to set them off. These medium-sized leaves are beautifully shaped, serenely smooth and simply veined. The lilac flowers are good too, standing tall on 3 ft/1 m stems.

— **univittata** is very similar to *H. undulata*; sometimes it is hard to tell the difference, but this one is a little taller, and more vigorous. (15–18 in./380–460 mm.)

ventricosa. This is perhaps the finest green-leafed *Hosta* with broad, heart-shaped leaves of rich dark green, evenly veined. Of all *Hosta* flowers, apart from the elusive white of *H. plantaginea*, this is the finest, with large dark lilac bells, more rounded in outline, with internal veining. (2 ft/600 mm.)

— **'Variegata'.** The variegation forms a butter-yellow border which partially seeps into the centre. As the leaf matures the variegation becomes pale cream, almost ivory, unlike some other hostas whose variegation turns to green. This makes it one of the best variegated hostas but it is not the most vigorous, needing patience as well as good conditions, moisture and good feeding. (2 ft/600 mm.)

HOUTTUYNIA, Saururaceae.

cordata is found in shady wet places from Japan, Formosa and China to the Himalayas. It can be grown in squelchy soil, even a few inches of water, or in any cool but moist border. One is warned that it has a creeping rootstock, but in several years mine has never become a nuisance; possibly it has been checked by occasional hard winters. Lax stems carry bluish-green heart-shaped leaves blotched and margined with rusty-tan. Little white flowers with cone-shaped centres stand up on short stems. There is a double form, *H.c.* 'Flore Pleno' in which the centres become a cone of white petals. The leaves smell of bitter Seville oranges—some people think it is vile. (18 in./460 mm.)

HUMULUS, Urticaceae.

lupulus. From damp or wet woodlands of Europe and central Asia.

— **'Aureus'.** The Golden Hop does best in deep rich loam. New shoots emerge in spring and rapidly make at least 10–12 ft/3–4 m of growth, decked with handsome yellow leaves. It can be trained over a wall, or allowed to run riot over an old tree or large shrubs; not a tidy plant but adds light and charm in suitable places.

HYLOMECON, Papaveraceae.

japonicum. There is some confusion about this name. The Japanese botanist J. Ohwi says it is a synonym of *Stylophorum* or *Chelidonium*. Other botanists make a distinction; it is apparently absent from Japan, and may come from China. Spring can come and go, when there is so much to see, without your noticing this modest woodland plant, but it is very pretty. Low growing with leaves cut into dainty leaflets over which hover clear yellow poppies. (12 in./300 mm.)

IMPATIENS, Balsaminaceae.

roylei. Found in the Himalayas, on damp disturbed ground. A wickedly self-seeding annual, only to be admitted to the wild garden pond, or stream-side. There its great juicy stems bearing wide heads of pale or rose-pink hinged and pouched flowers give out a strangely sweet perfume on late summer evenings. (5–6 ft/1.5–2 m.)

INULA, Compositae.

hookeri. From the eastern Himalayas. This is a lovely plant to fill up moist places in the sun. From a running rootstock come quantities of branching stems, 2½ ft/760 mm high, clothed with softly hairy leaves. Exquisite green woolly buds, like downy nests, are complete in themselves, especially filled with morning dew, but twists of yellow appear, unfolding as many fine-rayed pale yellow daisy flowers. August–October.

magnifica (*I. afghanica*, of gardens). The form is undoubtedly magnificent where there is room to show it off from top to bottom, and where it will not be caught by strong winds which will leave it tattered, or toppled. The leaves are shaped like a dock, but four times as large, of a rough matt texture. They make a handsome pile at the base of stout branching stems which can soar 6–8 ft/2–2.5 m in rich moist soil. The leaves ascend the stems in diminishing size to the wide branching head of flowers. These are large, 5–6 in./ 130–150 mm across, fine rayed yellow daisies. This plant I grow, and it conforms to all the reference books.

I have another version with similar form and foliage, but slightly smaller flowers whose petals are not so finely shredded, and which are orange, with brown centres. I also have a third version, which grows tallest of all, with scarcely branching stems, but instead forms stout but narrow spires of closely set knobby buds which open quite small yellow daisies not much more than an inch across. It makes quite the most dramatic outline, either in the garden or by the water-side. These last two must have specific names, but I have yet to find them.

IRIS, Iridaceae. The following are irises which need varying degrees of moisture, from the merely damp to several inches of water.

chrysographes. Found among bushes on brook-banks and damp valley sides in the high mountains of south-west China. It needs deep soil which does not dry out and makes clumps of light green leaves, with flowers in varying shades of rich violet-purple to velvety-black. (1½–2 ft/460–600 mm.) The broad drooping falls are just touched with a few specks of gold. There are several selected and named forms. The two I have are:

— **'Black Knight'**. The flowers are well formed, of dark indigo-purple, slightly larger than 'Black Velvet'.

— **'Black Velvet'**. The buds and newly opened petals, before the sun has dried the dew off them, are almost totally black, the texture of velvet. Twisted standards emerge between the broad central guards whose texture is of fine matt silk, a delicious contrast with the velvet-black falls. They flower in June. (1½–2 ft/460–600 mm.)

cristata. From the eastern USA. A wee thing for a damp pocket in the rock garden, it is inclined to be lost by even a small pool. From a tangled mat of slender rhizomes appear small tufts of leaves followed by pale lilac flowers with deep yellow throats. (6 in./150 mm.) There is a rare and lovely white form called *Iris cristata* 'Alba' (4 in./100 mm.) (*Iris lacustris* is very similar to *I. cristata* but much smaller, 3 in./80 mm.)

delavayi. From wet mountain meadows of south-west China (Yunnan). It is often considered a species, but may be a hybrid of *I. chrysographes*. The flowers are purplish. (1½–2 ft/460–600 mm.)

douglasiana. Confined to the coastal areas of southern Oregon and California, a stretch of almost 700 miles, and usually found on grassy hillsides and clifftops within sight of the Pacific. The flowers are variable from reddish-purple through lavender and blue to cream, marked with gold, blue or purple. The evergreen leaves are dark and glossy, making low, wide-spread tussocks, often with rose-red bases. Well suited in any reasonable garden soil, it flowers in June. (12 in./300 mm.)

foetidissima. The native Gladwin or Stinking Gladdon, from the woods of western Europe. I could not leave this out although it will grow in dry and dense shade. It is indispensable in any garden, however small, provided it is not soggy. It prefers retentive soil in part shade. (18 in./460 mm.)

— **'Citrina'** produces sheaves of larger, taller, rich evergreen leaves which some people think smell like roast beef when crushed. To my nose it is another pungent winter smell, in the same class as *Helleborus foetidus* with which it looks so well. Small yellow-ochre flowers are marked with brown pencilling, followed in November by bursting seed pods, full of large orange seeds. (2–2½ ft/600–700 mm.)

— **'Variegata'**. It is valuable in winter to have bright, well-preserved variegated leaves. These are lovely among shrubs, with fallen leaves, snowdrops and aconites. (12–18 in./300–460 mm.)

fulva. From marshy places in the Mississippi valley; needs warmth and better drainage in Britain. I once had this unusual *Iris* but through neglect I lost it. The flowers are sparsely produced and have a rather lax shape, but the colour is special, a soft warm terracotta-tan. I have since acquired something which must be *Iris* × *fulvala* but although its rich crimson-purple flowers are handsome and the plant more robust, it has not that special quality of *I. fulva* itself.

gracilipes. Comes from Japanese woodlands, in rich humus and light shade. This is another pretty dwarf, with pinkish-lilac flowers, with orange crests, held on 10 in./250 mm stems. It flowers in spring, and should only be transplanted then, never in autumn or winter.

graminea. From moist meadows of southern Europe. Thick clumps of narrow, dark green, grassy leaves almost hide the small flowers tucked in among them. The blue falls are in turn almost hidden by the broad central 'shields' of soft amethyst. The wiry standards are somehow fitted in between these two. Most people do not bother with this, but bury their noses into the little flower and breathe deeply the perfume of sun-warmed plums, preferably old fashioned greengages. (12 in./300 mm.)

innominata. Found wild in the Roque river area of south-western Oregon on rich, well-drained and wooded slopes. The original form introduced was yellow, with narrow leaves. In the wild the colours range from pale creamy-buff through yellow to orange, from orchid-pink to deep purple. They have been hybridized with *I. douglasii* and *I. tenax*, so that now in gardens it is impossible to distinguish them and they tend to be called the Pacific Coast Hybrids. They are all without exception exquisitely beautiful in many shades, including cream, yellow, greyish-lilac, sulphur-veined copper, rose-maroon veined blue and various shades of blue. They are as fascinating as a butterfly's wing. They make spreading tussocks of narrow dark ever-green leaves which emerge from rose-pink bases. Above them stand the frilled and fluted orchid-like flowers, to be followed by wide-opened seed pods, shaped like a flower, with pale beige linings. They need good drainage, but some sun and a retentive soil. (10 in./250 mm.)

japonica. From hilly woods of the southern parts of Japan, and China. The Japanese Iris sends up fans of shiny evergreen sword-leaves from its creeping rhizomes, which sometimes rise from the ground like small trunks. Its rather small flowers are carried in branching sprays some 1–2 ft/300–600 mm tall. They are soft lilac-blue, the frilly falls marked with a white central band spotted with yellow, recalling those of an orchid. Though this *Iris* is a woodlander needing a humus-rich soil and some shelter, it is shy to flower in shade in East Anglia and prefers a warm position, even in the sun, but must not be allowed to dry out.

kaempferi. It is now considered that the correct name for this plant is *I. ensata* (Thunberg) of Japan and eastern Asia. I have not yet become addicted to these although they are works of art, long hybridized, improved and enlarged, sometimes too much, over generations of gardeners in Japanese gardens and nurseries, and also in the USA. They make the most exotic-looking flower, which has predominantly enlarged falls with diminished standards. The colours range from white, pink, lavender, violet, purple and more, some plain, some splashed and striped. They like moist lime-free soil, or good rich border soil, and full sun. June–July. (3 ft/1 m.) I love my white form which I raised as a seedling years ago. I also value the variegated form:

— **'Variegata'**. The foliage goes through a dull patch as the plant is coming up to flower, but afterwards it produces splendid new leaves, fresh and handsomely striped in grey-green and white. The dark purple flowers always seem too good for a variegated plant. (2 ft/600 mm.)

kernerana. Found wild in damp places along the Black Sea coast in Turkey. A restrained and elegant *Iris* for June, with pale creamy-yellow flowers freely produced, and narrow green leaves. It likes a sunny place, in retentive, not waterlogged soil. (15–18 in./380–460 mm.)

laevigata. From shallow water and marshes from Japan to south-west China. This *Iris* loves squelchy soil, so it is ideal to plant in the water, to mask the pond edge. Unlike *I. kaempferi* it does not object to lime. Tussocks of soft green leaves are a setting for quantities of rich soft blue flowers, with broad drooping falls, like dogs' ears, with small upright standards of the same blue. (1½–2 ft/460–600 mm.)

— **'Alba'** has wide petals held out boldly with a central cream vein. The small standards are marked with a narrow vein of purplish-blue. (1½–2 ft/ 460–600 mm.)

— **'Rose Queen'** is a hybrid with *I. kaempferi*. It is taller than *I. laevigata*, and prefers a less saturated soil. The flowers are a rare shade of soft brownish-rose. There are others, white mottled with purplish-blue, and a plum-purple whose name escapes me.

— **'Variegata'** has the very best of variegated leaves for the water-side, most sharply striped in green and ivory-white. It can be smothered in big water garden plantings, but in smaller pools where it can be watched it makes spectacular clumps of foliage which remain fresh until autumn. (12–15 in./ 300–380 mm.)

pseudacorus. Found in shallow water and marshes, and boggy woods of Europe to central Asia. This is the wild Yellow Flag of our river-sides and ponds. It makes huge clumps of luxuriant dark green broad-bladed leaves, either in the boggy edge, or in several inches of water. It is adaptable and will grow in any retentive border soil in the garden. Better forms have been selected with larger, deeper yellow flowers. There is also one which has very pale creamy-yellow flowers, called 'Bastardii'. They flower in June. (3–4 ft/ 1–1.2 m.)

— **'Variegatus'** is one of the loveliest foliage plants in early spring. Pale cream and butter-yellow leaves last many weeks into the summer before changing to green. These last two, and any good deep yellow form, should be propagated by division, and care taken that seedlings from them do not root down and overpower them since they will be the common type. This can happen unnoticed all too easily. (2–2½ ft/760 mm–1 m.)

setosa. Found in marshes and bogs which are often peaty, from the Aleutians to eastern Siberia and the mountains of northern Japan. A free-flowering *Iris* for damp soil, in sun, in June. Above low arching clumps of grey-green leaves stand many branched stems crowded with flowers. From indigo-blue buds open wide drooping falls darkened with veins and shadows of deeper blue. Plenty of seed heads follow, rounded and pale brown in colour. (2 ft/600 mm.)

There is a dwarf form, about 10 in./250 mm. It has soft lilac-blue, broad, flaring falls, veined all over with deeper purple leading towards the white and cream centre.

sibirica. From damp and often peaty meadows of central Europe to east-central Siberia. This *Iris* has been grown in gardens since the sixteenth century. It is most accommodating, growing in ordinary moist or dry, but not too dry, soil. It flourishes best in moist or retentive soil, in sun, producing healthy upright sheaves of narrow leaves above which stand slender branching heads of flowers. There are many selected forms. I prefer the ones with upright narrow standards and broadly flaring falls. The type is blue, but as well as many blues there are now shades of plum, purple and white. The narrow, polished, chestnut-brown seed heads are a joy to flower arrangers. (3 ft/1 m.)

versicolor. Both foliage and flower set each other off in this shorter, sturdy-looking *Iris*. The branched flower stems carry rich purple-blue flowers with strong clear veining on a white and pale gold centre. These stand just above tidy fans of short broad leaves of a rich, almost bluish-green colour. (2 ft/600 mm.)

— **kermesina** has light wine-coloured flowers with a white and gold finely veined base to the petals. Both these irises like moist soil in sun, looking well with the orange-flowered *Primula bulleyana*. They flower in June. (2 ft/600 mm.)

JEFFERSONIA, Berberidaceae. A cool shaded situation, sheltered from drying winds in rich leaf-mould soil is needed for these woodland treasures.

diphylla (*J. binata*, *Podophyllum diphyllum*). A North American species found in woods on the eastern seaboard and in Tennessee. It is called 'Twinleaf' because each leaf is deeply divided into two halves. Pure white poppy-like flowers, about 1 in./25 mm across poised on 6 in./150 mm stems open in May.

dubia (*Plagiorhegma dubia*) comes from mixed conifer and summer-green woods in Manchuria and far eastern Siberia. Many tiny purple buds on thin wiry stems, about 4–5 in./100–130 mm tall open fragile-looking, pale lilac petals, commencing to flower before the foliage has unfolded, which finally forms low clumps of heart-shaped, blue-tinged leaves.

KIRENGESHOMA, Saxifragaceae. Wild in woodland on some of the Japanese islands, but rare even there.

palmata. This unique and lovely plant starts to flower about the end of August, until the end of September, later in cooler districts. Heavy clusters of fat, swelling buds cause the smooth purplish-maroon stems to bend low. The calyces are prominent, clasping the developing bud so that just before the petals open it looks not unlike a large hazelnut. When the petals are extended, the shuttlecock-shaped flower is about 2 in./50 mm long, pale butter-yellow, of a thick waxen texture. The flowers do not open very wide, but this does not detract from their beauty; it is the combination of buds and flowers, and the way they hang from the weighted purplish stems which is beautiful. Lush green leaves with irregularly cut edges clasp the stems in pairs. This plant must have deep moist soil, free of lime, and be sheltered from damaging winds. My plants have not suffered from slug damage, but probably because of the hostas nearby which will already have drawn the slugs to their doom. (3 ft/1 m.)

I have been given a plant which may be *K. koreana*, which holds its flowers more upright. I am not so well acquainted with it, but I notice it does not have those distinctive dark stems.

LAMIASTRUM, Labiatae.

galeobdolon (*Galeobdolon luteum*). Yellow Dead Nettle, or Yellow Archangel. From glades in woods, throughout Europe to the Caucasus. This plant can be bitterly regretted in the wrong place, where it will be smothering its neighbours, even climbing into shrubs or rose bushes. But under trees, or in rough hedge bottoms, its brilliantly frosted and evergreen leaves are much admired, as are the fine heads of lemon-yellow flowers. I have it as a carpet beneath bamboos, which seem to keep it in order. (10 in./250 mm.)

LAMIUM, Labiatae. Dead Nettle. From open woods from France to west Asia. These plants can make very useful and pretty ground-cover. Like ajugas they sometimes tend to be dismissed as rampant weeds, but both are hard to fault in their natural setting—in cool humus soil which never thoroughly dries out, under trees or shrubs. They also make very attractive edgings to cool borders, both in leaf and flower.

maculatum. The Spotted Dead Nettle has dark green crinkle-edged leaves with a broad silver stripe down the middle, rather like a badger's face. In flower there are three colour forms, a deep mauve-pink, a light rose-pink, 'Roseum', and white 'Album'. (6 in./150 mm.)

— **'Aureum'** is not nearly such a healthy plant, the leaves being totally warm tones of yellow. It needs rich leaf-mould soil which never dries out, and shelter from direct sunlight which scorches the delicate foliage. (4 in./100 mm.)

— **'Beacon Silver'**. This form has almost totally silvered leaves, a bonus for the shade garden among the many shades of green. The leaves become speckled with purple blotching as quantities of deep rose-purple flowers are produced, but provided there is adequate moisture new growth completely refurnishes perfect carpets by the autumn. (6 in./150 mm.) I have a charming white-flowered form sent to me by Mr Philip Levesley, called 'White Nancy', in which the leaves are not disfigured by purple blotching. (6 in./150 mm.)

— **'Chequers'**. There is little to distinguish this from 'Beacon Silver' except that the narrow green margin of the leaf is slightly broader and more indented. (6 in./150 mm.)

orvala. I first saw this beautiful Dead Nettle on a Chelsea exhibit of Messrs Bloom of Bressingham. Not at rest till I possessed it, it has taken several years to please it with a suitable position. It now thrives in part shade, in cool, well-drained but not dry soil. The large heads of flowers are a rare shade of coppery-pink. I also have the beautiful white form, but for me the unusual pink colouring is preferable. The leafy plants, which are non-invasive, stand about 15 in./380 mm high and flower in May.

LATHYRUS, Leguminosae. Apart from the perennial climbing peas there are these little, low-growing, bushy plants which cover themselves in spring with small pea-shaped flowers. They are easily grown in retentive soil, preferably in part shade, although they will take some sun.

aureus. Found at wood edges and in semi-shady places of Europe to the Caucasus. An unusual colour in the garden, it makes fresh, green, bushy plants about 18 in./460 mm high, carrying branched stems of orange-buff flowers, held in loose clusters. It is a quiet plant, but distinctive.

vernus. From forests, France to Russia and the Caucasus. It makes dwarf bushlets, not more than 12 in./300 mm high, set with pairs of small, oval leaves. Tiny pea-shaped flowers, purple and blue with red veins, cover the plants in early summer.

— **variegatus** ('Albo-Roseus'). In early May these low, bushy plants are smothered with dainty clusters of little pink and white pea flowers. (12 in./300 mm.)

LEUCOJUM, Liliaceae.

aestivum. From wet meadows, stream-banks and open wet woods, from southern France to the Caucasus. This is generally known as Summer Snowflake, although it flowers in spring, April–May. It makes large bulbs and leaves not unlike a daffodil. The white bell-shaped flowers are very like snowdrops, but with out-turned green tips, and hang gracefully in a loose cluster from the top of tall (2 ft/600 mm) stems. The best form is called 'Gravetye Giant'. It was selected by William Robinson, and named after his garden, Gravetye Manor. This bulb likes deep rich soil, and will flourish by the water-side where a large clump makes a good feature.

vernum. The Spring Snowflake from woods and meadows, France to the Caucasus. It appears earlier, in March, and is often mistaken for snowdrops as it is much the same height. It opens white bells almost at ground level, gradually pushing them up on stems about 6 in./150 mm high. They look like tiny lampshades with a rounded, yet arched, shape to the open bells, with rims of yellowish-green tips.

LIGULARIA (*Senecio*), Compositae. Another race of imposing plants, all needing deep, well-fed, moist soil. They need shelter from continuous strong sunlight and wind, both of which can wilt large soft leaves even if there is ample moisture. Slugs and snails too can ruin a fine display, so put the bait down early in spring and replenish it from time to tine.

dentata (*Senecio clivorum*). From damp mountain meadows of Japan to west China. Fine selected forms of this plant are sold under the names 'Desdemona' and 'Othello', but seedlings from them produce good plants, varying in intensity of leaf colour and size of flower. Branched heads of daisy flowers are held well above the leaves on maroon-black stalks. The flowers are orange, with soft brown centres. Some have shorter broad petals, others are longer and narrower; both are equally good. It is the impact of this rich orange colour held in large clustered heads which is so magnificent. The leaves, no less handsome, are large, roundly heart-shaped, almost beetroot-red when new, but becoming green on the surface, the undersides remaining purple marked with heavy veins. July–August. (4 ft/1.2 m.)

'Gregynog Gold' (*L. dentata* × *L. veitchiana*). This handsome hybrid has broadly heart-shaped leaves, richly veined, with neatly cut edges; 3–4 ft/ 1–1.2 m stems carry close-set conical spires of large, bright yellow daisies. July–August.

hodgsonii. From damp mountain meadows of north Japan and Sakhalin. This plant is similar but slightly smaller than *L. dentata*, and is usually seen with green kidney-shaped leaves, and heads of yellow daisies. (3 ft/1 m.)

macrophylla. Of damp mountain meadows of the Altai, and northern Tienshan, in central Asia. I do not have it, but it sounds and looks good in Graham Thomas's book, *Perennial Garden Plants*. He says it is rare: 'the tall horseradish-like leaves are of grey-green, and the dense spikes of yellow daisies stand aloft like paint-brushes in the August landscape.' (5 ft/1.5 m.)

przewalskii. Found in damp mountain meadows among forests, in north-west China. It differs from the others in having its leaves cut into many pointed fingers. The tall tapering stems are almost black, the top half making a spire of small, ragged-petalled, yellow daisies, effective against the black. (5–6 ft/1.5–2 m.)

'The Rocket' may be a good form of this plant, or of *L. stenocephala*. It has large rounded leaves with neatly cut edges, and purple-black stems which set off the long narrow spikes of lemon-yellow, groundsel-shaped flowers. The total shape and colour produce a most handsome addition to the garden design. They flower throughout July, followed by attractive spire-shaped seed heads. (6 ft/2 m.)

wilsoniana. From damp mountain meadows of west China. This makes a somewhat smaller plant, with roundish green leaves forming a comfortable mound about 2 ft/600 mm high and across, above which stand slender spikes of yellow flowers. It can easily be ruined by slugs or snails. (3–4 ft/1–1.2 m.)

LILIUM, Liliaceae. Most lilies need well-drained soil, so put plenty of grit into heavy soils, but add humus to conserve moisture during the growing season. Try to choose a site that gives shelter from damaging wind. From the vast field this species covers I select a few which like damp, but not water-logged, places.

concolor and its varieties. From mountain meadows of northern China and Mongolia to Japan. These lilies hold their star-shaped flowers upright in rounded heads on stems 1–2 ft/300–600 mm tall. They range in colour from scarlet to bright yellow, according to variety, some being spotted and some not. They have played a part in the breeding of the hybrid garden lilies now known as *L. × hollandicum*, which were once called *L. umbellatum*. Though I do not at present grow *L. concolor* or any of its varieties, I have some of its hybrids.

martagon. Turk's Cap Lily. From open rocky woods, wood-edges and rocky mountain meadows, central Europe to the Altai. High in the alpine meadows, tucked into a crevice between large boulders where the cows cannot reach them, you may find these lilies. In the garden they seem to like full sun or part shade provided the soil is deep. They make far taller stems, crowded with soft pinkish-purple flowers, than I have seen exposed in the wild. The white form is especially lovely in semi-shade. They flower in mid summer, and stand 3–4 ft/1–1.2 m.

pardalinum. From shady stream-banks and wet meadows in the mountains, from central California to British Columbia. This exception among lilies can be grown in the bog garden, creating a stately feature as it rises above lush foliage plants and grasses. In July stout stems will carry up to thirty bright sealing-wax red flowers, with recurved petals showing large purple spots on the lower half. (5–6 ft/1.5–2 m.)

— **'Superbum'** grows even taller, 6–8 ft/2–2.5 m, in really wet soil. Both these lilies have curious rhizomatous roots, making clusters of scaly off-shoots which can be split and replanted.

speciosum. Rare in the mountain meadows of south Japan (Shikoku and Kyushu). Flowering in August–September, these well-known pink and white lilies vary considerably in depth of colour, from white, to almost totally stained deep rose-red. The type has white wavy-edged petals partially suffused with deep rose. In rich soil they make large grapefruit-sized bulbs, and the stout stems stand 4–5 ft/1.2–1.5 m, carrying many nodding flowers. They look lovely peeping through *Polygonum amplexicaule* and *Salvia uliginosa*.

szovitzianum. There can scarcely be a lovelier lily, in shape, colour and texture. It opens large nodding, recurved, bell-shaped flowers, of cool creamy-yellow with thick waxen-textured petals in June (3–4 ft/1–1.2 m.)

tigrinum. Tiger Lily. From mountain meadows of Japan and Korea to west China. Although it may be considered common this easy lily looks magnificent in late summer. Strong stems, 4–6 ft/1.2–2 m, clothed with dark glossy leaves are topped with orange-red recurved petals, heavily dotted with black spots. Purplish-black bulbils are readily produced in the leaf axils.

LINNAEA, Caprifoliaceae. This name honours Carl Linnaeus, who originated classified plant names.

borealis. From shady conifer forests all round the northern hemisphere. This plant makes a dainty trailing evergreen over cool moist soil, ideal in partial shade, preferably in a peat bed. Tiny oval leaves are spaced along reddish prostrate stems. Small shell-pink bell-like flowers appear in mid summer at the end of short side shoots. (2 in./50 mm.)

— americana is more robust than the European plant, and seems to do better in garden conditions. (2 in./50 mm.)

LIRIOPE, Liliaceae.

muscari (*L. platyphylla*). Found among bushes and at wood edges of southern Japan to China, often in part shade. Provided it is planted in deeply dug and enriched soil this plant will grow and flower well in part or deep shade. The low clumps of overlapping, strap-shaped, evergreen leaves make interest in winter, while in September–October dense spires of lavender-violet buds on violet stems, scarcely opening to small flowers, are attractive offsetting goblet-shaped colchicums on north-facing borders. The flowers tend to be bleached by strong sunlight. There is a white-flowered form, but I have not seen it. (12 in./300 mm.)

— 'Variegata'. The leaves are cream, lightly striped with green. It always attracts attention, but with so little chlorophyll it is not very robust. (6–10 in./150–250 mm.)

LITHOSPERMUM, Boraginaceae.

purpureo-caeruleum. From open woods of central and southern Europe to the Caucasus. The Creeping Gromwell sends out long, arching stems which root at the tip, and are covered with narrow, dark green leaves, so forming wide mats. The flower stems are upright and rise from the rooted centres to about 12 in./300 mm, bearing forked clusters of quite large Forget-me-not flowers of an intense rich blue.

LOBELIA, Campanulaceae. The North American Cardinal flowers are among the most elegant for late summer, taking over from the candelabra primulas and needing the same deep, rich, moist soil. They are not averse to sunlight, but will flower in part shade.

cardinalis. From marshy meadows and shady brook-banks in all the eastern United States and Canada. Although it is a handsome plant, this is not often seen in gardens. It makes a basal rosette of green leaves followed by large spires of scarlet, lipped flowers which last from mid August until well into September. (3 ft/1 m.)

fulgens. From marshy places in Mexico, this plant much resembles *L. cardinalis* except that it has reddish stems and leaves and is not so hardy.

HYBRIDS

It is the hybrids from these two and other species which have become well-known as garden plants. 'Queen Victoria' and 'Bees' Flame', among the best known, have large, velvety, scarlet flowers and dark, maroon-red leaves. They should be covered with a mulch put down by mid November, and left until about mid March. This will protect the fat buds which are just beneath the soil surface. They flower throughout August and September, standing 3–4 ft/1–1.2 m tall.

syphilitica. Found in damp or wet meadows of the eastern United States. Looking very different from the scarlet lobelias this plant is more prim, with very erect stems clothed on the lower half with whorls of crinkled, light green leaves. The top half carries a narrow spire of small but intensely coloured tubular flowers, a combination of light blue flaring lips and darker shadowed throats. There is said to be a white variety, but I have not seen it. They need to be divided and replanted in fresh soil every few years. (2½ ft/760 mm.)

× **vedrariensis** is probably a hybrid of *L. cardinalis*, *L. syphilitica* and *L. fulgens*. It flowers later into September–October with long-lasting large spires of rich violet-purple flowers. This is a vigorous and reliable perennial, valuable in the autumn as a contrast to the many daisy-shaped flowers. (2½–3 ft/760 mm–1 m.)

LUNARIA, Cruciferae.

rediviva. Found in woods from central Europe to Siberia. This fine perennial is a relation of the well-known biennial, Honesty. Its four-petalled flowers are much paler, being a pretty soft lilac, and make a charming display for some weeks in spring, particularly among cream and white varieties of

Narcissus. It is also distinguished by its papery-white seed pods which are elliptical, not round. (2½–3 ft/760 mm–1 m.)

LYCHNIS, Caryophyllaceae.

chalcedonica. Maltese Cross or Jerusalem Cross, on account of the shape of the flowers; known since the time of the Crusades. This flat-topped Scarlet Campion does much better in rich moist soil in full sun and looks very good by the water-side, flowering in July–August, dramatic with *Phormium tenax,* especially the purple-leafed form. (3–4 ft/1–1.2 m.)

LYSICHITUM, Araceae.

americanum. Bog Arum. From peaty marshes of central California to Alaska. Large, rich butter-yellow arum flowers appear through bare mud in early spring, followed by clumps of huge smooth, spinach-shaped leaves which grow 4–5 ft/1.2–1.5 m in my garden, making dramatic features by the water-side all summer long. (I measured them!)

camtschatcense. From swampy places of north Japan and far eastern Siberia to Kamtchatka. This has pure white flowers. Neither these nor the foliage (2½–3 ft/760 mm–1 m) attain quite such large dimensions as *L. americanum*.

Hybrids sometimes occur between the two, producing cream-coloured flowers. They must both have very deep, wet soil.

LYSIMACHIA, Primulaceae. Yellow Loosestrife. All these plants will grow in full sun if the soil remains moist. They wilt and look miserable if the soil dries too much.

ciliata. From damp bush thickets, by streams and damp open woods, in the eastern and central United States and Canada. I value this plant highly in my bog garden. Although it spreads by underground shoots it is not dangerously invasive. In spring the new shoots produce a carpet of pale brown rosettes turning to light green as many stems rise, 3–4 ft/1–1.2 m. Half their length is topped with continuously flowering open heads of fresh yellow nodding flowers, each with a deep orange eye. They are not large, but are produced abundantly from July to September.

clethroides. Found on sunny hills, from Japan and Manchuria to China and Indochina. This plant also produces dense colonies of flowering stems (3 ft/1 m) from underground shoots. The flower spikes, rather like curved, miniature *Buddleia* heads are packed with tiny chalk-white flowers in late summer. Sometimes the foliage is tinted rich bronze and red in autumn.

ephemerum. From rich, damp river-banks and marshy places of Spain and south-western Europe. This also has white flowers but looks very different. It does not run, but makes a tidy clump of basal foliage which sends up 3 ft/1 m slender stems close set with leaves arranged in pairs. Seen in mass they are very distinctive, being long and narrow with wax-coated grey backs and a marked central vein. The general effect is grey, topped with long spires of tiny, round buds set close against the stem, opening to small, starry, white flowers with lilac centres which finally become dainty spikes of round brown seed capsules. Shorter, upright side shoots carry on the display which begins in early August and continues well into September.

nummularia. Creeping Jenny. From wet meadows and wet woods throughout Europe to the Caucasus. This makes a pretty carpeting plant for the water's edge, or along any damp cool border. It has small, rounded, dark green leaves set in opposite pairs along the prostrate, trailing stems. In early summer they carry bright yellow cup-shaped flowers. It can be too invasive in small gardens. (2 in./50 mm.)

— **'Aurea'** has golden foliage, exquisite as a flower among blue *Meconopsis* or blue-leafed hostas. It needs protection from scorching sunlight and is less vigorous. (2 in./50 mm.)

punctata. From shady damp places and along streams, often growing with *L. vulgaris*, from Scotland and Germany to south-east Europe. This plant is similar to *L. vulgaris*, whose place it takes in gardens, being more densely flowered with spires of bright yellow. In the wild garden, or around a lake-side or large pond, its invasive habit can be tolerated: it will establish broad sheets of bright yellow flowers with little or no maintenance. In smaller areas it is very enjoyable for a long while in mid summer, but the running clumps must be reduced. (3 ft/1 m.)

LYTHRUM, Lythraceae. Purple Loosestrife. These plants are remarkably adaptable—they will grow in saturated soil by the water's edge, even underwater, or in an ordinary border—but they grow finer, and the flowers last longer, where the soil does not dry out.

salicaria. From Britain to China and Japan, and North America. In its natural state, along most stream-banks, it is a rather strong magenta-pink. In gardens rather softer or brighter shades of rosy-pink have been selected and named. They make tall, leafy plants topped with long, flaming tapers which glow for weeks in late summer. They are great seeders, and the young plants quickly make tough deep roots, so beware—cut off the flower heads in time. (4–5 ft/1.2–1.5 m.)

virgatum. From western Asia. There are selected and named forms of this *Lythrum* which make much smaller, daintier plants (2–2½ ft/600–760 mm). They are ideal for the smaller bog garden, and could easily be lost in large areas where *L. salicaria* would naturalize. The leaves are much smaller and less dense on the much-branched stems, which carry close spires of rosy colour. Named forms include 'Rose Queen' and 'The Rocket'. They make very pretty plants, continuing to flower for many weeks, from July to September.

MACLEAYA, Papaveraceae. Plume Poppy. These stately plants have the advantage of lightweight flower heads so they need not be disfigured by staking. They are handsome from top to toe so need to be planted where other plants do not hide them, preferably not at the back of a border. They need deep, retentive but drained soil.

cordata. From open meadows in the hills of Japan and China. It makes a compact, scarcely running root. The foliage is similar to that of *M. microcarpa*, but the creamy-white flowers are of better quality. (5–7 ft/ 1.5–2.25 m.)

microcarpa. From open scrubby hillslopes in China. This is the plant we called *Bocconia cordata*, the Plume Poppy. It makes underground shoots which appear in unexpected places in spring, sending up a tall colony of 7 ft/2.25 m stems. The base and stem leaves are large, round and deeply indented, light olive-green above, with blue-grey backs. Slender panicles of creamy-white buds open to small fluffy white flowers which form tiny orange seed capsules. Although slight, the remaining seed heads are delicately colourful.

— **'Coral Plume'.** In this selected form the upper leaf surfaces are bronzed, and the dainty plumes of drooping flower buds are warmly tinted coral-pink, making a very pretty feature in August–September. (5–6 ft/1.5–2 m.)

MAIANTHEMUM, Liliaceae.

bifolium. From moist shady woods, especially those of conifers, of Eurasia and North America. The little May Lily forms spreading colonies of slender stems up to 9 in./230 mm high, carrying glossy, heart-shaped leaves, and at their tops fluffy spikes of little white star-shaped flowers.

MECONOPSIS, Papaveraceae. To most of us this name immediately calls to mind the exquisite Blue Poppy, but there are other coloured poppies in this genus.

betonicifolia (*M. baileyi*). From moist mountain meadows among forests of south-east Tibet, upper Burma and Yunnan. Like crumpled pieces of sky caught up on tall slender stems (4–5 ft/1.2–1.5 m) the petals expand to show a heart filled with yellow stamens. The leaves are covered with soft bristles. If allowed to flower too soon the plant usually dies; it must be well established, with several crowns, to be truly perennial. Plants grown from seed will vary in colour from sky-blue to rosy-lavender shades. Drying winds are death to these plants, whose home is in mist-drenched mountains. In gardens they must have deep, rich soil, moist but not stagnant, in a cool, sheltered position. In northern counties they can probably take more sun. In the south, light woodland creates both the right setting and micro-climate. But the north side of a wall, or a group of shrubs, might suit equally well. They flower in June.

cambrica. From rocky woods and open rock slopes in the mountains of west Britain to Spain. The prolific but lovely little Welsh Poppy with tissue-paper petals, in pale lemon or orange, hovers above dainty, ferny-green foliage. The only drawback is its birthrate, but that is an advantage in the right place, naturalized in semi-wild shrubbery or open woodland. There is a double form which curiously does set true seed, but not nearly so abundantly. They all flower for many weeks, from April to June, about 18 in./460 mm high— exquisite above a carpet of the Foam Flower, *Tiarella cordifolia*.

grandis. From moist, rocky meadows of the eastern Himalayas. Another Blue Poppy which varies from shades of blue to a purplish tint. It is larger than *M. betonicifolia*, but since it hybridizes freely with that poppy it is not often seen in its true form. (3–5 ft/1–1.5 m.)

napaulensis. From rocky, half-shady places in the eastern Himalayas to China. This is a monocarpic species, that is, it may live for several years but once it flowers it dies. The large rosettes of deeply cut evergreen leaves are covered with reddish bristles. The flower stem, thick as a walking stick, may be over 6 ft/2 m high. The flowers range in colour from white, light blue and pink to dusky purple.

quintuplinervia. The Harebell Poppy. From alpine turves of the north-west Chinese mountains. Perched on thin, leafless stalks are drooping bells of soft lilac-blue, hiding inside their silky petals pale cream stamens. They spread by underground shoots which form low mats of slightly hairy grey-green leaves, and are not nearly invasive enough in my unfavoured garden. They flower from May to June, on 15–18 in./380–460 mm stems.

regia. From the Himalayas of Nepal. A well-grown plant of this poppy allows no one to pass by without a second glance, and it is not blue, nor yet in flower. The huge bunched rosette, looking like some gigantic flower itself (it can become almost 3 ft/1 m across) lies flat against the dark, leaf-mould soil, every leaf covered with fine golden hairs, which catch the light or hold the dew. All its strength and beauty fade as the strong flower stem ascends finally to display a great head of fifty or more, downturned, pale lemon, saucer-shaped flowers. They set seed, and the plant is dead. (Up to 5 ft/1.5 m.)

× **sarsonsii** (*M. betonicifolia* × *M. integrifolia*). This sounds such a delight, with ivory-creamy flowers, that I obtained seed from the RHS seed list. Three seedlings came up, all looking slightly different in leaf. Despite slug bait, and daily visits after they had been planted out, two were devoured. One has survived. Will it be ivory white? I wonder. (4 ft/1.2 m.)

× **sheldonii** (*M. grandis* × *M. betonicifolia*). Progeny from this alliance have a great reputation for size of flower, brilliant colour and perennial habit. Seedlings from the RHS seed list have been much more successful, making strong leafy clumps in moist soil, sheltered from too much drying air by surrounding *Cimicifuga* and ferns, and by a screen of willow from the southern sun. The flowers should be 'splendid, of clear blue', but not overpoweringly large, I hope. (3–4 ft/1–1.2 m.)

villosa. From the Himalayas, from Nepal to Bhutan. This is a perennial with beautiful leaf rosettes in winter. The leaves are deeply lobed, covered with bronze-golden hairs which can be rotted by excessive winter wet so should not be immediately under the drip from trees, although they do need partial shade. The flowers are yellow, wide and nodding. (2 ft/600 mm.)

MELANDRIUM, Caryophyllaceae.

rubrum. From open woods and shady mountain meadows of Europe to west Asia.

— **'Flore Pleno'** is the double form of Pink Campion. It is an ancient cultivar, attractive with its rather loosely double flowers, easily grown in retentive soil and part shade. May–June. (2 ft/600 mm.)

MELITTIS, Labiatae. Bastard Balm.

melissophyllum. From open woods of central and southern Europe to west Asia. I like this curious Dead Nettle. In the upper half of its slightly bristly, green-leafed stems are whorls of large, white-lipped flowers with a difference. Each lower lip is stained pinkish-purple. It likes a little shade and leaf-mould, in a retentive soil. (18 in./460 mm.)

MENTHA, Labiatae. Mint. All mints prefer damp soil, but with their invasive habits they can make trouble if they are unwisely sited. One of my mistakes was to plant Water Mint, which has pretty mauve flowers, in my bog garden. It took a lot of moving; every small bit left undetected made feet of new shoots. Perversely it is possible to lose mints that you value. I had to move my 'Eau de Cologne'-scented mint from where it was contentedly confined and have not yet established it in a suitable home. The following mints are garden worthy, but could be dangerous nuisances in very small gardens, unless confined, perhaps in a bucket with the odd hole knocked in it for drainage.

× **gentilis** (*M. arvensis* × *M. spicata*). 'Variegata' has dark green leaves striped with gold, on reddish-purple stems. It needs sun to produce the best colour and can be useful and decorative on the edge of a shrub border that is not too dry. *Arum italicum* grows well through it, marking its position when the mint is dormant in winter, while the stems of juicy red arum fruits show up well among the green and gold of the mint foliage. (18 in./460 mm.)

longifolia. Horse Mint. From wet meadows and along water courses of central and southern Europe to central Asia. An attractive mint in leaf and flower: woolly, cylindrical heads of soft grey-blue flowers are offset by downy, grey leaves. (4 ft/1.2 m.)

pulegium. Pennyroyal. From marshes and wet meadows of mainly southern Europe to west Asia. This is used to make Oil of Pennyroyal. On damp soil it quickly makes flat-pressed mats of small shining green leaves, neat and useful as ground-cover. The whorls of lavender-blue flowers, 6–9 in./ 150–230 mm high are attractive.

× **rotundifolia** (*M. longifolia* × *M. suaveolens*). Rounded, crinkly and very woolly leaves are edged and irregularly blotched with pale creamy-white. Sometimes whole shoots are entirely white. (2 ft/600 mm.)

suaveolens. I think this is better-looking. The leaves are more evenly marked cream and green. (18 in./460 mm.)

MENYANTHES, Gentianaceae. Bog Bean.

trifoliata. From peaty bogs, marshes and shallow water all round the northern hemisphere into the Arctic regions. This is another plant to unite water and land, ideal to soften the hard edges of a large concrete pool. It is a spreading plant, and will cover yards when suited. Prostrate, branching stems are covered with smooth, grey-green divided leaves, not unlike those of the vegetable Broad Bean. These stems float like rafts onto the water from the moist pond edge. Clustered heads of white fringed flowers stand just above the leaves on 6 in./150 mm stems, in May.

MERTENSIA, Boraginaceae. Valued for their delicate blue bell-shaped flowers, these woodlanders are sometimes called 'Smooth Lungwort' to distinguish them from the bristly-leafed *Pulmonaria*. They need a little shade, in well-drained, cool, leaf-mould soil.

ciliata. Mountain Bluebell, or Languid Ladies. Found wild in subalpine meadows among spruce, or along mountain stream-banks in the Rockies from Montana–Oregon–Nevada to New Mexico. It is at its best in June, making 2 ft/600 mm high branched leafy stems dangling with small sky-blue bells which open from pink buds. In the wild it is found growing with the rosy-mauve musk, *Mimulus lewisii*.

paniculata. North America. This produces quantities of small turquoise-blue flowers which smother the sprawly bushy plants, harmonizing with grey-green smooth leaves. If tidied up in mid summer it will produce fresh flowers. (2–2½ ft/600–760 mm.)

sibirica. A close relative of *M. ciliata*.

virginica. Virginian Cowslip. From moist meadows and along streams, sometimes in open damp woods of eastern and central United States. This is one of the gems of the spring woodland garden. Arching stems 12 in./300 mm high, carry clusters of pink buds opening to cool violet-blue flowers. They droop, cowslip-like, over smooth blue-green leaves. The new shoots, as they appear through the soil, are purple. (18 in./460 mm.)

MIMULUS, Scrophulariaceae. Monkey Musk. Most of the musks quickly cover yards of wet soil, if allowed, with carpets of green rosettes and vivid flowers. They will grow in the squelchy mud at the pond margins, or on the edge of a damp border. The coarse ones are only suitable for large areas. The smaller ones are suitable for the really small pool edge, or damp cool spots in the rock garden, where they can be cherished.

× **burnettii.** A hybrid between *M. cupreus* and *M. luteus*. I find this neater growing than some. Low rosettes are smothered with pretty coppery-orange flowers in mid summer. (10–12 in./250–300 mm.)

cardinalis. Found along streams and in swamps of Oregon and California. This is an upright-growing musk which can take less-saturated soil, merely damp will do, provided it does not dry out. The light green leaves are downy, soft contrast for brilliant orange-red snapdragon-like flowers which come in long succession from mid summer onwards. Sometimes a seedling produces rich red flowers with dark centres showing sulphur-yellow stamens and throat. They stand 2½–3 ft/760 mm–1 m.

cupreus. From swampy mountain meadows in the Andes of central Chile. This is similar to *M. luteus* (*M. guttatus*), but more compact in habit. Many named clones have arisen from it, one of the best being 'Whitecroft Scarlet', which makes very small-leafed rosettes which are lost beneath bright scarlet flowers. It is best in a choice moist corner on the rock garden, where it can be cherished and where it will stand not more than 6–8 in./150–200 mm high.

guttatus (*M. luteus* of gardens). From stream-banks of California to Alaska, eastward to the Rockies. This is the familiar yellow musk spotted with brownish-red. Seedlings vary; some are more richly coloured than others. It is very rampant, lovely at the water's edge where its long trailers float out, full of flower, together with the Water Forget-me-not, *Myosotis palustris*. Included in this group would be the form 'Hose-in-Hose' in which one lipped flower sits comfortably inside another. There have been many hybrids bred from this plant, *M. cupreus* and *M. variegatus*, producing a variety of colours, but not all are reliably hardy.

lewisii (*M. bartonianus*, of gardens). Of damp mountain meadows and stream-banks in the Rockies and Sierra Nevada, from British Columbia to California and Utah. This is not one of the hardiest of musks but survives most winters, reappearing as a seedling or two if the parent has been killed. It makes low bushy little plants covered with flowers. They are such a pretty colour, warm rosy-mauve with yellow throats, continuing to blossom for several weeks in mid summer. Cool soil and part shade suit it well. It is lovely with *Polygonum sphaerostachyum*, and *Mertensia ciliata*, with which it grows wild. (15–18 in./380–460 mm.)

ringens. From swamps and along streams of eastern and central United States and eastern Canada. This needs a small-scale design to show it off. Dark green, narrow leaves ascend erect square stems, ending with a spire of narrow snapdragon-like flowers, soft lavender-mauve. (2½–3 ft/760 mm–1 m.)

× **'Wisley Red'.** This good hybrid makes compact plants with rich crimson flowers in mid summer. (8–10 in./200–250 mm.)

MITELLA, Saxifragaceae. I have long grown this plant under the name *M. breweri*, which comes from conifer woods in British Columbia. I have learnt that my plant is not *M. breweri*, but may be *M. caulescens*. In cool leafy soil, in part shade, this is one of my favourite trailing plants. It runs like *Tiarella cordifolia*, but is much smaller and daintier, its clumps and trailers covered with small heart-shaped lobed leaves. In May short stems carry inconspicuous flowers, creating a pale haze of green. When picked they are seen to be tiny green discs surrounded with whiskery fringes—such delicacy is too good to be overlooked in the garden. With choice woodlanders this little plant creates just the right floor for a miniature 'forest'. (6–9 in./150–230 mm).

MONARDA, Labiatae.

didyma. Bee Balm, or Oswego Tea. From moist woods and along streams of the eastern and central United States and Canada. The pleasantly aromatic leaves can be infused in boiling water to make a refreshing drink, and are also used still, I believe, to perfume certain blends of tea—possibly Earl Grey. These plants need a rich moist soil; they are much more prone to mildew if the soil becomes dry. They make running clumps which send up many tall, 3–5 ft/1–1.5 m leafy, branching stems topped with curiously constructed flowers. Each has a central boss of closely packed tubes from which emerge rings of curving, claw-shaped flowers. Among the cultivars are:

— **'Beauty of Cobham'.** Cyclamen-pink flowers spring from a deep purple centre while the surrounding and supporting large leafy bracts are also shaded purple—an altogether spectacular mixture. (2½–3 ft/760 mm–1 m.)

— **'Cambridge Scarlet'.** Brilliant scarlet flowers emerge from a soft maroon centre. Large bushy masses of flower are formed by late summer. (4–5 ft/1.2–1.5 m.)

— **'Croftway Pink'.** The packed centre is pale, in keeping with the delicate shell-pink flowers. (3–4 ft/1–1.2 m.)

fistulosa. This plant and its hybrids, although similar in appearance, will tolerate drier situations. Most of them are in shades of purple.

— **'Snow Maiden'** ('Schneewittchen') is pure white. (Up to 4 ft/1.2 m.)

MORINA, Dipsacaceae.

longifolia. From mountain meadows of the Himalayas. This is a plant of character. It makes clumps of thistle-like leaves, narrow, dark green and softly prickly. If you back into them when weeding you are not hurt, but are aware of the pleasant spicy smell which comes from the bruised leaves. In mid summer several tall stems, 2–2½ ft/600–760 mm appear, carrying at intervals upturned, cup-shaped calyces which are filled with pale green narrow tubes. From these come hooded, tubular flowers, first white, deepening to rose and finally crimson, all colours being seen at once on the same stem. When they have gone the best part is left, the green stem with its upturned spiny seed heads, reminiscent of the roof of a pagoda. They make a supremely decorative shape, green or dried. They need well-drained but deep retentive soil.

MYOSOTIS, Boraginaceae.

palustris. From stream-sides, marshes and sometimes wet woods of the northern hemisphere. The Water Forget-me-not of our ditches is happy along the muddy edge of the pond, even growing out into the water. In May and June it is smothered with branching stems of small blue flowers, delightful to trail among bog primulas and water irises. Once there were various forms available, with larger or darker flowers. Someone may have them still. *M.p. semperflorens* is more dwarf, and flowers nearly all summer. (6–8 in./ 150–200 mm.)

NARCISSUS, Amaryllidaceae. Most of the larger *Narcissus* species and hybrids, and several of the smaller wild ones, appreciate good moist soil. They have been much interbred, selected, enlarged and altered, and the resulting highly cultivated strains are out of the scope of this book. However, our own Wild Daffodil, *Narcissus pseudo-narcissus*, is beautiful and has yielded some delightful forms of its own, and there are some hybrids of other wild species which retain much of the grace of their ancestors, especially those of *N. cyclamineus* and *N. triandrus*. These are larger and more robust than the wild plants, and I value them and grow them in drifts, where they flourish in moist soil, or in part shade. I also grow forms of the Pheasant's Eye, *N. poeticus*, with its white perianth segments and little yellow and scarlet cups, and a few other less altered hybrids and also species, which I cannot describe here.

NEPETA, Labiatae.

govaniana. From Kashmir. This is a surprising catmint which does best in cool, moist conditions. The lower half of the plant provides a setting of light green scented foliage, while above it the erect branched flower stems are a-dangle with widely spaced clusters of lemon-yellow buds which open to paler, wide-mouthed, tubular flowers. The delicate display continues for weeks from late August into September. (2½–3 ft/760 mm–1 m.)

NIEREMBERGIA, Solanaceae.

repens (*N. rivularis*). From stream-sides and lake-shores of central Chile, Argentina and Uruguay. This is a choice and lovely little plant when grown well in sunny, well-drained but damp soil on the edge of a border, small pool or rock garden. It slowly makes close-spreading mats by means of underground stems. Surprisingly large, fluted, cup-shaped flowers—white with a yellow centre—nestle just above the leaves. (2–3 in./50–80 mm.)

OMPHALODES, Boraginaceae. These plants are valued for their lovely spring flowers, but also make good ground-cover in cool soil with ample humus.

cappadocica. Grows over damp rocks in woodlands of the south Caucasus and Turkey. This plant will grow in sun where there remains enough moisture or in part shade. It does not increase as readily as *O. verna* but makes slowly creeping clumps of grey-green oval leaves which are prettily ribbed and pointed. In spring they are smothered with dainty sprays of rich blue flowers, larger than forget-me-nots, and finer. (6 in./150 mm.)

verna. From open woods of southern Europe. 'Blue-eyed Mary' is fine for naturalizing in light woodland or shrubberies where there is ample humus and rainfall. It rapidly increases by runners when established, making dense carpets of heart-shaped leaves. Throughout spring it is decorated with waves of tiny blue flowers. (4 in./100 mm.) There is a nice white form called 'Alba'.

OPHIOPOGON, Liliaceae.

japonicus. From woods and shady places in the lowlands and hills of Japan. This is grown as a carpeting plant in Italy.

— 'Variegatus' would be very popular if it were more easily grown. The narrow strap-shaped leaves are striped yellowish-cream, with precious little green. It is not entirely hardy in my garden but increases slowly in the slight protection of a plastic tunnel. Possibly in warmer districts it would do better, but I suspect there is too little health in the plant to do well. (4–6 in./100–150 mm.)

planiscarpus. From woods and thickets in the hills of south-western Japan.

— nigrescens. This awkward name belongs to a plant which attracts attention by its very lack of bright colour. The arching, strap-shaped leaves are almost black, making spidery clusters against the soil, in summer and winter. In late summer short sprays of tiny mauve bells are seen tucked among the leaves. These have formed shiny black berries by the autumn. Both they and the leaves remain in good state all winter. This plant needs a choice site, in sun or part shade, in well-drained but retentive soil. It spreads slowly by creeping underground stolons. Seed sown produces a good proportion of purple-leafed forms. (10 in./250 mm.)

OURISIA, Scrophulariaceae.
Choice plants for damp, well-drained sites, either in the rock garden or on a raised north-facing bed. In nature they grow in the open, in moist areas by stream-sides, so in the garden provide shelter from scorching sun or drying wind. They make close carpets of foliage from creeping rhizomes, and are best in lime-free soil.

elegans (*O. coccinea*). From the Andes of Chile. This plant makes low tufts of bright green lobed and toothed leaves. Above them stand 8 in./200 mm stems of brilliant scarlet tubular flowers, not unlike tiny penstemons. They flower intermittently from mid to late summer.

macrocarpa. From moist, peaty, tussocky mountain grassland of western South Island, New Zealand, often with *Ranunculus lyallii*. This looks very different from *O. elegans*. It has large, thick, leathery leaves with finely cut edges. Above them are held large clusters of pure white flowers, rather like those of *Bergenia*, with yellow eyes, on stems 15–20 in./380–500 mm tall.

macrophylla. From tussocky mountain grassland of southern North Island, New Zealand. This plant is similar but smaller: the same exquisite flowers are carried in whorls on stems up to 12 in./300 mm high.

OXALIS, Oxalidaceae.

acetosella. From moist shady woods, including the northern conifer forests, of Eurasia and North America. The Common Wood Sorrel makes low carpets of clover-like leaves, but they are softer and of a fresher green, and fold down each night. It sends up large, frail white flowers pencilled with pink, each on a slender stem about 3 in./80 mm tall. It is thought to be the original Shamrock.

oregana. From the coastal forests of northern California to Washington, the Redwood Sorrel is a rather larger plant, its flower stems reaching 6 in./150 mm high, and its leaflets often having lighter green marks. The flowers are pale to rose-pink, veined with a darker shade. This is a superior plant to our native Wood Sorrel.

PACHYPHRAGMA, Cruciferae.

macrophylla (*Cardamine asarifolia*). From the deciduous forests of the Caucasus. This useful and pretty plant will grow and flower in quite deep shade. Bunched heads of small white cruciform flowers standing about 12 in./300 mm high appear in early spring like patches of snow among the first daffodils. They are followed by large, round, shiny green leaves, their overlapping mounds making handsome ground-cover.

PACHYSANDRA, Buxaceae.

terminalis. From the hill and lowland forests of Japan and China. This plant will make carpets of evergreen foliage in densest shade provided it is not too dry. In moist leaf-mould soil the underground stems of thick-textured, dark green leaves make dense but attractive ground-cover, topped in spring with loose spikes of creamy-green flowers. (12 in./300 mm.)

— **'Variegata'** has the toothed edges of its leaves painted creamy-white. It is a little less vigorous. (10 in./250 mm.)

PAEONIA, Ranunculaceae. Paeonies, whether species or cultivars, need to be planted in deeply dug holes, in a rich mixture of decayed vegetable matter. They last longer in flower if sited with some shelter from direct sunlight and damaging wind. A good mulch is beneficial and the occasional dressing of farmyard manure for feeding.

cambessedesii. Comes from the Balearic Islands so is rather tender and needs a sunny situation in well-fed soil. It makes a short, sturdy plant with outstandingly good leaves. Of neat and tidy shape they are, in spring, dark bluish-green with a silvered sheen on the surface, the undersides being rich crimson-purple. Deep rose-pink flowers with red filaments and purple stigmas crown this rare plant. (12–18 in./300–460 mm.)

delavayi. From openings in pine and evergreen oak forests of Yunnan and east Tibet. This makes a woody shrub, up to 5 ft/1.5 m. Its chief beauty lies in the foliage, which is finely cut, stained and veined with maroon. The downturned flowers are of wax-like texture, dark crimson in colour, sometimes blackish-crimson, lit with golden anthers.

emodi. Grows in openings in mixed forests of an evergreen oak, spruce and tree rhododendrons, in high mountain forests of the central and western Himalayas. In spring the new leaves are bronze and shining, each deeply cut to the vein. Thin, red-tinted stems carry two or three nodding white flowers. They are flat-faced, about 3 in./80 mm across, ivory-white petals centred with a golden circle of stamens. (3 ft/1 m.)

lactiflora. From north-east Asia. This beautiful and unsurpassed paeony is the forerunner of the large-flowered Chinese hybrids. Easily grown in reasonably fertile soil its huge, white, single flowers with their central boss of yellow stamens are well contrasted with healthy bronze-tinted foliage and stems. (3 ft/1 m.)

lutea. From openings in pine and evergreen oak woods of the mountains of Yunnan and east Tibet.

— ludlowii. This is another paeony I value more for its foliage and form than its flowers—which I often miss in the spring, being smallish, drooping, saucer-shaped blooms, clear yellow in colour, already concealed in the imposing foliage which clothes the large woody stems, up to 6 ft/2 m in height. I value it as a background shrub, while in autumn large fat seed pods dangle beneath the leaves, filled with shining black seeds, large as marbles.

mlokosewitschii. From the rocky sides of gorges in deciduous mountain woods, in two limited areas of the Caucasus, and west Elburz. It is true that the pale, lemon-yellow globular flowers are fleeting but the whole plant contributes colour to the garden for months. By the end of February fat, cherry-red buds are breaking through the soil, slowly unfolding pleated leaves of warm brownish-maroon, which only slowly fade to soft grey-green as the flower buds swell in May. It is worth the whole year of waiting to see the large, rounded petals open to filtered sunlight, sheltering in their hearts golden stamens surrounding a cherry centre. In the autumn tight seed pods split open to show blue-black 'pearls' nestling against a crinkled crimson lining. (2–2½ ft/600–760 mm.)

obovata alba. From glades in mountain woods, from Japan and far eastern Siberia to western China. You need to be in the garden every day in spring to make sure you do not miss such fleeting but memorable beauty. Perfectly round petals form translucent globes of alabaster-white, parting just enough to show a ring of yellow stamens enclosing a crimson stigma. The stems and leaves are lovely too, tinted with soft cherry and copper tones. Surrounded by soft spring colours it needs shelter from sudden cold winds, even though it be May. Late in the autumn there will be large satiny-blue seeds. (2–2½ ft/ 600–760 mm.)

veitchii. From openings in forest and bush on the mountains of south-west China. This pretty paeony is far removed from the heavy-headed double cultivars. It has dainty, finely cut, branched stems of foliage, dark green in colour, above which are carried flat-faced single flowers with slightly fluted edges. Their colour ranges from deep magenta to palest shell-pink, the centres filled with cream anthers on pink filaments. Grown from seed they vary in size and colour. All are pretty but it is worth selecting the larger flowered forms. They flower freely, followed by copious seed heads which are also attractive to pick—not too large and filled with dark blue seeds. The pale forms are known as *P.v. woodwardii*. (12 in./300 mm.)

PATRINIA, Valerianaceae.

triloba (*P. palmata*). From mountain meadows of Japan. A plant that flowers in July, in part shade, is worth knowing. Provided the soil has remained damp enough this little plant will produce cool sprays of lemon-yellow flowers above fresh green, deeply cut leaves. It spreads in a modest fashion, too nice to be a nuisance, not more than 12 in./300 mm tall.

PELTIPHYLLUM, Saxifragaceae.

peltatum. From mountain stream-sides of the northern Sierra Nevada in California. This is a plant for holding firm a muddy bank for its thick flattish rhizomes interweave over the surface of the clay. In early spring 2 ft/ 600 mm tall red-tinted, naked, hairy stems suddenly appear, topped with flat heads of pale pink flowers. As they fade scallop-edged parasol-shaped leaves, up to 12 in./300 mm across on 2–3 ft/600 mm–1 m stems cover the area with eye-catching splendour. In some gardens they turn beautiful coppery shades in autumn; in mine they disintegrate into dreary shades of brown.

— **'Nanum'** is a smaller version. The leaf stems are 6–12 in./150–300 mm tall, the rounded leaves bronze-margined on their shining surfaces. I find it a handsome leaf to plant on a damp corner by the edge of a grass walk. Both these plants will grow away from water, provided the soil remains damp.

PETASITES, Compositae. These plants should only be used with careful forethought, as they are very invasive. Where there is room, around large lake-sides, farm reservoirs or heavy clay banks that need binding and covering, they can be dramatic and handsome. If you do make a mistake it is now possible to use a systemic weedkiller to remove them. Before such inventions they were ineradicable.

fragrans. From southern Europe and north Africa. On a mild day towards the end of January or in early February, you may suddenly catch a sweet smell of almonds. It comes from this plant, Winter Heliotrope: 6 in./150 mm stems carrying up to ten little clusters of flower emerge before the leaves appear. Because there is little else to admire you look closely and see that the tiny starry flowers are white, with buds and calyces stained dull purple. Inside the flowers are little streaks and dots of purple. Rushing up to smother them are round, light green, heart-shaped leaves which will be from 6–8 in./150–200 mm across, making impenetrable carpets, well sited in hedge bottoms or waste land. This plant can be a pestiferous nuisance in the wrong place but I thought it looked beautiful along the road sides in Ireland.

japonicus. From along streams in the woods of Japan and China. The variety *P.j. giganteus* is from north Japan or Sakhalin, and makes overlapping mounds of enormous round leaves, almost as impressive as *Gunnera*, up to 4 ft/1.2 m across. They disappear in winter, leaving totally bare soil which is dotted in February with round green buds the size of cricket balls. Rows of pale green bracts turn back like a ruff to leave a central posy of tiny, white, close-packed daisy flowers. The effect is enchanting, in the right place.

PHLOX, Polemoniaceae. The United States of America is the home of our garden phloxes, which vary from creeping mats and cushions to the tall border varieties. There are many species and cultivars. The following are a few that prefer a cool and rather damp situation:

adsurgens. From shady rocky slopes and cliffs of the coast ranges of north California and Oregon. Too often thrust onto a hot rock garden, this lovely *Phlox* prefers a little shade and plenty of humus in soil that does not dry out. It makes a scrambling patch of lax stems covered with small, shining, evergreen leaves. Twisted buds open to shallow saucers of bright salmon-pink. *Phlox* 'Wagon Wheels' is the same colour, but the petals are narrower.

amoena (of gardens) (*P. × procumbens*, *P. stolonifera × P. subulata*). Since writing *The Dry Garden* I have decided that this lovely little plant does not really flourish in very dry conditions. I have had to provide it with rich humus soil, but have no doubt it would be no problem where there was more rainfall. The type makes fairly tight spreading mounds of narrow leathery leaves sending up clusters of pinky-lilac blossoms on 6 in./150 mm stems.

— **'Variegata'** is a splendid plant growing surprisingly well for a variegated plant. It excels itself by producing strong heads of silky pink flowers which actually add something to the already colourful foliage. (6 in./150 mm.)

'Chattahoochee', possibly a hybrid between *P. divaricata* and *P. pilosa*, is an outstanding plant. Lax stems 6–9 in./150–230 mm long are clothed in narrow, slightly hairy, dark green leaves. They are topped with wide heads of silky flowers. The petals are widely spaced, joined at the centre by a wine-red patch. The soft rich-blue bleaches to very pale blue as they fade, while the central zone deepens to purple, the whole making a striking harmony of blues on the same plant. I find it does best in cool shaded soil; tucked against a taller plant is sometimes enough shelter. It starts to flower in May, continuing until early July.

maculata. From moist woods and along streams of eastern North America. This is a tall plant reaching 3 ft/1 m high, with red-spotted stems and rather narrow oblong heads of pale purple flowers. I once grew this 'Wild Sweet William', as it is called in America, but unfortunately have lost it.

'Millstream', probably a hybrid between *P. amoena* and *P. stolonifera*, makes low, tidy carpets of small grey-green leaves. Loose heads of mauve-pink flowers stand above on 6 in./150 mm stems. It will take more sun than some, but will not tolerate drought.

paniculata. From woods of the eastern and central United States. This is the origin of many bright coloured border phloxes. It makes a tall willowy plant, up to 4 ft/1.2 m, and when well grown into a substantial clump the delicate lilac-mauve heads are very attractive. It is not often seen in gardens, but its offspring need deep rich soil with adequate moisture all summer. A border which does not stand in sun all day is preferable. Such conditions help the plants to resist attacks of eel worm, to which they are martyrs. There is also a white form, *P. paniculata* 'Alba'.

There are many named cultivars which I do not have space or climate to grow well, but I have the following variegated forms:

— **'Harlequin',** produced by Alan Bloom, has rather less cream variegation than *P.p.* 'Norah Leigh', but grows more strongly. The long narrow leaves have a shadowed central zone surrounded by an irregular border of cream, which becomes wider and more conspicuous on leaves nearest the top of the stems. Heads of suffused purple-violet flowers in August seem surprisingly good for a variegated plant. They smell delicious. (2½ ft/760 mm.)

— **'Norah Leigh'** has almost totally cream leaves, with only a thin central zone of green. The result is a plant of little vigour, but it survives and manages to produce pale lilac flowers. (1½–2 ft/460–600 mm.)

pilosa. From the prairies of the central United States and Canada, and also in the east. This *Phlox* runs about, sending up quantities of fine stems, 15–18 in./380–460 mm high, from underground shoots. Quite large loose pyramidal heads of soft pinky-mauve flowers, sweetly scented, provide colour for most of the summer, continuing on a succession of side shoots. This is a really good plant in retentive soil, and where it cannot engulf tiny neighbours. In drier soil it flowers well in part shade.

PHORMIUM, Liliaceae. These plants provide a sharp architectural feature, as yuccas do in the hot dry garden. They like heavy, enriched soil in full sun. In cold districts it is wise to protect them in winter with straw or bracken and finally a sheet of polythene tied around. Continuous freezing wet can kill them to ground level, if not outright. Winter inspection is necessary by water-sides to ensure that water voles are not making their larder in the succulent leaf bases.

cookianum (*P. colensoi*). From damp mountain scrub and grassland, and on wet rocks and cliffs in New Zealand. This makes a much smaller plant than *P. tenax*, with stiff sword-like leaves, valued in smaller settings as contrast among soft rounded shapes. It flowers more regularly. Wide-spread stems about 4–5 ft/1.2–1.5 m high carry rather dingy green and orange tubular flowers, but the almost black spikes of twisted seed heads are very decorative. There are several variegated forms to be had, imported from New Zealand, where they have been developed. They need protection from cruel north-east wind and frosts.

tenax. New Zealand Flax. From river banks and marshes, damp sandy or gravelly places of lowland New Zealand. While the smaller, colourful, variegated forms are very admirable this one, huge and imposing, beats them all for form and dignity. Sword-like leaves, 5–8 ft/1.5–2.5 m high of smooth grey-green, edged with a dark brown line, can make a clump many feet round and across, like a gigantic, stiffly upright *Iris*. The curious flower spike towers up to 12 ft/3 m, carrying clusters of dull red flowers which become black bunches of short banana-shaped seed pods.

— **'Purpureum'**. There are variations in size and tone of this form. The best have large, dark purplish-brown leaves and are propagated by division. Seedlings produce some purple-leafed forms, not necessarily as good—or they might be better. (4–5 ft/1.2–1.5 m.)

— **'Variegatum'**. There are now several different clones available; the best have bright yellow leaves thinly striped with green, others commence with cream-streaked leaves maturing to grey-green edged with cream. In frost-free districts they are breathtaking, looking like great bursts of sunlight, 6–8 ft/2–2.5 m high and across. In less favoured districts they are still impressive, but it is wise to protect them.

PHYSALIS, Solanaceae. Winter Cherry. Chinese Lantern. There are two separate species of this plant.

alkekengii is found in open woods and bushy places from central Europe to the Caucasus. This is the Bladder Cherry of the ancients, with rounded 'lanterns' of bright orange-red. (18 in./460 mm.)

franchetii. From Japan. This plant is more luxuriant, with bigger leaves and larger, more pointed lanterns. It will grow in almost any soil, but does better where it is not too dry. Tucked into some inconspicuous corner where its running roots will not be an irritation, it is a pleasure to come across in autumn, hung with brilliant orange-red papery 'lanterns'. (2–2½ ft/600–760 mm.)

PHYSOSTEGIA, Labiatae.

virginiana. The Obedient Plant. From damp places in the east-central United States and Canada. Running shoots send up many tall, slender stems, 2½–3 ft/760 mm–1 m high, alternately set with pairs of narrow green leaves. Tapering spires, sometimes branched, of close-set, narrow, tubular flowers in glowing pinky-mauve make a display for weeks in mid summer. The flowers stand out from the stem on rows of hinged 'ratchets', so that you can push them to face another way. I wonder why such a complicated mechanism has been evolved?

— **'Alba'** produces white flowers. It is not quite so adept at being pushed around, but I like the stems of close-set, upturned green calyces which remain to make interesting green spikes when the flowers have gone. (2½–3 ft/760 mm–1 m.)

— **'Vivid'.** This flowers later, in early autumn, and makes shorter, denser spikes of light purple flowers, good on the edge of the border, among colchicums, or in front of Japanese anemones. (12 in./300 mm.)

PHYTEUMA, Campanulaceae.

halleri. From mountain meadows and open woods of the central and southern European mountains. This is a tall strong rampion, growing to 2 or even 3 feet/600 mm–1 m, with heart-shaped leaves, and long columns of black-purple, curiously-shaped flowers which open halfway up but not at the tip. It seems to prefer damper meadows than most of its relatives.

PHYTOLACCA, Phytolaccaceae. These completely herbaceous plants take up a lot of room when well grown in deep, retentive soil. They make a huge woody rootstock which sends up thick, branching stems set with large, oval leaves up to 6 in./150 mm long. The foliage effect alone can be interesting as contrast among smaller-leafed shrubs, or at the back of herbaceous plants. All parts of these plants are poisonous.

americana. From river-banks, open woods and bushy wood edges of the eastern and central United States. Every branch holds an upturned spike densely set with small, starry, white flowers. Slowly they develop as small green fruits. Gradually the tiny stalks and calyces turn carmine-pink as each fruit, still showing itself to be made up of a cluster of seeds, turns purple and then shining black. (4–5 ft/1.2–1.5 m.)

clavigera. From Yunnan, south-west China. This species starts with pokes of vivid pink flowers but the final heads of evil-looking black fruits are made as much rounder, simpler berries containing a cluster of seeds inside. The contrast of black fruits with their crimson-stained stems and the surrounding yellows of autumn foliage can be very dramatic. (4–5 ft/1.2–1.5 m.)

PLATYCODON, Campanulaceae. Balloon Flower.

grandiflorus. Widely scattered through the mountains of the Japanese islands, also in China, Korea and Manchuria. Being a relative of the campanulas, I find these lovely plants do best in deep, fertile soil. They flower late, from July to September, so need some moisture in mid summer. Neat clumps made up of many short stems, up to 12 in./300 mm, are set with small blue-green leaves. They are topped with a spire of large buds which slowly inflate like a balloon, until the petals split open to show large, flat-faced flowers with pointed petals in shades of blue, pale pink 'Mother of Pearl', and pure white.

PODOPHYLLUM, Podophyllaceae. These plants when suited make slowly creeping rootstocks in cool, shady places in damp leaf-mould soil. They are curious, elegant specimen plants to be watched from the moment they unfold their pleated umbrella-like leaves, poised on the top of single stems.

hexandrum (*P. emodi*). From woods and among bushes in Sichuan, south-west China, to the Himalayas. Round, deeply lobed leaves are mottled brown when they first appear. On top of the leaf sits a solitary white-cupped flower. Later in the year, as the leaves begin to deteriorate, you will be astonished to see a large red fruit, as big as a bantam's egg, hanging just below the leaf. (18 in./460 mm.) *P.h.* 'Majus' is an extra-large form; *P.h. chinense* has rose-pink flowers.

peltatum. May Apple. From moist woods of the eastern and central United States and Canada. This is similar, with rose-coloured fruits. They say it is a good colonizer, but I don't seem to have just what it needs yet. (18 in./460 mm.)

POLEMONIUM, Polemoniaceae. These plants will grow in sun, or part shade, in retentive soil. Their pretty divided foliage and silky cup-shaped flowers will not stand very drying conditions.

caeruleum. From damp meadows of northern Eurasia and in mountains further south and in North America. This plant has long been known in gardens as Jacob's Ladder. At its base it makes a tidy mound of long, arching stems of narrow leaflets arranged in pairs. At the top of upright, branched stems, 2½–3 ft/760 mm–1 m, are clusters of innocent-faced flowers, wide open, sky-blue, the unmarked centre fading to white, holding out orange-tipped stamens. They are produced for weeks, even months on end, especially if not allowed to set early seed. There is a fine white form, and varying shades of blue. *P. reptans* is shorter, 2 ft/600 mm, with a more open, spreading head of flowers and less finely cut foliage.

carneum. From woods in the coast ranges of north California and Oregon. This makes tumbled stems smothered in loose heads of large shell-pink saucers which open from cream buds and fade to soft mauve, about 18 in./460 mm high and widely spreading.

foliosissimum. From the Rocky Mountains. This lovely plant produces throughout the summer a succession of rich purplish-blue cups, lit by orange stamens. It still looks good in late August with *Geranium wallichianum*

'Buxton's Variety' at its feet while *Ajuga reptans* 'Burgundy Glow' spreads its warm pink-toned carpet beyond them. (2½–3 ft/760 mm–1 m.)

POLYGONATUM, Liliaceae. Solomon's Seal. These are woodland plants that need to be left undisturbed in cool positions in humus-rich, retentive soil. They slowly make fat, white rhizomes which lie just beneath the soil surface. Polygonatums are indispensable among ferns and hostas for creating a lush, leafy background, and are much appreciated by flower arrangers whether for their arching stems of fresh green leaves, or for the little cream-green tipped bells which appear in spring. With hostas they die beautifully in autumn, glowing honey-gold before they become transparent and collapse.

falcatum (*P. japonicum* of gardens). From thin woods and open glades in the hills of Japan and Korea. I know only 'Variegatum', the variegated form. This plant has pink-tinted stems with smaller oval leaves narrowly edged with ivory-white. The stems stand more upright, and are not so tall as the following plant. (2–2½ ft/600–760 mm.)

× **hybridum** (*P. multiflorum* × *P. odoratum*). From woods and glades of Europe and northern Asia. This plant makes widely arching stems, 3–4 ft/ 1–1.2 m in length with large, shining, ribbed leaves flaring to left and right on the upper side of the stem. As the stems unroll in spring, beneath them hang clusters of four or five small, green-tipped ivory bells, about ¾ in./20 mm long, and narrow.

I have another form whose name I do not know. Although similar, it has a special difference. It produces shorter, more upright stems with smaller, more close-set leaves with wax-blue undersides; the small flowers are followed by a fine crop of berries. First they are dark bloomy-green, finally almost black—lovely for autumn arrangements. (1½–2 ft/460–600 mm.)

— **'Flore Pleno'.** This I have not seen, but I hope one day I shall find a plant. Graham Thomas says the double flowers are like ballet dancers' skirts.

— **'Variegatum'.** This plant is also rare in gardens. Its leaves are strongly striped with creamy-white and slightly twisted. It is slow to increase, which is why it is scarce. (1½–2 ft/460–600 mm.)

verticillatum. Distributed over the temperate Himalayas and pretty general in the northern hemisphere, in woods and rocky glades in woods, mostly in the mountains. This plant is not often seen, although found in Perthshire in 1792, and cultivated by John Tradescant as early as 1656. It is not showy, but I like its vertical form. Tall, slender stems, 4–5 ft/1.2–1.5 m, in rich soil, make graceful columns set with whorls of long, narrow, pointed leaves. They diminish towards the top of the stems where, at the nodes, are clusters of tiny, drooping, greenish-white bells. These become clusters of little red berries by the autumn.

POLYGONUM, Polygonaceae. The Knotweeds. These plants range from

M. Several kinds of *Polygonatum*

the jungle-forming canes of *P. sachalinense* to the flat-spreading mats of *P. vaccinifolium*. Although alarming in unsuitable places, the larger ones are noble in the wild garden. The rest provide some of our most attractive plants in the damp garden. They all need retentive soil, some needing more moisture than others, especially those with large leaves.

affine. From the Himalayas, where it grows on rocky river-banks and meadows, and hangs in rosy clumps from moist precipices, often with *Anaphalis triplinervis*. In gardens it will stand less wet soil, but must not dry out. The type has short thick spikes of salmon-pink flowers. A form called *P.a.* 'Darjeeling Red' starts with thin rat-tail spikes, white at first, deepening to pink and finally filling out and deepening to dark crimson-red, all shades seen at the same time. The warm, reddish tints of the winter foliage are especially good. (10 in./250 mm.)

— **'Donald Lowndes'** has short, thick pokers of seemingly double salmon-pink flowers. They flower from mid summer until the autumn frosts, and then the low carpeting foliage turns bright reddish-brown, remaining a feature all winter. (8–10 in./200–250 mm.)

amplexicaule. From the Himalayas. This makes both a feature and a fine background plant. Although it will grow in any good border soil, in rich, damp soil it makes huge leafy plants, 5–6 ft/1.5–2 m high and across. From mid summer until the first frosts it is alight with slim, vivid, crimson tapers. There are also a pale pink and a white form. Lovely behind *Aster × frikartii*, *Aconitum carmichaelii* 'Arendsii' or *Lilium speciosum*.

— **'Arun Gem'** may be related to *P. amplexicaule*, but its habit is very different, making small, compact, leafy plants, covered with downward-tilting flower heads curved like a bird's head, ending in a shining bronze tip. It flowers from August until cut by frost. (12–15 in./300–380 mm.)

bistorta. From damp meadows of northern Eurasia far into the Arctic. It is a mountain plant further south.

— **'Superbum'.** This selected form produces in May–June fat pokers of densely packed flowers 3½ in./90 mm long, more than 1 in./25 mm across, of soft mauve-pink. Large dock-like leaves are almost 10 in./250 mm long and 6 in./150 mm wide. It must have ample water, and loves to grow by the water's edge; slowly invasive. (2½–3 ft/760 mm–1 m.)

campanulatum. From damp places in the Himalayas. This has lovely foliage as well as pretty flowers. It starts at ground level in spring, covering damp land with clusters of crinkled, dark green leaves. As the colonies of flower stems grow, up to 3 ft/1 m, one admires the ribbed leaves with pale buff-coloured backs set along the entire stem. Finally they are smothered with drooping panicles of tiny, pale pink bell flowers which open from buds of deep rose. Although this plant spreads by surface shoots it is easily dislodged, never a nuisance. Its frothy heads of colour are a pleasure for weeks in late summer, early autumn. It will flower in sun or part shade.

carneum. This plant belongs to the *P. bistorta* group, but is much more suitable for small gardens. It does not invade but makes tidy clumps of long, narrow leaves which are both undulating and curving. The almost bare flower stems are topped with fluffy bottle-brushes of coral-pink. It flowers prolifically, at its best in early summer, but can make a fine show in autumn. It will stand less moist soil than *P. bistorta*. (1½–2 ft/460–600 mm.)

cuspidatum. From damp, sunny places in the hills and mountains of Japan, Korea and China; a dwarf form high in the Japanese mountains. Unfortunately this plant can only be considered in very large gardens or areas of wild garden: from colonizing underground roots it sends up many branched stems, handsomely clothed with large, pale green, oval leaves which are hung with frothy chains of little creamy-green flowers. Sometimes it can be considered as a specimen group in grass, controlled by frequent mowing. (5–7 ft/1.5–2.25 m.)

— **'Compactum'.** I originally bought this as *P.* 'Reynoutria', said not to spread. But soon it was popping up in all the wrong places. Where no harm can be done, and where colourful ground-cover in clay soil is required, it is very pretty, with shortish (2–2½ ft/600–760 mm) stems crowded with round leaves and showy clusters of raspberry-pink flowers followed by crimson seed heads, in late summer and autumn.

— **'Spectabile'** is as colourful as a parrot in early spring, as bright red stems, thick and jointed like bamboo, unfold buds and leaves that are first washed with cherry and yellow but gradually simmer down until a large leafy plant, more than 6 × 6 ft/2 × 2 m is left, covered with large, oval leaves striped and marbled in shades of green and butter-yellow, with touches of pink. Sometimes there is a spray of entirely cream leaves. It needs heavy, damp soil and shelter from scorching sun and wind, and is no less invasive than the plain form.

miletii. From moist stony alpine turf in the west Chinese mountains and Tibet borderlands. Another plant in the *P. bistorta* class, but I find it one of the less easy ones. It needs really moist soil, and can be overlaid by large calthas or ligularias in late summer and autumn. It makes slowly increasing clumps of dark green, narrow, undulating leaves, producing on almost bare stems flower heads the size and shape of rich, ripe loganberries, a dark crimson-red. (18 in./460 mm.)

paniculatum. From damp places in the Himalayas. This makes a handsome plant where there is room. A woody rootstock sends up a mass of fresh leafy growth which sets off feathery sprays of creamy-white flowers. These appear in mid summer, continuing to produce odd panicles for weeks. (Up to 5 ft/1.5 m.)

polystachyum. From rich ground and snow hollows of the high mountain grasslands of west China to the Himalayas. I used to be confused with these two, but *P. paniculatum* does not spread whereas this one must only be used in large, damp landscapes where it makes spreading, weed-smothering clumps of handsome, pointed foliage, with red veins and stems. Frothing sprays of small white flowers are a feature in early autumn when their fresh appearance is welcome. (4–5 ft/1.2–1.5 m.)

sachalinense. Found along mountain streams and in damp mountain gorges of north-west Japan and Sakhalin. This is the giant of them all, only suitable along river-sides, reservoirs or lake-sides, with other great herbs such as *Petasites japonicus giganteus* and *Heracleum mantegazzianum*; or it may be isolated in grass and mown around. The thick, hollow, jointed stems which grow up and die down every year soar to some 10–12 ft/3–4 m high. They are hung with large, oval, green leaves, at the base of which, in mid summer, dangle catkin-like sprays of small greenish-white flowers. They create a tropical effect but can be bitterly regretted in the wrong place.

sphaerostachyum (*P. macrophyllum*). From moist stony alpine turf in the west Chinese mountains and Tibet borderlands to the Himalayas. Here is another late-flowering and lovely *P. bistorta* type. In moist soils, in sun, it flowers continuously throughout late summer and autumn. It makes neat compact clumps of narrow, wavy, dark green leaves. The flowers are small pokers on 1½–2 ft/460–600 mm stems, made of smooth buds which do not open to show their stamens, the waxy texture adding to the almost luminous shade of amethyst-pink.

vacciniifolium. From bouldery slopes among birches and dwarf rhododendrons in the Himalayas. This is one of the smallest and prettiest of the polygonums. Completely prostrate reddish-brown stems will spread flat mats across paving or flow down a rock face, covered with tiny oval green leaves. In late summer the little flowers begin to appear, carried in upright tiny spikes, covering the plants with glowing pink; they flower from August to November. (3–4 in./80–100 mm.)

weyrichii. From gravelly mountain slopes of north Japan and Sakhalin; also on shingly sea-shores. This plant makes handsome rosettes of large, dark green, pointed leaves, and produces branching spires of tiny creamy flowers very like those of rhubarb, followed by flat, transparent, brownish-red seed cases. Its habit of growth and size of leaf make this a useful buffer between one type of plant and another. (2–2½ ft/600–760 mm.)

PONTEDERIA, Pontederiaceae.

cordata. Pickerel Weed. From the shallow water of ponds and streams in the eastern and central United States and east Canada. Here is a handsome plant for shallow water, ideal to break the hard line of the pond edge. Standing above the water on 1½–2 ft/460–600 mm stems are clumps of beautiful leaves of an elongated heart shape, very smooth, almost wax-like, with a swirling pencilled pattern of light and dark green covering the surface. They are not veins—you can scarcely see a vein at all, just feel a thickening along the centre. In August there appear, just above the leaves, narrow spikes of closely set deep blue flowers, something like a small hyacinth, but much smaller, and softer textured.

POTENTILLA, Rosaceae. These are easy herbaceous plants in almost any soil in full sun or part shade. Poor dry gravels do not suit them but a retentive soil ensures a long display of bloom.

alba. From open woods and rocky meadows of central and southern Europe.

argyrophylla (*P. insignis*). From valley meadows or grassy mountain sides of the Himalayas, Kashmir to Nepal. Neat clumps of strawberry-shaped leaves heavily silvered with silky hairs are the setting for free-flowering, wide-flung sprays of yellow flowers, each with an orange heart. (18 in./460 mm.)

atrosanguinea (*P. argyrophylla atrosanguinea*). This has larger, dark green leaves, and fewer stems (18 in./460 mm), carrying sprays of large, single, blood-red flowers. Both of these flower early in mid summer.

Possibly derived from these two, among others, is my favourite late-summer *Potentilla*, 'Gibson's Scarlet'. This plant produces a long succession of brilliant scarlet, velvety flowers with black centres, throughout late summer and autumn. The wide-sprayed branching stems are held rather flat. (18 in./460 mm.)

nepalensis. From Himalayan meadows. There are several named forms or hybrids from this source. The two I have are:

— **'Miss Willmott'**, which produces delicious raspberry-pink flowers over a long season, mid to late summer. (18 in./460 mm.)

— **'Roxana'** has warm orange flowers with brick-red centres. (18 in./460 mm.)

rupestris. From wooded rocky slopes in rock clefts in the mountains of central Europe and Asia. This pretty thing is a joy among unfolding *Hosta* leaves and primroses in late spring. Neat clusters of finely cut pinnate leaves are followed by slightly hairy, pink-tinted stems topped with branching heads of pure white saucer-shaped flowers, each with a yellow eye. (18 in./460 mm.)

'Tonguei'. Too good to leave out, this little *Potentilla* will thrive almost anywhere, but in good retentive soil scarcely stops flowering from early summer until autumn. It makes flat clusters of small dark green leaves, touched with copper. Low, wide-spreading stems carry a long succession of small apricot-coloured flowers suffused with dark red. (15–18 in./ 380–460 mm.)

PRATIA, Campanulaceae. It seems there are several of these creeping plants grown in gardens. They come mostly from Australasia, also from Asia and South America.

angulata comes from New Zealand, where it is found on shingly river plains in the west of South Island, growing with *Acaena sanguisorba*, *Cotula squalida* and *Mazus radicans*. In the far south of South Island it is found with *Blechnum penna-marina*, *Astelia montana* and *Celmisia longifolia*. (2 in./50 mm.)

treadwellii (*or tredwellii*) is the form well known in gardens. It is a charming mat-forming plant on soil that does not dry out. Creeping stems carry small, rounded leaves, thick textured with prettily pointed edges. By June it is covered with starry white flowers, continuing for weeks. By the autumn they have become small rose-madder berries; the low green carpets are strewn with them. (2 in./50 mm.)

PRIMULA, Primulaceae. Certainly in areas of low rainfall you need moist retentive soil for the following species. Heavy soil, well enriched with humus, with shelter from too much sun and drying winds, are all essential. In areas of heavier rainfall they might be treated with less reverence. Of all plants they are among the most desirable, whether planted in drifts along the water-side, or as groups of two or three caught in a shaft of light beneath the shade of trees. There are hundreds of different species, many of them just the thing to torment those who pride themselves on growing difficult plants. The following I have learnt to know and grow without too much pain.

altaica 'Grandiflora' (of gardens). The species is a native of the Caucasus with the advantage of flowering earlier than our native; this garden form produces crowded bunches of pale mauve-pink flowers. (6 in./150 mm.)

bulleyana. From wet valley meadows in the mountains of north Yunnan, south-west China. It was named in honour of Mr Bulley, the owner of the firm of Bees, who did much to finance plant collecting in China at the beginning of this century. It is one of the easiest of bog primulas, provided you have continuously damp soil. Set in whorls around the stem are bright orange-peel-coloured flowers, maintaining a vivid display for weeks, and followed by tiers of round green seed capsules which finally dry pale brown. Given the right conditions they seed easily, making good ground-cover with their large oval leaves. (2–2½ ft/600–760 mm.)

calderiana. Widespread in high alpine meadows in west China, Bhutan, Tibet and Nepal. I am proud to grow this lovely plant in one of my few choice damp and sheltered spots. It dies back in winter to fat, ground-level buds. In spring the leaves emerge, pale green and upright, dusted with gold specks. The tall strong flower stems, 15–18 in./380–460 mm, carry drooping gold-dusted bells in deep purple or pale creamy-yellow, all with yellow eyes. They look like an extra-large form of *P. alpicola* which I have not succeeded in keeping long.

denticulata. From open birchwoods and meadows in the Himalayas. These hardy warriors thrive in sticky soil enriched with humus. With snowdrops still in flower, round fat buds emerge at ground level and immediately open a mauve eye or two, while the thick short stems, 9–12 in./230–300 mm, slowly push up the round, tightly packed balls of flower which have suggested the name, Drumstick Primula. There are several colour forms, shades of lavender, and rich carmine-red to purple. There are also white ones. Not all are good; in some, the individual flowers are small or washy-coloured. If grown from seed, select the best and propagate these from root cuttings, taken when the plants are in flower. Pot the trimmed cuttings and keep in cool shade. Replace the parent plant with flowers removed and leaves reduced, also in a sheltered spot.

elatior. From woods and moist meadows of Europe to the Caucasus and Iran. This is the true Oxlip, differing from the Cowslip in having a cluster of creamy-yellow primrose-like flowers nodding from the top of each stem. It prefers part shade and damp leaf-mould. (8–10 in./200–250 mm.)

farinosa. From wet meadows of the northern hemisphere, far into the Arctic; a mountain plant further south in all the great mountain ranges. It is included here because it is native in Great Britan, the Bird's-eye Primrose of moist northern meadows. It is short-lived in the drier south, but is worth attempting and retaining with seedlings in cool damp spots in the rock garden, or on a north-facing raised bed. Small leaf rosettes are dusted with meal, so they appear pale whitish-green. Above them short stems carry dainty heads of pinky-mauve flowers, yellow-eyed. (3–4 in./80–100 mm.)

florindae. From wet mountain meadows in south-east Tibet. The Giant Himalayan Cowslip, described by Kingdon-Ward when he found it in stream-beds with its bright red roots showing under water. It does well enough in heavy damp soil, but my plants are pygmies compared with what they can do in Scottish gardens. Flowering July–August, it prolongs the *Primula* season with its large cowslip-shaped heads of sulphur yellow bell-like flowers. The flowers and stems are powdered with pale greenish powder, or farina, as are the handsome seed heads. I have a form in which the outside of the bells is red, the inside pale primrose. Sometimes a seedling has copper-tinted flowers. These used to be known as 'art shades', but they are neither better, nor worse, than the type. (Stems 2–4 ft/600 mm–1.2 m, according to condition.)

helodoxa. From marshy meadows and stream-sides of the Yunnan–upper Burma border mountains. This is a lovely buttercup-yellow candelabra *Primula*, with no farina (mealy powdering). The large flowers are set in as many as six whorls around the tall stems which can be up to 3 ft/1 m high. An easy plant in moist soil.

japonica. From wet stream-sides of Japan and Taiwan. Possibly the best-known of the candelabra primulas, and the first to flower in May. Large, broad, crinkled leaves are pale green, harmonizing with other soft spring greens, complementing the glowing crimson or rich pink tiers of flowers. Two named forms are 'Millar's Crimson', which is dark red without any trace of mauve, and 'Postford White', both illuminated with yellow eyes. (1½–2 ft/460–600 mm.)

polyneura. From shady bouldery slopes among grass. Discovered by E. H. Wilson in west Sichuan around the beginning of this century, this plant is good in part shade. Downy, scallop-edged leaves nestle among the leaf-litter, producing in late May large blotting-paper-pink primrose-like flowers. Grown from seed you may have other shades, from pale rose to deep purple, all with yellow eyes. Good forms can be increased by division in early spring, their soft foliage making good ground-cover. (5–6 in./ 130–150 mm.)

pulverulenta. From damp, part-shaded meadows of a limited area in the mountains of west Sichuan, China. This is a favourite among the bog primulas; its flowers follow *P. japonica*. The leaves are smaller, narrower and heavily wrinkled. The 2 ft/600 mm flower stems are white with meal, and so are the buds which open deep wine-coloured flowers with purple eyes. Among its most famous offspring is:

— **'Bartley Strain'** which has palest pink flowers, as many as five and seven whorls to a stem, enhanced with orange eyes, dancing like ballerinas in white tights among the floating balls of Cotton Grass, *Eriophorum angustifolium*. (2–2½ ft/600–760 mm.)

rosea. From the north-west Himalayas. I include this because it is so good in early spring, but I have lost it among my large water-side groupings. Situated in a moist, cool pocket of the rock garden many people could enjoy its low clusters of large bright rose flowers, 4–9 in./100–230 mm high.

secundiflora. From damp mountain meadows, often with *P. sikkimensis* in north-west Yunnan and Sichuan. This *Primula* has rather narrow leaves, and mealy stems from which the flower clusters tend to droop rather one-sidedly. The downturned bells are a rich wine-purple while the calyces are striped with black, a very elegant *Primula*, flowering in June. (12 in./300 mm.)

sieboldii. From wet, grassy river-sides in Japan, Korea and Manchuria. This delicate-looking *Primula* manages well in shady leaf-mould, provided it does not dry out. It increases by creeping shoots which lie just beneath the surface, and so pop up unexpectedly, making spreading clumps of small clustered leaves. In spring, just above them, float fragile-looking flowers in pale shades of pink, lilac and white, several on dainty branching heads. (4–6 in./100–150 mm.)

sikkimensis. From wet meadows, with a wide range, including Nepal, Burma, Sikkim, Tibet and Bhutan to Yunnan and Sichuan in west China. Plants grown from seed may vary, some larger or deeper than others. A smaller plant than *P. florindae*, with bright yellow flowers, no farina, but a sweet scent, it needs wet soil. (18 in./460 mm.)

viali (*V. littoniana*). From moist grassy openings in pine forests on the mountains of Yunnan and west Sichuan in south-west China. Although not one of the easiest, most people who see this *Primula* crave to grow it. At a quick glance (apart from its leaves) it looks like a weird little Red Hot Poker. Imagine a 12 in./300 mm stem topped with a narrowly pyramidal head of bright scarlet buds. Some time in June the bottom row of buds opens small, mauve *Primula* flowers. Gradually all open, disposing of the wildly contrasting red tip. It is a worrying plant, its leaves not appearing through the soil until late May. Although supposed to be perennial, flowered plants often die unaccountably, so it is wise to collect seed to maintain young plants. It will grow in sun, but prefers part shade, in damp, humus-enriched soil.

vulgaris. From woods, usually on heavy soil, and shady places of west-central Europe and the mountains of southern Europe to the northern Caucasus. This is our native Primrose, to be treasured, for it is every bit as lovely as any of the foregoing exotics. It loves heavy soil, well enriched with humus, preferably in a cool, shady position, not dried out by shrub roots. This applies to all the many cultivated hybrids and forms. There are primroses to be had in almost every colour of the rainbow, as well as doubles, hose-in-hose, polyanthus, etc. They are all fascinating, but none better than the perfect, cool pale yellow form of our native primrose. Of the many forms and varieties I can only describe a few.

DOUBLE VARIETIES—OLD FASHIONED KINDS

There are still to be found some of the genuine old fashioned primroses with romantic names, delicate flowers and miffy constitutions. Among them I have *Primula* 'Lilacina', also known as 'Quakeress' or 'Quaker's Bonnets', whose flowers are pale lavender-lilac. *P.v.* 'Alba Plena' has perfectly formed double white flowers, also on lax stems; and *P.v.* 'Marie Crousse', a rich mauve-red, has petals edged with silver. Alas, they are not very robust. Given the best of treatment, rich moist soil in part shade, sheltered from wind, they *can* make astonishing growth, and be crowded with hundreds of flowers. But after two or three years they begin to deteriorate unless you dig them up, separate the crowns and cut away the ugly warty bases, just leaving the newly forming roots to each piece. Do this early in the season, cut off all the flowers and reduce the foliage. Pot up or box the pieces, growing them in a sheltered frame until strong enough to plant out in damp conditions.

DOUBLE PRIMROSES—MODERN STRAINS

In recent years the interest in all kinds of primroses has become almost a cult. The Barnhaven primroses originated in America with Mrs Florence Bellis, who began in 1934 with Sutton's Seed Catalogue. After much cross-fertilizing, endless patience, and the passage of many years Mr Jared Sinclair, of Barnhaven *Primula* fame, continues with her strains in Cumbria, adding his own little bits of magic and writing seductive descriptions and titles for his offspring. His own double primroses, selected from hundreds of thousands that are discarded, have to be seen to be believed, not only for their perfect shape but the infinite range of colours. They are lovely.

After several years of seed sowing and rejection I have a few passable new doubles. Thus far they are neither so good as Mr Sinclair's, nor have they that indefinable something that have the old double white and 'Quakeress'. From seed I have a new double white, with flowers not quite so perfect as *P.v.* 'Alba Plena', but it is amazingly floriferous, with firm stems on strong-growing plants, and a few others, yellow, blue and purple. But the list of colours in the Barnhaven catalogue sets your teeth on edge with envy, not to mention an ability to describe colours.

Having obtained any kind of double primrose, there are still problems. If the leaves suddenly look drained and yellow, it is more than likely they are having the life sucked out of them by red spider mites—minute, red, dot-like creatures, almost invisible on the backs of the leaves. Just as likely, they might have an aphis attack. It is better to be forewarned and spray them with something unpleasant to catch those devils before they have wrecked the precious primulas. But sometimes you can find no obvious reason for their discontent and can only suppose they disapprove of their situation.

THE GOLD-LACED POLYANTHUS

As unlike the modern, large-flowered, bedding polyanthus primroses as could be, the hallmark of these little antiquities is the small size of their flowers. Small, neat petals of deep velvety-maroon, sometimes almost black, are edged with a fine gold or silver edging. There used to be named varieties; I have none of those, but have selected those I thought best from seedlings. Again I find they need regular division to keep them strong and healthy.

× **pruhoniciana.** This is a collective name for hybrids which are crosses between *Primula juliae* (small purple-crimson flowers from moist mountain meadows in a limited district on the southern slopes of the Great Caucasus, often with *Gentiana lagodechiana*) and other high mountain pasture primroses. Well known in this section are the following:

— **'Wanda',** whose vivid crimson-purple flowers over dark purple leaves are well known. I am pleased to have a rather more fragile-looking type, a 'hose-in-hose' 'Wanda' which has two little flowers sitting inside one another. I also have a white form of 'Wanda' which may be the one called 'Schneekissen', its generous posies of white primrose flowers set off by maroon buds, stems and calyces. (4 in./100 mm.)

× **'Garryarde Guinevere'** is one of the best-known, with its polyanthus head on a very short stalk, making crowded bunches of light amethyst-pink flowers, intensified with maroon calyces and stems. The leaves, neat and narrow are shaded and veined maroon. (6–8 in./150–200 mm.)

× **'Kinlough Beauty'** may perhaps be included in this group. Neat, small flowers in light and dark shades of rosy-pink, each petal marked with a cream slash down the centre, leads to a bright yellow eye, making clustered heads of old world charm. This plant has a healthy constitution. (6–8 in./ 150–200 mm.) I am not certain of this plant, as I was once sent something with the same name with larger, clumsier flowers. I prefer my form with its small, very neat flowers.

Before leaving the primrose hybrids I cannot leave out the old fashioned 'Jack in Green' primroses, whose calyces have developed into conspicuous green ruffs behind the flowers, still decorative when the flowers have dropped. I select only the yellow and white forms, preferring them to the rather strident purple and red tones.

The old 'hose-in-hose' primroses I do not have. I suspect some of those I have seen to have been 'improved'; in health and vigour, no doubt, but I would like to see some genuine old forms, if they still exist.

viride. I have a green primrose but cannot get excited about it. If it had green petals in place of the yellow ones of our lovely native, it might have great appeal, but my plant produces flowers which rarely open properly, looking more like a modified calyx than proper petals. Mrs Fish mentions two forms—the other one with a poor constitution which easily fades away. She implies that it has a better flower. I wonder if there is still any of it about.

PRUNELLA, Labiateae.

grandiflora. Large Self-heal. From rather dry mountain meadows and open woods of south-central Europe. It makes a splendid edging plant, or good ground-cover, in damp soil, not too sun-scorched. It creeps over the soil with prostrate stems covered with small, dark, rough-surfaced leaves. Just above them stand crowded spikes of nettle-like flowers. The type is rich purple, but in gardens one usually sees 'Loveliness', which is pale lilac. There is also *Prunella* 'Pink Loveliness', with warm rose-pink flowers, but this is descended from another species. There is a white form too, 'White Loveliness'. (6 in./150 mm.)

PULMONARIA, Boraginaceae.
This is another of my favourite plants. There are several distinct forms. They tend to interbreed, so the best forms are propagated by division, some from root cuttings. They provide two seasons of interest. In spring they are among the first to flower, and continue to do so for several months. Later in the year their robust clumps of fresh basal leaves, which are produced after the flowering season, make both a feature and ground-cover until the following spring. Their large leaves tend to wilt in sun; they need shade or part shade, in humus-rich, retentive soil. There is a tendency to mildew if they suffer too dry conditions.

angustifolia 'Azurea'. From woods and moist meadows of the hills and mountains of central and southern Europe. This is the one which has totally plain, unspotted leaves, slightly bristly to touch. There are several forms, including:

— **'Mawson's Variety'**. This is larger in leaf and flower than 'Munstead Blue'. It also flowers later—in April–May, with bold clusters of deep gentian-blue flowers, held well above strong clumps of dark, holly-green matt leaves. (12 in./300 mm.)

— **'Munstead Blue'**. This charming plant opens pink-tinted buds just as its small, oval green leaves are unfolding, often in February if it is mild. Soft clusters of pure blue flowers smother the low carpet of leaves, creating long-lasting pools of blue beneath early-flowering shrubs. (6 in./150 mm.)

longifolia. From woods and shady meadows of west and south-west Europe. Flattish rosettes of long, narrow, pointed leaves, dark green but heavily spotted with silvery-white, lie like sharp petalled flowers against the dark soil. During spring and early summer they produce quaint heads of small, deep blue flowers, held well above the leaves. (8–10 in./200–250 mm.)

officinalis. From rather moist open woods of central and eastern Europe to Russia. This is the most commonly known form, with many local names, including Lungwort. (The even spotting on the leaves suggested the Latin name to the old botanists.) Soldiers and Sailors and Spotted Dog are among others. This plant has smallish, heart-shaped leaves, heavily spotted with silvery white. The flowers open in early spring, first rosy-pink, changing to purplish-blue. There is also a white-flowered form. (10–12 in./250–300 mm.)

— **'Cambridge Blue'** opens rose-pink buds which quickly change to a clear lighter blue, one of the earliest to make a show. (6–8 in./150–200 mm.)

rubra. From openings in the beechwoods on the mountains of south-eastern Europe. While searching for snowdrops in January you may well see a glowing eye looking at you from the leafy depths of this plant. Its flowers are bright coral-red with no hint of blue. They are at their best in March and April. The leaves are large and long, in plain apple-green, their hefty clumps very useful as contrast among the spotted types, extremely good ground-cover in shade. (12 in./300 mm.)

saccharata. Origin uncertain, but a similar plant has been noted in the woods of north Spain. Plants under this name vary slightly in foliage and flower. All make large clumpy plants with very handsome basal rosettes of leaves. Some may be dark green with large, paler green spots, others will be smothered with bright silvery-white spots. In yet another the spots have joined together to make almost totally silvered leaves, and this we call *P. saccharata* 'Argentea'. These last two are outstanding in the shade garden, in late summer and autumn, when their fresh, dramatic appearance is needed. In early spring they all open pink buds from conspicuous dark purplish calyces, the flowers passing through mauve to rich blue as they age. Seedlings will vary in quality of flower. There is a very fine white form, *P. saccharata* 'Alba', with flowers twice as large as those of *P. officinalis* 'Alba', vying with snowdrops for attention. (12 in./300 mm.)

This does not dispose of all pulmonarias. I have two unnamed clones which I value as distinct. One produces large clusters of dark blue flowers in late spring, held well above scarcely spotted leafy clumps. (12 in./300 mm.) The other, collected in Portugal by my old friend and teacher, Sir Cedric Morris, we call 'Mournful Purple'. It is economical with foliage: a few dark, narrow leaves bearing broad pale green blotches in no way detract from the drooping clusters of amethyst-purple flowers held in bristly maroon calyces. (12 in./300 mm.)

PULSATILLA, Ranunculaceae. I would not include *Pulsatilla vulgaris* among damp-loving plants, but the yellow-flowered 'Shockheaded Peter' of high alpine meadows will tolerate neither drought nor starvation.

alpina. From steep mountain grasslands of central and southern Europe to the Caucasus, and North America. This plant has white flowers with exquisite blue backs to the petals. (15 in./380 mm.)

— sulphurea has light, lemon-yellow, shallow bowls filled with stamens, wonderful when sunlight slants through hundreds and thousands as they blow just above the short turf. It is almost as lovely when the flowers have become silky, silver seed-heads. A well-grown clump with finely cut woolly green leaves standing in full flower, in May and June, is one of the loveliest things we can grow. (18 in./460 mm.)

There seems to be confusion and contradiction as to whether these are lime-tolerant or not. In the Pyrenees the white form is found on acid formation, and the yellow one on lime. In gardens I suspect that sufficient moisture at the root is the most important ingredient, although they must not be put in ill-drained soil.

RANUNCULUS, Ranunculaceae. All will grow in sun with retentive soil.

aconitifolius. From rocky stream-sides and wet, shady places in the mountains of central and southern Europe.

— 'Flore Pleno'. This centuries-old garden plant, slow growing and rare, has the lovely name 'Fair Maids of France'. When well grown it makes quantities of wide-spreading branches, which divide and subdivide, and so can carry a huge bouquet of small double white flowers, exquisitely perfect, tinted green in the centre. The dark green pointed foliage remains discreetly in the background, doing nothing to detract from the sense of lightness and space in which these enchanting blossoms float. (2–2½ ft/600–760 mm.)

— platanifolius (*R.a.* 'Grandiflorus'). From drier rocky places further east. This is a selected form with tall branching stems, 2½–3 ft/760 mm–1 m, crowded in May and June with showers of shallow white cups.

acris. The Common Buttercup. From moist meadows of temperate Eurasia.

— 'Flore Pleno'. Another historical plant found in Lancashire in the sixteenth century and called 'Batchelor's Buttons'. Long lasting and lovely, and much easier to grow than 'Fair Maids', it does not run but makes well-behaved tidy clumps which produce slender-stemmed bouquets crowded with glistening, densely double, green-centred buttercups. It flowers in June, standing at 2½ ft/760 mm.

ficaria 'Aurantiaca'. This attractive celandine has mottled green and grey leaves, with glistening orange single flowers. It flowers in February–March. (3–4 in./80–100 mm.)

— 'Flore Pleno'. A double-flowered celandine—such a clean shade of yellow with a tight centre of green which opens layer upon layer of shadowed petals. (3 in./80 mm.)

— 'Foliis Purpureis'. Clusters of rich, bronzed-brown leaves are a good foil for large single yellow celandines. (3 in./80 mm.)

lingua. Greater Spearwort. From marshes and water-edges of temperate Eurasia. This is an invasive bog-loving buttercup, only to be used where it cannot become a nuisance, or else strictly confined in a container. It will colonize shallow water, where its long, spear-shaped leaves piercing the flat surface and large shining yellow buttercup flowers provide a tempting scene. There is a selected form called *R. lingua* 'Grandiflorus'. (2–3 ft/600 mm–1 m.)

lyalli. From moist, sunny, subalpine herb fields and scrub of the wet mountains of western South Island, New Zealand; often found in large colonies. The New Zealand Buttercup is rare to find, and next to impossible to grow in the drier counties. It must have ample moisture and shelter from drying winds. It is said to have large waxy-white flowers, and large, round, saucer-shaped leaves for a bonus, and stems up to 4 ft/1.2 m tall.

speciosus plenus (sometimes found as *R. gouanii*). From mountain meadows of the Pyrenees to the western Alps. It needs moist soil in sun to produce a long display of flowers, 1½ in./40 mm across, densely double with row upon row of shining enamelled petals with bitter-green centres. It has rough bristly leaves, rounded with cut edges, not so divided as most. (18 in./460 mm.)

RHEUM, Polygonaceae. The ornamental rhubarbs are among the most statuesque and handsome of foliage plants, invaluable to create a grand, lush atmosphere, even when space is limited. They like deep humus-enriched soil, and some shelter from both wind and scorching sun. Part shade suits them well. Ill-drained soil will cause the great woody crowns to rot.

alexandrae. From rich, boggy, high mountain meadows, or among scrub in north Yunnan and Sichuan, west China. This is quite different from the rest. It has much smaller leaves, shaped like overgrown Greater Plantain leaves, strongly veined—pale veins against dark shining green—and makes vigorous clumps in moist soil. In June a 2½–3 ft/760 mm–1 m flower spike is set from top to bottom with large, pale cream, overlapping, papery bracts, beneath which are hidden little clusters of typical rhubarb-like flowers, sheltering from the wild Tibetan rainstorms which they are expecting. In cultivation it never produces many flower heads, but one alone sets off the whole garden.

palmatum. From west Sichuan, China, at great heights—by streams in rocky ravines, among alpine plants in rocky turf, or round alpine lakes in scrub. The type is not generally overpraised, but I think it could have wider recognition and use. In many gardens where *Gunnera* can neither be accommodated nor obtained this plant provides those huge, cool, simple leaves that are needed to give style and atmosphere. Each apple-green leaf, up to 3 ft/1 m across, is less cut than the red-leafed forms, and produces a more tranquil effect as it stands in a great overlapping pile. The towering stems, 6–7 ft/2–2.25 m, of creamy-white flowers are softly harmonious.

— **'Atrosanguineum',** also found as 'Rubrum'. The tall flower spike (6 ft/2 m) carries large leaves, 2½–3 ft/760 mm–1 m across, which are deeply cut. As they unfold in March–April, from fist-sized, shining scarlet buds, crumpled and creased, they are stained deep mahogany-red, but as the leaves quickly expand, the colour fades from the surface, remaining on the undersides, so that a rustle of wind will reveal them as carmine-pink under-skirts. In May the tall flower spike carries a froth of tiny crimson-pink flowers which later become transparent brown seed cases. There are several other forms, one called 'Bowles' Variety', and another I have seen with very scallop-edged leaves. I also have a form, whose name I do not know, which produces larger, more richly coloured leaves, continuing to do so for longer. It has white flowers.

RODGERSIA, Saxifragaceae. These are among the finest of foliage plants for the water-side, or for cool, damp soil. They will grow in sun if the soil is very moist, or in shade, in soil which does not dry out. They can suffer from sun-scorch and damage by wind. Their roots are thick, slowly spreading rhizomes which can be divided.

aesculifolia. From openings and clearings in forest on moist slopes of west Chinese mountains. This makes handsome clumps, 3–4 ft/1–1.2 m high, according to the amount of moisture. The leaves are shaped and arranged like those of the horse chestnut.

pinnata. From openings in forests, stream-sides and moist meadows of south-west Sichuan and north Yunnan, China. This plant arranges its leaves in pairs, on either side of a central stem. The foliage is not quite so handsome as some of the others, but it flowers more freely, with flower spikes similar to *Astilbe* but more substantial. It can be found with white or pale pink flowers. (3 ft/1 m.)

— **'Superba'** is a very fine form with brilliant pink flowers, and copper-tinted leaves. (3 ft/1 m.)

podophylla. From mountain woods of Japan and Korea. The young leaves have wonderful rich bronze tones in spring, turning to green as they expand, but often copper-tinted when they are mature. Usually five leaves are arranged at the top of a stem, broadly triangular in outline with jagged tips. (3 ft/1 m.)

tabularis comes from China. Unlike all the rest, this produces large, round, teatray-sized leaves, dimpled in the centre where they are attached to the stem which may be 2–3 ft/600 mm–1 m tall. The edges of the leaves are slightly scalloped. It is one of the most beautiful, large, simple leaves. A strong flower stem rises high above the leaves carrying heavy drooping clusters of white starry flowers. (3–4 ft/1–1.2 m.)

ROSCOEA, Zingiberaceae. These are exotic-looking plants as well they might be, related to the root we candy and call ginger. Their flowers may be described as halfway between an orchid and an *Iris*. Their roots are fleshy, liking deep soil that does not dry out. They will grow in sun or part shade.

cautleoides. From turfy glades in mountain pine-oak forests of Yunnan, south-west China. This plant has long, light green leaves, ribbed and curving, which clasp the stem alternately. The light yellow flowers, of which there may be several in a close spike, emerge just above the leaves. Sometimes there are purple forms.

procera. From openings in woods of the Himalayas. The flowers have an upright purple petal. Below are two white, beak-like petals which enfold the precious stamens and stigma, while below them falls a broad and inviting flared petal which probably acts as an alighting board for some pollinating insect. (12–15 in./300–380 mm.)

RUDBECKIA, Compositae. Coneflower. These are North American daisies, flowering in late summer and autumn, distinguished by their hard, cone-like centres and somewhat drooping broad petals. They are happy in full sun, so long as the soil is retentive, which also means the flowering period will be longer.

fulgida (*R. speciosa, R. newmanii*). From damp meadows of the eastern and central United States. The problem of names is multiplied by there also being several good forms to be found in gardens. Basically they all make tidy clumps of very dark green leaves which, in late summer, produce compact branching heads set with bright yellow daisies with dark brown central cones, hence their common name Black-eyed Susan.

Among the named varieties are 'Deamii' and 'Goldsturm'. They may have slightly longer (or narrower) petals. Or they may flower a week sooner or later. All are a joy to have. (2–2½ ft/600–760 mm.)

laciniata. From brook-banks and damp thickets of the east and midwest United States and Canada. This and *R. nitida* are closely related. They too can be found in named selected forms. The main characteristic is the height, from 5–7 ft/1.5–2.25 m tall. *R. laciniata* has more deeply dissected leaves than *R. nitida*. Both produce sheaves of clear yellow daisies, enhanced by slender green central knobs. They are good in large gardens not troubled by wind.

RUMEX, Polygonaceae.

hydrolapathum. From muddy edges of streams and ponds, sometimes in shallow water, of central and northern Europe and into Asia. The big, smooth, rather narrow leaves of the Great Water-dock sometimes turn rich red in the autumn, and its flower-plumes, which stand 5 ft/1.5 m or more high, are soft brownish-pink in late summer, becoming rusty-red as the seeds ripen. It is not a very choice plant, but handsome by large ponds.

SAGITTARIA, Alismataceae.

sagittifolia. From the quiet water at the edges of ponds and rivers of Europe and Asia. The Common Arrowhead sends up shiny leaves of perfect arrowhead shape above the water on juicy stems. From among these rise its flowering stems bearing whorls of a few rather large white flowers with conspicuous black-purple centres. If growing in faster running water, the leaves become strap-shaped and do not emerge into the air. It needs to be kept under control, as it spreads fast. (18 in./460 mm.)

SALVIA, Labiatae. Most salvias need sunny positions and well-drained soil; some will tolerate quite dry conditions. The following flower late in the year and need a reasonable amount of moisture to keep their foliage healthy to the end of the season.

glutinosa. Jupiter's Distaff. From open mountain woods of south-central Europe to the Caucasus and Himalayas. Another coarse plant for the wild garden, making branching stems set with rough, crinkled leaves, heart-shaped and pointed, as much as 7–8 in./180–200 mm long, so making quite a foliage feature. The chrome-yellow flowers, which appear in late summer, are arranged in a broad spike above the leaves. (2½–3 ft/760 mm–1 m.)

guaranitica (*S. ambigens, S. caerulea*). From moist places in Paraguay. This plant is not reliably hardy in very cold soils, but it is worth covering the roots with a mulch, when it usually sprouts again in the spring. Stems 4–5 ft/1.2–1.5 m high carry scented matt-green leaves. At the tip of every branch are short spikes of indigo-blue buds which open in September deep blue, lipped and hooded flowers. They are larger than those of *S. uliginosa*, but in a less dense spike.

uliginosa. From moist places of southern Brazil and Uruguay. Another slightly tender plant, but it is well worth protecting the roots in winter. Graceful, branching 5–6 ft/1.5–2 m stems are set with narrow, toothed leaves. They are topped with a continuous display of pure sky-blue and white flowers held in drooping, clustered heads until the first frosts destroy them. September–November. Both this plant and *S. guaranitica* need a warm, sheltered position in soil that does not dry out.

SANGUINARIA, Papaveraceae.

canadensis. From rich woods of the eastern and central United States and Canada. The common name Blood Root refers to the red sap which oozes from the thick rhizome if wounded. This choice woodland plant needs a shady site in damp leaf-mould. Some time in April fat flower buds push through the soft earth, their short, waxy, purple stems wrapped around in a frilled, glaucous leaf, like a shawl, for protection. The single, cupped flowers look not unlike large white celandines, but the very full, double form, *S. canadensis* 'Flore Pleno', with many narrower incurved petals, has you down on your knees to gasp and marvel. Each exquisite flower lasts several days. When they have gone the leaves expand to become quite large and round, with deeply indented margins, reminiscent of *Bocconia* leaves. But the rhizomes spread slowly. When large enough they should be divided in August. (4–6 in./100–150 mm.)

SANGUISORBA, Rosaceae. These plants are valued for their elegant pinnate foliage and long fluffy flowers. They increase fairly vigorously in moist soil, thriving in full sun. They are not tiresome invaders.

canadensis (*Poterium canadense*). From swamps and wet meadows of eastern Canada and the United States, becoming less common inland. Sometimes the green pinnate foliage turns to vivid autumn tints. Above it stand stiffly upright stems whose branching heads are topped with narrow white bottle-brushes. When the multitudes of fluffy stamens and petals have disintegrated the remaining green tapers are interesting, and useful for flower arranging. August–September. (5–6 ft/1.5–2 m.)

obtusa. From certain high mountain meadows of north Japan, where it is rare. The plant we cultivate may be *S. hakusanensis*, also from north Japanese mountain meadows with deeper-coloured flowers, or a hybrid (?). It has beautiful light blue-grey leaves to set off larger, fluffier, deep rose bottle-brushes which nod and quiver at the end of long, slender, branching stems, in mid to late summer. (4–5 ft/1.2–1.5 m.)

officinalis. From damp meadows throughout Europe and Asia to Japan, mainly in the mountains and reaching the Arctic. Our common Burnet is not generally considered garden-worthy but a selected form, 'Rubra', produces very effective, small, hard, blackish-crimson heads, massed at the top of tall branching stems in July. It is worth growing for the lovely silvery-grey foliage alone. It is invasive, so only for the large or wild garden. (4 ft/1.2 m.)

SAXIFRAGA, Saxifragaceae. From this enormous and important family of alpines I select only a few which are large enough to be associated with general garden plants. They all like a cool situation, a little shade and humus-enriched soil.

cuneifolia. From damp rocks in mountain woods of central and southern Europe and Spain to the Carpathians. This is a very easy plant, looking like a miniature London Pride. Small, neat, evergreen rosettes gradually spread into ground-covering mats. There is a variegated form, slightly speckled and spotted with creamy-yellow spots. In June 6 in./150 mm sprays of creamy-white flowers are more generously produced from rosettes planted in fresh soil.

fortunei. From wet shady mountain rocks and ravines of Japan and Sakhalin to Manchuria and China. Round, veined leaves of wax-like texture are green above, pinkish-tan on the undersides. A late spring frost sometimes dissolves them, but new ones appear. In gardens the red-leafed forms *S.f.* 'Wada's Variety' or *S.f.* 'Rubrifolia' are bronze-red above, shining crimson-pink on the reverse. It is lovely to come upon these beautiful plants on an October evening when the wide, airy sprays of dainty white flowers appear to float over richly coloured leaves. Looking closer you see they have cherry-red stems, and the little flowers have yellow centres which become green pointed pods. One petal of each tiny star becomes an elongated ribbon ¾ in./20 mm long. (12 in./300 mm.)

stolonifera (*S. sarmentosa*). Mother of Thousands. From damp rocks and wet places of south Japan to west China. Although not reliably hardy this will stand most winters tucked in among leaf-litter. Rounded leaves are veined and marbled with pale green. Young plants are produced on the ends of long trailing runners; and 12 in./300 mm stems carry dainty sprays of white flowers, the lower petals several times as long as the upper ones.

There is a beautiful variegated form, richly coloured in red, cream and green, with young plantlets dangling from red runners. It is definitely not hardy, but very lovely hanging from a pot in a window or conservatory.

From the mossy saxifrages I have selected these three which I enjoy on the edge of a cool, shaded bed. They would be among the first plants to go on my north-facing raised bed—or a cool, shady pocket in the rock garden.

'Bob Hawkins' makes neat low cushions of finely cut leaves held in fairly large rosettes. The new young growth is strongly variegated cream and green, while around the edges the tips of the old leaves are crimson. The flowers, on 6 in./150 mm stems, are white, making a long lasting display in May–June.

'Cloth of Gold' makes beautiful mossy carpets of light yellow rosettes which are vivid all the year round. In May they are studded with white flowers on short stems. There must be enough light to maintain the colour, but not direct sunlight which will cause scorching. (3–4 in./80–100 mm.)

'Flowers of Sulphur' has creamy-green flowers over low compact green carpets, in April. (2–3 in./50–80 mm.)

SCABIOSA, Dipsacaceae.

caucasica. From rich subalpine meadows of the Caucasus. I include this plant because although it needs full sun and good drainage it has taken me a long time to learn to grow it successfully, and I have concluded that it likes a reasonably fertile soil with enough moisture in its busy flowering season. The addition of lime in acid soils may be helpful. It does not do well in poor dry soils. When suited it is one of the most beautiful flowering plants. The best known is probably 'Clive Greaves'; there are also several white forms. I have a creamy-white form which starts flowering in early summer, and continues non-stop, producing armfuls of flowers until the frosts. All are beautiful, poised on long, scarcely leafed stalks. (2–2½ ft/600–760 mm.)

SCHIZOSTYLIS, Iridaceae. The Kaffir Lily.

coccinea. From South Africa. This is another plant needing far more moisture than you might imagine. It needs a warm, sunny situation in continuously damp soil if it is to flower well. The plants increase readily, sending up quantities of light green, blade-shaped leaves. Slender spires of buds appear in September, continuing to flower into the winter if it is mild enough. Autumn frosts damage the open flowers, but do not harm the unopened buds. Although likened to a miniature *Gladiolus*, the Kaffir Lily has evenly shaped, beautifully rounded petals, satin-textured, which open flat in warm autumn sunshine. (1½–2 ft/460–600 mm.)

There are several named forms. *S.c.* 'Major' or 'Gigantea' has extra-large flowers, ripe cherry-red. There are also some good pink ones, including 'Mrs Hegarty', 'Viscountess Byng', and Alan Bloom's 'November Cheer', which has especially fine pink blooms. I particularly like Eric Smith's 'Sunrise', with flowers over 2 in./50 mm across in bright salmon-pink.

SCIRPUS, Cyperaceae.

lacustris. From usually quite deep water of lakes and quiet rivers over most of the world. The green, nearly leafless stems of the Bulrush rising out of the water, and up to 8 ft/2.5 m tall, with their heads of large red-brown spikelets, are handsome but only suitable for large sheets of water. The stems of the variety *S.l. zebrinus* have horizontal bands of pale yellow, while those of *S.l. pictus* are vertically and broadly lined with greenish-white, giving an attractive pale effect. Both these varieties seem to spread more slowly than the wild plant, but need a fairly large pond.

SCROPHULARIA, Scrophulariaceae.

aquatica. From stream-sides and wet places in Europe.

—'Variegata'. This can be one of the most spectacular variegated plants when well grown. Square stems, much branched, form a stiff frame set with clusters of leaves. Each leaf is a narrow oval, of crêpe texture, with finely cut edges; a central zone of rich green is surrounded by an irregular border of startling cream. As the leaves get smaller, towards the tips of the branches, they are almost totally cream. Finally they produce funny little spires of small, fig-shaped, brown flowers. It needs rich, damp soil, and shelter from wind, and too much sunlight as may be made by other great herbs, perhaps ligularias, or a tall grass such as *Miscanthus*. (3–4 ft/1–1.2 m.)

SELINUM, Umbelliferae.

tenuifolium. From the Himalayas. This is a Cow Parsley, but so delicately lovely no one passes it by. Light overlapping fronds of finely cut, almost fern-like leaves are stiffly held out, like elegant filigree fans. Above them rise maroon-red, *branching* stems 3 ft/1 m high which support delicate white parasols. The struts which carry the flat heads of multitudinous little white flowers are ghostly white. It is in flower in July.

SEMIAQUILEGIA, Ranunculaceae.

ecalcarata. From high mountain meadows and grasslands, and among bushes, of the China–Tibet borderlands. This plant is related to and closely resembles an *Aquilegia* in growth and foliage, and stands about 15 in./ 380 mm high. It does not make a vivid show but its open sprays of spurless flowers are a soft, pale purplish-brown, and have quiet charm.

SENECIO, Compositae.

smithii. From southern Chile, Tierra del Fuego and the Falkland Islands, on the banks of pools and streams, often with *Gunnera magellanica* and marsh marigolds. This unusual plant likes to have its roots in rich, moist soil, even in soggy mud. It makes a coarse plant with huge basal leaves, broadly spear-shaped, 18 in./460 mm long and 9 in./230 mm across. They are rich, glossy green, somewhat puckered and tooth edged. A thick stem, 4–5 ft/1.2–1.5 m tall supports a densely clustered flower head, sometimes 12 in./300 mm across, made of many yellow-eyed white daisies, each over 1 in./25 mm across. Fluffy seed heads follow.

SMILACINA, Liliaceae.

racemosa. From woods all across the eastern and central United States and Canada to the Rockies. In good, deep soil, sheltered from sun and wind, this plant can grow to over 3 ft/1 m. Slightly arching stems carry upturned leaves, more deeply veined (almost ribbed) than Solomon's Seal, to which it is related. They clasp the stem alternately to left and right, stopping before the tip which carries a soft spike of fluffy, creamy flowers. As the flowers age they become tinged with pink. Mine give every promise that later I shall see little berries, like 'vitrified drops of blood' but the promises drop off. Perhaps they need a moister atmosphere? I do enjoy the heady, lemon perfume.

SMYRNIUM, Umbelliferae.

perfoliatum. From open woods, bushy and rocky places of southern Europe to the Caucasus. This plant is not a perennial; it can take two or three years

N. *Senecio smithii* (foreground) and *Lysichitum americanum*

to reach flowering size and then, having made seed, will die. It could be called a weed, but such a pretty one in the right place, among shrubs or in rough grass under spring-blossoming trees. An angular, ribbed stem appears to pass through the centre of heart-shaped leaves. These leaves diminish in size as they near the tips of the branches when the green dissolves into a delicious yellow tint, intensifying the effect of small heads of tiny cow parsley-type flowers. (1½–2 ft/460–600 mm.)

SOLIDAGO, Compositae. Golden Rod. I have to confess that along with the tall heleniums these are not my favourite plants. The tall, gawky ones I have not left space for, but I do like some of the low-growing, late summer flowering varieties which seem to have less awkward-shaped heads. Among some of the named forms I grow 'Golden Thumb', alias 'Queenie', which is a very nice little plant for a damp edge, and 'Lemore', with pretty heads of lemon-yellow flowers, on 2–2½ ft/600–760 mm bushy plants.

SPEIRANTHA, Liliaceae.

gardenii. From China. This plant is related to Lily-of-the-Valley (*Convallaria majalis*). I was attracted by the light green, broad-bladed leaves which slowly spread into good clumps. I have not yet seen the flower sprays of pure white, fragrant, starry blossoms which should appear in spring. Perhaps it does better in the warm, damp counties of the south-west, liking cool shady places in humus-rich soil? (12 in./300 mm.)

STACHYS, Labiatae. Most of this family grow happily in dry, free-draining gravel.

macrantha. From wood edges and mountain meadows of the Caucasus. This member of the genus does not like dry soil. Apparently it used to be called 'The King of Splendour'. Regal and splendid it is in mid summer when its 2½ ft/760 mm stems are set with whorls of large, lipped flowers in rich mauve-purple. For the rest of the year it covers the soil with thick mats of dark crinkled evergreen leaves.

STOKESIA, Compositae.

laevis. From eastern North America. Not just another daisy, but a very distinctive one, with its own special character for late summer and early autumn. It is ideal for the front edge of a sunny border, in retentive soil, where it may spend the summer creating a healthy clump of long, narrow, soap-smooth leaves, slightly toothed at the base, capable of sending up 1½–2 ft/460–600 mm branched, flowering stems. By August curious buds are enclosed in rows of narrow, bristle-edged calyces which almost give the effect of a green flower themselves. But gradually they open to expose a pale, round bud which in turn opens lilac-blue with fine-cut petals surrounding a creamy-white centre. New flowers continue to open well into the autumn. Apparently there are purple, pink, and white forms. I should like to see them.

STYLOPHORUM, Papaveraceae.

diphyllum. From shady woods of eastern North America. Sometimes called the Celandine Poppy, this plant likes cool, humus-rich soil in part shade. Its blue-grey divided leaves catch the eye as they appear through the soil in early spring, enhanced by purplish stems and veins. In April nodding yellow poppies make just the right contrast, followed by large seed pods. (15–18 in./380–460 mm.)

SYMPHYTUM, Boraginaceae. These plants will grow in part or full shade, flowering and making total cover among shrubs or under trees where few other plants would flourish. They can be too successful; it helps to know which are dangerously invasive. Having delved into the RHS *Dictionary* I hardly dare offer names for my plants. There is obviously much confusion with illicit offspring, so my mind is no clearer.

caucasicum. From along water courses in damp soil in the Caucasus. When in flower in spring, this plant is irresistible, with graceful sprays of forget-me-not-blue tubular flowers drooping over mats of well-shaped grey-green leaves. The danger is that it colonizes by means of strong underground shoots, eventually covering a wide area. Every small piece left in the ground produces a new healthy plant. However, where I came to regret a planting I found that painting the leaves with a systemic weedkiller removed my problem. Now it is confined to my heaviest clay banks, invaluable where little else would grow. (2 ft/600 mm.)

grandiflorum. From mountain forests of the Caucasus. Invaluable as ground-cover in large shrubberies where it colonizes by means of underground shoots. It makes close carpets of slightly bristly, dark green leaves which remain until new ones replace them in spring. Very early in the year little croziers of orange-red buds unfold themselves to become small primrose-yellow tubular flowers. (8 in./200 mm.)

— **'Hidcote Pink'** and **'Hidcote Blue'**. These look so different I feel they must be hybridized with something else. They make larger leaf clusters, and the flowers stand well above them throughout May, held in conspicuous and very attractive sprays. 'Hidcote Pink' has flowers in shades of pale and rosy-pink, while 'Hidcote Blue' we used to call the 'Red, White and Blue' Borage, because all those colours are seen in the uncurling heads of flower. (18 in./460 mm.)

— **'Variegatum'**. This is another good plant selected by Eric Smith. Low, neat clumps of matt, oval leaves have dark green centres surrounded by broad, bright yellow margins. The flowers are similar to those of 'Hidcote Blue'. It makes much less invasive plants. (8–10 in./200–250 mm.)

rubrum. Probably a garden hybrid. This is not nearly such an invasive spreader, but makes clumps of long, narrow, bristly, dark green leaves. Crozier-heads of vivid garnet-red flowers hang just above the leaves, lasting for weeks in early summer, with another show of welcome colour in the autumn. (15–18 in./380–460 mm.)

× **uplandicum.** Could also be *S. peregrinum*, a hybrid of uncertain name and origin.

— **'Variegatum'.** Whatever its name may be, this foliage plant stands out above all else in the late summer and autumn border. During the early part of the year nothing will stop it doing its duty and sending up tall, leafy stems topped with indifferent pink and blue flowers. They are fussy compared to the grandeur of the basal foliage to come. By the end of July, with the flowering over, they start to create a huge, overlapping cluster of large, long leaves, like giant-sized dock leaves in shape, with a matt texture, shadowed greyish-green down the centre, surrounded by a broad irregular margin of cream. Occasionally a leaf is almost entirely creamy-white. Deep retentive soil in part shade is essential for this plant. (2½ ft/760 mm.)

TELLIMA, Saxifragaceae.

grandiflora. From shady rich woods, central California to Alaska.

— **'Rubra'** is the best form usually seen in gardens. (The type is not so well coloured in winter.) Although it will survive in dryish soil, in shade, it certainly does better where the soil does not dry out. One of our most valued winter-foliage plants; tidy clumps of scallop-edged leaves are, with the first frosts, flooded with rich carmine-red shades, brighter on the undersides. In spring multitudes of tall, slender wands carry tiny, pale green bells edged with rolled-up pink fringes, delicately pretty in a shady setting. (18 in./460 mm.)

TEUCRIUM, Labiatae.

scorodonium. From open woods and glades, often on rather sandy loam, of Europe.

— **'Crispum Marginatum'** will also tolerate fairly dry shade, but this lovely foliage plant selected by Eric Smith is worthy of a quiet place in cool leaf-mould where it makes good cover for snowdrops. The intricately ruffled edges of this Wood Sage are rimmed with white, while little spires of tiny cream lipped flowers are pretty in small posies. (12 in./300 mm.)

THALICTRUM, Ranunculaceae. Meadow Rue.

aquilegifolium. From moist mountain meadows, wood edges and rocky ravines of the mountains of Europe and Asia to Japan. This is beautiful in every part. The leaves, not unlike those of *Aquilegia* but smaller and greyish-green, ascend with diminishing size purple-stained stems and side branches. During June and July the tips erupt into wide heads of amethyst-pink fluff, rather like giant powder puffs. Later there are loose clusters of flat green seed cases, still good to look at. The white form, 'Album', is also very good. (3–5 ft/1–1.5 m.)

delavayi (*T. dipterocarpum* of gardens). From valley stream-sides, often among bushes, at comparatively low levels in the mountains of Yunnan. Wide airy sprays, held 5 ft/1.5 m or so above the ground, consist of tiny lilac flowers filled with dangling, greenish-yellow stamens; star-shaped seed capsules mature before the petals have dropped. There is also a white form. The tall slender stems carrying more finely segmented leaves need some support and shelter from wind damage, preferably among other plants rather than clumsy staking. August–September.

— **'Hewitt's Double'** does not have quite such delicate charm, but the tiny pom-poms of deep lilac are very attractive and last well. (5 ft/1.5 m.) Both these plants need rich, deep soil, in sun or part shade.

diffusiflorum. From south-east Tibet, in moist, part-shady places. This treasure needs well-drained but damp leaf-mould soil in a cool, sheltered spot. In my garden it grows to about 3 ft/1 m, but it can be more in damper climates. Delicate stems set with sprays of very tiny greyish-green leaves are topped with drooping heads of surprisingly large lilac blossoms.

kiusianum (*T. microspermum*). From the mountains of south Japan (Shikoku and Kyushu). This is a tiny pygmy, about 3 in./80 mm high. It is difficult to distinguish petals from stamens, all so narrow giving the effect of tiny balls of lilac fluff floating on purple wiry stems over sparsely leafed plants. It runs a little if well suited, in moist humus soil.

speciosissimum. From stream-sides and wet places in the lowlands and mountains of Spain, Portugal and north-west Africa. This has perhaps the most handsome foliage of all thalictrums. Large fans of blue-green leaves, finely divided, are held stiffly from the central stem. The clustered heads of small, greenish-yellow flowers seem exactly right for the tall, waxy-grey stems and bluish leaves. This plant will grow almost anywhere, from the back of an ordinary border to the pond-side, where it will thrive among *Lythrum* and *Lysimachia*. (5 ft/1.5 m.)

TIARELLA, Saxifragaceae. With masses of fluffy white flowers and especially pretty leaves these are perfect for the woodland garden, among shrubs, or in cool pockets of the rock garden. They prefer light, humus-rich soil, not too dried out by tree roots.

collina. I do not know the origin of this plant, and the name may be incorrect but it is distinct from the others which I list. It does not run, but makes neat clumps of soft green foliage, warmly bronzed in winter. In May, dainty spires of pink-tinted buds open white starry flowers. (12 in./300 mm.)

cordifolia. The Foam Flower. From rich moist woods of the eastern and central United States and eastern Canada. Running trails of pretty, heart-shaped, pointed leaves make attractive ground-cover, copper-tinted in winter; in spring covered with creamy-white flower spires. (9 in./230 mm.)

wherryi. From woods of the south-east United States. Tiny mounds of exquisite foliage, shaped like ivy, are velvety-textured in shades of moss-green with dark brown accents along the central vein. Spikes of pink buds followed by creamy-white starry flowers are produced throughout the summer. (10 in./250 mm.)

TOVARA, Polygonaceae.

virginiana (*Polygonum virginianum*). From woods and thickets of the eastern and central United States, eastern Canada and Japan.

— filiformis 'Painter's Palette'. This is similar to *T.v.* 'Variegata', but the centre of each leaf is marked across with a distinct V-sign which runs parallel to the end tip. This V is almost brick-red when fresh, but darkens to blackish-bronze. The newest leaves are sometimes almost entirely cream, just faintly brushed with delicate touches of pink and pale green. Tiny rat-tail wisps of little brown flowers show its relationship with *Polygonum*. (2 ft/600 mm.)

— 'Variegata' is the form we grow in gardens. Its branching stems are covered with large, oval leaves, slightly ruched and wrinkled, irregularly marbled in all shades of cream and green. Individual plants may be about 2 ft/600 mm high and across, clothed with leaves to the ground. It makes a beautiful light feature, against a plain green background, in soil that does not dry out, and sheltered from sun and wind which can damage the delicate foliage.

TRACHYSTEMON, Boraginaceae.

orientale. From the forests of the Caucasus, Turkey and the south-east Balkans. Wonderful, great, heart-shaped leaves, of fine sandpaper texture, dark green in colour, make a grand feature as well as impenetrable ground-cover in large shrubberies or woodland borders. This plant is invasive, so needs watching where space is limited. Curious flower spikes appear very early in spring, pinkish-mauve buds roll back clear blue petals, while black-tipped stamens are thrust forward like darts from white centres. (18 in./460 mm.)

TRADESCANTIA, Commelinaceae. Named in honour of John Tradescant, gardener to Charles I.

virginiana. Common Spiderwort. From the rich prairies of the central United States and in meadows further east. The forms commonly seen in gardens are probably of hybrid origin and are now listed as *T.* × *andersoniana*. They are easily grown in full sun and any reasonably fertile soil. Their shape provides useful contrast of form among large-leafed plants; they make large clumps of long, narrow leaves deeply grooved to form cradles at the top of the flower stems, out of which tumble many buds, opening three-petalled flowers, each with a conspicuous fluffy centre. They have a very long season, from the end of May until the autumn. The flowers close in the afternoon. They can be found in several shades of blue, also white, purple and pink. (2 ft/600 mm.)

TRICYRTIS, Liliaceae. These curious flowers are welcome in September and October as a change from the wealth of daisy flowers. They need moist retentive soil, in sun or part shade, and are lovely among hostas. They make slowly spreading clumps which produce many slender stems. From a distance their colour is dingy, but close to they have much to offer.

formosana. From the forests of Taiwan. Shining green leaves, alternately clasping 3 ft/1 m stems are deeply veined and spotted with dark green freckles. Dark maroon flower stems emerge from the axils of the leaves along the upper half of the stems, producing a fine, open head of flowers which last many weeks. The buds are dark purple-maroon, opening upturned lily-shaped flowers with petals so densely spotted with reddish-purple they appear purple overall. The complicated arrangement of stamens and stigma, protruding from a gold-ringed centre, adds to the weird charm. (2½–3 ft/760 mm–1 m.)

— **stolonifera** is similar, but grows taller, up to 3½ ft/1.1 m, and increases somewhat faster. The flowers appear paler, having fewer spots on cream petals.

hirta. From the woods of Japan, where it is quite common. This plant has softly hairy matt-looking leaves, with mauve flowers held more closely to the stem, forming a spire rather than a branching head. The petals are white, finely peppered with purple. (2½–3 ft/760 mm–1 m.)

— **'Alba'.** Green-washed buds open to show white wax-like flowers, with the important central heart of stigma and stamens in cream. It needs a warm site to encourage the flowers, which come rather late in the season. (2½–3 ft/760 mm–1 m.)

macropoda. From the woods of south-western Japan. This plant flowers earlier, about August. The flowers are pale creamy-yellow, finely peppered with maroon. These dots become fewer and larger towards the heart of the flower. The leaves are pale green and curled at the tips. (2 ft/600 mm.)

TRIFOLIUM, Leguminosae.

pratense 'Variegata' has green velvety leaves strongly veined with creamy-yellow. The leaves are larger, the flowers are pink. (6 in./150 mm.)

repens. From the meadows of Europe and western Asia, from the Mediterranean to the Arctic.

— **'Purpurea'.** Clovers will not last in poor, dry soils, but like heavy, retentive soil where they will make handsome ground-cover in sun or part shade. This one has leaves of rich chocolate-brown, with faint green edges, which close up in the evening, and white flowers. (3 in./80 mm.)

TRILLIUM, Liliaceae. These are woodland treasures needing cool conditions in rich, leaf-mould soil that does not dry out. Patience also is needed to establish handsome clumps which are slowly formed by underground rhizomes. There are several species and forms; all are distinguished by the division of three—three leaves, three calyces and three petals. I have selected only the most popular.

chloropetalum. From low woods of the coast ranges from central California to Washington. This plant is sometimes confused with *T. sessile*, but is a much larger plant in every way. Large maroon-red or (rarely) white petals emerge from the sheath-like calyces, standing stiffly upright, and attached directly to the large, flat 'collar' of three mottled broad leaves which are poised on 18 in./460 mm stems.

grandiflorum. The Wake Robin. Found in woods, from Quebec to Florida and west to the Great Lakes. The best-known and possibly the loveliest *Trillium*. It makes a dome-shaped plant of veined and shining leaves which set off the pure white, open, funnel-shaped flowers. The pale pink form, *T. grandiflorum* 'Roseum', is a great treasure with foliage warmly tinted also. (15 in./380 mm.)

— 'Flore Pleno'. It is breathtaking, in April, to see these perfectly formed, double white flowers, as lovely as little camellias. (10 in./250 mm.) I had, but am ashamed and sad to say have lost, a form of *T. grandiflorum* which had white flowers splashed with green.

sessile. From woods of the mid and eastern United States and Canada. Three large leaves, strongly marbled chocolate and green, are held at the top of a 10–12 in./250–300 mm stem, centred by the flower whose dark maroon petals are held stiffly upright. By July the colouring in the leaves has faded to shades of silvery-green.

TRITONIA, Iridaceae.

rosea. Although related to *Crocosmia* this plant has a more delicate, less flamboyant character. Fresh green, narrow, blade-like leaves form the base for 3–4 ft/1–1.2 m slender stems of flower which are held close on branching spires, gently curved. Each lily-shaped flower is ½ in./12 mm long, in a peculiarly attractive shade of pink. It is soft rose with a hint of brown about it, so thin petalled the light shines through. They produce new flowers for many weeks during August and September, if planted in full sun in deeply fertile soil.

TROLLIUS, Ranunculaceae. Globe Flower.

asiaticus. From wet mountain meadows of central and northern Asia. This Globe Flower has leaves resembling those of the European one, but rather smaller and often somewhat brown-coloured. Its flowers are carried on stems 1–1½ ft/300–460 mm high, and are open (not globe-shaped) and deep yellow. It has produced beautiful orange varieties, and has been used in breeding some fine garden hybrids. I do not grow the wild plant, but have some of its progeny.

× **cultorum.** This name covers numerous named garden varieties, derived from *T. europaeus* × *T. asiaticus* × *T. chinensis*, varying slightly in size and shades of yellow and orange. They include 'Alabaster', whose soft ivory-cream flowers are much admired, but the plant is not very robust. They stand 2½–3 ft/760 mm–1 m, making clumps of healthy divided green leaves. Their main display is in June–July, but they often give a second display in autumn, if in rich moist soil, in full sun.

europaeus. From damp meadows and damp woods of north and central Europe to the Caucasus, mostly on mountains. This wild form can scarcely be improved upon, in colour or form. *T. e.* 'Superbus' is a selected clone, but still has the right shape and colour—soft, light lemon-yellow, like a very large buttercup, with petals so rounded they form a globe, slightly translucent. (2½ ft/760 mm.)

ledebouri (of gardens). *T. ledebouri* comes from damp meadows of the Amur, in far eastern Siberia, but is said not to be in cultivation. This garden form flowers after *T. europaeus*. The flowers are the colour of orange peel, consisting of an outer cup of broad petals, with the central ones slashed to ribbons and held upright to form a palisade around the precious boss of orange stamens and stigma. (2½–3 ft/760 mm–1 m.)

pumilus. From damp meadows and stream-sides of the mountains of west Sichuan, China. This little plant stands about 9 in./230 mm high, so you must kneel down to look into an enamelled buttercup-like flower with vivid orange stamens. They stand above a tiny clump of crinkled, cut leaves speckled with curious white spots. It is free flowering and lovely for a cool pocket in the rock garden, or on a damp raised bed.

yunnanensis. From high, wet mountain meadows of west China and the Tibet borderlands. This has long-stalked leaves cut into threes or fives, and stems reaching 2 ft/600 mm bearing large, rich yellow, buttercup-like flowers, one to each stem.

TYPHA, Typhaceae.

angustifolia. From shallow water or mud at the edge of ponds and quiet rivers of Eurasia and North and South America. The Lesser Reedmace has stiffer, narrower leaves which are less grey than those of *T. latifolia*, and narrower brown 'pokers', with a gap between the lower (female) and upper (male) parts. It stands some 4 ft/1.2 m or more high, and spreads rapidly, so is not suitable for small ponds.

latifolia. From generally rather deeper water than *T. angustifolia*, round lakes and slow-flowing rivers of Eurasia and North America. The Great Reedmace or Cat's-tail stands 6–8 ft/2–2.5 m tall, its strap-shaped, upright leaves are smooth and ashy grey-green, and its thick 'pokers' are rich dark brown. It is rampant, and will soon fill a small pond, but is one of the most handsome plants for the margins of lakes.

minima. From shallow water and mud around ponds and along slow rivers of eastern Europe to the deltas on the Caspian and Aral Seas, and eastward, sometimes in brackish mud. This little Reedmace only grows from 1–2½ ft/300–760 mm high, with very narrow grassy leaves, though there are none on the flowering stems, which are topped by oval or very short rusty-brown 'pokers'. In the wild it sometimes grows with the Flowering Rush, *Butomus*. I had one once, but have lost it.

UVULARIA, Liliaceae. Related to Solomon's Seal, these strange little plants like cool leaf-mould or peaty soils, in part shade.

grandiflora. From rich woods of the eastern and central United States and eastern Canada. In spring succulent-looking olive-green stems, about 18 in./460 mm high, partially unroll narrow, pointed leaves along the stem. Between them, at the upper end, hang slightly twisted yellow petals, forming open bell-flowers. When they have faded the leaves straighten out and remain fresh for the rest of the summer.

perfoliata. From moist woods of the east and central United States and Canada. This is similar to *U. grandiflora* but not quite so robust. The flowers are paler, and a little smaller. (10–12 in./250–300 mm.)

VANCOUVERIA, Berberidaceae. These plants closely resemble the epimediums of Eurasia, but are found along the west coast of North America, in the deep shade of redwood, Douglas fir and other conifer forests, from central California to Oregon.

hexandra flowers later than epimediums, in June. Suddenly you find in a shaded spot fairy sprays, 10 in./250 mm tall of stiffly held, tiny white flowers, on wire-thin stalks. Dainty leaves, lobed like small ivy leaves are light green, held in clusters of three, on red-tinted wiry stalks.

VERATRUM, Liliaceae. Beautiful, large, deeply pleated leaves slowly expand in spring to make arching mounds of foliage. Later they send up statuesque flower spikes, 5–6 ft/1.5–2 m tall. They must have deep, damp soil, with generous dressings of farmyard manure. Slug bait must be put down as soon as they emerge. All these plants tend to be scarce because of the time it takes to raise them from seed, and then several more years to establish them as handsome clumps in the garden. But they are worth the time and patience needed, there being nothing like them for shape and style. The seed heads are good in autumn.

album. From moist or wet mountain pastures, from central Europe to the Caucasus. Related forms are found in boggy places in Siberia and Japan. At the top of a stout stem is a large, branched spike of densely set, greenish-white, star-shaped flowers. (4 ft/1.2 m.)

nigrum. Found in mountain pastures, from central Europe to Siberia and China. It is similar in shape to *V. album* but can be taller, over 6 ft/2 m, with short, branched spikes of darkest maroon stars.

viride. From marshes and damp woods, across Canada to Alaska, south to the eastern United States. This plant has totally green flowers. (4 ft/1.2 m.)

VERBENA, Verbenaceae.

corymbosa. From Chile and southern South America. This plant will spread freely in moist soil, and makes an attractive tangle around the edge of the golden-leafed *Cornus spaethii*, or small shrubby willows. Its dense, branched heads of violet-blue flowers are produced for most of the summer. (18 in./460 mm.)

VERNONIA, Compositae.

crinita. From the south-central United States, in moist places. This makes a large, columnar plant of narrow, dark green leaves which clothe stiff 6 ft/2 m tall stems topped with flat clusters of small, tightly double, daisy-like flowers of bright reddish-purple. At a different time of year they might be considered small for such a leafy plant, but the intensity of colour makes an interesting companion for *Chrysanthemum uliginosum*, *Aconitum carmichaelii* 'Arendsii', or even colchicums planted at the base.

VERONICA, Scrophulariaceae. The following all prefer soil which does not dry out.

gentianoides. From mountain meadows of the Caucasus. This low-growing plant makes neat clumps of broad, shining green leaves. In May, delicate 2 ft/600 mm spires of pale-washed blue flowers look charming on the edge of a border, in sun or part shade. There is a variegated form, with smaller leaves heavily splashed with cream, which is less vigorous. (18 in./460 mm.)

prostrata 'Trehane'. From central and southern Europe in dry grassland. This garden form is a pretty carpeting plant for the edge of cool-facing borders. Bright golden foliage makes contrast among neighbouring plants all summer. In June it is startling, covered with short spires of deep blue flowers. (6 in./150 mm.)

teucrium. From central and southern Europe to the Caucasus and northern Asia in dry grassland, open woods and wood edges.

— 'Crater Lake Blue'. Low tuffets of small, bright green leaves are topped with 12 in./300 mm spires of vivid blue flowers, a lovely edging plant with *Erigeron* 'Dimity'.

virginica (*Veronicastrum virginicum*). From meadows, moist woods and thickets of the central and north-eastern United States and Canada. An elegant plant: tall, strong but slender stems, clothed in whorls of narrow, dark green leaves are topped with fine spires of tiny flowers, in pale blue, lilac-pink, or white (*V.v.* 'Alba'), which is the best of all. Slowly making an imposing clump, it is an ideal companion for border *Phlox*, flowering during August and September.

VINCA, Apocynaceae. Periwinkles make excellent ground-cover in damp or dry shade, especially if the ground can be mulched after planting. The dwarf form, *V. minor*, has flowers in rich blue, plum or white; there are also doubles in blue and plum. *V. major* is too rampant, with too few flowers per yard of trailer, but the variegated form, *V. major* 'Variegata' is lovely, and there are variegated forms of *V. minor* also.

In Ireland I have seen, in February, *V. difformis* which is found wild in the west Mediterranean, in moist and bushy places, and I realize why I do not grow it successfully. At Mount Usher it was trained up the walls of a potting shed, smothered in large white flowers, just faintly tinted with blue. They said it flowered all the year round. It probably does well in the south-west counties, in warmer, wetter conditions than in East Anglia.

VIOLA, Violaceae. The following violas, especially in warmer, drier counties, need cool-facing borders with plenty of moisture-holding humus.

cornuta. From the Pyrenees, and elsewhere sparingly in the Alps in mountain meadows. It is easily grown in sun, in soil that does not dry out, or in part shade. It makes spreading carpets of small, neat, light green leaves, smothered with tall-stemmed, large, violet-shaped flowers, backed by a long spur or horn. Violas come in white, lilac-blue and deep blue, and are in flower for months in summer. If cut back as they begin to look shabby, and the soil remains damp, they will refurnish themselves and flower again in autumn. (6 in./150 mm.)

cucullata. From damp, shady places of the eastern and central United States. The plant I have under this name. *V. cucullata* 'Bicolor', has tall-stemmed white flowers marked with thin purple veins. It flowers in April and May. (6 in./150 mm.)

— 'Freckles'. The base colour of these large violet-shaped flowers is pale blue, covered with dark blue freckles. Both these plants make thick, scaly rhizomes, and after flowering continue to produce quantities of large, healthy green leaves, which make effective ground-cover. (6 in./150 mm.)

elatior. From central and eastern Europe and western Asia, in marshy places. It is easily grown in gardens in soil that remains damp, making erect, leafy plants, about 12 in./300 mm high, smothered with pale blue, violet-shaped flowers, during June and July.

gracilis. From eastern Europe and the Balkans. Mine may not be the true species, but whatever it is I treasure my plant from Sir Cedric Morris's garden. It makes low mats of dark green, finely toothed leaves and in spring and early summer carries quantities of medium sized *Viola* flowers, of deep velvety purple-blue, the petals slightly twisted, giving them butterfly grace. (4–5 in./100–130 mm.)

labradorica. From the northern United States, Canada and Greenland, in damp or shady places; probably only a northern variety (*minor*) of *V. adunca*.

— **'Purpurea'** makes carpets of small, heart-shaped leaves, dark green suffused with purple. In April small, light purple, scentless flowers are produced with abandon. It both seeds and runs about, making pretty ground-cover in semi-shade, among primulas, ferns and hostas. (4–5 in./ 100–130 mm.)

septentrionalis. From moist open woods, especially of conifers, of eastern Canada and the north-east United States. This plant increases like *V. cucullata*, both by seed and by thick scaly rhizomes which can easily be pulled apart for propagation. Towards the end of April until mid May low clusters of fresh, round leaves are lost beneath generous bunches of large, white violet-shaped flowers. They are so lovely it scarcely matters they are not scented. The leaves continue to expand, to make weed-smothering clumps for the rest of the season. (6 in./150 mm.)

WALDSTEINIA, Rosaceae.

ternata. Found in eastern Europe, Siberia and Japan in mountain woods. Much valued for its glossy, dark green, strawberry-like leaves, it makes thick-spreading carpets in sun or shade, in almost any soil, but revels in a cool moist situation. Sprays of bright yellow strawberry-like flowers are more abundant in sun, produced chiefly round the edges of the mats. (3 in./80 mm.)

ZANTEDESCHIA, Araceae.

aethiopica. From stream-sides and damp low places of South Africa. The well-known Arum Lily, handsome in leaf and flower, grows well in deeply prepared soil kept moist in summer. The leaves will collapse but the crowns must be protected in winter with heavy mulching. They will survive in deep mud in natural clay-based ponds. (3–4 ft/1–1.2 m.)

— **'Crowborough'.** This form was found established in an open sunny border in Sussex. Slightly smaller in flower and leaf than some of the florists' forms, it is an excellent plant, and grows vigorously in well-prepared holes. (3 ft/1 m.)

— **'Green Goddess'** grows equally well in water or in a deeply prepared pit in a cool border. It has enormous, broadly spear-shaped leaves, and green flowers with white throats and will stand well over 5 ft/1.5 m when established in damp soil. In flower from July to September.

ZIGADENUS, Liliaceae. From moist meadows and woods in the Rocky Mountains.

elegans. This unusual bulb sends up firm, grass-like foliage, above which stand elegant spires, 1½–2 ft/460–600 mm tall, of creamy-green, star-shaped flowers in July–August. Retentive, well-enriched soil produces the best results.

A few bamboos

I used to think of bamboos as plants for large and park-like gardens, but I have seen a narrow London garden transformed into a leafy bower with bamboo planted against the boundary wall, blotting out any surrounding ugliness, the tall, arching canes creating a leafy oasis within the garden. They can be grown in any retentive but not waterlogged soil, sheltered if possible from damaging wind. It is a good idea to prune them occasionally, cutting out the very old canes, removing damaged ones, making room for new young canes. I now use my strongest canes for staking beans, while the more slender canes are often useful to support delicate plants.

ARUNDINARIA, Gramineae.

japonica (*Sasa japonica*). From central and southern Japan and south Korea. This is the largest, heaviest-looking bamboo, best in large gardens. In good moist soil it makes dense, invading thickets of olive-green canes which can reach 12–15 ft/up to 4.5 m, heavily clothed with dark green, glossy, ribbon-shaped leaves. It is the better for being tidied up occasionally, to remove wind-bedraggled canes.

murieliae. This bamboo was introduced from China by Ernest Wilson and named after his daughter. Not so invasive, this is medium-sized, 6–9 ft/ 2–3 m. The foliage seems to be halfway between *A. japonica* and *A. nitida* in size, of a light shade of green. The young canes are bright green, aging to dull yellowish-green. Making slowly increasing, rounded clumps this bamboo can be used as a specimen, or in tubs.

nitida. From the wooded mountains of west Sichuan, west China, where the Giant Panda lives. The most beautiful of the tall bamboos. Although it may be 10–12 ft/3–4 m high, and a wide, dense clump several feet across, the effect is of delicate grace and elegance. The slender canes, stained dark purple, carry very narrow leaves, green above and grey on the reverse, so creating a light effect. It is ideal as a specimen plant in grass, in large tubs or in the town garden, provided its roots are restricted.

viridistriata (*A. auricoma*). The Golden-Leafed Bamboo. As a feature this is perhaps the loveliest bamboo, safe in any garden, in good retentive soil. The leaflets are about 5 in./130 mm long, 1 in./25 mm wide, of soft, warm yellow, varyingly striped and shaded with light green, as though they were hand painted. I cut the canes down in spring so that the new canes shoot up with bright new foliage, unspoilt by tattered remains. In very sheltered gardens they could be left to create a taller feature.

SASA, Gramineae.

veitchii. From southern Japan. This bamboo makes low thickets (2–3 ft/ 600 mm–1 m) of purplish-green canes, furnished all summer with rich green leaves, about 6 in./150 mm long, almost 2 in./50 mm wide. In the autumn the colour is withdrawn from the edges, leaving a central zone of green, with creamy-white margins of varying widths. This variegated effect, seen in a low-growing mass, remains handsome all winter. Cut and put to dry in a cool place the leaves remain in perfect state, slightly curled, but most acceptable for winter 'drieds', with far more 'life' than pressed foliage, and a change from leaves preserved in glycerine. However, it is very invasive: you may need to dig up and give most of it away from time to time.

This is a very short list of bamboos. There are many others which I do not know or grow, including the genus *Phyllostachys* which, I am told, includes some of the finest bamboos, less invasive than the arundinarias and sasas. However, due to the large size and hungry roots of many bamboos and the wickedly invasive habits of the low-growing ones, only a very small selection can be grown in any but the largest gardens. Finally, not all are equally hardy, so it is wise to discover which will suit your conditions.

Some grasses and grass-like plants

ALOPECURUS, Gramineae.

pratensis. From moist meadows of Europe and central Asia.

— 'Aureus'. The Golden Foxtail Grass makes vivid clumps of low-growing foliage (12 in./300 mm), brightly striped with strong yellow and green. It is much stronger than *Milium effusum* 'Aureum', Bowles' Golden Grass, and useful as an edging plant where its form and colour make good contrast among such plants as *Geranium* and *Hosta*. It will stand sun provided it is in retentive soil.

ARUNDO, Gramineae.

donax. From damp sandy places, often among river and sea dunes of southern Europe to Iran, India, China and Japan. The Giant Reed is the most stately of all grass-like plants. Tall, thick-jointed stems form a slender column from which cascade, evenly spaced, long blue-grey leaves. In warmer countries the stems tower 12–15 ft/3.5–4.5 m, but in the southern counties of England it is usually about 8 ft/2.5 m. It is wise to take a little trouble with winter protection around the base, cutting off any damaged stems in spring.

— 'Variegata'. This lovely form has leaves broadly striped with ivory-white. It cannot be called hardy. I keep some plants boxed up, protected with straw in a plastic tunnel. They survived one particularly hard winter. Planted out in May they make handsome features by late summer and autumn, 3–4 ft/

1–1.2 m tall. We are now experimenting by covering some of the outdoor plants to see if they will make large plants more quickly. This lovely grass would make a fine feature plant in a conservatory.

CAREX, Cyperaceae. Sedge. All these plants need fairly moist soil, when they will grow in full sun.

buchananii. From stream edges of South Island, New Zealand. It is not reliably hardy, but survives most winters in warmer counties. We tuck bracken or straw around our plants for the winter, cutting off their weather-beaten tops in spring to make way for fresh new growth. This springs up to make a fountain shape: hundreds of shining, rounded stems in shades of buff and bright pinky-copper are curved with slender flower spikes meshed in curling wisps of leaf. There is not a hint of green. (2–2½ ft/600–760 mm.)

morrowii 'Aureo-Variegata'. Also called 'Evergold'. This eye-catching Sedge makes a focal point, winter and summer, on the edge of a damp border. The narrow, grass-like foliage is bright yellow with narrow green margins. Spiralling out from the centre of the plant it makes spider-shaped clumps, showing off each leaf against the dark soil. (12 in./300 mm.)

CORTADERIA, Gramineae. The well-known Pampas Grass is sometimes devalued, either by being planted in unsuitable positions, or by the use of inferior varieties. Grown from seed both good and bad forms may be obtained, the bad ones having poor, skimpy flower heads, often of a dirty colour. ˙

fulvida (*Cortaderia* or *Arundo conspicua fulvida*, of gardens). I lost this grass by dividing it as I should have done, in spring, but not attending to it sufficiently thereafter, when it died from desiccating winds. Now we protect all newly divided grasses for several weeks in a plastic tunnel until they have made new roots. *C. fulvida* is found wild in damp places along river-sides and in dune hollows, often with *Phormium tenax*, in New Zealand. It is slightly tender so succeeds best in southern and western counties. It looks like a refined version of the South American Pampas Grass, starting to flower early, towards the end of June, with more delicate, less bulky plumes which hang gracefully to one side from the tips of tall (7 ft/2.25 m) slender stems. When the flowers are young there is a hint of pink in the silvery-beige colour which changes to ivory with age. This lovely grass is worth protecting in very cold districts.

selloana. (*Gynerium argenteum, Cortaderia argentea.*) Found wild along water-courses and in moist places in Argentina and Chile. There are many forms, so it is worthwhile to check both the eventual size of the plant and the shape of the plume.

— 'Pumila'. This name means dwarf but do not be misled. By comparison it is a valuable, more compact plant with shorter, beautifully arching foliage which makes an all-year-round feature. But in good deep soil the flower stems stand 5–6 ft/1.5–2 m tall. The flower heads are dense and upright, of a soft creamy-beige colour. They look best seen with the sun directly on them, not through them.

— **'Sunningdale Silver'**. Where there is room for a giant this is my favourite. Huge mounds of wickedly sharp-edged leaves form a base for the flower stems which soar 8–10 ft/2.5–3 m tall. The drooping plumes are open and delicate, gleaming like silvery-white pennants among the rich copper and gold of autumn-tinted trees and shrubs which form a frame around them. They are equally beautiful with the light behind or in front of them.

There are other named forms of *C. selloana* which I have not grown. 'Monstrosa' has immense creamy-white plumes. 'Rendatleri' is also a giant, with pink-tinted plumes. I am not yet enamoured of the so-called Pink Pampas Grass. In those I have seen the colour tends to be a dark purplish shade hidden among the silvery silkiness of the flower and can, in the wrong light, look dingy. Well placed it may look magnificent. *C.s.* 'Aureo-lineata' is possibly the form now seen listed as 'Goldband'. It is a variegated form with leaves striped yellow and pale green. There is said to be a white-striped version called 'Albo-lineata', but I have not seen it. It is rare.

CYPERUS, Cyperaceae.

longus. From wet meadows and stream-sides of southern Europe and south-central Asia. The Galingale is a graceful, tall, grassy plant for the water's edge—where there is room, for it is invasive—ideal to bind the banks of large ponds or reservoirs. The drooping clusters of chestnut-brown flowers and seed heads are attractive. (3–4 ft/1–1.2 m.)

vegetus. From South America. A plant enjoyed by flower arrangers: fresh green clumps of rushy foliage are topped in late summer by flower heads of curious green spikelets. (1½–2 ft/460–600 mm.)

DESCHAMPSIA, Gramineae.

caespitosa (*Aira caespitosa*). Tussock Grass. From damp meadows of Europe, central and northern Asia to Japan and the northern USA and Canada. One of the prettiest of our native grasses, it forms dense tussocks of narrow, arching leaves which send up a shower of needle-thin flower stems topped with foaming sprays of tiny flowers. I have recently acquired the form 'Goldschleier' ('Gold Veil'), whose conspicuous stems are pale sulphur-yellow, making a pretty specimen plant in retentive soil. (3–4 ft/1–1.2 m.)

GLYCERIA, Gramineae.

maxima (*G. aquatica*). From stream-sides and shallow water of Europe, temperate Asia and North America.

— **'Variegata'**. In spring the young leaves are flushed deep pink as they push through the mud at the water-side. They quickly change to rich creamy-yellow stripes on green as the leaves lengthen, eventually making stems 3–4 ft/1–1.2 m. This plant will climb the bank out of the water, and can be grown in any heavy retentive soil. It is very handsome, making bright patches from a distance, but it is invasive.

HAKONECHLOA, Gramineae.

macra. From wet mountain rocks and cliffs of Pacific central Japan, where it is rather rare.

— **'Albo-aurea'.** A pity it has such an offputting name, but few people pass by a well-grown clump of this lovely grass. It needs a cool-facing site, in deep moist soil. The ribbon-shaped leaves, set alternately along a red-tinted stem, are 9–12 in./230–300 mm long, creating a light, arching effect. They are warm golden-yellow, finely striped with green, sometimes stained pink or bronze, and this fine colour lasts throughout the summer. This grass is slow to reappear and get going again, not usually until warmer weather in early summer. (12 in./300 mm.)

LUZULA, Juncaceae.

maxima (*L. sylvatica*). Great Woodrush. From moist woods, mostly in the hills of western, southern and central Europe.

— **'Marginata'.** The form most generally used in gardens. Quite handsome when used as a contrast of form, but valuable as ground-cover in rough places, in damp shade, or to stabilize steep banks of heavy soil. It forms clusters of broad, grassy leaves which form dense creeping carpets. The leaves are narrowly edged with creamy-white, while bare stems hold airy sprays of little brown and yellow flowers in May. (18 in./460 mm.)

nivea. From sunny openings in mountain woods of the Pyrenees to the Alps. This Woodrush is more suitable to grow among plants, as it is not invasive. It makes neat, low tuffets of slender, slightly hairy leaves. Above them stand 18 in./460 mm stems topped with graceful panicles of parchment-coloured buds which open beige-white fluffy flowers. They look quietly elegant behind a foreground of the richly tinted foliage of *Astilbe* 'Sprite', and will grow in sun or part shade, in retentive soil. May–June.

MILIUM, Gramineae.

effusum. Wood Millet. From moist woods of Europe, across Asia to Japan, also in the northern United States and southern Canada.

— **'Aureum'.** 'Bowles' Golden Grass' is much more delicate, its thin-textured foliage brightest in spring when it competes with the daffodils, fading to yellowish-green when its dainty sprays of tiny bead-like seeds shimmer in the cool shade of the woodland garden. Seedlings come true, never too many to be a nuisance. (1½–2 ft/460–600 mm.)

MISCANTHUS, Gramineae. This race of noble grasses will grow in moist or dryish soils. I would not consider them to be drought-lovers, but they will grow in sandy soils providing there is sufficient rainfall. They grow best in deep, retentive soil.

sacchariflorus. From river-sides and wet places of Japan, Korea, Manchuria and north China. This grass makes as grand and imposing a plant as bamboo. Slowly increasing clumps of strong, jointed stems shoot up annually to 8 ft/2.5 m, clad from top to bottom with fluttering, ribbon-shaped leaves. It makes ideal contrast for *Gunnera*, or large rheums, and can be used as wind protection or shading for the late summer.

sinensis. From drier, often sandy slopes, or on river sands of Japan and Korea to south-west China and Indo-China.

— **'Gracillimus'.** This plant is more suited to the smaller garden where it can be used as a superbly elegant specimen grass. The narrower leaves help to create a more delicate effect, curling gracefully round the narrow columnar shape as they lengthen. As the colour is withdrawn in late autumn, the stems and leaves become palest straw colour, too lovely to cut down until winter gales destroy them. (5–6 ft/1.5–2 m.)

— **'Silver Feather'.** This fine form flowers regularly in September— upturned feathery shuttlecocks, pale pinky-fawn in colour, fluffed out when it is dry, tight closed when it is wet. It can be used as an isolated specimen, or as background to late summer flowers. (6 ft/2 m or more.)

— **'Variegatus'.** Strangely this has broader leaves than the last two, which helps to make the bold white stripes more effective. (4–5 ft/1.2–1.5 m.)

— **'Zebrinus'.** Throughout the early summer one feels cheated by the healthy columns of plain green leaves, but some time in July the cross bands of gold begin to show along the rich green foliage. From then until the frosts it catches the eye, as do the feathery flower heads which are regularly produced in October. (6 ft/2 m or more.)

MOLINIA, Gramineae.

caerulea (*M.c. altissima*) (*M. litoralis* of gardens). From wet heathy grass-lands, and wet woods of Europe and temperate Asia. This grass is grown for its strong flower stems, up to 6 ft/2 m tall, which are topped in August and September with heavy heads of dark greenish-purple flowers. They may be overlooked, because not until the oaks are russet-brown does this grass really play its part in the scene, and then it can dominate the garden. Every leaf and stiff, rounded stem becomes transformed, gilded to glowing honey-gold. (4 ft/1.2 m or more.)

— **'Variegata'.** Wherever there is retentive soil, or reasonable rainfall, no garden should be without this exquisite small grass. On the edge of a damp border it makes neat, dense tufts of narrowly arching leaves, conspicuously striped with cream. In autumn the pale colour is intensified as thin cream flower stems appear like a fountain. Finally the whole plant fades to parchment, beautiful to the last dead days of winter. (Foliage: 18 in./460 mm; flower stem: 3 ft/1 m.)

PHALARIS, Gramineae.

arundinacea. From river banks and marshes of Europe and north-central Asia to Japan; also northern United States and southern Canada.

— **'Picta'** ('Elegantissima', Ribbon Grass or Gardener's Garters.) This differs from *Glyceria maxima* 'Variegata' in that its variegation is sharply green and white. It too is very invasive, will grow in wet or surprisingly dry soil, usually about 2–3 ft/600 mm–1 m tall, but can be taller in rich wet soil.

SPARTINA, Gramineae.

pectinata. From marshy hollows in the prairies of the midwestern United States.

— **'Aureo-marginata'** makes tall graceful stems from which hang long, narrow, ribbon-like leaves, edged with yellow. This grass likes moist soil. It is invasive but handsome in large landscapes. (6 ft/2 m.)

STIPA, Gramineae.

arundinacea (*Calamagrostris* or *Apera arundinacea*). From New Zealand. This is another grass which draws attention when looking its best. It makes dense clumps of fine, arching leaves which become tinted bronze, red and orange in late summer, remaining so all winter, looking like little mini-bonfires when caught in the sunlight. No less lovely are the long sprays, up to 3 ft/1 m long, of soft, silky bronze-brown seed heads which make one think of newly washed hair. It needs a retentive soil, and can be killed by very hard winters, but seedlings always appear. (Foliage: 2½ ft/760 mm.)

Ferns

Most ferns need a cool, damp, sheltered site. Some need more moisture than others. These are all lime tolerant, except *Blechnum* and *Thelypteris*.

For bog or water-side
Matteuccia, Onoclea, Osmunda, Thelypteris.

For soil which never dries out (i.e., has ample rainfall)
Adiantum, Asplenium, Athyrium filix-femina, Athyrium goeringianum, Blechnum chilense, Blechnum penna-marina, Blechnum spicant, Dryopteris erythrosora.

For somewhat drier soil (but still needing shelter from drying winds, especially in spring)
Crystopteris, Dennstaedtia, Dryopteris filix-mas, Dryopteris goldieana, Hypolepis, Polypodium, Polystichum.

I am not an authority on ferns, gardening as I do in the least favourable part of the country. The following I grow in the limited areas that have evolved in making the garden. For those readers with the right conditions, who could be tempted to start a fern collection, two very helpful books are: *Hardy Ferns* by Reginald Kaye, and *Ferns for Garden and Greenhouse* by A. J. Macself.

ADIANTUM, Filices, to which family all the following genera belong.

pedatum. From rich, moist, hilly woods of most of the United States and Canada; also Japan, eastern Siberia, Manchuria and China. This choice, hardy Maidenhair Fern is unusually shaped. From a slowly increasing rootstock it produces shining, purplish-black wiry stems which hold elegant divided fans composed of bright green rounded leaflets. (12–15 in./ 300–380 mm.) This and the following fern particularly need shelter in my garden from drying winds.

venustum. From woods in the Himalayas. This hardy Maidenhair Fern increases more readily, especially in warm, damp counties. In my garden it makes small, lace-like fronds which remain all winter when they become bronzed. This fern deeply resents being buried, even shallowly. To propagate it it is best to detach a rhizome carefully, keeping its roots intact, place it on leaf-mould soil, and cover with pieces of flat stone. (9 in./230 mm.)

ASPLENIUM. Spleenwort.

scolopendrium (*Phyllitis scolopendrium*). The Hart's Tongue Fern. From shady rocky slopes and banks of central and southern Europe to the Caucasus, also Japan and North America (rare and local in the east). So common in the damper counties, so valuable in the garden, where there is not another leaf to take its place, it has long, undulating ribbon-shaped leaves arranged in open shuttlecock form. It will grow in any soil, including chalk, but will not tolerate drought. It can be grown by water, provided the crowns are not waterlogged, or in cool rocky crevices. There are several forms to be found with names such as 'Crispum' and 'Undulatum', whose edges are gently or intricately fluted. There are others with crested tips to the fronds which, to my mind, do not improve them, but are quaint. They vary in height, are usually about 12 in./300 mm. I have a form which makes almost 2 ft/600 mm.

ATHYRIUM. From moist woods of Europe, central and northern Asia and west North America.

filix-femina. This species includes a large number of very varied ferns, collectively known as the Lady Fern, because of their slender, graceful appearance. They range from fronds standing 4 ft/1.2 m high to only a few inches. They all need shelter from drying wind. They can be found under a variety of names, suggesting that they also come in crested, tasselled, plumed and congested forms.

goeringianum. From hilly woods of southern Japan.

— **'Pictum'.** Delicate fronds look as though they were washed over with pale grey paint, while the purple-tinted stems seem to cast a shadow down the central frond. This fern needs the most sheltered position, in moist leaf-mould, in a moist atmosphere. (6–9 in./150–230 mm.)

BLECHNUM. These ferns need lime-free soil.

chilense. From damp woods of central Chile. A magnificent evergreen fern for a cool, damp site. The great fronds look as though they were stamped out of leather. Each pinna, set in pairs along the centre stem, is single and entire with undulating edges. They look like rows of little Hart's Tongues, making together one huge arching leaf of dark matt green. The roots are slowly but steadily invasive. It needs a little protection in winter in very cold districts. (2½–3 ft/760 mm–1 m.)

penna-marina (*Lomaria alpina*). From damp woods, thickets and tussocky moors of southern New Zealand to southern Chile. This little fern looks charming in rock crevices, or can make effective ground-cover in moist shade, with its crowded colonies of small evergreen fronds, each a single stem set on either side with simple pinnae, dark leather-green surfaces with rusty backs. (8–10 in./200–250 mm.)

spicant. Common Hard Fern. Deer Fern. From forests and damp moors of Europe, north-east Asia and north-west America. This makes dense clumps of longer, larger fronds. The infertile bright evergreen fronds, shaped like ladders, spread outward from the centre which is filled with taller, upright fertile fronds. These are green at first with much narrower pinnae. When they have matured and scattered their spores they wither, standing in winter as curling, light brown skeletons. Size depends on moisture: 12 in.–2 ft/ 300–600 mm or more. This fern does well in retentive soil under trees and shrubs, or in damp, shady rock work.

CYSTOPTERIS

bulbifera. From moist, rocky woodland banks of eastern and central North America. It differs from *C. fragilis* in bearing bulbils under the leaves which sow themselves in cool areas where the plant grows well. I do not have it. (18 in./460 mm.)

fragilis. From shaded moist rocks and banks in the mountains of the cooler parts of the northern and southern hemispheres. This is so pretty and fragile-looking in spring: delicate sprays of tiny lace-like leaves, very light green when they first appear in spring, are held on wiry stems. It must be sheltered from wind and strong sunlight, in light leaf-mould or peaty soil through which its creeping stems can wander. (9–12 in./230–300 mm.)

DENNSTAEDTIA

punctilobula. From open sunny woods of eastern and central North America. This can be a menace in the wrong place, among shade-loving treasures, but it is very pretty in woodland, or among shrubs. It runs underground, like bracken, sending up very finely divided bright green leaves, about 12 in./300 mm high.

DRYOPTERIS

erythrosora. From hilly woods of southern Japan to the Philippines, Korea and China. The most remarkable thing about this fern is the young foliage which is a warm brownish-red in spring, remaining so for a while, then fading to light glossy green as the fronds mature. It needs really moist, shaded conditions. (18 in.–2 ft/460–600 mm.)

filix-mas. From woods and shady places of Europe to central Asia, also the Andes and in Africa. This is the most widely distributed of British ferns and includes a large range of variations, including crested, congested and other aberrations. Some are beautiful, but hard to beat is this, our Common Wild Fern, the Male or Buckler Fern. It will put up with almost any situation (except boggy soil), and is the only fern for quite dry shade. It never fails to unroll elegant sheafs of typical fern-like fronds, light green deepening to dark green, remaining well into the winter, but not really evergreen. (Fronds: 3–4 ft/1–1.2 m.)

goldieana. From rich woods of the north-east and central United States and north-east Canada. There is a distinctly yellowish tinge to the extra-large, boldly divided leaves when they first appear in spring. This is not always apparent when first planted. (3–4 ft/1–1.2 m.)

phegopteris. From moist shady forests, including those of conifers, of Europe and Asia Minor to the Himalayas, China, Siberia and Japan, and North America. The Beech Fern forms running carpets, 6–12 in./150–300 mm high, of delicate, once-cut fronds on long, slender stems. The divisions are also cut, but not into separate sections as in the Oak Fern (*D. linneana* or *Gymnocarpium dryopteris*).

spinulosa. From rather moist woods of Europe, north-east Asia and eastern North America. The Broad Buckler Fern resembles the Male Fern (*D. filix-mas*) but is generally smaller, its more divided fronds some 1–2 ft/300–600 mm long, and with the lowest divisions (pinnae) as long as or longer than the upper ones.

HYPOLEPIS

millefolium. From mountain woods and scrub and wet tussocky moors of New Zealand. This is another invasive ground-covering fern, similar to *Dennstaedtia*, welcome where its foraging roots can do no harm, and where the finely cut, dark green, woolly leaves will be an enchantment. (12 in./300 mm.)

MATTEUCCIA

struthiopteris. Ostrich Plume Fern. From moist, shady places, especially along streams of the north-east and central United States and Canada, also Europe to Siberia, China and Japan.

ONOCLEA

sensibilis. From damp or wet shady places of the east and central United States and Canada; also Japan, Korea, eastern Siberia and Manchuria. This is another much firmer textured fern, but not quite so leathery as *Blechnum*. Broadly segmented, light green leaves make an arching mass in damp or wet soil. An accommodating fern, it will grow in fairly dry soil in shade or, if allowed, will spread in dense carpets over the surface of water. It makes lovely contrast with bog primulas and water irises. (18 in./460 mm.)

OSMUNDA. Named after Osmund, a Saxon chieftain who hid his daughter in a clump of this fern, to protect her from the Danes.

regalis. The Royal Fern. From marshy woods and wet places of Europe to the Caucasus, the Himalayas to Japan, eastern North America to the West Indies, South America and South Africa. This is the largest, most handsome fern we can grow out of doors in the British Isles. It revels in wet, boggy soil, making an ideal feature by still water where its elegance can be reflected. Large elegant fronds tower above bog irises, stand up to ligularias, and finally outshine them all in autumn, as they assume glowing tints, from orange-copper to russet-brown. They tolerate sun, provided their roots can reach water, and wax larger on a diet of peat, fibrous loam and vegetable compost. (4 ft/1.2 m.)

POLYPODIUM. Polypody.

vulgare. From steep, shady banks and rocks, often on tree trunks, of Europe and Asia to Japan, eastern and central North America and South Africa. This is the one fern which may be seen in hedge bottoms in dry East Anglia, most often where there is chalk in the soil. But that is not to say that it cannot be enjoyed in damper places together with its many variants—fronds broader, much divided, fringed, feathered, etc. It is often seen on tree branches in the moister west. It is a colonizing fern, making effective ground cover. (12 in./300 mm.)

POLYSTICHUM. This family includes some of the most beautiful and varied ferns.

aculeatum. Hard Shield Fern. From woods of Europe to central Asia, North America, Chile and elsewhere in the southern hemisphere—almost cosmopolitan. This is a strong, stout fern, distinctive to look at but slow to increase, the individual crowns remaining in my garden as one, for years on end. (Perhaps it increases more elsewhere.) It is one of the few good evergreen ferns, with tall, narrow fronds of hard, leathery pinnae, neatly cut, producing a firm effect. The colour is yellowish-green in spring, shining olive-green in winter. (3 ft/1 m.)

lonchitis. Holly Fern. From shady, rocky mountain slopes of Europe and Asia to Japan. It looks as though one had taken the scissors to the Hart's Tongue Fern and cut it across to the vein, into many fine segments; similar in shape but smaller than *P. munitum*. (18 in./460 mm.)

munitum. Christmas Fern. Sword Fern. From conifer woods of Alaska to California, common under the giant redwoods. This is the finest evergreen fern, perfect in the shade garden as background for hellebores and snow-drops. With large, curving, dark green leaves, simple in shape, but with narrowly divided pinnae as *P. lonchitis*, it creates an imposing feature. (3 ft/1 m.)

setiferum (*P. angulare*). The Soft Shield Fern. From woods; nearly cosmo-politan. There are many variations. I give only two:

— **'Acutilobum'.** One of the very best of delicate-looking ferns, yet it will grow in comparatively dry shade. However, it grows twice as tall in damper gardens. From among the old leaves, which do not collapse until late spring, unroll new fronds of exquisite lace-like delicacy. Fully extended they form ladder-shaped fronds. Hard little buds can be found along the stems, already sprouting little leaves in late spring. If laid in a box of moist soil and kept shaded they will root down and make new plants. (1½–3 ft/460 mm–1 m.)

— **'Densum'.** This form is less elegant, but no less attractive. The light green pinnae are longer at the base, forming broadly pyramidal-shaped fronds. They are also more closely packed, creating a heavily ruffled effect. This fern needs a cool, moist spot to show its best. (18 in./460 mm.)

10 *The Homes of Some Hardy Garden Plants*

In this chapter I would like to share a little of the invaluable background knowledge which my husband, Andrew Chatto, has patiently collected over forty years of reading and research, as it has been such a help to me. He has had the difficult task of reducing his work into one chapter. Of course, he has not, in every case, visited and studied on the spot the flora, climate and geology of all these distant lands, so relies for information from those who have. Unfortunately, most of this is in scientific books and papers published in many countries. A short bibliography appears at the end of this chapter.

Several good books have recently been published, mostly on the European mountains and Mediterranean countries, to help holiday visitors recognize the flowers they come across, and many now include brief descriptions of their environment. There are also articles in the *Journal* of the Alpine Society, and that of the Royal Horticultural Society, especially those on particular groups of plants, and there are *Floras* obtainable for most European countries.

The substance of this chapter is written by my husband, the scholar, linked here and there by comments from myself, the gardener. His lifetime's study has been my inspiration, to make my garden and write this book. Where I have a rather dank shady place, for instance, I have learnt from him to look for plants whose natural home is woodland; or where I have a sun-scorched stretch of gravel to think of using plants from sunny Mediterranean hills.

We can none of us reproduce the dark, wood-scented shade of a mountain forest with its moss-covered boulders and cascading brooks, or suggest the rich meadows just before hay time, where we would recognize many of our well-loved garden plants. But it is, I think, interesting to know where a plant comes from, and helpful when planting to have some idea of the natural environment and associations of those plants we try to grow.

Our garden plants have been brought home from countries that lie in the temperate belts of the world, both north and south of the Equator, by brave and dedicated travellers and collectors over several hundred years. Those plants that have been brought from warmer regions have to be grown in heated houses. We admire them in the steamy, tropical glasshouses of the Royal Botanic Gardens; or we find ourselves desiccated in an atmosphere that is constantly hot and dry in the cactus houses. With the increased use of central heating a small selection of these plants have been introduced into our homes as house plants. But more often than not the poor things pine away because the conditions are designed for humans, not plants. It is either too dry, too inconsistent in temperature or too dark.

I am writing mainly of 'species plants', that is, plants found growing wild in their native homes, not those plants which we have 'improved' by selection or hybridization, which now bear little resemblance to their ancestors. These latter are known as cultivars, obvious examples being roses and chrysanthemums. The enormous variety in shape, colour and form of these two genera alone adds greatly to our pleasure in the garden, and although I am addicted to species, it would be absurd to deny the value of cultivars to the garden. Any visitor to my garden could not fail to notice the old fashioned roses, double primroses and selected clones of variegated plants, none of which would survive for long in the wild.

Not all wild plants would be suitable for cultivation in gardens. Some that have been introduced have been greatly improved by the plant breeders, while others could still be enhanced by careful selection or hybridization. But although that is so, I am constantly amazed and enchanted by the vast numbers of plants that we grow which are just as they were when they were found in the wild. The study of the habitats of our garden plants is, of course, an enormous subject, and one in which continuing study will produce fresh information. There will, without doubt, be corrections made, both in nomenclature and statements, but also we hope new evidence to fit into the jigsaw of our knowledge.

Plants have had to adapt themselves to the conditions in which nature has placed them—and they in turn, as the plant community has developed, have played a part in recreating that environment. Swamps have been colonized by tall reeds and grass-like plants, for example. In the course of time, as the roots have matted and rotted, as the silt has been held and built up around them, more plants have grown up on top of the lower layers until a substratum has been formed which provides a foothold for tree seeds, like poplar or willow, blown in by the wind. So a forest may eventually be formed with firm soil to walk upon where once a boat may have been punted through the still water. We can see this type of change in our gardens where, with careful use of colonizing plants, we help to turn a previously windswept and empty site into a sheltered haven for plants that need quite different conditions. This is what is meant by creating a microclimate.

Although most of our colourful shrubs and stately trees were also originally found growing wild, I shall not have space to write much about them. It is the plants which clothe the floor of the temperate world with which I am concerned, and of these I shall talk almost entirely of the herbaceous perennials.

Herbaceous perennials—those which make a long-lived rootstock, from which leaves and flowers grow up to produce seed, and which then die down again, to reappear next year—have evolved where there are regular seasons of good growing conditions long enough for them to develop their strong roots and underground resting buds. They are only overcome in such situations, in nature, by taller-growing bushes and trees; but even in forests many can make do with, or even prefer, half-light.

Annuals are plants which are adapted to take advantage of short periods of good growing conditions between long ones when growth is impossible. There are not many of them where perennials form communities, as there is no room for them to seed (so strong perennials make excellent ground-cover) but they are very common, as we know to our cost, on poorly cultivated land and disturbed ground, or in countries where winter cold and spring moisture are quickly followed by drought. They must rely on a sharp burst of growth producing blooms and setting seed by the thousand with all speed. Some can manage this in such a short time that they can complete their lifecycle more than once a year, and are called ephemerals.

Biennials are in a sense modified annuals which take two years before completing their lifecycle. There are also some plants needing several years to build up enough strength to flower and set seed, after which they die, such as 'Century plants' and some bamboos. These, together with the annuals and biennials all of which flower only once in their lives, are known as monocarpic plants.

Now to return to our specific subject, which is to look briefly at the natural homes of moisture-loving plants. I find that I have at least two main groups of plants that need moist growing conditions. First there are those that like sunlight, and come from open places, either in lowland water-meadows and swamps, or from damp mountain meadows. Second there are those that need shelter from strong sunlight and wind, and come from shady forests or open woods.

I can only try to describe a few of the regions from which our garden plants come, and only a very few of those plants which grow in them. Not all of the plants mentioned in these wild groupings are in my alphabetical descriptions, as I would not want to grow them in my garden, but they are included to paint the scene, for they help to form the background. These associate plants, which many people might call weeds, I have put with brief descriptions in a separate list (together with a few garden-worthy plants which I do not grow) at the end of this chapter. For them I would substitute more decorative plants of similar growth from other regions of the world, or varieties of them selected and 'improved' in gardens. In place of the European Hemp Agrimony, *Eupatorium cannabinum*, for instance, I plant the stronger-coloured *E. purpureum*, or for *Thalictrum flavum* I might use *T. speciosissimum* or even *T. aquilegifolium*. There are so many fine plants from which to choose! Incidentally, I find it interesting to notice that where similar conditions occur in widely separated parts of the world, the same, or closely related plants, are to be found—for instance, the various species of *Trollius* or *Caltha* along the brooks in their mountain meadows, or the different species of *Anemone* and *Viola* carpeting the summer-green forests in spring.

You must understand that most of the plants I shall mention are adaptable within limits, or we could not grow them in our gardens. For instance many plants which are typical of water-meadows may also be found in man-made grasslands if they are damp enough, or even in open moist places among trees where enough sunlight can reach them.

Flood-meadows, Marshes and Swamps

Before embankment or other control, rivers and streams, if they flowed through gently rolling lowlands and plains, meandered this way and that, thus more or less levelling their valley bottoms. As the snows melted in the spring, or after heavy rains, they broke through low places in their banks and spread over these plains. As the floods subsided, the water flowed back to the main river, leaving a fresh layer of rich, fine silt on the flats and gentle rises, on which grew lush meadows; there were also undrained wet hollows and ponds. In the growing season the level of the water in the ground was (and is) never far down, even on the higher parts of flood-plains, and often stands just below the surface, causing marshy places.

As spring comes in Britain, and the cooler parts of Europe and west Asia, the glistening yellow cups of the Marsh Marigold, *Caltha palustris*, open, with pale lilac Lady's Smock, *Cardamine pratensis*, among fresh green grasses and the dark clumps of rushes. Very locally in Britain, but more common further south in Europe, the Snake's Head Fritillary, *Fritillaria meleagris*, hangs its maroon-chequered bells. Later, among yellow butter-cups and pink Ragged Robin, the rusty plumes of Sorrel, *Rumex acetosa*, the nodding brownish-pink heads of Water Avens, *Geum rivale*, and locally the rosy-lilac spikes of orchids, or the flat, white sprays of Sneezewort, *Achillea ptarmica*, come into flower. Contrasting with these colours are the black-red drumsticks of the Great Burnet, *Sanguisorba officinalis*.

Common further north are the heads of soft, blue cups of Jacob's Ladder, *Polemonium caeruleum*, and the fluffy pink spikes of Bistort, *Polygonum bistorta*. Groups of the creamy-flowered Meadowsweet, *Filipendula ulmaria*, stand along the waterways, where Creeping Jenny, *Lysimachia nummularia*, runs; here and there, colonies of the Marsh Violet, *Viola palustris*, show pale lilac flowers, and the Marsh Spurge, *Euphorbia palustris*, though not native to Britain, spreads its yellow heads on tall, leafy stems.

Where the meadows rise higher above the water-table are red and white clovers, the Common Daisy, *Bellis perennis*, the blue spikes of Bugle, *Ajuga reptans*, the white plates of Yarrow, *Achillea millefolium*, yellow potentillas and many more.

A jungle of taller plants which are not often found in the open meadows grows under the alders and other trees and bushes, along the banks of streams and lakes, especially where there is broken sunlight. Colonies of Yellow Loosestrife, *Lysimachia vulgaris*, tall plants of Hemp Agrimony, *Eupatorium cannabinum*, with fluffy heads of dusty pink, the purple or white croziers of comfrey, *Symphytum officinale*, pale yellow Meadow Rue,

Thalictrum flavum, and the rosy-white wild Valerian, *Valeriana officinalis*, compete with nettle beds on the soggy soil. Here and there are clumps of the Marsh Fern, *Thelypteris palustris*, or the Marsh Helleborine, *Epipactis palustris*, sends up spikes of white orchid-flowers, lined with pink.

The water's edge is lined with the slender crimson-purple spikes of Purple Loosestrife, *Lythrum salicaria*, among sedges, pink 'Codlins and Cream', *Epilobium hirsutum*, and locally the Great Spearwort, *Ranunculus lingua*, with its large yellow buttercups, both of which spread fast and can become bad weeds in gardens. Spreading into the water are the Yellow Flag, *Iris pseudacorus*, the Water Mint, *Mentha aquatica*, with its whorls of lilac, and tall grasses, one of which, the Reedgrass, *Phalaris arundinacea*, has produced the white-striped 'Gardener's Garters'. Also rooting on the edge and in shallow water are the Water Forget-me-not, *Myosotis palustris*, Watercress, *Nasturtium officinale*, and in the north, the creeping white Arum, *Calla palustris*, and the Bog Bean, *Menyanthes trifoliata*, which reaches the Arctic. Only in more southern marshes grow clumps of the Summer Snowflake, *Leucojum aestivum*, hanging its green-tipped white bells.

In the quiet water itself, to a considerable depth, grow rustling beds of reeds, *Phragmites communis*, with their purple plumes, or the tall, grey leaves and brown pokers of reedmaces, *Typha*, or other tall plants, with the dark green, leafless stems of Bulrush, *Scirpus lacustris*, in deeper water, with water-lilies, *Nymphaea*, and *Nuphar*, in some places, leaves and flowers floating between. Growing in shallow water not far from the edge are Arrowhead, *Sagittaria sagittifolia*, the Water Plantain, *Alisma plantago-aquatica*, and the beautiful Flowering Rush, *Butomus umbellatus*.

Many plants of the flood-meadows, marshes and swamps, or closely related species and varieties, grow in such situations all over temperate Europe and Asia, and several grow in North America too. The Marsh Marigold is ubiquitous, and so is the Reed and the Great Reedmace, while a great many others are only absent from limited areas.

Growing among these widespread plants are others which do not spread so far. In Eurasia some are more common eastwards, or confined to the east, while others are found only in the west. The tall clumps of *Iris sibirica*, with their rich blue flowers, grow in damp or wet peaty meadows from central Europe to the River Lena in Siberia, often with the Great Burnet, and there is a closely related *Iris* as far as Japan. The long, slender, lilac spikes of *Veronica longifolia* appear in central Europe also, and spread to the flood-meadows of the River Yenesei and beyond, among spires of *Delphinium elatum* of a dark blue, the stout plants of *Veratrum album-lobelianum* (an eastern form) raising columns of greenish-white stars, above the pale lavender flowers of the Cranesbill, *Geranium sylvaticum*, and pink Bistort. The yellow Day Lily, *Hemerocallis flava*, opens new flowers every morning in drier meadows from south-eastern Europe to far eastern Asia. It is also found in the open, rich grassland of central Siberia known as the steppes.

The Sweet Flag, *Acorus calamus*, grows wild in swamps and in shallow water along rivers from eastern Europe across Asia to Japan, and is also common in eastern North America, but not western Europe. This curious gap is probably due to its extermination in the last Ice Ages, when mountains and the Mediterranean blocked retreat southwards; and many other trees, shrubs and plants, or closely related ones, once widespread, are also found only in eastern Asia and eastern North America.

Quite different in their range are the two magnificent species of *Lysichitum*. The Asiatic one, *L. camtschatcense*, pushes up its big, white, arum-like spathes, and then its vast leaves, from the mud at the edges of ponds and rivers, from north Japan to Kamchatka and east Siberia. On the other side of the north Pacific, its American cousin *L. americanum*, with canary-yellow spathes, grows in similar situations from Alaska to northern California. Another plant of much the same range, though not strictly of water-meadows, but growing in damp, peaty, stony grassland, or in partially shady glades of peaty conifer forests, is the Black Sarana, *Fritillaria camtschatcensis*, which hangs its black-maroon bells from Washington to Alaska, and the north Pacific islands and Kamchatka to north Japan, always within the influence of the Pacific.

True water-meadow and swamp plants of eastern Asia are the two irises, *I. ensata*, which has given rise in Japanese gardens to the forms and varieties known as *I. kaempferi*, and the beautiful soft blue *I. laevigata* which grows in wetter places, and even shallow water, from Japan and Manchuria to south-west China.

Growing among many plants which are also common in Eurasian water-meadows and marshes are some confined to North America, a few of which I will mention here.

Among the tall grasses of swamps and river banks of the eastern USA and Canada, as far west as the Rocky Mountains, stand the blazing scarlet spires of the Cardinal Flower, *Lobelia cardinalis*. It reappears, with a gap of hundreds of miles between, in the mountains of southern California. Though it grows where the winter temperatures may drop many degrees below zero in the northern part of its range, it is liable to be damaged, or even killed by spring frosts in Britain, where it is usually unprotected by snow, and starts into growth too soon during mild periods. This is also true of a number of other plants from Canada and even the coldest parts of Siberia, where the intense frost is uninterrupted until summer warmth quickly comes and melts the snow once and finally. A plant of the eastern United States and Canada which does well in Britain, if given the right conditions, is the Pickerel Weed, *Pontederia cordata*. In America it forms colonies in the shallow water of ponds, lakes and quiet streams, and is common everywhere. In British ponds, the water protects its roots from unseasonable changes in the weather.

North America is rich in tall members of the daisy family, many of which grow in the water-meadows and marshes, and many of which flower late in the season. The parent of many of our tall, large-flowered Michaelmas daisies, the lilac-blue *Aster novi-belgii* is abundant in marshy places from Canada to Georgia, mostly not far inland from the Atlantic, while another commonly grown Michaelmas Daisy, the rosy-lavender *Aster novae-angliae* grows in less wet meadows and spreads further west. Contrasting with the rose-purples, blue-mauves and pale lilacs of the asters, of which there are many species, and colouring the damp meadows and marshes in the autumn sunshine, are the rich yellows of the Golden Rod, *Solidago, Helenium autumnale*, a few small sunflowers, *Helianthus*, the big plants of one of the Cone Flowers, *Rudbeckia laciniata*, which prefers damp river-side thickets, and other yellow-flowered daisies. *Solidago canadensis*, which extends west to damp valleys in the prairies, is the chief parent of our tall garden Golden Rod, and most of our garden sunflowers also come from among the tall grasses of such damp places in the prairies.

Mountain Meadows

I am going to talk about the meadows in the zone of the upper forests and just above the tree-line, not the short, high alpine turfs, the plants of which grow under harsher conditions, and often need special treatment in gardens.

The mountain meadows usually grow on the bottoms and more gently sloping sides of the high valleys, where rich humus soil can collect among the fragments of rock. They are kept damp all summer by water from the melting snow above, seeping through the soil and stones, or trickling in innumerable little runnels, as well as by rain; but only where the water is held up are there boggy patches, especially along the smaller streams. On either side, on steeper slopes consisting mainly of broken rock with some leaf-litter soil, grow the forests, or at higher levels bushland, often of rhododendrons. The vegetation in these high valleys, with the snow peaks above, therefore, varies greatly within quite short distances, from lush, open, sunny meadows with marshy places, and partially shaded forest edges, to buttresses of rock, screes and cliffs, some also in full, hot sun, and very dry.

There is much discussion about the plants of limestone (calcareous) and non-limestone (siliceous) mountains. You will find I do not mention many plants typical of limestone soils. Rainwater dissolves limestone, enlarging the cracks and sinking away quickly, in some districts forming caves and underground rivers. The soil therefore tends to be drier than on siliceous mountains, where most of the water runs off on or near the surface. I successfully grow many plants from the calcareous mountains on my rather acid soil, but only in well-drained, drier parts of the garden, while many plants from siliceous mountains are happy in the damper parts. There are certainly plants which are adapted to acid peat soils, and generally fail on limy ones, especially members of the heather family, and those which, when wild, seem to be able to compete better, and are more abundant on calcareous soils and are absent on acid ones. But, in gardens, where there is little competition, I am coming to the conclusion that the amount and continuous availability of water, and the speed of drainage, are more important than the amount of lime initially present in the soil. Perhaps to bear out this theory, plants usually confined to acid soil, such as heathers, grow on hard limestone in the very wet climate of western Ireland, where they form a surface layer of peat from which the lime is washed out. Also the plant explorer, George Forrest, emphasizes that in Yunnan in south-west China, with a wet climate, the mountains are mostly of hard limestone, yet are covered with notoriously lime-hating rhododendrons.

So consider your annual rainfall, and your drainage, as well as the nature of the bedrock under your soil.

Grasses do not play such an important part in the mountain meadows as they do in the lowland ones, and in the height of the season the mountain meadows become sheets of varied colour.

In the central European mountains, among the first to flower at the edge of the melting snow is *Crocus vernus*, varying from white to purple, and the parent of the big Dutch cultivated forms. The Pyrenees and north Spain seem to be the headquarters of the daffodils. Several yellow species flower early, and a little later whole meadows are covered with the white *Narcissus poeticus*, often standing above sprawling mounds of the Horned Pansy, *Viola cornuta*, their violet flowers on long stems. The taller meadow plants grow up quickly, and are soon in flower. The lavender *Geranium sylvaticum*, the blue of bellflowers (*Campanula*) and Mountain Cornflower, *Centaurea montana*, the cream or purple of rampions (*Phyteuma*), one of which, *P. halleri*, is nearly black, a pleasing contrast to the more vivid flowers, and the burnt orange of *Crepis aurea*, are set off by colonies of pink Bistort in damp places, and yellow globe flowers, *Trollius europaeus*, along the streams. Several other lowland plants ascend to these meadows, white yarrow and Ox-eye Daisy in great numbers on drier slopes, and buttercups. The Red Campion, *Melandrium rubrum*, is rather unexpectedly common, being a woodland plant in the lowlands. Pink and rose-purple orchids add their colours. The season ends with the lilac cups of *Colchicum autumnale* and, in the Pyrenees, the lavender *Crocus nudiflorus*.

Taller plants grow at the edges of the woods, and in part shaded torrent gullies, where there is ample water trickling through the rich humus soil among rock fragments. The tall bellflower, *Campanula latifolia*, the yellow foxglove, *Digitalis grandiflora*, the beautiful fluffy lilac heads of *Thalictrum aquilegifolium*, blue-purple and pale yellow monkshood (*Aconitum*) and the Fair Maids of France, *Ranunculus aconitifolius*, can all be found, while *Lilium martagon* raises its spotted mauve-pink turkscaps among the rocks and sometimes in the open meadows.

Many beautiful plants come from the high meadows of the Caucasus and Minor Caucasus mountains between the Black and Caspian Seas, especially in the west which receives more rain and melt-water from deeper snow. The soil of these meadows is always nearly black with humus, often deep, and where it is shallower, as in the drier east, the meadows are shorter and thinner, though most of the same plants are to be found. The meadows grow among the highest woods, and extend above them for some distance.

The large-flowered, soft blue *Scabiosa caucasica* is common everywhere, with the sprawling *Gentiana septemfida* lifting rich blue trumpets, and the much paler blue spires of *Veronica gentianoides*, while *Chrysanthemum coccineum*, cultivated in gardens as *Pyrethrum roseum*, adds its daisies which are almost white to rosy-red, with the pincushion heads of *Astrantia maxima*, surrounded by their petal-like bracts, all of crushed-strawberry pink, in damp places. There are the big plants of *Geranium ibericum*, with their rich mauve-blue flowers, the smaller mounds of beautifully crinkled leaves and white, violet-pencilled ones of *G. renardii*, yellow species of *Primula*, clovers, vetches and the tall spires of *Digitalis ferruginea*, with its tight-packed, small trumpets of golden-brown, and which prefers the edges of the woods, as do the large spreading clumps of *Stachys macrantha* showing its big whorls of crimson-purple.

Where there is an even greater abundance of water always trickling through deep, humus-rich soil, such as in sheltered, steep gullies, jungles of huge plants crowd together. The big spreading leaves and pale straw-yellow flowers on tall stems of *Cephalaria gigantea* are characteristic, not only of these wet ravines, but all over the damper parts of the meadows. With them in the wet gullies grow enormous cow parsnips, blue and yellow monkshoods (*Aconitum*), the dark blue *Delphinium elatum* and other tall larkspurs, the magnificent *Campanula lactiflora*, a man's height and crowned by heads of soft blue bells, and big thistles, while at the edges of the jungles stand the lemon-yellow turkscaps of *Lilium monadelphum* (in the Great Caucasus) or *L. szovitzianum* (in the Minor Caucasus), which also often grow in part shade near the woods, and the rich yellow suns of *Inula glandulosa* and *I. grandiflora*.

Half choking the mountain streams is the large and spreading Marsh Marigold, *Caltha polypetala*, while the sky-blue comfrey, *Symphytum caucasicum*, runs on the banks.

As the meadows fade in the autumn, and the surrounding woods shed their foliage, leaving only the dark conifers, the great lilac goblets of *Colchicum speciosum* appear, and in the east, especially on the Minor Caucasus, the nearly blue *Crocus speciosus* gives the last colour to the meadows.

The vast wall of the Himalayas is drier at its western end in Kashmir than on its eastern part, where it checks the full force of the south-west monsoon, the wettest place on earth being on the hills near its foot. As the mountain chains rise from a tropical climate to everlasting snow, the only plants hardy in Britain come from the upper forest zone and above. Many are unique to the Himalayas, mixed with more widely distributed plants, and to the east, ones also found in China. I shall mention here a few plants from the damp valley meadows of the central Himalayas, with their boulder-strewn torrents and side gullies, their marshy level places, and with their steep rocky slopes rising on either side, where woods of birch and conifers grow, or scrub of low rhododendrons.

The sloping or fairly level meadows are lush and very flowery. Growing among such widespread plants as *Caltha palustris* in wet places, *Polemonium caeruleum* and *Aruncus dioicus*, are the open heads of white blue-backed flowers of *Anemone rivularis*, other anemones, the slatey-blue violet-stained ones of *Delphinium brunonianum*, the purple-marked yellow lilies of *Nomocharis oxypetala* and the purplish-blue ones of *N. nana*, the straggling plants with silvery-silky leaves of *Potentilla argyrophylla* sending up open sprays of rich yellow, orange-eyed blooms, with the blood-red ones of its close relative or variety *P. atrosanguinea*, and the spiky spires of *Morina longifolia* showing whorls of white trumpets which turn crimson as they age.

The sprawling plants of *Geranium wallichianum* show their purple-blue, white-eyed flowers with those of other geraniums, and the short *Trollius acaulis*, its yellow ones which open wide. *Codonopsis rotundifolia* twines among the taller plants, hanging its large yellow-green bells veined with purple. (*Codonopsis clematidea* scrambles over rocks in the damp valleys further west, from the Himalayas to the Hindu Kush and the Tien Shan.) *Primula denticulata* lifts its lilac drumsticks in the meadows with other small primulas, and also in the birch woods. Where the streams fall steeply and the banks are of rocks, a few bushes find roothold, and silver-grey mounds of *Anaphalis nubigena* and *A. triplinervis* with their papery-white heads spread over them, contrasting with the deep green ones, studded with pink spikes, of *Polygonum affine*, which also colours rocky hill-sides. (*Polygonum vacciniifolium* is not a meadow plant, but forms wide mats over loose boulders in the light birch copses and among dwarf rhododendrons.)

Accumulations of settled or lodged rocks and boulders at the foot of slopes and in small side gullies provide the damp, sheltered pockets which some plants prefer. The small *Bergenia stracheyi* is one of these, and also grows in damp grassy patches among the dwarf rhododendrons. The blue poppy, *Meconopsis aculeata*, which dies after flowering, also favours such pockets under boulders, and *Corydalis cashmeriana* spreads sheets of vivid blue among the rocks and low rhododendrons. Where the meadows have been broken up by grazing animals or other causes, and bare soil exposed, tall stands of *Impatiens roylei* spring up, hanging their large, curiously shaped pink flowers.

The mountains of west China in the Province of Sichuan on the border of Tibet (old spelling Szechuan) rise abruptly in a broad series of fore-ranges from the Red Basin, which is subtropical, with palms and tall bamboos.

Westward beyond these fore-mountains, an enormous wall, with peaks of 20,000 ft/6000 m and over, forms the border of high, rolling tablelands at 13,000 to 14,000 ft/4500 m, extending into northern Yunnan Province, covered by rather monotonous short mountain grassland. Other isolated, permanently snow-covered mountain massifs rise from the grassy table-lands, and the large rivers, including the upper Yangtze, have cut tremendous gorges through them. The bottoms of these river chasms are thousands of feet below the plateau, especially in north Yunnan, and the precipitous lower parts of their sides, being walled off from the rain, are hot and dry. The tributary streams also flow through steep, narrow rock defiles in their lower courses, but become wider with more gently sloping floors higher up. These upper valleys usually have damp meadows along their streams, with bushes where it is rocky, and on their sides grow fine conifer forests, interspersed with grassy slopes. It is in these upper valleys and mountain meadows, and in the higher meadows in the fore-mountains, that a large number of beautiful plants, hardy in Britain, have been found, though many are not yet common in gardens, and some, especially species of *Primula*, seem difficult to cultivate.

The fore-mountains receive much rain in summer from the south-east monsoon, except where shut off by mountains, as well as winter snow. On the high tablelands and their mountain ranges the winters are bitter, and the summer weather, in the thin atmosphere, is very changeable. Hot sun quickly changes to hail showers or cold misty rain, and there are almost daily monsoon thunderstorms in June and July. This country and the eastern Himalayas, with its very varied conditions, has an extremely rich flora, and seems to be the central home of rhododendrons and primulas. I can only mention a very few plants which are common and easily grown in Britain, and first of all I must speak of some which perhaps are not strictly meadow plants.

In bottom lands and along torrents in the fore-mountains, and spreading up the damp, rocky, once-forested sides, at comparatively low altitudes, are communities of tall herbaceous plants, most of which appreciate partial shade or some shelter, and before deforestation grew in open places in the summer-green woods. With *Aruncus dioicus* stand the tall green-leafed stems of *Artemisia lactiflora*, the large creamy-white plumes of *Astilbe rivularis*, and the slender rosy-purple ones on their red stems of *A. davidii*, the deep orange daisies of *Ligularia dentata*, and on more open rocky slopes the rosy-pink *Anemone tomentosa*. The big horse-chestnut leaves of *Rodgersia aesculifolia* with their tiered flower heads spread from the wood edges over damp rocky slopes, while *R. pinnata* grows in glades further south in Yunnan. *Bergenia purpurascens* (*B. delavayi*) prefers more open and drier rock slopes, often with lilies.

The lilies are most abundant on the steep sides of the dry, warm valleys, several of the species being confined to one valley. *Lilium regale* grows only on the sunny, rocky sides of the upper Min valley. Also growing in hot valleys and ravines in Yunnan is the beautiful, lilac-flowered *Thalictrum delavayi*, on stream-sides among bushes.

At much greater altitudes, in valleys and high basins among the conifer forests, are true mountain meadows. Growing among more ordinary plants of damp meadows, such as a Marsh Marigold, *Trollius yunnanensis* and the smaller *T. pumilus*, both with large, wide-open, yellow flowers, the fringed pink *Dianthus superbus*, the pink spikes of Bistort and *Anemone rivularis*, are whole marshy stretches and stream-sides coloured by species of *Primula*. The tall stems of *Primula sikkimensis* hang their yellow bells from the eastern Himalayas to China, as do the mealy ones, topped by heads of the rosy-purple nodding flowers of *P. secundiflora*, often in the same meadows; but some seem more local, though abundant in their own district, such as some of the candelabra primulas, their flowers in whorls on tall stems. The soft orange *P. bulleyana* of north Yunnan, and the shorter but more brilliant red-orange *P. aurantiaca* of the same country, are two, and *P. pulverulenta* is another, its wine-purple whorls on white-mealy stalks being found only in a limited area in Sichuan. The bright yellow candelabra *P. helodoxa* is more southern, on the Yunnan-north Burma border mountains, growing among irises and sedges. The plant explorer Kingdon-Ward found the Giant Cow-slip, *P. florindae*, growing in groups along the mountain streams, nearly blocking their flow, in damp meadows full of *P. alpicola* of varying colours, in south-east Tibet, above the gorge of the Yarlung Zangbo (once spelt Tsangpo) which becomes the Brahmaputra on entering India. These high meadows have much the same character, with their conifer-forested sides, as those further east in China. They are also the home of the beautiful Blue Poppy, *Meconopsis betonicifolia*.

In the high mountains of Sichuan and Yunnan, where the streams flow swiftly, and their banks are stony and rocky, bushes grow, and the deep violet-purple *Iris chrysographes* with its yellow pencillings takes shelter, with violets and primulas, and at the edges, *Semiaquilegia ecalcarata*, which also grows all over the high grasslands, hangs its pale, brownish-lavender, spurless columbine flowers.

In high marshy basins, especially where manured by yaks, stand the pale pagodas of *Rheum alexandrae* above yellow marsh marigolds and sometimes with colonies of tall blue irises. Another rhubarb, the huge *Rheum pal-matum*, prefers rocky places on the borders of mountain lakes and streams, sometimes among low bushes.

The mountains of north-east China and Manchuria have hard winters with bitterly cold, dry winds out of Siberia, and rather short rainy seasons in the hot summers. They were once forested with summer-green trees and pines at lower levels, passing to spruce and larch woods higher up, much of it now reduced to bush. In the meadows and openings among the woods grow such widespread Eurasian plants as the Great Burnet, *Sanguisorba officinalis*, Jacob's Ladder, *Polemonium caeruleum*, and the Meadow Cranesbill, *Geranium pratense*, while higher up where the conifers become scattered and grow mainly on the rocky sides of the valleys, appear the Bistort, *Polygonum bistorta*, blue and yellow monkshoods (including *Aconitum vulparia*), and the dark blue columbine, *Aquilegia vulgaris*.

Growing with these are Asiatic plants, the orange-yellow, wide-open flowers of *Trollius asiaticus*, the grassy clumps showing lemon-yellow lilies of *Hemerocallis minor*, and the beautiful Lady's Slipper Orchid, *Cypri-pedium macranthum*, its single large bloom veined with crimson and with a crimson-purple pouch. *Anemone rivularis* grows along the brooks, with the white or rose plumes of *Astilbe chinensis*, while the leavy plants of *Dracocephalum sibiricum* raise their whorls of lavender in the meadows.

These meadows pass into shorter, soft alpine turfs up to the craggy peak ridges and rock slides, with familiar Eurasiatic plants of high mountains, such as Edelweiss, gentians and forms of the Iceland Poppy, *Papaver nudicaule*. Sheltering among piled rocks, from the woods right up to the peak ridges, are the big plants of the rhubarb, *Rheum emodi*, while in light mountain woods of birch and oak, and not a meadow plant, is the pure white *Paeonia lactiflora*, a parent of many garden paeonies, growing with *Lilium concolor pulchellum* showing heads of upright, scarlet, saucer-shaped flowers, columbines, yellow day-lilies and geraniums.

Japan is much more influenced by the surrounding seas, and has a wet climate with rain for most of the year, and with much snow in the north and on the Japan Sea side of the main island. Due to a warm Pacific current washing the south-west, and a cold one the north, the summers in the two are different, hot and muggy in the south, and cool and foggy in the north. Several huge plants, copiously watered by snow-melt and misty rain, grow along the streams in the mountains of the north, and some extend to Sakhalin and even south Kamchatka. Colonies of 10 ft/3 m, arching, bamboo-like stems of *Polygonum sachalinense*, with their big leaves and rather small white flower-spikes, and the Meadowsweet, *Filipendula kamtschatica*, raising its white or pink-stained fluffy plumes to more than a man's height, which also colonizes brook banks in the mountain ravines, are two of these.

Most of Japan's high mountains are in the centre and the north, and are of granite, hard metamorphic or volcanic rocks. They yield sandy soils, which become enriched with humus if not disturbed.

The subalpine conifer forests give way upwards in the north to thin woods of a birch, *Betula ermanii*, or bush thickets on the rocky slopes, with meadows in the valleys, and these in turn to dense elfinwood of Dwarf Pine, *Pinus pumila*. Growing only in north Japan and Sakhalin in the damp meadows is *Ligularia hodgsonii*, spreading heads of big yellow daisies, where the nodding deep rosy-red bottle-brushes of *Sanguisorba hakusan-ensis* also stand (*S. obtusa*, of gardens). Two rather small but beautiful day-lilies grow in the high meadows of the north, *Hemerocallis midden-dorfiana*, its soft apricot-orange flowers overtopping its leaves, and *H. dumortieri*, with its orange-yellow ones which are brown-backed, among its foliage.

The mountain meadows and ravines of Japan share a number of plants with the mainland of Eurasia, but often as a Japanese variety. The Marsh Marigold has its Japanese and east Asiatic race, as does *Aruncus dioicus*, but the Bistort, *Thalictrum aquilegifolium*, and *Ligularia dentata* have not developed a local form. Growing with these in the damp meadows and along streams throughout Japan are more strictly Japanese or east Asiatic plants, of which I will mention only the purplish-crimson candelabra *Primula japonica* of wet stream-sides, and *Filipendula multijuga*, which raises flattened heads of fluffy rose-pink flowers, and which is a parent of the garden plant called *F. purpurea* or *Spiraea palmata*.

The magnificent Golden-rayed Lily, *Lilium auratum*, grows in colonies in rocky, sometimes shady, lower mountain meadows, in the main island only, often with tiger lilies, *L. lancifolium* (*L. tigrinum*), which also are found in Manchuria and China.

Lastly I will talk of a few of the plants of damp mountain meadows among the upper conifer forests of western North America, the Cascades, the Rockies and the Sierra Nevada, but not of the alpine mats and rocks. Many plants are found on all these mountains, but others are confined to one system of ranges.

Beginning the season, and closely following the melting snow-banks, whole mountain-sides in the Rockies become coloured by the yellow Glacier Lily, *Erythronium grandiflorum*, which is often mixed in the north-west, though in separate colonies, with the white *E. montanum* with an orange throat, but which is difficult to cultivate in Britain.

As the summer advances, in both the Rockies and the Sierra Nevada, and lining the stony mountain brooks through the meadows, is the deep rose-pink *Mimulus lewisii*, often growing with the narrow sky-blue bells of *Mertensia sibirica*, or *M. ciliata*, the white *Caltha leptosepala* in marshy places, and the pale creamy-yellow or white open flower of *Trollius laxus albiflorus*, the last three in the Rockies only. The spotted, yellow Monkey Musk, *Mimulus guttatus* also climbs to timber-line on marshy stream-sides on all the western mountains, sometimes spreading into the water, whereas the heads of pink flowers on tall stems of *Peltiphyllum peltatum*, followed later by big umbrella-leaves, form their creeping colonies only along the brooks and torrents in the northern Sierra Nevada.

Growing in the open meadows of all the ranges are the heads of pale or dark rose, dart-shaped flowers on their tall stems, of several species of *Dodecatheon*, all rather alike, and each growing in its own mountains. The spikes of dark blue stars of *Camassia quamash* are seen in large colonies in damp places, the lavender or white daisies of different species of *Erigeron* colour the meadows, as do the deep yellow ones of *Arnica*, tall cluster-headed blue gentians, and the tall blue spikes of *Lupinus polyphyllus*, a parent of many garden lupins, and which is confined to the meadows of the Cascades and the Sierra Nevada.

Where the woods meet the meadows, and along half-shaded brooks, hang the vivid scarlet flowers of *Aquilegia formosa truncata*, among blue monkshoods and larkspurs (*Aconitum* and *Delphinium*), and the tall stems of the Leopard Lily, *Lilium pardalinum*, topped by many scarlet turkscaps with yellow, spotted centres, standing in colonies on damp stream-banks, but only in the coastal mountains and the Sierras. The beautiful blue and white *Aquilegia coerulea* is confined to grassy meadows among the dark conifer forests of the central Rockies, where it is abundant.

Shade Plants from Summer-green Forests of Europe, America and Japan

Few of our garden plants can survive in permanent deep shade, such as under dense evergreens. Most require some light, but protection from the scorching midsummer sun, and shelter from strong, dry winds. Most of them, therefore, grow in woods where they benefit not only from the comparatively still air, but also from its moisture, due to transpiration of the trees and bushes.

There is another class of plants, not strictly shade plants, which grow on the margins of woods, and in open glades and bushy places, such as hedges. They can flourish in sunlight, and die out in too much shade, but also need protection from wind, some leaf-mould and a good water supply. I have already mentioned some of them, as they often grow on the borders of meadows. Some true woodland plants can also survive in such positions, even in open grassland in damp cloudy climates.

Now I want to give a very brief description of different types of forest from which our garden plants come.

All round the northern hemisphere is a broad forest zone of mainly coniferous trees. Similar woods also occupy the upper cloud belt on most mountain chains in the temperate parts of this hemisphere. The climate in which most of these coniferous forests grow is one of long, cold winters, often with much snow, and short, misty or rainy summers. There is little evaporation, and the movement of water is almost constantly downward in the soil, causing layers to form. The basic salts are washed down, the rotting of the needle carpet is therefore very slow, and these soils are acid and infertile. Many of the plants on the forest floor are specialized, and many are nearly world-wide. We do not get many garden plants for ordinary conditions from these forests.

The conifer forests give way southward, through a region of mixed woods, to trees which drop their leaves in winter (summer-green trees), but only in those lands within reach of winds from across oceans, which bring them adequate water, spread throughout the year. The interiors of the continents are too dry for trees, and grasslands or deserts take the place of forest. The winters in the summer-green forest lands may be cold with deep snow, or rainy with little snow, but with periods of sharp frost. The summers are longer than in the coniferous forest zone, with spells of warm, dry, sunny weather between rainy times. Thus water moves up and down in the soil, bringing salts and enabling the leaf-litter to rot down to mild humus. These forest soils are usually rather acid, especially on top, but are fertile, and most of our best shade plants come from the woods growing on them.

Southward still, in warmer climates, the summer-green forests merge into woods of predominantly evergreen trees, but with broad leaves, not needles. These are of two main types, those of lands with fairly heavy rainfall throughout most of the year (Japan, central China, the eastern United States, New Zealand), and those with adequate rainfall in winter, but long, dry summers, typically round the Mediterranean, but also in southern California, parts of Chile and elsewhere. A number of shade-loving plants from these warm woods can be grown in Britain, mostly from cool, moist valleys in the mountains.

I would like to leave the conifer forests till later, and talk first of the familiar summer-green forests of Europe and their shade plants, and then discover how they differ from those of other parts of the world. The summer-green forests of Europe are predominantly either of various species of oak, or of beech. Other trees mingle with them, and locally may be numerous, especially in the south. On deep, moist soils of the lowlands (often clays or silts) the main oak is the Pedunculate Oak, *Quercus robur*, growing all over Europe to the Urals. Also widespread, but not so far east, is the Durmast Oak, *Q. petraea*, which needs a moister climate but can flourish on shallower, rockier or more sandy soils. Other oaks grow in the south. The beech can grow on fairly shallow soils, whether calcareous or not, but requires a damper, more equable climate than the oaks. It therefore becomes a mountain tree in the south and east, forming a zone in the cloud belt above the oaks, but below the conifers. In the central European mountains the beech often mixes with silver firs (*Abies*) and other trees. Where the beech woods are nearly pure and dense, there is very little underwood and the ground plants are also scanty.

Many shade plants grow in all the European summer-green forests, whether of oaks, mixed trees or beeches, wherever there is enough light and plenty of moist leaf-mould. The ground plants are more influenced by the dryness or wetness of the soil, and the amount of light which can reach them, than by the species of trees forming the canopy, but some plants are much more abundant, or confined to the wet Atlantic climate of the west, while others are only found in the woods of the more continental east, or the southern mountains.

Mature lowland oak woods, not thinned, coppiced, grazed or otherwise modified by man (which are now very rare), do not cast such a deep shade as pure beech forests. They allow enough light for some bushes and many plants to grow on the forest floor. Most flower in the spring sunlight before the canopy is fully developed, to be pollinated by flying insects, and provide the beautiful woodland scenes we love.

Our own pale yellow primrose, *Primula vulgaris*, does not extend to north-east Europe, but carpets woods on heavy loams, being especially common in the west. Another western plant is the bluebell, *Hyacinthoides nonscripta*, which is most abundant on lighter, sandy loams, avoiding very damp soil, and reaches along the Mediterranean to Italy. Its place is taken in Russian oak woods by the smaller, purer blue *Scilla sibirica*, which pushes up to flower through the melting snow, and by *S. bifolia* in south-east Europe. So we find bluebell woods, followed later in the season by open stands of bracken, *Pteridium aquilinum*; and primrose woods, usually with wood anemones, though they will sometimes all grow in the same wood, often in patches according to the texture and dampness of the soil. Much more widespread on both heavy and light though moist soils, is the Wood Anemone, *Anemone nemorosa*, carpeting the woods of both oaks and beeches, and even the northern conifers far into Siberia, with its delicate white cups; while from central Europe eastwards to Russia the yellow *Anemone ranunculoides* becomes common in well-lit oak woods.

The foliage of many of the spring plants disappears as the shade of the canopy deepens, such as that of the two similar, lilac-flowered *Corydalis* species, *C. cava* and *C. solida*, and of the Lesser Celandine, *Ficaria verna*, which is abundant in damp places in the woods as well as in water meadows, as is the Bugle, *Ajuga reptans*, whose mats remain green; and *Geranium sylvaticum*. Others keeping their foliage all summer are the Lungwort, *Pulmonaria officinalis*, its white-spotted leaves not fully spread till its pink buds have opened to pale blue bells, while *Lamium maculatum* not only keeps its leaves but continues in bloom later. Both grow throughout Europe, as do the violets (*Viola odorata*, *V. riviniana* and others) which produce their showy flowers early, but their inconspicuous self-fertile ones later. Another method of securing pollination is that of the widespread Asarabacca, *Asarum europaeum*, which takes advantage of the beetles foraging in the leaf-litter and produces its liver-coloured, foul-smelling flowers under its foliage.

The Cuckoo Pint, *Arum maculatum*, sends up its green, or occasionally purple, spathes in moist woods all over Europe, while the delicate little Wood Sorrel, *Oxalis acetosella*, opens its pencilled white flowers and folds its shamrock-leaves every night, in all damp, shady forests whether of oaks, beeches, or northern conifers right round the northern hemisphere. Another plant of the northern woods, including those of the conifers, is the baneberry, *Actaea spicata*, which prefers damp soil. The Lily-of-the-Valley, *Convallaria majalis*, is also mainly northern, in oak, beech and conifer forest, often in large colonies, but wide districts are without it.

In open glades in the woods, where the sun filters down more freely, grow the Wood Spurge, *Euphorbia amygdaloides*, the Red Campion, *Melandrium rubrum*, and the scrambling Yellow Archangel, *Galeobdolon luteum*.

When the oaks are in full leaf in midsummer, only a few, not very showy flowers bloom in the shade, most relying for pollination on the breezes, and including woodland grasses such as the Wood Millet, *Milium effusum*. The bracken is now tall in open sandy woods. Other ferns are still green in damp places, though they are not very numerous, the Lady Fern, *Athyrium filix-femina*, the Male Fern, *Dryopteris filix-mas*, and *D. spinulosa* being the commonest. There is little autumn display in the woods.

Beeches often form nearly pure forests with very little underwood between the tall grey trunks, which cast deep shade, but even when these are mature, and the stronger trees have killed out the weaker ones, there is a rather sparse growth of spring-flowering plants. In the deepest woods few plants grow among the slowly rotting leaf-litter; several of those that do are plants with no green chlorophyll that live on decayed vegetation. In the mature forests on good soil, especially if other trees share the canopy, many of the same spring plants as in the oak forests shoot up as the beeches come into leaf, such as the Wood Anemone, violets, Wood Spurge, Yellow Archangel and Wood Sorrel. There are others which are more abundant in beech forests, especially on calcareous soil, or which are not often found in other woods, and which give them a character of their own.

On the Balkan mountains the early-flowering Lungwort, *Pulmonaria rubra*, and toothworts (including the Coralroot, *Dentaria bulbifera*), some of which also grow in the oak woods, but not so abundantly, are characteristic, often with *Geranium macrorrhizum*. Growing among the widespread snowdrop, *Galanthus nivalis*, and Spring Snowflake, *Leucojum vernum*, is the blue *Scilla amoena*, a plant of the eastern beech woods, as is *Helleborus purpurascens*. The Perennial Honesty, *Lunaria rediviva*, grows in the central European beech woods, where *Lathyrus vernus* and *Cardamine trifolia* are common. The Christmas Rose, *Helleborus niger*, and *Cyclamen europaeum* grow in the beech woods of the Alps, as well as in other types of forest, as does *Hepatica triloba*.

Not common, but characteristic of the British beech woods on thin soil over chalk are *Helleborus viridis occidentalis, Polygonatum multiflorum*, and here and there in open places *Aquilegia vulgaris*, which is widespread over Eurasia in semi-shady places. Several white orchids (*Epipactis, Cephalanthera*) are almost confined to these woods. The ramsons, *Allium ursinum*, and the Lily-of-the-Valley form wide drifts locally.

The forests on the western Great and Minor Caucasus, within reach of winds off the Black Sea, differ from those of central Europe in having a milder and wetter climate. Hard frosts occur in winter but do not last long, and the summers are hot. The woods are of mixed summer-green trees, predominantly of various oaks, with the eastern beeches higher up the mountains and in damp gullies down to sea level, but much of the underwood is of evergreen bushes, such as the common Cherry Laurel, *Prunus laurocerasus*, the holly and *Rhododendron ponticum*. The summer-green forests give way to those of conifers on the wet heights above.

Between the bushes, in this comparatively mild climate, several of the plants growing on the forest floor still have their old leaves when they flower in the early spring, such as the forms of *Helleborus orientalis*, and *Epimedium pinnatum colchicum*, while *Cyclamen coum caucasicum* sends up its leaves before the winter is over, and also flowers very early. Even the Mediterranean *Arum italicum*, also in leaf all winter, grows in these woods. Some of the many ferns are evergreen too, the Hard Fern, *Blechnum spicant*, forms of the Prickly Shield Fern, *Polystichum aculeatum*, the Ribbon Fern, *Pteris cretica*, which is not hardy in Britain, and the Hart's Tongue Fern, *Asplenium scolopendrium*, both usually growing in rocky places.

Flowering before the canopy becomes too shady are leaf-losing plants with big, lush foliage not yet fully spread, the clumps of *Brunnera macrophylla*, and the quickly spreading colonies of the borage-like *Trachystemon orientale*, both of which climb to the mountain woods. Mats of

Omphalodes cappadocica hang over shady rocks in the south, where the evergreen *Iris lazica* covers banks. Among the eastern plants are woodland ones widespread in Europe, the pale yellow primrose, *Primula vulgaris*, but only in the north-west, its pink close-relative further south, the Wood Spurge, *Lathyrus vernus*, the pale yellow-flowered sage, *Salvia glutinosa*, and many more.

The upper, cooler, mountain forests show a spring display more like that of central Europe. Very early to flower are the cyclamen, the blue *Scilla cernua*, the snowdrop, *Galanthus plicatus* and other snowdrops, followed soon by *Pachyphragma macrophyllum*, blooming before its foliage has carpeted the forest floor, as does that of the low comfrey, *Symphytum grandiflorum*, which flowers later in damp places. The pink *Corydalis angustifolia*, and the larger, mauve-purple *C. caucasica* are early flowering Caucasian and Iranian plants, while the toothwort, *Dentaria bulbifera*, *Anemone ranunculoides*, the baneberry, *Actaea spicata*, the Creeping Gromwell, *Lithospermum purpureo-coeruleum*, and the Sweet Violet grow over much of Europe. The Lady Fern and the Ostrich Fern, *Matteuccia struthiopteris* inhabit damp places. The huge plants of *Buphthalmum speciosum* are common, following the streams from the lowlands up to the subalpine meadows, as they do in the Balkan woods also. The Willow Gentian, *Gentiana asclepiadea*, the Calamint, *Calamintha grandiflora*, and *Lathyrus aureus* grow in half shade at the edges of the woods, where they open out to glades and meadows.

The summer-green woods of eastern North America are of more varied trees, climbers and underwood bushes than those of Europe. They once stretched from the Canadian conifer forests nearly to the Gulf of Mexico, and from the Atlantic westward to beyond the Great Lakes, where the climate becomes too dry, and they give way to the prairies. The leaves of many of them colour vividly before they fall, and the forests are very beautiful before the first winter blizzards. The colouring of some of them is not so reliable in Britain, perhaps because the climate of the eastern United States is less oceanic than that of west and central Europe, more influenced by hot air from the interior and the south in summer, and by arctic winds in the winter, especially in the north, where the winters are much colder, with deep snow. The rainfall is 40–60 in./1–1.5 m or more, heaviest in the southern mountain forests.

The forests vary over such a vast area, but most of the main trees can grow over the whole range where soils and sites are suitable. On the best soils and in cool sites, both in the north-east and southward on the Appalachians, the predominant trees are the American Beech and the Sugar Maple, with Lime, Yellow Birch, various oaks and sometimes Canadian Hemlock growing among them. On drier sites and in drier climates the main forest trees are several oaks and hickories, again with many other trees. These oak–hickory forests form the general western forest limit. From Virginia southward the lower and mid slopes of the Appalachians are covered by forests of more southern oaks (and American Sweet Chestnuts before they were destroyed by imported disease), while tulip trees, magnolias and many others are common. These southern mountain forests are the richest and most varied summer-green woods in America.

Many of the ground plants grow throughout the whole range of the summer-green forests, from east to west, provided their needs for moisture, shade or drainage are satisfied. However, a number which grow in the forests of the south do not extend to those of the north.

Very early to flower, as the trees are breaking their buds and coming into leaf, are the Adder's Tongues, the yellow *Erythronium americanum* of damp woods, and the white *E. albidum* of rather drier forests of the Mid West, neither as easy to grow in gardens as the far western species, blue *Hepatica triloba*, white anemones very close to the European Wood Anemone, the pink Rue Anemone, *Anemonella thalictroides*, the Blood Root, *Sanguinaria canadensis*, and the pale pink or white Dutchman's Breeches, *Dicentra cucullaria*. Soon several Wake Robins (*Trillium*), white, deep brownish-purple or occasionally greenish-yellow, including the beautiful *T. grandiflorum*, open their flowers, with the bellwort, *Uvularia perfoliata*, and the running Jacob's Ladder, *Polemonium reptans*. The Jack-in-the-Pulpit, *Arisaema triphyllum*, sends up its striped and hooded spathes, and violets, of which there are many eastern American species, show their white, lilac, yellow or deep purple-blue flowers, some preferring open, damp places, others dry, sunny woods.

The False Solomon's Seal, *Smilacina racemosa*, and true Solomon's Seals (*Polygonatum*) flower a little later in the spring, and some woods are carpeted by the lilac-blue *Phlox divaricata*, or in the Appalachians, by *P. stolonifera*. The beautiful cool lilac to rosy-purple *Geranium maculatum* blooms in rich moist woods, as does the Foam Flower, *Tiarella cordifolia*, and the May Apple, *Podophyllum peltatum*. Growing in boggy places in the woods are colonies of the tall, white and carmine-pink Lady's Slipper Orchid, *Cypripedium reginae*, while the Moccasin Flower, *C. acaule*, prefers damp sandy or rocky woods. The scarlet and yellow *Aquilegia canadensis* and *Heuchera americana* which grow mainly in the Mid West states both grow in rocky but somewhat drier woods.

In the deep shade of midsummer in the woods, few but coarse weedy plants with inconspicuous flowers are to be found, but where sunlight can reach the ground, such as along streams, the Bee Balm, *Monarda didyma*, the tall *Phlox maculata*, *P. paniculata*, *Cimicifuga racemosa* in cool places, and the Indian Physic, *Gillenia trifoliata* in the Appalachian woods, are all in bloom.

As the canopy begins to thin in the autumn, woodland species of Michaelmas Daisy (*Aster*) and Golden Rod (*Solidago*), with some other members of the daisy family, such as Boneset (*Eupatorium*), here and there, come into flower after all else is over, especially in more open oak forests.

Apart from nearly cosmopolitan ferns, eastern North America shares some with Japan and east Asia only, such as the Northern Maidenhair,

Adiantum pedatum, of moist, usually hilly woods, the Sensitive Fern, *Onoclea sensibilis*, of damp, open places, and which will flourish with its roots in wet mud, the Cinnamon Fern and the Interrupted Fern, *Osmunda cinnamomea* and *O. claytoniana*, both of damp or even wet forests. The Eastern Lady Fern, *Athyrium angustum*, and the Common Wood Fern, *Dryopteris spinulosa intermedia*, take the place of their European relatives, while the Hay-scented Fern, *Dennstaedtia punctilobula* is confined to America, where it runs in open woods. There are many more.

The summer-green forests of Japan resemble those of eastern North America more closely than they do those of Europe. They are of equally varied trees and bushes, and also show vivid colouring of their leaves in the warm, dry autumn, after the hot, wet and humid summer. The winters in the summer-green zone are cold, dry and frosty, except on the Japan Sea side of the central mountains, and in the north, where the snow lies very deeply. The yearly rainfall is everywhere high, averaging 60 in./1.5 m over much of Japan.

The summer-green forests extend from the lowlands and hills of south-west Hokkaido (the northern island) and the northern part of the main island (Honshu) southward, becoming mountain woods further south and west, where they merge into those of evergreen oaks on the hills and lower mountain slopes. The lowlands of the south-west are subtropical. Above the summer-green forests on all the higher mountains, and in the north of Hokkaido, are forests of conifers. In the forests of the warmer lower slopes and hills, the main trees are oaks, chestnuts and magnolias, with many others, and on the central mountains, with cypresses, Umbrella Pine and other conifers growing among them, or forming groves. Higher in the mountains beeches become much more common, still mixed with many other trees.

As in other summer-green forests, many plants shoot up and flower quickly in the spring, before the shade becomes deep. Several east Asiatic anemones and violets, not often grown in Britain, Japanese forms of *Hepatica triloba*, and Dog's Tooth Violet, *Erythronium dens-canis japonicum*, and a winter aconite, *Eranthis pinnatifida* with yellow-eyed, white flowers are all early, though the latter is rather local and rare in south-west Honshu. Japan has many species of *Asarum*, most with beautifully marbled leaves and making attractive ground-cover, but many are southern and local, and perhaps not very hardy in Britain. There are also many species of Jack-in-the-Pulpit (*Arisaema*), few of which are grown in gardens. More well-known and cultivated are the barrenworts, especially the large-flowered lilac to white *Epimedium grandiflorum*, which is also a parent of beautiful garden hybrids. Others that flower in the early spring are *Disporum sessile* and *D. smilacina*, Asiatic species of *Trillium*, the rosy-purple *Paeonia obovata*, usually grown in Britain in its pure white form, the low yellow poppy, *Hylomecon japonicum*, and the evergreen, orchid-like *Iris japonica* of the centre and south-west. Another evergreen, which makes carpets, is *Pachysandra terminalis* which produces its fluffy white spikes in the spring. The posy-shaped flower heads of *Petasites japonicus* appear before its huge leaves, along shady mountain streams.

Late spring and early summer is the flowering season of the species of *Hosta*, of which Japan has nearly all. Many are very local, a few inhabiting boggy places, some of the smaller ones damp crevices and pockets in cliffs, and those with larger leaves, such as *H. sieboldiana* of the wet, western side of Honshu, are plants of rich woods. Growing only in the woods on the high mountains of central and north Japan, *Glaucidium palmatum* also opens its large lilac flowers now, while *Rodgersia podophylla* spreads its big, bronzed foliage in glades in the same districts, blooming a little later.

In high summer, when much monsoon rain falls, members of the nettle family, umbellifers and other coarse plants, and the many ferns, predominate in the shade, but in more open places species of *Smilacina* and the Giant Lily, *Cardiocrinum cordatum*, come into bloom. Two plants, native in Japan only, and rare even there, are the tall *Anemonopsis macrophylla* of the woods on the mountain ranges of central Honshu, and *Kirengeshoma palmata*, scattered here and there on a few mountains of the southern islands of Shikoku and Kyushu, and probably a relic of an earlier age. Several species of toad lily, *Tricyrtis*, some local and rare, though *T. hirta* is rather common except in the far north, produce their curious spotted white or pale yellow bells in late summer and on into autumn, with the White Rue, *Boenninghausenia japonica*, in the central and southern mountains. Last to flower in the woods are species of Michaelmas Daisy and other, mostly tall members of the daisy family, and the white fluffy spires of *Cimicifuga*.

Conifer Forests

The northern conifer forests in rainier climates, and on damp, close-textured soils, often glacial clays, are mostly of spruces (*Picae*), mixed with Silver Fir (*Abies*) towards the south. Similar forests grow in the upper cloud belt of many mountain ranges all over the temperate northern hemisphere where there is enough rain. The forests on drier sandy or rocky soils (and even dried-out peat hillocks), and in rather warmer climates, are mainly of pines (*Pinus*). In central and eastern Siberia, which has the coldest and harshest winters in the world, apart from Antarctica, and at the uppermost limit of tree growth on many mountains, leaf-losing larches (*Larix*) replace the evergreen conifers.

The spruce-fir forests, the typical 'taiga' of the Russians, cast a dense, year-long shade. There are practically no underwood bushes, and the ground is covered by a thick, silent carpet of spreading mosses among the fallen needles. Only a few low-flowering plants and ferns are scattered in these sombre woods, where the trees grow well. The Wood Sorrel, *Oxalis acetosella*, the running Beech Fern, *Dryopteris phegopteris* and a few other ferns, the mats of *Linnaea borealis*, and May Lily, *Maianthemum bifolium*, *Trientalis europaea*, *T. borealis* in Canada, the Whortleberry, *Vaccinium myrtillus*, and several wintergreen *Pyrola,* including the One-flowered Wintergreen, *Moneses uniflora*, are characteristic. Several plants without chlorophyll live on the rotting needles in the deepest shade. In Canada (and east Siberia) the creeping *Cornus canadensis* and *Mitella nuda* are also common. The thick moss carpet and most of these little plants are also characteristic of pine and larch forests on moist soil and in moist climates. Larger plants only find enough light along streams, or where the spruces grow poorly, and are not very typical, many being also found in water-meadows or summer-green forests.

Finally I cannot leave out the magnificent conifer forests of the coasts and coastal mountains of western North America, from British Columbia to northern California, as some fine shade plants come from them. They are of mixed, huge conifers, hemlocks (*Tsuga*), thujas, spruces, the Douglas Fir, cypresses (*Chamaecyparis*) and, in the south, the redwoods (*Sequoia*), tallest trees in the world.

The rainfall here averages 60 in./1.5 m, reaching 80 in./2 m in places most exposed to the Pacific winds, and dropping to 30 in./760 mm, mostly in winter, at the southern limit of the redwoods, but there are frequent sea fogs in the summer where they grow, which condense and drip from the trees. The temperatures are never very low in winter, even in the north where there is snow, and the summers are cool.

There is an abundant underwood of shrubs, between which, on the mossy ground, grow colonies of the tall Sword Fern, *Polystichum munitum*, and other ferns, creeping mats of the Wood Sorrel, *Oxalis oregana*, with rosy-white flowers and of *Asarum cordatum* with curious, spider-like blooms, *Dicentra formosa*, the Fringe Cup, *Tellima grandiflora*, the Coast Trillium, *Trillium ovatum* which is closely related to *T. grandiflorum* of the east, *Heuchera micrantha*, a parent of many garden hybrids, Fairy Lantern, *Disporum smithii* and its relatives, the delicate little *Vancouveria hexandra*, *Linnaea*, *Trientalis* and many others. The beautiful *Erythronium oregonum* grows in the lowland forests only, and *E. revolutum*, also of the lowland woods, often at the edges of bogs, is found further south, while the flesh-pink Jacob's Ladder, *Polemonium carneum*, is a rather rare plant in the woods of north California and Oregon.

Short Descriptive List of Plants Mentioned but Rarely Grown in Gardens

There are a number of plants in the foregoing descriptions which you will not find in my classified lists in Chapter 11, or in my alphabetical descriptions in Chapter 9. I have left them out either because they are not so decorative and garden-worthy as other, similar plants, or because they are both difficult to cultivate and often, to obtain. There are a few I have omitted because I have not grown them myself, and so cannot say much about them from personal experience.

I shall describe them now, giving my reasons for their omission from the main lists.

Anemonella (Syndesmon) thalictroides. The Rue Anemone is a delicate, *Anemone*-like little woodlander, with heads of pale pink flowers in spring. I have yet to obtain it.

Arum maculatum. Our own common Cuckoo Pint or Lords and Ladies is a much inferior garden plant to its close relative *A. italicum*, and can become a weed.

Codonopsis rotundifolia. A vigorous scrambler with greenish bells veined blue-purple. I do not grow this one, and have lost some others of its relatives, but will try again.

Corydalis angustifolia. A low, ferny-leaved woodland plant with heads of pale pink or white flowers.

C. caucasica is larger, with mauve-purple flowers. I do not grow either of these, but am fond of *C. bulbosa* or *C. solida*, which I substitute for them.

Cypripedium acaule. The Moccasin Flower, with rust-coloured, mottled 'wings' and a curiously infolded deep rose 'pouch'. I have failed to establish it, though it is said to be one of the easiest, given the right conditions.

C. macranthum of east Europe and Asia has very large rosy-purple flowers. There are many other very beautiful Lady's Slippers in North America and Asia which are tempting to try, but they are not generally easy to cultivate, or to obtain, and I do not think they should be dug up from the wild, only to be lost, especially as several are not common.

Dentaria bulbifera. Coralroot is similar to several of its close relatives, and is not the most decorative.

Dicentra cucullaria. Dutchman's Breeches is a little, early spring plant, less than 6 in./150 mm high, its stems drooping with a few locket-shaped white or pale pink, yellow-tipped flowers, fancifully resembling a man in baggy trousers. It has several larger and more colourful relatives. I have had this plant but, sad to say, have lost it.

Eranthis pinnatifida is a little white winter aconite with frilly leaves, which I have not yet obtained.

Erythronium albidum. The White Adder's Tongue sends up a two-leaved stem from which hangs a white or pale pink, open-mouthed bell.

E. americanum. The Yellow Adder's Tongue has yellow bells. Both woodlanders seem to be poor growers, and often shy to flower.

E. grandiflorum. The Glacier Lily shows very recurved 'turkscap' flowers of rich yellow.

E. montanum has similarly shaped flowers which are white with an orange throat. Both these two are high mountain plants and are also not easy to grow. There are many easier and equally handsome ones, which can take their place in the garden.

Eupatorium cannabinum. The Hemp Agrimony is a handsome plant, but I prefer the similar *E. purpureum*.

Filipendula kamtschatica. From mountain ravines, often in colonies along streams, of north Japan, Sakhalin and Kamchatka. The Kamchatkan Meadowsweet stand 3–6 ft/1–2 m high, with big leaves of a large, divided end leaflet and very small side ones, and spreading wide branching heads of little white to pale pink flowers, fluffy with stamens.

Heuchera micrantha is one parent of several garden hybrids, though its own tiny flowers are yellowish-white or faintly pink. The hybrids are finer garden plants.

Meconopsis aculeata only flowers once, then dies. It is a beautiful sky-blue poppy, but not a regular inhabitant of my garden.

Mitella nuda is a little member of the saxifrage family which runs about in cool shady woods, forming mats of rounded leaves, and sending up spikes of fluffy greenish-white flowers. I grow another charming *Mitella*, resembling it, but which I have been unable to identify with certainty.

Moneses uniflora. The One-flowered Wintergreen is next to impossible to grow in gardens. The related wintergreens of the genus *Pyrola* are also difficult, except under special conditions and care.

Nasturtium officinale. The Common Watercress is not very decorative and spreads alarmingly fast. If you wish to grow it for eating, you must be sure that the water is clean and cannot infect you with disease.

Nomocharis nana, *N. oxypetala*. Both these beautiful members of the lily family, and their relatives, with their nodding, lily-like flowers on leafy stems, are very difficult to please in my garden, being better suited to Scotland or the west of England. I have tried them, but failed so far to establish them.

Osmunda cinnamomea. The Cinnamon Fern sends up large, barren fronds, reaching 2–3 ft/600 mm–1 m long on stems 1 ft/300 mm in length. Its fertile fronds are distinct and much smaller. The whole plant is thick with rusty wool when young.

O. claytoniana. The Interrupted Fern forms an outer circle of once-divided, arching barren fronds 1–2 ft/300–600 mm and ones bearing fertile divisions standing upright in the centre of the clumps to a height of 3–4 ft/1–1.2 m. The fertile pinnae (divisions) are halfway up these fronds and are small, cylindrical, and velvety brownish-green.

Phlox divaricata (*P. canadensis*). This creeping *Phlox* carpets some American woods with its lilac flowers as do bluebells in England. I do not have it, but substitute the form called 'Chattahoochee', which may be a variety of it, or one of its hybrids.

Phragmites communis. The Common Reed is handsome with its tall canes and purple plumes, but much too invasive for any but the largest lakes.

Rumex acetosa. The Common Sorrel is not a decorative garden plant, but its leaves have a pleasant acid flavour. The French have selected some forms with very broad, soft foliage, one of which I grow, and often use in the kitchen. It needs well-enriched soil in the vegetable garden, where two or three plants will provide ample leaves for soup and sauces in the spring, and then again in late summer and autumn, after it has finished flowering. (Foliage 18 in./460 mm.)

Scilla amoena is a squill with several strap-shaped leaves, and a head of a few starry blue flowers on a rather weak stem some 4–6 in./100–150 mm tall.

S. bifolia has only two narrow leaves, and its smaller flowers are more numerous and bright blue. Both are occasionally white or pink. (I grow this in drifts, and its early blue is welcome.)

S. cernua is very like *S. sibirica*, and is often considered a variety of it.

S. sibirica. This early spring squill has produced several cultivated varieties of deeper or paler colour (one is white) and larger size. The wild plant has drooping and more bell-shaped flowers than the others mentioned, of a beautiful, slightly greenish-blue, with no hint of mauve. All these squills grow perfectly well without shade, and will tolerate considerable drought in summer so they do not strictly come into the confines of this book. *S. sibirica* is often found in high mountain pastures of Turkey, the Caucasus and Iran. I grow two varieties.

Symphytum officinale. The Common Comfrey is a large plant with heads of bell-shaped dull purple or yellowish flowers. There are several much more decorative comfreys to grow in its place.

Thalictrum flavum. The Common Meadow Rue is quite handsome, with graceful, much-cut foliage and pyramidal heads of fluffy pale yellow flowers in dense clusters, standing 3 ft/1 m high. I do not grow it, but substitute the grey-leaved, bright yellow-flowered *T. speciosissimum* from the river-sides of south Spain.

Trientalis europaea is a little, slowly creeping, woodland plant with stems about 6 in./150 mm high, and bearing a whorl of shining leaves at the top. Above these leaves rise several starry flowers, each on its own stalk, and white or pale pink with a yellow eye. I have not yet grown this plant. *T. boreale* is smaller.

Trollius acaulis is a globe flower with much-cut leaves, and stems from 3–12 in./80–300 mm high, each bearing a single, large, rich yellow open flower (not globe-shaped).

T. laxus albiflorus. This is a high mountain form of a globe flower, widely distributed in America. It has much-divided foliage, rather weak, slender stems, and its open flowers are creamy-yellow to white. I have not grown either of these.

Valeriana officinalis. The Common Valerian or All-heal misses being a garden plant, as its flat heads of small flowers are indeterminate pinkish-white, and it is too large a plant (2–4 ft/600 mm–1.2 m) for their size. Its foliage is handsome, each leaf cut into a number of leaflets on either side of a central axis (pinnate), but it spreads vigorously. I collected a rather similar valerian (which may be a form) in the Pyrenees, which is not so big and rampant, with clear rose flowers, but I have not been able to identify it yet.

Veronica longifolia. This is a tall, upright plant, 2–4 ft/600 mm–1.2 m, with narrow, pointed leaves, often in whorls up its stems, which are topped by slim, dense columns of lilac flowers. It has produced several forms or local varieties with purple, pink or white flowers. I have not yet grown it.

Ecological Bibliography

I have concentrated in this short bibliography on those works with ecological or plant-distributive interest, rather than those of value for plant identification. Of course there are many more which I have not managed to study, especially more recent works.

Alpine Garden Society *Bulletin*. Woking, Surrey, England. Many articles.

CLEMENTS, E. S. and CLEMENTS, F. E., 'Flower Pageant of the Midwest', *National Geographic Society Magazine*, Vol. LXXVI, No. 2. Washington DC.

COCKAYNE, L., 'The Vegetation of New Zealand', *Die Vegetation der Erde*, Vol. XIV. W. Engelmann, Leipzig, 1921.

CONARD, H. S., *The Background of Plant Ecology*, a Translation of 'The Plant Life of the Danube Basin' by A. Kerner. Iowa State College Press, Ames, Iowa, USA, 1950.

COX, E. H. M., *Plant-hunting in China*. Collins, London, 1945.

Ecology, the Journal of the Ecological Society of America. Duke University Press, Durham, N. Carolina, USA. Many articles.

Ergebnisse der Internationalen Pflanzengeographischen Exkursion durch die Tschechoslowakei und Polen, 1928. H. Huber, Bern-Berlin, 1930. Several contributions by European botanists.

FOURNIER, P., *Les Quatre Flores de la France*. P. Lechevalier, Paris, 1946.

The Garden, Journal of the Royal Horticultural Society. New Perspectives Publishing Ltd, London.

Journal of Ecology, the Journal of the British Ecological Society, Cambridge University Press. Many articles.

LAVRENKO, E. M. and SOCHAVA, V. B., *Descriptio Vegetationis USSR ad Tabulare Geobotanicam Annotationes.* Academie Scientarum, Leningrad, 1955.

LIMPRICHT, W., *Botanische Reisen in den Hochbergen Chinas und Ost Tibets.* Dahlem bei Berlin, 1922.

OHWI, J., *Flora of Japan.* Smithsonian Institution, Washington DC, 1965.

PARSONS, M. E., *The Wild Flowers of California.* Dover Publications Inc., New York, 1966.

RADDE, G., 'Grundzüge der Pflanzenverbreitung in den Kaukasusländern', *Die Vegetation der Erde*, Vol. III. W. Engelmann, Leipzig, 1899.

REICHE, K., 'Grundzüge der Pflanzenverbreitung in Chile', *Die Vegetation der Erde*, Vol. VIII. W. Engelmann, Leipzig, 1907.

SCHIMPER, A. F. W., *Plant Geography on a Physiological Basis.* Clarendon Press, Oxford, 1903.

SMYTHE, F. S., *The Valley of Flowers.* Hodder and Stoughton, London, 1947. Deals with the Central Himalayas.

TANSLEY, A. G., *The British Islands and their Vegetation.* Cambridge University Press, 1939.

TAYLOR, N., *Flora of the Vicinity of New York*, Memoirs of the New York Botanical Garden. 1915.

THOMPSON, H. S., *Alpine Plants of Europe.* G. Routledge, London, 1911.

THOMPSON, H. S., *Subalpine Plants of the Swiss Woods and Meadows.* G. Routledge, London, 1912.

TURRILL, W. B., *The Plant Life of the Balkan Peninsula.* Clarendon Press, Oxford, 1929.

WALTER, H., *Die Vegetation Osteuropas.* Paul Parey, Berlin, 1943.

WEAVER and CLEMENTS, *Plant Ecology.* McGraw-Hill Book Co., New York.

WILKOMM, M., 'Grundzüge der Pflanzenverbreitung auf der Iberischen Halbinsel', *Die Vegetation der Erde*, Vol. I. W. Engelmann, Leipzig, 1896.

WILSON, E. H., *A Naturalist in Western China.* Methuen, London, 1913.

11 *Classified Lists to Help with Garden Planning*

I may tend to overstress the need for dampness for certain plants in the garden, but I should remind you that my part of East Anglia has a very low average rainfall (20–22 in./500–550 mm per year). Half of that falls in summer, but it is then often whisked away by a couple of days of destructively drying winds. Also the foliage of trees, bushes and plants themselves prevent some of this precious moisture reaching the roots. Those who live in areas of heavy rainfall—I imagine the Lake District, and much of the western half of the country—will probably grow many of these plants without too much difficulty.

There is, however, another point I should like to make. I am advocating the idea of gardening without regular resort to watering. Although I have ample supplies of water in the form of large spring-fed pools which we have made, we do not irrigate the garden. I try to plant each different section with plants chosen for their ability to survive there, whether it be hot, sunny, totally drained gravel, including dry shade (as I described in *The Dry Garden*); or heavy clay, saturated at the pond edges; meadow silt watered by springs which run just beneath the surface; or yet again, areas where enough moisture is conserved because of shade, shelter from wind and the ample addition of humus, both in the soil and protectively as a mulch. Of course I do not disapprove of watering plants well in at planting time. But it is always when we need most badly to use the garden hose that we may not because of serious water shortages. My theory of gardening without irrigation would make it impossible for many people to contemplate growing such plants as astilbes, or even some of the polygonums, for example. I confess that in my previous garden there were many plants I craved. I planted them, and suffered as I watched them wither away in utterly the wrong conditions no matter what I tried to do to please them. So I abandoned the idea of growing damp-loving plants and stuck to those I could grow reasonably well. For the last twenty years I have been creating a garden on a site that has almost every kind of condition from free-draining gravel to deep silt fed by underground springs.

Grouping Plants from Similar Environments

When I come to plant a new bed in my garden, I find it too confusing to consider all the possible plants from which I can choose, so it has helped me to classify the enormous range of plants into groups, so that my choice becomes simplified. In the following lists the plants are grouped into sections, each of which need roughly the same kind of conditions or situations, where I hope you may find some which suit your climate and soil.

It is sometimes possible to mix plants from bordering groups, but not from extreme conditions. These lists will not be grouped strictly ecologically. In my garden design I choose plants from different countries around the temperate world and plant them together, provided they all share a similar environment. In the Munich Botanic Garden the rock gardens are a delight for any student of plant ecology. They have planted different areas using only those plants and grasses which grow naturally together. I found it fascinating, but although the faithful reproduction of a specific piece of mountain-side reminded me of very happy plant-hunting holidays in the Alps, it is not, I think, something we can reproduce in our English gardens, certainly not in table-flat Essex with unsuitable imported rock. Nor would I wish to do so. Basically it is common sense to put plants where they will survive. Aesthetically I have found it very helpful to have a little knowledge of the native environment of my plants, to know something of the landscape, the trees, bushes, grasses and other plants with which they grow in the wild.

The art of gardening, I think, is to select plants from similar environments and group them so that they complement each other, not vie with each other for attention. We should consider scale, observe form and outline, be aware of textures, study nature's gentle colour harmonies. If we could practise all this we would have a dissolving and constantly re-forming tapestry emerging throughout the growing season and, in some cases, throughout the year.

Now for the lists. I shall include both variegated and double versions of plants which are familiar to us in gardens. It would be impossible to include every plant that may be known or grown. I tend to include those most familiar, and which I have grown myself.

The Pond Edge and Shallows

These are swamp plants, that is, those which need to be in very wet soil throughout the growing season. Some, indicated by a 'W' will also grow in shallow water. To be saturated in winter and then dried out in summer will not do. I am not including water-lilies, or the many submerged and floating aquatics which are dealt with fully in *Water Gardening* by Frances Perry. Those marked 'R' are very rampant, or too huge for a small garden.

W	*Acorus calamus* 'Variegatus'		*Caltha palustris* 'Alba'
	Acorus gramineus 'Variegatus'		*Caltha palustris* 'Flore Pleno'
W	*Alisma plantago-aquatica*		*Caltha polypetala*
W	*Butomus umbellatus*		*Cardamine latifolia*
W	*Calla palustris*		*Cardamine pratensis* 'Flore Pleno'
	Caltha leptosepala		*Geum rivale* 'Leonard's Variety'
	Caltha minor radicans	R	*Gunnera manicata*
	Caltha palustris	R	*Gunnera scabra*

Houttuynia cordata
Houttuynia cordata 'Flore Pleno'
Iris laevigata
Iris laevigata 'Variegata'
Iris pseudacorus 'Bastardii'
Iris pseudacorus 'Variegata'
Iris setosa
Iris sibirica
Iris versicolor
Iris versicolor Kermesina
Leucojum aestivum
Ligularia stenocephala 'The
    Rocket'
Lysichitum americanum
Lysichitum camtschatcense
Lythrum salicaria
Lythrum virgatum
W Menyanthes trifoliata
Mimulus cupreus 'Hose-in-Hose'
Mimulus cupreus 'Whitecroft
    Scarlet'
Mimulus guttatus
Mimulus lewisii

Mimulus ringens
Myosotis palustris
W Orontium aquaticum
Peltiphyllum peltatum
Phormium tenax
Polygonum bistorta 'Superbum'
Pontederia cordata
Primula bulleyana
Primula florindae
Primula helodoxa
Primula japonica
Primula pulverulenta
Primula pulverulenta 'Bartley
    Strain'
Primula sikkimensis
RW Ranunculus lingua
RW Sagittaria sagittifolia
Senecio smithii
Trollius europaeus
Trollius ledebouri
W Zantedeschia aethiopica
Zantedeschia aethiopica 'Green
    Goddess'

Grasses and Grass-like Plants for Boggy Conditions or Shallow Water

Carex riparia 'Variegata'
Carex stricta 'Bowles' Golden'
Carex trifida
RW Cyperus longus
R Eriophorum angustifolium
RW Glyceria maxima 'Variegata'
Miscanthus sacchariflorus

RW Phalaris arundinacea 'Picta'
W Scirpus lacustris 'Pictus'
W Scirpus lacustris 'Zebrinus'
RW Typha angustifolia
RW Typha latifolia
Typha minima

Ferns for Wet Conditions with Partial Shade

Onoclea sensibilis
Osmunda regalis

Thelypteris palustris

All of these plants will tolerate saturated soil, even shallow water at the pond edge. Some of them can be planted a little further from the water's edge—or even in a garden where there is no visible water, but where plenty of moisture can be maintained all the year. So some of them will turn up again in the following lists, where I shall group the plants according to size and situation.

Large Plants for Damp Soil in Sun

These are plants for soil that is not saturated, but remains damp all summer. Some shelter from drying winds is vital for the larger leafed plants. Sometimes north-facing sites can be a blessing, where there is adequate light overhead, but not direct scorching. These plants are superb where there is plenty of room, where invasive plants, in particular the polygonums, will not be forever regretted, and where the scale of planting requires handsome architectural features.

However, they are not only for owners of parks and lake-sides. Many can be used, in smaller numbers and in smaller groupings, provided that the invasive members are avoided. It is astonishing how one really magnificent plant can add style and dignity to a small and simple setting.

Those marked 'R' are rampageous or heavy seeders, and must be used with care.

Aconitum carmichaelii 'Arendsii'
R Angelica archangelica
Aralia cachemirica
Artemisia lactiflora
Aster novae-angliae, varieties
Aster novi-belgii, tall varieties
Astilbe rivularis
Boltonia latisquama
Campanula lactiflora
Centaurea macrocephala
Cephalaria gigantea
Chrysanthemum uliginosum
Delphinium elatum, varieties
R Epilobium angustifolium 'Album'
Eupatorium purpureum
R Filipendula rubra 'Venusta'
Gunnera manicata
Gunnera scabra
R Heracleum mantegazzianum
R Impatiens roylei

Inula magnifica (I. afghanica)
Ligularia dentata
Ligularia × hessei 'Gregynog Gold'
Ligularia przewalskii
Lilium pardalinum
Lythrum salicaria
Phormium tenax
Phytolacca americana
Phytolacca clavigera
R Polygonum cuspidatum
R Polygonum sachalinense
Rheum palmatum 'Atrosanguineum'
Salvia guaranitica (S. ambigens)
Salvia uliginosa
Sanguisorba canadensis
Thalictrum speciosissimum
Vernonia crinita
Veronica virginica
Zantedeschia aethiopica 'Green Goddess'

Large Plants for Damp Soil Needing Shelter from Wind and Sun-scorch

Aruncus dioicus
R Buphthalmum speciosum
Cardiocrinum giganteum
R Petasites japonicus
Rodgersia aesculifolia
Rodgersia pinnata

Rodgersia podophylla
Rodgersia tabularis
Rudbeckia laciniata
Thalictrum delavayi
Thalictrum delavayi 'Hewitt's Double'

Large Grasses for Damp Soil

Arundinaria, and other bamboos
Arundo donax
Cortaderia selloana
Cortaderia selloana 'Pumila'
Cortaderia selloana 'Sunningdale Silver'
Miscanthus sacchariflorus

Miscanthus sinensis 'Gracillimus'
Miscanthus sinensis 'Silver Feather'
Miscanthus sinensis 'Variegatus'
Miscanthus sinensis 'Zebrinus'
Phalaris arundinacea 'Picta'
R Spartina pectinata 'Aureo-marginata'

Medium-sized Plants for Damp Soil in Sun

Achillea decolorans 'W. B. Child'
Achillea millefolium, varieties
Aconitum × bicolor 'Ivorine'
Amsonia tabernaemontana
Anaphalis yedoensis
Anemone hupehensis
Anemone tomentosa; A. × hybrida
Aster lateriflorus
Aster × frikartii 'Mönch'
Aster, other species and cultivars
Astilbe taquetii
Astilbe; hybrids
Astrantia major
Astrantia maxima
Bergenia, species and varieties
Camassia leichtlinii, varieties
Campanula 'Burghaltii'
Campanula latifolia
Cautleya spicata 'Robusta'
Centaurea montana
Chelone obliqua
Chrysanthemum maximum, all forms
Cirsium rivulare
Dracocephalum sibiricum
Echinacea purpurea
Eupatorium ageratoides
Euphorbia griffithii 'Fireglow'
Euphorbia palustris
Euphorbia sikkimensis
Filipendula palmata 'Elegantissima'
Filipendula ulmaria 'Variegata'
Gentiana asclepiadea
Gentiana lutea
Geranium endressii
Geranium himalayense
Geranium pratense, and varieties
Geranium 'Kashmir White'
Geranium sylvaticum
Geranium wallichianum
Helenium autumnale, varieties
Hemerocallis, species and varieties
Heuchera, varieties
Hosta sieboldiana
Incarvillea delavayi
Inula hookeri
Inula royleana
Iris chrysographes
Iris delavayi

Iris ensata (I. kaempferi)
Iris sibirica
Knautia macedonica
Leucojum aestivum
Liatris, species
Lobelia cardinalis, and varieties
Lobelia syphilitica
Lobelia × vedrariensis
Lychnis chalcedonica
Lysimachia ciliata
Lysimachia clethroides
Lysimachia ephemerum
Lysimachia punctata
Lysimachia vulgaris
Lythrum virgatum
Mimulus cardinalis
Monarda didyma, and varieties
Morina longifolia
Nepeta sibirica
Phlox pilosa
Phlox, cultivars
Phormium cookianum
Physostegia virginiana
Polemonium caeruleum
Polemonium foliosissimum
Polygonum campanulatum
Polygonum carneum
Polygonum sphaerostachyum
Polygonum weyrichii
Potentilla argyrophylla
Potentilla atrosanguinea
Potentilla × 'Gibson's Scarlet'
Potentilla nepalensis 'Miss Wilmott'
Ranunculus acris 'Flore Pleno'
Ranunculus speciosus plenus
Rheum alexandrae
Rudbeckia fulgida, and varieties
Sanguisorba obtusa
Scabiosa caucasica
Schizostylis coccinea
Stachys macrantha
Stokesia laevis
Tradescantia × andersoniana
Tradescantia virginiana
Trollius, species
Verbena corymbosa
Zigadenus elegans

A Few Medium-sized Grasses and Sedges for Damp Soil in the Open

Alopecurus pratensis 'Aureus'
Dactylis glomerata 'Variegata'
Deschampsia caespitosa

Luzula nivea
Molinia caerulea, varieties
Panicum virgatum 'Rubrum'

Lilies

I cannot give a list of all the species and hybrids that can be grown in damp soil. They suffer if they are dried out in summer, especially the stem-rooting ones, but they will also fail if their bulbs become waterlogged in winter. Though they flourish in the sun, they can tolerate some shade, and shelter from surrounding bushes is often helpful to check the wind. The few I shall list are species which enjoy these conditions, and which I grow with no trouble.

Lilium bulbiferum croceum
Lilium hansonii
Lilium lancifolium (L. tigrinum), and a
    number of hybrids
Lilium martagon, and varieties

Lilium pyrenaicum
Lilium regale
Lilium speciosum
Lilium szovitzianum

Small and Low-growing Plants for Damp Soil in Sun

Adonis amurensis, and varieties
Adonis vernalis
Ajuga reptans, varieties
Aquilegia flabellata (A. akitensis)
Aster alpinus
Aster yunnanensis
Astilbe chinensis 'Pumila'
Astilbe, dwarf hybrids, including 'Sprite'
Bellis perennis 'Dresden China'
Bergenia stracheyi
Campanula glomerata, varieties
Campanula, other low species
Cardamine pratensis 'Flore Pleno'
Carex morrowii 'Variegata'
Colchicum autumnale
Colchicum speciosum, and varieties
Colchicum, other species
Crepis aurea
Delphinium brunonianum
Delphinium tatsienense
Dodecatheon meadia, and species
Erigeron 'Dimity'
Erigeron 'Roseus'
Erythronium dens-canis
Filipendula hexapetala
Francoa sonchifolia

Fritillaria meleagris
Fritillaria pallidiflora
Gentiana acaulis (of gardens)
Gentiana farreri
Gentiana septemfida
Gentiana sino-ornata
Gentiana, other species
Geum 'Borisii'
Geum rivale, forms
Heracleum minimum 'Roseum'
Iris cristata
Iris setosa, dwarf form
Lysimachia nummularia
Lysimachia nummularia 'Aurea'
Mentha pulegium
Narcissus pseudo-narcissus
Narcissus, smaller hybrids
Nierembergia repens
Ourisia coccinea
Ourisia macrophylla
Parochetus communis
Polygonum affine
Polygonum miletii
Polygonum vacciniifolium
Potentilla aurea
Primula denticulata

Primula rosea
Primula veris
Sisyrinchium angustifolium, and
   varieties

Solidago, dwarf varieties
Trifolium repens 'Purpurea'
Veronica gentianoides
Viola cornuta

Plants for Shade and Part Shade

The site may be shaded by trees and tall bushes, or it may be a generous border along a north wall. Every effort must be made to conserve moisture by enriching the soil and mulching, especially where tree and bush roots are present below. If there are many of these roots near the surface, such as close under hedges, or immediately under some large, densely shady trees, the soil will be too dry, and most of the following plants will not survive (except where rainfall is plentiful).

Large and Medium-sized Plants for Part Shade in Damp Soil

There are few large plants which can grow in deep shade, but many flourish best in, or even need, the moister atmosphere and shelter from wind provided by surrounding bushes and trees. Most of them enjoy direct sunlight for part of the day (preferably not mid-day), especially if it is partly flecked and broken by tree foliage high above. In the garden they grow well in gaps between tall bushes, at the edge of plantings of trees and in sunny woodland glades, or in north, north-east and north-west-facing borders with open sky overhead but little direct sun (*not* bone-dry under eaves).

Aconitum × *bicolor*
Aconitum carmichaelii
Aconitum vulparia
Aconitum, other species and hybrids
Anemone × *hybrida* (*A. japonica*)
Anemone tomentosa (*A. vitifolia*)
Aquilegia formosa truncata
Aquilegia, long-spurred hybrids
Aquilegia vulgaris
Arum italicum 'Pictum'
Aruncus dioicus
Aruncus dioicus 'Kneiffii'
Cardiocrinum giganteum
Carex morrowii 'Variegata'
Carex pendula
Dactylorrhiza (*Orchis*) *elata*
Dactylorrhiza (*Orchis*) *foliosa*
Dicentra spectabilis
Digitalis grandiflora
Digitalis purpurea
Doronicum, garden hybrids
Euphorbia amygdaloides 'Purpurea'

Euphorbia robbiae
Gentiana asclepiadea
Geranium maculatum
Geranium phaeum
Geranium sylvaticum
Geranium wallichianum
Geranium, other species
Gillenia trifoliata
Heuchera americana
Heuchera cylindrica 'Greenfinch'
Hosta, including variegated forms
Lamium orvala
Lilium, species
Meconopsis cambrica
Melandrium rubrum (*Lychnis dioica*)
Mertensia ciliata
Mertensia sibirica
Paeonia emodi
Paeonia lactiflora
Paeonia mlokosewitschii
Paeonia obovata alba
Paeonia veitchii

Phlox paniculata, and varieties
Phlox, garden hybrids
Phytolacca, species
Polygonatum × hybridum
  (P. multiflorum)
Polygonatum verticillatum
Polygonatum, other species
Polygonum (Tovara) filiforme
Ranunculus aconitifolius
Reineckia carnea
Roscoea cautleoides
Roscoea purpurea

Salvia glutinosa
Scopolia carniolica
Selinum tenuifolium
Teucrium scorodonium 'Crispum'
Thalictrum aquilegifolium
Thalictrum delavayi
Thalictrum delavayi 'Hewitt's Double'
Thalictrum diffusiflorum
Valeriana phu 'Aurea'
Veratrum album
Veratrum nigrum
Veratrum viride

Low Scramblers for Part Shade in Damp Soil

These will scramble into bushes or make ground-cover, but some are very rampant.

Aconitum volubile
R Galeobdolon luteum 'Variegatum'

R Rubus tricolor
   Tropaeolum speciosum

Low-growing Plants for Part Shade in Damp Soil

Ajuga reptans, varieties
Arisarum proboscideum
Chiastophyllum oppositifolium
Convallaria majalis
Corydalis cheilanthifolia
Corydalis lutea
Corydalis ochroleuca
Eranthis hyemalis
Erythronium californicum
Erythronium dens-canis
Erythronium oregonum
Erythronium, garden hybrids
Fragaria × ananassa 'Variegata'
Galanthus, species
Hacquetia epipactis
Hosta, dwarf species and varieties
Lamium maculatum
Lathyrus (Orobus) vernus, and varieties
Leucojum vernum

Lithospermum purpureo-caeruleum
Lysimachia nummularia 'Aurea'
Omphalodes cappadocica
Omphalodes verna
Ophiopogon planiscapus nigrescens
Potentilla alba
Primula denticulata
Primula elatior
Primula, hybrids ('Polyanthus')
Primula viali
Ranunculus ficaria
Rubus calycinoides
Rubus nepalensis
Shortia galacifolia
Viola cucullata, and varieties
Viola labradorica
Viola odorata
Viola, other species
Waldsteinia ternata

Plants for Shade in Damp Soil

These are plants that do not need direct sunlight, which can be harmful to many of them by wilting and scorching their leaves. But they do need subdued light, perhaps speckled through the overhead foliage of trees. Some, with hard leaves, will stand more sun, but flourish best in shade.

Large and Medium-sized Plants

Actaea, species
Anemonopsis macrophylla
Boenninghausenia japonica
Brunnera macrophylla
Caulophyllum thalictroides
Cimicifuga, species
Deinanthe bifida
Dentaria digitata (D. pentaphylla)
Dentaria pinnata (D. heptaphylla)
Dentaria, other species
Dicentra formosa, and varieties
Diphylleia cymosa
Eomecon chionantha
Epimedium pinnatum colchicum
Epimedium × versicolor 'Sulphureum'
Geranium phaeum
Glaucidium palmatum
Helleborus niger
Helleborus orientalis, and varieties
Hosta sieboldiana
Hosta, other large species and varieties

Iris foetidissima
Kirengeshoma palmata
Lunaria rediviva
Melittis melissophyllum
Mertensia virginica
Pachyphragma macrophyllum
Pachysandra terminalis
Petasites japonicus
Podophyllum emodi
Polygonatum falcatum 'Variegatum'
Smilacina racemosa
Tellima grandiflora
Tolmeia menziesii
Trachystemon orientale
Tricyrtis hirta
Tricyrtis macropoda
Tricyrtis, other species
Trillium chloropetalum
Trillium grandiflorum
Trillium, other species
Uvularia, species

Low-growing Plants for Shade in Damp Soil

Anemone nemorosa, and varieties
Anemone ranunculoides
Anemone, other low species
Asarum, species
Asperula odorata
Cardamine trifolia
Clintonia andrewsiana
Coptis trifolia
Cornus canadensis
Cortusa matthioli
Corydalis bulbosa (C. cava)
Corydalis, other species
Cyclamen, species
Epimedium grandiflorum
Epimedium, smaller species
Galax urceolata
Hepatica triloba, and varieties
Heucherella × 'Bridget Bloom'
Hylomecon japonicum
Jeffersonia dubia

Linnaea borealis
Maianthemum bifolium
Mitella breweri
Oxalis acetosella
Oxalis oregana
Phlox divaricata 'Chattahoochee'
Phlox stolonifera
Primula vulgaris, and varieties
Pulmonaria angustifolia 'Munstead
   Variety' and 'Mawson's Variety'
Pulmonaria, other species
Sanguinaria canadensis
Saxifraga cuneifolia
Saxifraga fortunei
Saxifraga × umbrosa
Symphytum grandiflorum
Vancouveria hexandra
Viola septentrionalis
Viola, other species

Ferns for Shade or Part Shade in Damp Soil

Adiantum pedatum
Adiantum venustum

Asplenium (Phyllitis) scolopendrium
Asplenium trichomanes

Athyrium filix-femina	*Hypolepis millefolia*
Athyrium goeringianum 'Pictum'	*Matteuccia struthiopteris*
Blechnum chilense	*Onoclea sensibilis*
Blechnum penna-marina	*Osmunda regalis*
Blechnum spicant	*Osmunda*, other species
Cystopteris bulbifera	*Polypodium vulgare*
Cystopteris fragilis	*Polystichum aculeatum*
Dennstaedtia punctilobula	*Polystichum lonchitis*
Dryopteris erythrosora	*Polystichum munitum*
Dryopteris filix-mas	*Polystichum setiferum*
Dryopteris goldieana	*Polystichum setiferum* 'Acutilobum'
Dryopteris linneana	*Polystichum setiferum* 'Divisilobum'
Dryopteris phegopteris	*Polystichum setiferum* 'Plumosum'

Some of these, such as *Dryopteris filix-mas* and *Polystichum setiferum* will grow in surprisingly dry (if shaded) sites, but they will grow twice as large where there is more moisture.

There are many more forms available of some of these ferns; those listed are most generally obtainable. On the whole I prefer the simple forms as found generally in the wild to the excessively feathered and crested ones which were sought and treasured in Victorian times, the heyday of the fern collector.

A Few Grasses and Sedges for Damp Shade

Carex morrowii 'Variegata'	*Luzula nivea*
Carex pendula	*Luzula sylvatica* 'Marginata'
Cyperus vegetus	*Milium effusum* 'Aureum'
Hakonechloa macra 'Albo-aurea'	

Bamboos

I used to dislike bamboos, perhaps because too often they are not tidied up occasionally. By cutting out some of the oldest shoots you allow room for the young canes, and also remove tattered-looking pieces which have suffered from an extra-cold winter, or been much buffeted by wind.

There are many kinds to choose from. Some become much too large and overpowering for small gardens. Others may be low-growing, but are much too invasive, quite unsuitable for mixed groupings. Both these kinds are ideal where there is plenty of room, and are particularly valuable, I find, around the edges of farm reservoirs or private lakes that take up several acres and need variation from endless reeds and sedges. Their great charm is that they remain live and shining in winter, the very large ones looking particularly graceful when partnered by fine willows, alders and coloured-stemmed dogwoods.

In small gardens, where the soil remains moist, *Arundinaria pygmaea* 'Viridistriata' is probably the best, being not so invasive. Its beautiful foliage is best on the new canes, so it pays to cut this bamboo practically to ground level each spring. It looks very well in a tub in a town garden. Those I grow include:

Arundinaria murieliae	*Arundinaria pygmaea* 'Variegata'
Arundinaria nitida	*Arundinaria pygmaea* 'Viridistriata'
Arundinaria pumila	*Sasa japonica* (*Arundinaria japonica*)
Arundinaria pygmaea	*Sasa veitchii*

I intend to try some species of *Phyllostachys* recommended to me as being among the most beautiful of bamboos.

Bibliography

ASLET, KEN, *Water Gardens*. Wisley Handbook No. 29, Royal Horticultural Society, London.

BECK, CHRISTABEL, *Fritillaries*. Faber and Faber, London.

BLOOM, ALAN, *Moisture Gardening*. Faber and Faber, London.

BOWLES, E. A., *My Garden in Spring*. David & Charles, Newton Abbot.

BOWLES, E. A., *My Garden in Summer*. David & Charles, Newton Abbot.

BOWLES, E. A., *My Garden in Autumn and Winter*. David & Charles, Newton Abbot.

FARRER, REGINALD, *The English Rock Garden*. T. C. & E. C. Jack Ltd, London and Edinburgh.

HILLIER, H. G., *Manual of Trees and Shrubs*. Hillier and Sons, Winchester.

INGWERSEN, WILL, *Manual of Alpine Plants*. Will Ingwersen and Dunnsprint Ltd.

LLOYD, CHRISTOPHER, *Foliage Plants*. Collins, London.

LLOYD, CHRISTOPHER, *The Well-tempered Garden*. Collins, London.

MACSELF, A. J., *Ferns for Garden and Greenhouse*. W. H. Collingridge and Transatlantic Arts Inc., New York.

MATTHEW, BRIAN, *Dwarf Bulbs*. B. T. Batsford, London.

PERRY, FRANCES, *Water Gardening*. Country Life, London.

ROBINSON, WILLIAM, *The English Flower Garden*. John Murray, London.

ROYAL HORTICULTURAL SOCIETY, *Dictionary of Gardening*. Clarendon Press, Oxford.

SACKVILLE-WEST, V., *In Your Garden*. Michael Joseph, London.

THOMAS, G. S., *Perennial Garden Plants*. Dent, London.

THOMAS, G. S., *Plants for Ground-Cover*. Dent, London.

Index

Numbers in bold refer to illustrations.